ABOUT THE AUTHOR

JOHN SEDGWICK is an award-winning journalist, novelist, memoirist, biographer, and historian who has written many books, ranging from *The Peaceable Kingdom*, about the Philadelphia Zoo, the basis of a dramatic series on CBS; to *In My Blood*, his bestselling multigenerational family memoir; to *War of Two*, about the fatal rivalry between Hamilton and Burr, a finalist for the George Washington Prize for the year's finest book on America's founders. He has published articles in *Vanity Fair*, *GQ*, *Newsweek*, *The Atlantic*, and other magazines. The father of two grown daughters, he lives with his wife, the *Financial Times* columnist and CNN analyst Rana Foroohar, and her two children in Brooklyn. Visit his website at johnsedgwick.biz.

ALSO BY JOHN SEDGWICK

NONFICTION

War of Two

In My Blood

The Peaceable Kingdom

Rich Kids

Night Vision

FICTION

The Education of Mrs. Bemis

The Dark House

BLOOD MOON

AN AMERICAN EPIC OF
WAR AND SPLENDOR
IN THE CHEROKEE NATION

JOHN SEDGWICK

SIMON & SCHUSTER PAPERBACKS

NEW YORK LONDON TORONTO SYDNEY NEW DELHI

Simon & Schuster Paperbacks
An Imprint of Simon & Schuster, Inc.
1230 Avenue of the Americas
New York, NY 10020

First Simon & Schuster trade paperback edition April 2019

SIMON & SCHUSTER PAPERBACKS and colophon are registered
trademarks of Simon & Schuster, Inc.

For information about special discounts for bulk purchases,
please contact Simon & Schuster Special Sales at
1-866-506-1949 or business@simonandschuster.com.

The Simon & Schuster Speakers Bureau can bring authors to your live event.
For more information or to book an event, contact the Simon & Schuster Speakers
Bureau at 1-866-248-3049 or visit our website at www.simonspeakers.com.

Interior design by Ruth Lee-Mui
Maps by Jeffrey L. Ward

Manufactured in the United States of America

10 9 8 7 6 5 4 3 2 1

Library of Congress Cataloging-in-Publication Data is available.

ISBN 978-1-5011-2871-4
ISBN 978-1-5011-2869-1 (pbk)
ISBN 978-1-5011-2872-1 (ebook)

For Rana, and for Logan and Kyla of the next generation

Come to the window, sweet is the night-air!
—MATTHEW ARNOLD

CONTENTS

PART TWO

THE DESCENT INTO HELL

PART THREE

VENGEANCE BE MINE

PART FOUR
FATEFUL LIGHTNING

LIST OF MAPS

Thousands of Europeans are Indians, and we have no examples of even one of those Aborigines having from choice become Europeans!
—J. Hector St. John de Crèvecoeur,
Letters from an American Farmer, 1782

One does not become enlightened by imagining figures of light, but by making the darkness conscious.
—Carl Jung, *Alchemical Studies*, circa 1929

A NOTE ON THE TITLE

A blood moon is a rare form of lunar eclipse. For the Cherokee, any vanishing from the night sky was troubling, as it threw their cosmos out of order. A blood moon was especially terrifying, since the moon did not disappear, but turned bloodred. Meteorologists now see that a blood moon is actually lit by an unusual sunset glow picked up from the earth's atmosphere as the sunlight brushes past. But the Cherokee considered the sight an ill portent. The moon was red with rage over what lay below.

BLOOD MOON

INTRODUCTION

T his is the last big surprise of the Civil War: It was fought not just by the whites of the North and South, and by the blacks who mostly came in after Emancipation. It was also fought by Indians,* as many as 30,000 of them, from the Seneca and Shawnee of the Northeast to the Creeks and Seminoles in the Southwest, nineteen tribes altogether. They fought at Second Bull Run, Antietam, Wilderness, Spotsylvania, and Petersburg in the East. But most of their battles were fought west of the Mississippi, beyond the range of the eastern newspapers that covered the war.

While the Indians were skilled as scouts, trackers, horsemen, and sharp-shooters, their greatest value may have been their fighting skills. Shaped by

---

*I use the now somewhat antiquated word "Indians" because it was universally accepted by the country's indigenous people and everyone else during the period of this book. I mean no disrespect.

a warrior culture, most were used to violence, and they took to battle. Their long black hair spilling out from under their caps, their shoddy uniforms ill-fitting, their faces painted in harsh war colors, they surged into battle with a terrifying cry, equipped not just with army-issue rifles but also with hunting knives, tomahawks, and, often, bows and arrows. Even when mounted on horses, they exhibited a deadly aim, and their arrows sank deep, leaving their victims as much astonished as agonized. They'd close fast, whip out a toma-hawk to dispatch their man, then pounce on the corpse with a bowie knife to shear off a scalp to lift to the sky in triumph. The *New York Tribune* fulmi-nated against an "Aboriginal Corps of Tomahawkers and Scalpers" among the rebels, but President Jefferson Davis was not embarrassed enough to order his Indians to stop. The natives killed as Indians, and they often died as Indians, too. When one dwindling band of sharpshooters, fighting for the Union at Petersburg, Virginia, in the yearlong siege at the close of the war, found them-selves out of bullets, surrounded by a tightening ring of Confederates, they lifted the blouses of their uniforms over their heads and chanted their tribal death song until the end came.

If that is the last big surprise, another one lies hidden within it—about the mysterious behavior of the Cherokee in the conflict. Of all the tribes that fought in the Civil War, the Cherokee were one of the very few to come in on both sides, and, of those few, by far the most notable. The internal nature of their own conflict doubled the slaughter, and also drew the fight into their territory, bringing more sweeping devastation. Nearly a dozen battles were fought on Cherokee land, more than on any other Indian territory, starting with Caving Brooks in 1861 and Cowskin Prairie the following year; continu-ing through Pea Ridge just outside it, the greatest pitched battle in the West; and running through other battlegrounds that have been ignored by history. By the time of the surrender in 1865, the war had devastated the Cherokee Nation.

At first, virtually all the Cherokee sided with the Confederacy, identify-ing with the Southern plantation owners, and proud of the black slaves they themselves had bought to pick their cotton. And, complicit with the state of Georgia, the Union had been responsible for the land theft that had cost them their ancestral territory and packed them west in the forced migration known as the Trail of Tears three decades before.

But why did the Cherokee not stay united against a common enemy? How could they have divided against themselves? To answer this, we need go back three decades to the terrible winter of 1838 and the issue that would never go away. Removal—the cruel shorthand for the Trail of Tears—was to the Cherokee Nation what slavery was to America, an issue so profound as to be bottomless and unending. To the outside world, it pitted the Cherokee against Andrew Jackson and his nefarious Indian Removal Act. To the Cherokee themselves, the matter was more complicated and far more divisive. The Cherokee Nation did not stand as one against the threat of removal; it stood as two, one side agreeing that, given the relentless white encroachment, the Cherokee had to go, and the other insisting that they stay forever, come what may. Stay or go—the question could not have been more essential or more agonizing. On this, there could be no compromise. Follow the past, or chase the future? Hold to tradition, or start afresh? Philosophical as these questions might seem, they were as real as children, as houses that had been built by hand, as crops that had been teased from the earth, as the deer that gamboled in the forest, as the sun that rose over the mountains.

The two sides were given body and voice by two proud Cherokee who loomed over the great debate like two great peaks on either side of a valley split by a raging river: John Ross and a man known as The Ridge. One the longtime principal chief, the other his primary councillor, and then his fiercest opponent. Their philosophies and personalities were so distinct as to name the two political parties that rose up over the issue. The Ross Party and the Ridge Party. One to stay, the other to go.

Everything about them expressed their differences. The Ridge—short for He Who Walks on Mountaintops—was a big, imposing, copper-skinned Cherokee, a fearsome warrior turned plantation owner, whose voice quieted any room, and whose physique awed anyone who crossed his path. Smaller, almost twenty years younger, Ross was descended from Scottish traders and looked like one: a pale, unimposing half-pint who wore eastern clothes, from laced shoes to a top hat. If The Ridge radiated the power of a Cherokee who could drop a buck at a hundred paces, Ross could have strolled into an Edinburgh dinner party without receiving undue attention. Tellingly, The Ridge spoke almost no English, and Ross almost no Cherokee.

Raised at either end of the string of Cherokee settlements from Tennessee down into Alabama, they were each a combination of Cherokee and Scottish, but in radically different proportions, and so demonstrated the startling variety of a seemingly homogeneous population: Cherokee skin ranged from a glowing tan to parchment white. In adulthood, the two men emerged as the two great leaders of the nation, statesmen both, united in their devotion to their Cherokee heritage, although no two men could have seen it more differently. Together, they created the first national Cherokee government, with a constitution, a legislature, and a supreme court, which certified the Cherokee as the most "civilized" tribe in America.

In those halcyon years of the 1820s, the two worked together in back-slapping harmony. It wasn't hard to picture them, on a warm evening, sitting together in the shade of the elms under the porch of The Ridge's fine house, sipping whiskey, although both professed not to drink it, and laughing into the night.

But President Andrew Jackson's hard push for removal touched something in them—a tension over whether to resist or to accommodate—that set each against the other, permanently. What started as an honest disagreement between friends developed into an active distrust that hardened into antagonism and then became a blinding hatred that consumed everything. A blood feud, in short, that went from personal vendetta to clan war to a civil war that swept through the entire Cherokee Nation before it got caught up in the even greater cataclysm of the American War Between the States.

It was Ross against Ridge, but of course it was much more than that. It was a great battle over the truth about who the Cherokee people really were. The times had given the Cherokee such a shake that they'd lost track of themselves. Were they a people of the mountains, believers in the Great Spirit, attuned to the flight of a hawk across the sky? Or were they a people who'd largely abandoned their ancestral past, ready to start over with modern ways? Did their passions still run to the wild—or to the bright promise of industrial civilization? Did they want what the Cherokee had always wanted, or did they seek something new that would make them new? Identity should be obvious, the face in the mirror. But in their own uncertainty, the Cherokee turned to their leaders to tell them what *they* thought they were. Two leaders in particular. And, of course, John Ross and The Ridge saw wildly different things—tradition-bound for one, enterprising for the other—and when they described these, such was the power of their telling that the differences grew, and the two visions became so distinct there was no reconciling them: it was one or the other. And then it got even worse. Each of these two great men grew monstrous in the other's eyes, and so did his ideas, and, following suit, the Cherokee Nation broke into two wrathful countries, each bent on annihilating the other before the other could annihilate it.

As for the two men behind all this—things went no better for them. And that was the tragedy, right there. Their differences might have added to their understanding and joint strength, but led instead to division and acrimony—and ultimately to a disaster that was all the more excruciating because they had inflicted it on themselves. Their tragedy became the tragedy of their own nation, and also the tragedy of the greater nation they so uneasily inhabited.

The tragedy did not begin with removal—that was simply when the sorrows hit hardest. It began earlier, at The Ridge's birth just before the American Revolution, although its sources could easily be tracked back even earlier. And it took its shape as the Cherokee Nation did, its aspirations rising even as its borders were being squeezed by the settlers pushing in on every side.

The resulting pressures on the Cherokee were tremendous, but hardly unique. Their story was the story of all Americans, really, as everyone in this land of emigrants tried to fit into a foreign nation. The difference, of course, was that the Cherokee were not emigrants; they had been here all along. By rights, everyone else should have been trying to get along with *them*, not the reverse. So, on top of all the other brutal hardships the Cherokee faced in being forcibly removed from their land, there was this one, which was possibly the worst of all: a terrible, grinding, and utterly legitimate sense of injustice that they should have to endure such suffering.

The Smoky Mountains of the Cherokee.

PART ONE

PARADISE
LOST

1771–1814

THE CHEROKEE LANDS
1700–1835

PA

OHIO

INDIANA

ILLINOIS

Ohio River

Ohio River

KENTUCKY

WEST VIRGINIA

1700

1775

1770

VIRGINIA

Cumberland River

1798

1783

• Nashville

Knoxville

1791

TENNESSEE

1798

NORTH CAROLINA

1798

Chattanooga

Tennessee River

1835

SOUTH CAROLINA

MS

1755

ALABAMA

1721

0 Miles   100   200

0 Kilometers   200

GEORGIA

© 2018 Jeffrey L. Ward

This map shows the diminishment of the Cherokee Nation—from 1700, when it spread out over eight present-day states; to 1783, after the Peace of Paris concluded the Revolutionary War; and finally to 1835, before the Treaty of New Echota ceded the last of the nation to the United States. The dates in smaller type refer to six treaties mentioned in the text: the first, from 1721, gave the nation's southeastern tip to the South Carolina of Royal Governor Francis Nicholson; the one in 1755 ceded much more to the South Carolina of Royal Governor James Glen; the treaty of 1770 surrendered a good deal of what's now Virginia and West Virginia to the Virginia Colony; the treaty of 1775 transferred almost all of today's Kentucky to Richard Henderson of the Transylvania Company; the Holston Treaty of 1791 gave away what's now northeastern Tennessee to the nascent United States; and Doublehead's treaty of 1798 stripped off three prime holdings near Knoxville.

1

A BIRTH ON THE HIWASSEE

Its walls made of branches slathered with red clay to keep out the wind, the little hut was alive with the pine scent of the wilderness as she writhed, her copper skin gleaming, on a bed of crosshatched reeds. She was O-go-nuh-to-tua, a Cherokee of the Deer Clan. Although her father was a Scottish trader who didn't stay long, she bore the high cheekbones and delicate features of most Cherokee women, and perhaps some of the exquisite "coquettishness" that exceeded even that of the French—or so said the Duke of Orleans, later the French king, when he came through to view these astonishing tribespeople. He couldn't fail to be struck by the women's supple beauty, the bewitching way they dipped their heads and angled their forearms, their skin lightly tattooed, with flickers of jewelry off their ears.

A few attendants fluttered over her, doing what they could to ease the mounting pain. A fire was going in a pit in the middle of the earthen floor, the dark smoke rising up toward a hole in the ceiling. Beside it, a long-robed shaman sat hunched, scrutinizing the ashes for portents.

Her husband, Tar-chee, knew better than to come anywhere near his wife in labor. He was a man of stout and boastful armbands, massive hoop earrings, and impressive nose ornaments, his hair in a topknot, the back of his head jauntily adorned with a sprig of feathers. He'd stay with the men, or simply go off by himself, to wait over a long-stemmed pipe.

Her face bore the look of birthing mothers everywhere: skin tight, eyes wild, as she strained, her belly impossibly huge, her head swinging this way and that, her black hair whipping about. She'd gone through this hell three times before, producing three sons, all three of them dead now. It was enough to put fear in anyone, but here the tale turns mystical. For the Cherokee, the spirits were as real as the wind. To believe the shaman, her sons had fallen to a primal malevolence that struck like lightning or a flash flood and needed now to be watched for in the fire that burned in the little hut.

There is much to see in a fire. The exact color of the flames, the heap of the ashes, the way the smoke rises. All could convey the intentions of the Great Spirit. The shaman sprinkled some tobacco leaves onto the embers and watched the smoke rise. It went straight to the hole above. That was a relief. No witches were about tonight.

It was safe for the attendants to ease O-go-nuh-to-tua outside on a stretcher of deer hide and into the cooling breeze that blew off the river. Remaining inside at his post by the fire, the shaman let out a shriek. The tobacco smoke was curving north! In the Cherokee compass, north was the place of ice and darkness. It bred witches. To dispel them, the shaman loudly recited chants and poked the embers. All to no effect. The smoke still leaned north.

Outside, the pains came faster, until a baby was brought forth, slick with blood. A boy. The midwives lifted him into the air in praise of the Great Spirit, wrapped him in cloth, and handed him to his mother. She was about to bring him to her breast when the shaman rushed out and snatched the boy from her. If he was to survive, he must drink nothing but tea for seven days. The shaman's tea, following his recipe. It would do more than just protect him from witches. It would give him special powers. He would be able to see the invisible, to leave his body, to take any form he chose. Crawl about as an ant or fly as a hawk. All the forces of the world would be his. He would be a magnificent hunter and a deadly warrior. He would be a force of nature. So said the shaman.

The mother gladly fed her son the shaman's tea from a leather nipple. But she let him suck her breast, too. Power was one thing, love another. She wanted both for her son, and both would be needed for what lay ahead.

It was 1771, the season now unknown, in a small Cherokee settlement along the wide-swinging Hiwassee River that wound through the steep blue-green mountains of what would soon be called Tennessee, veering off east from the wide, U-shaped river that would give the state its name. The headwaters of the Hiwassee were said to have poured down from a cleft in the towering ridgeline, as if spilling from a vast, invisible sea pooled on the far side. Down and down the waters tumbled, until they finally hit bottom to glide quietly through the meadows.

The whites called the place Savannah Ford, since its waters were passable, and it lay about twenty miles north of the future Chattanooga, near where the states of Alabama, Georgia, and Tennessee would converge. The Cherokee name for the settlement does not survive; there may not have been one. To the villagers, this stretch of shore may have been all the world there was. To them, it was simply *here*. It was the same impulse that inspired the Cherokee to call themselves the Real People. It fell to the neighboring Choctaw to call them, derisively, Cherokee—cave dwellers.

It was one of about sixty Cherokee villages spread out across the southern Appalachians, those great long slabs that angled across the Northeast, from the mystical Great Smokies that traced the future Tennessee's jagged eastern border across to the river-riddled Cumberland Plateau that lay to their west. All of the settlements were approximately like this one, with rough-hewn dwellings arrayed about a central "town house," round, with a conical roof, where official business was conducted amid clouds of tobacco smoke. Beside it was a ceremonial square for the stomping war dances of nearly naked, enraged men about a roaring fire, and the zesty fertility dramas of the harvest Green Corn dance, among other exuberant festivities of a ceremonial people.

In summer the fields were sprinkled with the rapturous red of strawberries; beyond them rose trees laden with peaches and plums. And there were crop fields for corn, beans, pumpkins, and sweet potatoes. Life was so rich in sunshine and rainfall that everything grew—twelve varieties of berries alone. It was almost as if a seed would merely have to touch the ground for a plant to hit the sky.

A heavy forest climbed up the mountainside, straight up in places, all of it thick with unchanging spruce and pine, and also with chestnut, oak, maple, sourwood, and hickory trees whose leaves turned from the deep, lush green of spring to the fiery orange of fall. The lofty mountaintops were often enswirled in a heavy mist that veiled the source of the terrifying lightning, booming thunder, and fierce winds that periodically shook their world and confirmed the Cherokee belief that there were far greater powers beyond the ones they could see.

When the doughty naturalist William Bartram, the aspiring son of the botanist to the king of England, scrambled over Cherokee territory in 1773 determined to catalog every species, flora or fauna, that he encountered, he saw the sublime in the "divine and inimitable workmanship" of the "glorious Magnolia," in the "expansive umbrageous" live oak, and even in the "pride and vanity" of the daylily. Bartram's literary raptures inspired Coleridge to write his phantasmagoric "Kubla Kahn," and Emerson and Thoreau to develop their heady Transcendentalism. At a mountain peak, Bartram imagined he'd reached the top of the world as he looked out on "ridges of hills rising grand and sublimely one above and beyond another, some boldly and majestically advancing into the verdant plain, their feet bathed with the silver flood of the Tanase"—the Tennessee River, into which the Hiwassee drains—"whilst others far distant, veiled in blue mists, sublimely mount aloft, with yet greater majesty lift up their pompous crests and overlook vast regions."

The Cherokee left no descriptions of themselves, so much of what we know comes from outsiders. The most prominent was James Adair, a swarthy Irish trapper who arrived in the New World in 1735. Among the first Europeans to come upon the Cherokee, he married one, a widowed full-blood of the Deer Clan called Mrs. Go-ho-ga Foster, and lived with her for forty years. Of a surprisingly scholarly bent for an uneducated man, in 1775 Adair wrote a massive *History of the American Indians*, the first account of the Cherokee, and still the best.*

Adair found Cherokee men surprisingly tall, much taller than Europeans, virtually all of them at least six feet, with an erect carriage, fine taut muscles, and exquisite proportions, as if they'd been designed by Leonardo. Bartram considered Cherokee faces "open, dignified and placid," their forehead and brow suggestive of "heroism and bravery," their black eyes "full of fire," their noses a "royal aquiline," and their hair "long, lank, coarse and black as a raven." Worn long, their hair was likely to be pulled up into a topknot clasped with a silver brooch. Both sexes plucked out their body hair—by the roots with a tiny corkscrew twirled by a stick—hair by hair from chin to "privities," leaving the skin baby-smooth.

Sharp-eyed, strong, and resilient, most Cherokee men seemed to Adair to be made for war. "Martial virtue" was the only quality they admired. Warriors slew their enemies with arrows that flew silently through the air, or bludgeoned them with tomahawks up close, and then, with a hunting knife, hacked off a trophy from the top of their heads. Steady-handed killers, the Cherokee had taken easily to the firearms the Europeans brought.

But not Tar-chee. He was far more hunter than warrior, alert to life in the forest, so precise with a bow and arrow he could hit a deer in the heart atop a high ridgeline, and with a puff of a poison-tipped blowdart, bring down a squirrel leaping from the highest branch of a chestnut. He had to his credit only a single scalp, hacked off in a skirmish with some renegade Indians of the Wabash. But war was coming, and he would have to join it.

A young Cherokee bears not just one name, but a series of names, each one reflecting his identity at a particular stage of life. At first, the little boy was Nung-noh-hut-tar-hee, for He Who Slays the Enemy in His Path, or Pathkiller, which surely reflected his parents' ambitions for him, whatever the fears

---

* It is a remarkably clear-eyed piece of ethnography to modern eyes, with one howling peculiarity: Adair devotes the entire book to his argument that the American Indians were a lost tribe of Israel. A "kink," Thomas Jefferson called this, no doubt chuckling, when he told John Adams about it later. Not that Jefferson himself didn't have more than a few delusions about the Indians, as his own infamous *Notes on the State of Virginia* attests.

of the shaman. Despite his Scottish grandfather, the little Pathkiller looked all Cherokee, with his copper skin and jet-black hair, and he was tall for his age, and hardy. Tar-chee taught him the lore of the forest and the ways of the Great Spirit. But it was a boy's life there in the village, a life of swimming and ball games, of going naked everywhere, and no particular work to do. He might have been a forest creature, the way he slipped so smoothly through the trees, or a fish when he swam in the river. But the freedom wasn't just a luscious tumble in the world. It meant exposure to the elements, right on his bare skin. Burning sun, scratching brambles, icy water, hard rock—all left their lessons. There were no books. He learned by living, by seeing what happened. All of it was guided by his father, Tar-chee, the hunter. The only account of The Ridge's childhood comes from Thomas McKenney, who served years later as the superintendent of Indian Affairs when Indian removal was becoming a national policy under Jackson. McKenney took it upon himself to collect biographies and lithographic images of the more notable Indian chiefs whose lives were being sharply altered by his own office, and one can hear a wistfulness in McKenney's romantic account of the young Ridge stealing through the forest of his childhood.

> His father taught him to steal with noiseless tread upon the grazing animal—to deceive the timid doe by mimicking the cry of the fawn—or to entice the wary buck within the reach of his missile, by decorating his own head with antlers. He was inured to patience, fatigue, self-denial, and exposure, and acquired the sagacity which enabled him to chase with success the wild cat, the bear, and the panther. He watched the haunts, and studied the habits of wild animals, and became expert in the arts which enable the Indian hunter at all seasons to procure food from the stream or the forest.

Tar-chee's instructions went past the practical details of hunting into mystical elements that McKenney found hard to track, as he detailed how a hunter, if he hoped to be rewarded with prey, needed to "go to water" in the evening to whisper an incantation to the river: "Give me the wind. Give me the breeze." Likewise, before a hunter lit his evening fire, he needed to ask the fire to warm him while he slept, and never to assume it would on its own. And before he let loose an arrow, he must ask for the consent of his prey—

whether it be a deer or a hawk—to be killed. Whatever his quarry, once it was killed he must cut out its tongue and pitch it into the fire as an offering to the spirits, to square the account after having taken something.

As he grew, Pathkiller learned the ways of the mountains, and his talents and daring earned him the name he would bear for the rest of his life, The Ridge, for He Who Walks on Mountaintops. Even as a boy, he ranged everywhere, for days and then weeks at a time, going without food or water, barely clothed if clothed at all, alert to any movement in the quiet, ready with his bow, poised to kill. And he would invariably return with a pack full of fresh meat for his family, which soon grew to four with the birth of a brother, David Oo-watie.

As he grew, The Ridge could see that it was the men's lot to roam the mountains hunting. Women were to stay home and tend the crops. The genders were separate, one staying close, the other going far, but they were equal. Society had no ranks. No one was fundamentally different from anyone else; no one should receive more than a fair share; anyone who could not provide for himself should be provided for by others. This was the Cherokee way— everyone was in it together. While there was a village chief, he ruled by consensus, and everyone had a voice, wearying as it must have been to hear them all. While men ran the councils, women selected those men and exerted such an influence over them that Adair memorably scoffed at the Cherokee as a "petticoat society."

The women held everything of value, from property to children. Tarchee may have built the marital hut, but O-go-nuh-to-tua owned it. And as the wife she would be the one to determine when a marriage was over. She'd let her man know by gathering up all his belongings and setting them outside the hut. Done. He knew better than to come back. This is probably why O-go-nuh-to-tua's father vanished from the record, leaving no trace beyond a slight lightening of his descendants' skin, and a softening of their features. He would have had no claim on his wife, or on their children. He'd been charmed by a comely Cherokee, who was slow to divine his intentions. Sharing no language, they communicated only by gesture and act, one in particular. When he left, his wife's oldest brother would have taken over as the man in the family, the father of the children, since he was related by blood, not marriage. And it was through the women that the all-important clans were arranged—seven of them, including the Deer Clan of The Ridge, the Bird, the Wolf, the Paint, and the Blind Savannah, all of which served as tribes within a tribe, extended families, and points of absolute loyalty. A man joined his wife's clan; she did not join his. The clans formed the basis of political society, too: every council house had seven sections. Among the Cherokee, anyone without a clan might as well not exist.

To the Cherokee, balance was everything. It started with men and women, but extended to sun and moon, winter and summer, war and peace. In the grand Cherokee cosmology, everything was poised against its opposite. There was a White Chief for times of peace, and a Red Chief for times of war. Both were essential to life, and each deserved its turn. Nothing was so distressing as when one went missing. Adair was there one night when the moon disappeared from the sky during a lunar eclipse, and he had never seen the Cherokee in such squawking pandemonium. "They all ran wild, this way and that way, like lunatics, firing off their guns, whooping and hallooing, beating of kettles, ringing horse-bells, and making the most horrid noises that human beings possibly could." They were afraid the moon was gone forever, devoured, they decided, by a monstrous bullfrog in the night sky.

The whites, coming in such numbers, were no less threatening, but they weren't about to consume their prey in a single gulp. Coming first in ones and twos to live like Adair among the Cherokee, the settlers were now pushing ever deeper into Cherokee territory, building solitary huts, then villages, then fortifications with stout blockhouses and a stockade perimeter, and a garrison of soldiers, ostensibly to protect the Cherokee, but also to protect themselves from the Cherokee. Either way, such forts advanced white society ever deeper into the virgin forest and invited still more settlers. None of these encroachments was yet visible from Savannah Ford, but Tar-chee knew, as everyone knew, they were out there, and coming closer. With so many settlers about, war was in the air in 1771, and the villagers were alert for any strange sounds brought in on the wind.

2

CONTACT

On feast days, the villagers turned out to hear the conjurers tell the stories of their people, and young Pathkiller would have been among them, gaping at these frisky characters in leggings of white deerskin who fanned themselves with colorful turkey wings as they told their spooky stories of how things got to be the way they were. The Cherokee were a people largely without history, that grand pageant of progress and disaster, possessing mostly legends about what had come before, legends only the conjurers knew. Pathkiller's eyes must have widened when he learned that all the land of the Cherokee was a vast, flat square that hung down from the vault of the sky on four long chains. It had been created by a humble water beetle who'd plunged from the sky vault where all the animals first lived, clear to the bottom of an ocean that lay below. There, he'd pulled up some grains of mud, which expanded dramatically when they reached the surface, creating all the earth that everyone now trod on. Initially, it was spread out as flat as any valley, but then the

Great Buzzard, an enormous flying beast, swooped through sculpting it with each flap of his broad wings into the magnificent high mountains that stood all around them.

It was the animals who first organized things, and kept tabs on them even now. They created the sun to pull the day from night, and made the moon to take over the darkness. Thunder had placed fire in a hollow sycamore tree on an island, but a little water spider had brought back a coal in her tusti bowl to share with everyone. To the Cherokee, big things often were the product of the tiniest of all the creatures. Fire was the expression of the Divine Spirit, which governs all life, and shamans were its interpreters. But a long, winding river like the Hiwassee brought life, too. To the Cherokee, any river was the Long Man, an unimaginably tall, slender, twisting giant whose head was way up at the mountaintop, whose feet were down in the valley, and whose rippling waters spoke in low murmurs only the shaman could understand. The Long Man ran through everything, high to low, slaked all thirst, brought cleanliness and purity. As a newborn, Pathkiller had begun his life as a Cherokee with a startling plunge into the cool water of the river. And all the Cherokee stripped to purify themselves at each new moon, even if doing it meant clearing off a thin sheet of ice in the depth of winter.

But there was more to life than what anyone could see—that was the point. Below the visible world lay an underworld full of ghastly spirits that governed things. And every animal, too, from the soaring eagle to the hopping rabbit, had a say. No one controlled his own destiny. And, it went without saying, no one owned even the smallest portion of the earth. The land, the water, the air, the woods, the mountains—no one could possess any of it any more than a rabbit could.

All this the young Pathkiller believed, just like everyone else.

The conjurers spoke mostly about the past, but of late they'd started to include some dark words about the future, reflecting the startling new ideas brought in by the settlers who were closing in around them: that the Cherokee occupied just a portion of a vast continent that fronted on an even vaster sea that led to a whole other land peopled by strangers whose skin was the color not of red clay but of pale sand; who wore clothes not of deerskin but of cloth; who hunted not with arrows but with bullets that flew out of a gun with a thunderclap; who did not regard the animals as possessors of spirits to be mindful of, but worshipped a God who'd died by torture but was to be worshipped for his vast powers; who carried papers that had the force of speech; who thought gold to be the very stuff of happiness; who drank firewater that allowed them to feel spirits inside their heads; who thought the land, the *land*, could be bought for a keg of whiskey or a sprinkle of coins, and then owned forever by virtue of a scrap of paper with ink on it.

Of course, the full truth was almost inconceivable. That this continent had a vast ocean at the other end, too, and virtually all of humanity had once lived on the far side of it—on a prodigious landmass called Euro-Asia—until maybe 20,000 years ago, when a few audacious souls ventured across the Bering Strait during an ice age that for about 1,000 years drew back the waters to create a passage of dry land to the New World.

All the people, millions of them, who remained on the far side of the globe carried on to build the Pyramids, the Great Wall of China, the Parthenon, and Chartres; to create vast empires, only to lose them; to invent writing, mathematics, the printing press, gunpowder, and the musket; to write the Bhagavad Gita, the *Divine Comedy*, and the *Canterbury Tales*; to sing English madrigals, accompanied by the harpsichord; to paint the murals of Giotto and erect Brunelleschi's dome; to create cities with coffeehouses and bustling markets; to develop elaborate, all-consuming politics; to think up scientific notions about the sun and the stars, the nature of matter, and life itself; to set down radical ideas so potent that people fought over them; to look into their own souls to write poems and plays; to create things of such astonishing beauty that people wept over them; to hunger always for more.

But those early bands of adventurers dispersed into the tundra, or filtered down into the forests of the Pacific Northwest, and farther down, all the way to the tip of South America, or spread across the Great Plains clear to the eastern shore, all of them to create a bewildering array of devil-fearing, sun-worshipping civilizations, many with inventive cosmologies, fantastic ziggurats, extensive agriculture, kinship societies, and war strategies. A few became quite imposing—the Aztecs, Mayans, and Incas to the south. But most left little trace of themselves. The ones who spread east culminated in the fearsome Iroquois, who spread over much of the Northeast but left few monuments. From them, a smaller tribe broke off, the Cherokee, an inventive, social people who spread to the Southeast to claim as their exclusive hunting ground as much as 125,000 square miles of the southern Appalachians, covering what would one day be eight American states, while they hunkered down in settlements on what would become Tennessee, Alabama, Georgia, and the Carolinas.

For thousands of years, neither race had any idea about the existence of the other. Until 1492, when an Italian seafarer crossed the Atlantic in three Spanish ships bound, he thought, for the Orient, and ended up in the Bahamas. He never did reach North America proper, and merely grazed South America, but he gave all the inhabitants of the New World the name they, in an ignorance that perfectly matched his, accepted as their own. Indians.

The Cherokee, tucked away in their fastness of the Appalachians, were far removed from the *Niña, Pinta*, and *Santa Maria* of Christopher Columbus that beached on a Caribbean shore. The tribe remained utterly unknown to Europeans until the iron-hearted Spanish conquistador Hernando de Soto, who'd conquered the Incas with the ruthless Francisco Pizarro, came plundering for gold in 1539. He crashed deep into the American wilderness to be the first to come eye to eye with the distant relations he termed "savages," his progress culminating, one fine day, in an encounter with the Cherokee. *Contact*, this is now termed. It was a moment that might have demonstrated the fundamental unity of all mankind, but did not.

With a small armada, de Soto landed in present-day Tampa Bay, on the greater landmass he called La Florida, with 500 soldiers, all in pointed *cabasset* helmets that gleamed in the bright sun. They splashed down into an Edenic bay of white sand fringed with coconut palms and mangroves; the azure sky streaked with ducks, egrets, and herons; the water and breezy air delightfully warm. De Soto knew, or thought he knew, enough metallurgy, to hunt for gold in the mountains, and he marched north to the higher elevations. Along the way, he rounded up as bearers 100 *tamemes*, or Indian slaves, who'd been too terrified to resist this devil's army of men in metal. De Soto's men fastened heavy collars to the Indians' necks, chained their ankles, and forced them at gunpoint to carry his burdens through the dense woods until they fell dead from exhaustion or disease. If they tried to flee, he unleashed a pack of fierce dogs to rip them apart. Rude, noisy, oblivious, the grand *entrada* snaked through the moist woods, de Soto up ahead on a chaise, the soldiers trudging behind, and then 100 more attendants, some female to provide for de Soto's wants, and finally a mob of snorting pigs that scrambled along, as a mobile larder.

Along de Soto's path, bewildered chiefs welcomed his surly army with gifts. To the Cherokee, these aliens might have dropped from the vault above the sky. But de Soto ransacked their villages all the same, and set fire to anyone who annoyed him. He took whoever might be useful. The most illustrious captive was the "Lady of Cofitachequi," said to be a nubile beauty, whose territory extended into the Blue Ridge Mountains, where de Soto had decided the gold was. Seeing no alternative, the Lady agreed to show de Soto the route to her supposed mines. As the *tamemes* bore her through the forest like an enslaved Cleopatra, she took a meandering route through the western expanse of her empire, from present-day Hickory, North Carolina, into the hollows of the Blue Ridge Mountains, over the Swannanoa Gap and along the French Broad River to today's Asheville. The daily log of one weary participant is astonishing for its lack of curiosity about the ancient civilization they were witnessing, to say nothing of the countryside. Mountaintops lost in primal mist, dreamy forests seemingly filled with every animal but the elephant, more twittering birds than in the tropics. They were there for gold; nothing else existed.

Tuesday, May 18: *In Guaquili. Here the Indians came forth in peace and gave us corn, although little, and many hens roasted on Baracoa and a few little dogs, which are good food. They also gave us tamemes.*

Friday, May 21: *Today we reached Xuala, which is a town on a plain between some rivers; its cacique is so well-provisioned that he gave us much of what we asked for: tamemes, corn, little dogs, petacas, and however much he had. Petacas are baskets covered with leather for carrying clothes and whatever they might wish.*

Tuesday, May 25: *We left Xuala and crossed a very high mountain range, and spent the night in a small forest.*

On they marched, this heavy-footed, clanging army of insolence, living off broiled dog, every scratch festering and stinking with pus, desperate to be

drunk, and dreaming of a poke at one of the lithe Indians flitting about half
naked. Whether or not the Lady of Cofitachequi felt those looks on her, she
grew increasingly miserable as the *tamemes* under her trudged along; each
step eroded her faith that the long-bearded, angry-eyed de Soto would ever
release her. Finally, the procession entered modern-day Knoxville, Tennessee,
in the heart of Cherokee territory.

It was here the Lady of Cofitachequi employed the oldest of ruses. As the
Gentleman from Elvas, one of five chroniclers of de Soto's journey, sheepishly
explained afterward, the Lady "stepped aside saying that she had to attend
to her necessities. Thus she deceived them and hid herself in the woods; although they sought her she could not be found." She'd taken four attendants
with her, and a slave who may have been her lover. De Soto must have gone a
little soft on her himself, for he did not unleash his dogs to tear her apart; he
only dispatched some men to track her halfheartedly. The forest was dense;
the trails were nonexistent. The hunters came back. The Lady had vanished.

This was the deepest de Soto penetrated into the Cherokee country. None
of the five chroniclers of his journey makes any note of the tribe, which may
have been difficult for them to distinguish from any other. The diary continued much as before.

Friday, May 28: *We spent the night in an oak grove.*

Saturday, May 29: *We marched alongside a large creek, which we crossed
many time*s

Monday, May 31: *The Governor left from Guasili and took the army to an
oak grove alongside a river.*

And so the greatest army that had ever assembled in North America and
the tribe that was on its way to becoming the most sophisticated on the continent passed by each other without the slightest engagement, possibly without
even noticing. The Spanish may have seen the Cherokee as just more Indians,
nothing memorable. And the Cherokee might have seen the Spanish as beyond comprehension, like a river that turned into a raven and flew away.

It was a bad dream, nothing more. If it had ever stayed with anyone, the conjurer would have taken that man to the river wearing just a shirt, had him step into the water, immerse himself, and then pull off the shirt to let the current bear the dream away.

Nonetheless, as the American Revolution was brewing in the early 1770s, the conjurers were coming to fear the East, but they feared the West more. "This is what our forefathers told us," they said by the night fire, eyes blazing. "Our feet are turned toward the West—they are never to turn around." It was the white settlers' doing, they went on, gripped by certainty. The white man would tell the Cherokee to give up their ancient ways of the hunt, and turn to farming instead, while the women spun cloth. "These are means to destroy you, and to eject you from your habitations. He will point you to the west, but you will find no resting place there, for your brother will drive you from one place to another until you get to the western waters." But not, the conjurers said, until we are "dead and gone. We shall not live to see the misery which will come upon you." Along the Hiwassee, protected by high mountains, keeping to the ways of their forefathers, and their forefathers before them, the Cherokee would feel a stir among themselves when a conjurer said such a thing, for it was well beyond anyone's comprehension.

True contact did not come until much later, on July 15, 1673, to be exact, when a couple of knockabout Virginians named James Needham and Gabriel Arthur suddenly appeared on horseback in the Cherokee village of Chota on the Little Tennessee River, which drains water off the Smokies into the Tennessee River well to the southeast in Tennessee's present-day Monroe County. As agents of Abraham Wood, a merchant at Fort Henry in what is now Petersburg, Virginia, they'd come to open trade relations between Chota and the Virginia Colony. They sought pelts, beeswax, and bears' oil for export to England in exchange for guns, axes, metal tomahawks, cloth, beads, looking glasses, and ribbons, which they had brought by wagon into the wilderness. But Needham and Arthur came for furs, chiefly beaver, as beaver hats were all the rage for the nobles just starting to be called gentlemen; hunters had already removed most of the beavers from Siberia to supply them. Cheap and worthless as many of the items they brought for sale were to the sellers, they were breathtaking to many of the Cherokee, who had never even heard of them before.

Even more remarkable to the Cherokee was the color of Needham's and Arthur's skin—or, more exactly, its absence of color. White. A pinkish white, to be sure, and reddened here and there from the sun, but far more white than not. The Cherokee were a people of color, in a place of color. The only white they knew was in the clouds and the snow that fell from them. The better to show it off, the Cherokee asked the two Virginians to mount a scaffold atop the town's parapet so that all the Cherokee who'd gathered for the astonishing spectacle could get a good look. This the two white men did, sheepishly.

The Cherokee were only too happy to trade with these materialists, fully stocked in firearms and other figments of modernity, and so made their first foray into the world of capitalism. It proved a rocky passage. When the two men's interpreter, a "flat, thick, bluffe-faced fellow" the whites called Indian John, got into a ferocious argument with Needham over something, Needham flung a hatchet at Indian John's feet. Furious, Indian John snatched up one of the guns he'd just purchased with deerskins, pressed it to the side of Needham's head, and blew his brains out. Not done, Indian John, in Wood's account, then "drew out his knife, stepped across ye corpse of Mr. Needham, ript open his body, drew out his hart, held it in his hand and turned and looked to eastward, toward ye English plantations and said he valued not all ye English." It would be a cry that he would not be the last to make.

To be done with these irksome traders, Indian John had a Weesock Indian tie Arthur to a stake and prepare a bonfire beneath him. Hearing about this, and fearful of losing English trade, a nearby chieftain rushed to Arthur's aid and, so goes the story, shot the Weesock just as he was bending down to set the Englishman on fire. Freed, Arthur did something remarkable. He did not rush back to civilization, desperate to be done with these terrifying heathens, as one might expect. Instead, he remained with the Cherokee, actually smearing his skin with a thin film drawn from the powder of red clay to pass as one.

He joined a band of Cherokee warriors to take on the Spanish in Florida. When the Shawnee captured him on the Ohio, they discovered that his red skin was faked, but were surprisingly tolerant of the deception. They allowed him to return to Chota, and from there to his employer, Wood, at Fort Henry, to whom he brought a detailed letter book recording his adventures. Thus was established the pattern of the British invasion—trade followed by conflict, death, destruction, loss of identity, and convulsive change on an unimaginable scale. But, as with any trade, there is a buyer and a seller, and both are complicit.

The guns, at least, were visible, as was the damage they inflicted. When they acquired firearms, the Cherokee knew what they were getting in the exchange, and that was true for most of the hard goods the Europeans had for sale. But the Europeans threw into the bargain other things that were impossible to see, yet no less potent. Foremost, of course, was the very idea that things were to be bought and sold on any kind of cash basis, not simply given to tribesmen in need, or bartered haphazardly. The Cherokee were a sharing culture; they made sure that everyone had enough. Trade introduced the invidious notion of comparative advantage to the exchange, as the English never intended the benefits to be equal on both sides, and the Indians quickly learned not to intend this, either, and so unleashed a new emotion, greed. And that brought on all the things greed leads to, such as selfishness, materialism, status, and class—startling ideas for a people who had always considered everyone more or less the same.

But the things these English brought were not just things, either, as they also carried implications that went well beyond their physical nature. Rum, for one. Unknown before the Europeans brought them, spirits were wonderfully enticing to the Cherokee not just for the heady warmth they delivered even on the coldest days, but for their spiritual qualities, as the intoxication was transporting, a little taste of heaven. And it was pleasing to take part in a refined European custom. It took a while to recognize that drinking also led to arguments, lethargy, dissolution, stupidity, disrepute, and fights over nothing. And, on the part of too many female Cherokee, who were not immune to the charms of the bottle, to errant sex with the white traders who dispensed it, which then introduced into the Cherokee line a foreign element that made the Cherokee noticeably less Cherokee.

And then there was disease. The Cherokee rarely infected the whites with anything they couldn't handle; but the whites brought with them toxic contagions, which had been brewed for centuries in congested European cities and for which the Cherokee, safe from them on the other side of the ocean, had developed no defenses: among them dysentery, typhus, influenza, scarlet fever, diphtheria, whooping cough, mumps, yellow fever, and even bubonic plague, all of them, passed invisibly, as baffling as they were devastating. But by far the greatest and most hideous threat was smallpox, a scourge that in its sweep and horror undermined their faith in the fundamental rightness of things. Smallpox often bubbled up first in the gums, then on the tongue and throughout the mouth, and then spread down deep inside the throat and nasal passages, and out over the lips to the face, sometimes even popping out the eyeballs, and then to anywhere it would cause the greatest torment, the soles of the feet, palms of the hands, forearms and genitals, from there out across great swaths of skin, where the crusty bubbles oozed together, raising a stink that the Cherokee recognized as the stench of coming death, and then crusted over in crinkly sheets that cracked open with the slightest movement as if pierced by a knife, opening the body to raw sinew, making every breath, every pulse of the heart, an agony of its own, bringing even the most hardened Cherokee into a vast new world of pain.

Horrible as this was for the sufferer, it proved more destructive to Cherokee society, as the disease defeated the chants and herbs of the near-sacred medicine men, bringing their power into question. For they not only failed to bring about a cure but worsened the onslaught, as their remedies made the disease more deadly, and more widespread. They preached immersing the sick in the life-giving waters of the river—but the sudden chill only shocked the system and hastened the end. Or they put their patients in common sweat houses, where the virus rode their breath to the lungs of others, widening the contagion.

Even more than the avarice of the white settlers, their diseases rocked the Cherokee, for these assaulted their essential faith in the Great Spirit to protect them. Horribly disfigured, in excruciating pain, wheezing, doomed, the afflicted fell into primal despair, and many brought about their own end before the virus could. "[A] great many killed themselves," Adair reported. "Some shot themselves, others cut their throats, some stabbed themselves with knives, and others with sharp-pointed canes; many threw themselves with sudden madness into the fire, and there slowly expired, as if they had been utterly divested of the native power of feeling pain."

These plagues cost the Cherokee nearly half their already scanty population, reducing it, by one estimate, from the 25,000 who greeted the first settlers in the late seventeenth century to little more than 10,000 a half century later. Into the bargain, the viruses savaged the Cherokee warrior class as no war ever had. By the time The Ridge was born, the number of Cherokee warriors was down to just 3,000. Meanwhile, the number of the settlers, and the soldiers to protect them, only rose.

But the greatest exchange of all involved the land, the very foundation of life itself. By the time the two Virginians encountered the Cherokee, the tribe controlled those 125,000 square miles of what would one day become the American Southeast, an almost inconceivably vast territory for such a small number of people. Without maps, land surveys, or territorial markers, the expanse was also curiously abstract. Kings might know their lands to the last inch, but the Cherokee territory extended to a blurry horizon in every direction. As late as the 1770s, even the finest English maps were theoretical at best. They gave no hint of the actual location of any settlements, Cherokee or white, and could place none of the many mountains, let alone describe their height or contours or give their names. They were precise only in depicting the navigable rivers that were used to penetrate this territory. The Cherokee, of course, had scarcely any maps at all, merely collective memories of a few critical landmarks—a particular hill, a bend in the river, a hut—that might allow them to find their way.

Even as they were starting to negotiate for furs and hunting rifles, they had no conception that land, too, had a price, let alone a fair price, since to them it was no more salable than the sun. But they did recognize that they had some to spare, especially if a sale—or "cession"—would win them something of obvious and immediate value like a gun or a period of peace with a colonial governor who might slaughter them otherwise. But in this exchange, as in all the others, there was no mechanism to establish a fair price. It was too one-sided. The English were experienced at determining land's value; the Cherokee had no idea at all. Few lived on the land in question, and they weren't the ones to sell it anyway. That fell by law to representatives of the entire Cherokee Nation, who could often be bought off with trinkets. Since everyone had a stake in the land, no one did, and that drove the price down to nearly nothing.

• • •

But once those first two traders came to the Cherokee, trade expanded in-exorably, even though it rarely went in the Cherokees' favor. Once unleashed, temptation rose on both sides. It started with the furs, and then consumed everything. The first traders followed "traces" or pathways to the Indians for the brazen thefts they called fair exchanges; when settlers came along, they developed a trading network to extend the exploitation; that development drew in the colonial government to support them; and the whole scheme soon reached such a scale that in 1730, the British government started casting about for a Cherokee to serve as the equivalent of the English king—George II at the time—with whom to conduct business more efficiently on a national scale, turning the Cherokee Nation into a giant fur factory.

The Cherokee, of course, were hardly an empire, but an assemblage of settlements whose residents shared a similar ancestry, and with it a common cultural outlook, and were willing to band together on occasion to protect their hunting rights, or even, as of late, to mount a common defense. Each settlement had a "headman," but the headmen rarely assembled even region-ally on any formal basis. There was a national council that met sporadically, but it was conceived as a "general convention of the entire nation" that re-flected the Cherokee impulse to govern by consensus, and was not intended to guide the national will actively to any particular agenda. To be sure, there was a "principal chief," but that chiefdom was more an honorific bestowed on some esteemed eminence than a position of genuine power.

Finding no one in authority with whom to talk trade on a national basis, a shameless Scottish adventurer, Alexander Cuming, took it upon himself to create such a personage and do it in the name of the British king. This was in the spring of 1730, when the England of old was emerging into the daunting British Empire that would become the greatest, and most encircling, power on the planet. To make the post enticing, Cuming gave it the impossibly grand title "emperor," a notion he doubtless had to explain. Surveying the landscape for an appropriate recipient, Cuming settled on an unassuming local chief named Moytoy, who formally accepted this great honor in a grand backwoods ceremony of Cuming's devising that featured, in Cuming's program, "Singing, Dancing, Feasting, making of Speeches, the Creation of Moytoy Emperor," probably in that order.

Once Moytoy was installed, Cuming invited this Cherokee emperor across the Atlantic to meet King George II and his royal court so they could talk official business. When Moytoy realized that he would have to traverse an ocean he may well never have heard of, aboard an assemblage of planking and canvas called a sailing ship, to a country he could not visualize, to meet an English person called a king, he seems to have grown uneasy, and he begged off, claiming his wife was sick. That left Cuming to scramble to create another august representative in a position to trade away the Cherokees' commercial interests, and he found another unexceptional local headman, named Oukah-Ulay, to fill the bill. Since Moytoy remained emperor, Cuming decided to award Oukah-Ulay the title of king, and so was he known in the British newspapers. To ensure that Oukah-Ulay actually made the ocean voyage, Cuming persuaded six other Cherokee chiefs to join him.

One of them was Moytoy's serious, peaceable son Attakullakulla, soon known to the English as Little Carpenter for his obliging manner and diminutive size. As Bartram gently put it, he was "of remarkable small stature, slender, and delicate frame." In the one surviving image, he has an eagle's beak, and a creased forehead, as if he was used to looking on things with suspicion, and is decked out rather stylishly, in a gray jacket with curling lapels and a plume of feathers. But this was after he came back. Going, he was a different man.

One might think the Cherokee would find the royals the silly ones. The doughy, paper-white King George under a haystack of a wig, encrusted with jewels, piled up with ermine and velvet, bearing a scepter that would be useless in battle, was dependent for his every need on liveried attendants hovering about. The king, however, was startled by these Cherokee, clothed only in a measly breechcloth decorated with a horse tail behind, their bare skin brilliant with green, red, and blue dots, and a feather poking up off the back of each chief's head. One astonished court observer was shocked to see that Attakullakulla bore "two large scars on each cheek," and "his ears were cut and banded with silver"—heavy hoop earrings that hung down to his shoulders. Probably most of the others were similarly decorated. Only "King" Oukah-Ulay was in anything close to proper English dress, as he was outfitted in a scarlet jacket and a pair of pinching satin breeches. All seven were induced to kneel before King George while Cuming solemnly "laid the Crown of the Cherokee Nation at His Majesty's Feet, with the five Eagle Tails, as an Emblem of His Majesty's sovereignty, and four Scalps of Indian Enemies." He left it to the official court observer to add: "All of which His Majesty was pleased to accept of."

To show how little about the occasion the Indians actually grasped, one of the chiefs had brought his bow and arrow and, when taking in the view from the royal balcony, he had to be discouraged from piercing an elk in the park below. Later, when a leg of mutton was served, the Cherokee eschewed the silverware and ate it with their bare hands. The king had the seven all fitted out in "rich garments laced in gold" for a tour of the London hot spots— St. James's Park, Westminster Abbey, and the Houses of Parliament. They were entertained in the fine homes of English noblemen, and sat for commemorative portraits, all of which showed that the bewildered chiefs, unfamiliar with the idea of such pictures, didn't quite know where—or how—to look. Everywhere they went, Londoners gathered by the thousand to get a glimpse of these mountain primitives, and responded as they might to the zoo creatures just coming into vogue, simultaneously transfixed and spooked. For Attakullakulla's part, when he was asked later whether he felt awkward to be put on display, he said not at all. "They [the crowds] are welcome to look upon me as a strange creature. They see but one, and in return I have an opportunity to look upon thousands."

Finally, they were driven in two royal coaches to pay a call on the lord commissioners, who reviewed with them the terms of an agreement they could not possibly have understood, for these native emissaries all signed their lives away with an X. The display of English superiority, in numbers, finery, and power, had done its work. The Cherokee were nothing, the English everything. Since Attakullakulla had a little of the mother tongue, he spoke for the group in the grave and thoughtful style that is characteristic of high Cherokee speech, but the message was tragic. "We look upon the Great King George as the Sun, and as our father, and upon ourselves as his children," he intoned, no doubt solemnly. "For though we are red, and you are white yet our hands and hearts are joined together. What we have seen, our children from generation to generation will always remember it. In war we shall always be with you."

3

THE BLOODY LAND

The doom of the Cherokee was foretold right there; all that followed was the details. It is not hard to imagine why a proud and innovative tribe like the Cherokee would debase themselves before a crusty, bejeweled foreign potentate. They may have seen the truth of it: these English were infinitely more powerful, more numerous, and, if one measures progress in material goods, far more advanced than the Cherokee would ever be. On some level, they accepted the depressing English view that, while the Cherokee might be marvels, they were marvels of a lesser order, little better than the Pygmies, the hermaphrodites, and the extremely deformed who had, by then, been staples of freak show entertainment in London taverns for a full century. The king might dress them in fine clothes, but they were savages.

If Attakullakulla went to London the proud son of a Cherokee chieftain, he returned a daunted man, overawed by these powers across the sea. The American settlers might defy King George, but they could do that only be-

cause they too were English. The Cherokee were much less. Following Attakullakulla, they came to regard themselves as the "children" of this great
king, their "Great Father," a title they would eventually give the American
president who defeated them. To the Cherokee, it was an honor to be related
at all. This would define the relationship with whites for decades to come. The
white men were more than just different from the red men. They were better.
And the only way that the red man could get better was to turn white.

Moytoy never made much of his powers; and, raised to glory by his visit
to King George, the frail little Attakullakulla was awarded his father's title to
make of it what he would. He was also called principal chief, a term more sensible to the Cherokee. Attakullakulla lived in Chota, on the banks of the Little
Tennessee River. Chota was the closest thing to a Cherokee capital city, and
he styled himself the White Chief of peace, not the Red Chief of war, to fit his
disposition and to mark his commitment to the alliance he had formed with
the king. When the endless English war against the French spilled over from
Europe into the New World, Attakullakulla tried always to take the side of
the English, even as they betrayed him time and again. When some renegade
Cherokee stormed the British Fort Loudon and took the British commander
John Stuart prisoner, Attakullakulla had him freed, and tightly befriended
him, giving Stuart a Cherokee name that translated as "Bushyhead" for his
shock of ruddy hair. Meanwhile, the Red Chief, Ostenaco, complicated relations by having no compunctions about going after the English for laying
waste to fifteen Cherokee towns.

Attakullakulla was the one to try to calm things down, and ask the British for peace. When it was finally secured, a British soldier, Henry Timberlake, escorted the war chief Ostenaco and several other chiefs to see King
George III. But the English had gotten everything they needed from Attakullakulla's delegation back in 1730, and the king kept the chiefs waiting for three
weeks before granting them an audience that proved a brief formality. The
most lasting thing that came from it was Ostenaco's meeting with the writer
Oliver Goldsmith. The Cherokee Red Chief gave the Londoner such a tight
embrace that he left Goldsmith's face smeared with face paint, to the amusement of everyone.

Meanwhile, Attakullakulla had been propitiating the English with transfers of land that were growing in number and expanse as the pressures from

the settlers rose. It was as if the Cherokee were a bear encircled by an ever-larger pack of wolves. Formidable as the bear might have seemed, it was wildly outnumbered, and once the first wolf landed a bite, the others were emboldened to sink their fangs deeper. Strictly speaking, the transfers were sales—or, more formally, "cessions"—but the conditions were so one-sided that they hardly merit this term. The first one had occurred before Attakullakulla left for London, and it was fairly modest: the royal governor of South Carolina Colony came away with just over two thousand square miles of Cherokee territory that lay on its distant eastern border. In 1755, however, his successor, Governor James Glen, took almost 9,000 more that lay closer inside. In 1770, the colonies of Virginia, West Virginia, and Kentucky grabbed almost 10,000 acres among them; and on it went in 1772 and 1773 before the Cherokee gave in to the greatest landgrab of them all in 1775, just as the colonists' war against mother England was heating up, when along came a sharpy, Richard Henderson of the Transylvania Company, which specialized in acquiring mammoth parcels of land for a song. He managed to win all of present-day Kentucky, first explored by the intrepid Daniel Boone, and much of Tennessee—a total of 25,000 square miles. All for a handsome display of arms and ammunition that had been enticingly laid out for the Cherokee in a log cabin beside their council ground, with a sweetener of a few thousand pounds. The fateful deal was struck at a place along the Watauga River, well to the northeast of Tennessee, called Sycamore Shoals for its graceful trees, on flatlands long used as a gathering spot for Cherokee hunting expeditions. With war rising all around, the munitions were irresistible to the rising chief, Oconostota. It was the prospect of maintaining easy relations with the settlers that moved Attakullakulla, now nearing ninety, haggard from decades of futile struggle against outsize adversaries, even though it violated his agreement with King George to sell land only to the crown.

Attakullakulla's son Dragging Canoe was there at Sycamore Shoals, and he was apoplectic to realize that his father and Oconostota would give up so much land to the enemy. Already sixty himself, Dragging Canoe was everything his father was not—his face scarred by smallpox, he was a fearsome spectacle of coiled wrath invariably depicted in the habit of war—breechcloth, knee-high leggings, and beaded breastplate, spear in hand. He earned his name by dragging a heavy canoe down a river shore as a small child, and he was always ready to shoulder any difficulty and haul it to the end of the earth. When his two elders signed the treaty, Dragging Canoe stormed out of the council house in a fury, only to stomp back moments later, his face blazing. He pointed toward Kentucky and roared at Henderson the words that would echo for some time. Just try to occupy your new purchase, he declared. "You will find its settlement dark and bloody!" Ever after, the territory was known to the Cherokee as the Bloody Land. It was Dragging Canoe who brought war to quiet Savannah Ford on the Hiwassee as he gathered an eighty-man force to roust these settlers from this ill-gotten Transylvania, as the ceded lands were now called. He enlisted two other fiery chiefs to assist him: the Raven was to slash at the settlers in Carter's Valley, and Abram would go after a settlement in Watauga, which the whites were claiming as their own private state; both places were well to the northeast. Dragging Canoe himself would raid the settlements on the long, meandering Holston River near a small forti- fied village called Eaton's Station, up by the present Kentucky border, on what had long been called the Great War Trail.

The Cherokee never raised an army by the sort of general conscription relied upon by other nations; rather, they made a full-throated appeal to the men of each town, hoping to inspire them to give up the hunt for a time and fight. Raging with indignation at these vile settlers, Dragging Canoe swept down the Hiwassee to win warriors. He drew a band of a few dozen from Savannah Ford, the peaceable Tar-chee among them.

To mark the glorious occasion of war against the infernal whites, the townsmen built a great fire in the middle of the ceremonial square. Just five years old, The Ridge must have watched, transfixed, as his father joined the other brave men, stripping off his long deerskin robe and thigh-high boots to don the flapping loincloths and soft moccasins of war, and then to streak their sweat-glistened skin with terrifying war paint and loop bold circles of black and red, the colors of death, around their eyes.

As the flames leaped up, the women set a kettle boiling, and then poured out a steaming brew of black tea to spread fearlessness through the veins of these warriors and to protect their bodies from the blades and bullets of the enemy. Before anyone drank, the shaman lifted a ceremonial swan's wing high over the kettle so the Great Spirit would bless their mission. Then the pound- ing grew louder, and the men grabbed their war clubs—red and black like their frightful painted faces—and formed a line to the east. The beat was slow at first, and the men stomped their feet into the well-trodden earth. Then they all shouted out a war cry—*Yeh! Yeh!*—and the beat quickened until, in a fury, they chopped their war clubs onto the heads of an imaginary enemy, making the brains run out. Finally, the beat slowed once more, and the men's arms dropped to their sides, and they slowed to a walk until the pounding ceased altogether and silence spread across the fields to the trees to represent the great peace that comes after a great victory.

Then the warriors disappeared silently into the forest, their tread light, the night air all over their skin. They bore an assortment of rifles, bows and arrows, knives, tomahawks, spears—anything deadly that was at hand. Unlike their enemy, the Cherokee had no regulation arms. Once they'd made their way through the valley to close in on the Holston River, a good twenty-five miles distant, they made their plan. They broke into small raiding parties of perhaps a dozen Cherokee each to attack the farmhouses of the pioneer families who'd ventured away from the settlements to live off a few acres they'd cleared from the woods. Hardly visible in the starlight, the Cherokee, Tarchee among them, made their way silently through the woods. They'd creep up to the edge of the cleared fields, and wait there, fully armed, in their fierce war paint, for the first light of dawn.

At a signal, they'd come roaring toward the house, letting loose with wild ululating cries like turkey gobbles, and then, when they drew near, let fly with everything they had—bullets, arrows. The settlers would scramble at the sound, rushing for their guns, but rarely in time. The Cherokee would surge across the yards, hack open the doors, and burst inside to bring their tomahawks down on everyone they saw, from doddering elders to babies in cribs. It was a war of shrieks, gun blasts, and blood everywhere as the blades fell.

Dragging Canoe's men surged on toward the main Holston settlement, leaving behind scalped corpses lying prone in a muddy field or draped across a table or curved protectively on a scarlet-stained bed around a hacked-up child. Horror was Dragging Canoe's way.

They arrived at the village in the pitch dark, and, as they had early that morning, stayed silent in the trees until first light, thinking the surprise was theirs to give. Attakullakulla's half-blood niece, Nancy Ward, lived in nearby Echota. The daughter of a British officer, whose own daughter was in love with an American, she'd heard whispers of Dragging Canoe's coming attack and told the men there to be on the alert. When a couple of lissome white girls, blissfully unaware of the danger, insisted on bathing in a nearby stream, the commander let them go—but had a few men secretly watch over them. If any Cherokee came, attracted by the sight of the beauties, these men were to lure the Cherokee back to the fort, pretending to be taken by surprise. Sure enough, the Cherokee were drawn to the girls, and then saw the men guarding them, and they gave chase, keen for the scalps. But hundreds of the white men's comrades were waiting for them, out of sight. When the Cherokee came tearing toward them, they opened fire from the trees and mowed the unsuspecting Cherokee down. In minutes, Cherokee lay everywhere on the ground. Dragging Canoe's right leg was shattered. His brother, Little Owl, took thirteen bullets, but somehow survived. They both managed to limp away to safety. But thirteen other men lay behind, to be scalped by whites seething over what the Indians had done to their dead.

Tar-chee, happily for him, was not among them. When the remnants of this hacked-up Cherokee regiment returned to their villages, Dragging Canoe made sure the men bore some scalps high atop a hemlock bough. There were thirty-seven scalps in all. But far more Cherokee had died. Dragging Canoe also brought back a small boy, Samuel Moore, he'd caught as he tried to scramble away. His hands were bound, and he was tethered by the neck to minders who jerked him along. Dragging Canoe had the boy tied to a stake atop a mount of wood, and then set a fire blazing.

Although Dragging Canoe's men had taken the worst of it, their assault provoked a ferocious counterstrike from a vast army drawn from the colonial governments of Virginia, Georgia, and the Carolinas, in the belief that any dead settler needed to be avenged a hundred times over. Putting aside their war with the British, the settlers formed an army of 6,500, one of the largest fighting forces ever assembled in the New World, to smash the Cherokee into oblivion.

Dragging Canoe had fled to South Carolina to recover from his wounds but, hearing of the American offensive, he charged back into Cherokee country in time to see waves of American soldiers sweep over a broad swath of valley towns from every direction, slaughtering everyone they saw. The inveterate Indian fighter General Griffith Rutherford was in charge of this apocalypse, and, after his men shot all the Cherokee they could see, they went on to kill their horses, destroy their fields, make off with their possessions, and burn their villages, thirty-six in all, to the ground.

Tar-chee fled before the slaughter reached Savannah Ford. He had already grown sick of war, and he'd seen too many families lose the father who provided for them. Tar-chee gathered up his wife and two young sons, grabbed all the possessions they could carry, and loaded everyone into a long dugout canoe, which they paddled downriver, desperate to stay ahead of Rutherford's marauders. Other Cherokee were fleeing south with them, most of them headed to Chickamauga, just across the Georgia border from present-day Chattanooga. Since this was Dragging Canoe's stronghold, along the southern curve of the Tennessee by the flatland of Muscle Shoals, they hoped to find safety. But Tar-chee wanted no part of Dragging Canoe. He curved his canoe north up a slender tributary to Sequatchie, as the Cherokee called it, "the place of the grinning possum," below the high mountain of that name. The Sequatchie was a quiet waterway on the far side of Walden Ridge from the mighty Tennessee, running northeast from the vicinity of today's Chattanooga. Tar-chee would settle there with a few other families, in a quiet glen well back from the river, protected from behind by a towering granite cliff topped by a ridge of trees.

The place was so well chosen that Tar-chee must have scouted it beforehand. Away from the other settlements, both Cherokee and white, the mountainside was not yet hunted out, at least not for a man of Tar-chee's talents, and the river ran with fish. Tar-chee's wife, O-go-nuh-to-tua, sowed corn and other crops on the rich soil of the flatland, while he returned to the hunt, taking The Ridge with him.

The Cherokee who'd fled to Chickamauga must have been shocked by what they found. Dragging Canoe had sent out his warriors to chase off the Americans encircling British positions in Georgia, leaving only women and children behind at Chickamauga when Americans bent on devastation surged down the Tennessee in canoes. So now the refugees from Savannah Ford found no haven, but smoldering villages, scattered corpses, and ruined crops. When Dragging Canoe himself returned to see the ruin, he refused to yield. "Now we live on grass," he declared. "But we are not conquered." He moved his stronghold farther downstream to a Sequatchie of his own, concealed by the river's windings, and protected by steep mountains behind. But it was larger, and would serve as the capital of the Cherokee resistance. From there, Dragging Canoe dispatched lightning raids against the hated American forces, even though they torched whole Cherokee towns in brutal retaliation.

When the British finally blundered at Yorktown, Virginia, in 1781, surrendering an army of nearly 10,000 men and ending any hope of reclaiming their rebellious colonies, Dragging Canoe was determined to assemble a confederation of Indian tribes to fight on against the detested Americans. Even after the British accepted the American terms for peace in Paris in 1783, Dragging Canoe joined with Spain to continue his attacks on the Virginia settlements. He agreed with Don Esteban Miró, the brazen governor of Spanish Florida. Without a king, these Americans "are nothing of themselves," scoffed Miró. "They are like a man that is lost and wandering in the woods."

And so, bolstered by Spanish military supplies, Dragging Canoe fought on. Safe in Sequatchie, Tar-chee was done with war. But not The Ridge. Even as a boy, The Ridge knew what his father did not—that this war with the Americans was not over, and might never be over. There could never be peace with so many American settlers bent on seizing every last piece of Cherokee land. The Ridge was only twelve, but he'd already reached his father's height; his voice had lost its girlish pitch; the muscles had thickened on his arms, chest, and legs; hair had grown in unexpected places; and bold thoughts filled his head. It was time for him to prepare to join this war. It was time for him to become *a-sga si-ti*, as the Cherokee said: dreadful.

Everyone assembled by the water at dawn one morning for the ceremony as The Ridge climbed up onto a flat rock to stand naked before the spectators for the last time as a boy. A stern old warrior joined him up there. The warrior held up a menacing wolf bone that had been whittled at one end to a claw with four nail-sharp points, two inches across. Anyone would have gasped to see it, but The Ridge remained silent, impassive. He lifted his arms toward the old warrior, palms up, as the warrior asked the Great Spirit to fill the boy's mind with war and his heart with courage.

A "Scratching Ceremony," McKenney called it, but he was a bureaucrat, writing forty years later. For these weren't scratches, but cuts deep into the skin, yielding an "effusion of blood," as McKenney observed. The old warrior placed the wolf bone up against the tender flesh inside one arm, and then pressed down the row of teeth, slicing a good quarter inch into the boy's skin, then drew the claw slowly up his forearm to the elbow and then, inch by inch, to his armpit. How the blood must have streamed down his arm, pooled on his open palm, dribbled between his fingers! The wolf bone left four bloody tracks as it climbed up to The Ridge's armpit, now darkening with hair, then across his thickening chest and ever so slowly down the other arm. Then the warrior dragged the wolf bone back up the outside of his other arm to his shoulder, then across his back, and down. Slowly, slowly, drawing out the pain as the blood welled up and slid down his body. Then from the boy's heels up the backs of his bare leg over his rump, up his back to the top of his broadening shoulders once more, and all the way down again. It must have been a bonfire of hurt, yet the boy did not cry out, did not even wince. He remained silent, unmoving, to live in the pain as the place where a boy goes when he becomes a man.

When the ordeal was finally over, The Ridge dived into the cool waters of the river to chill the senses, and then lay down on a blanket while the conjurer salved with herbs and potions the oozing cuts all over his body. A memory would remain on his skin in those scars. After this, he was to stay clear of women for seven days—but he was free to indulge himself as a man on the eighth, and on all the other days to follow. This was the joy of manhood, after all. He'd celebrate with a meal of roast partridge, a bird silent on the ground but thunderous in flight. Like a warrior who crept up on his enemies—and killed with a roar.

4

THE FIRST KILL

When the British formally surrendered in Paris, leaving their Cherokee allies to fight on with the Spanish if they dared, they gave up not
just the colonies, but all the uncharted territory past the Alleghenies
to the Mississippi. This was a broad patch of land that, on American maps,
was called the Southwest Territory, and left largely blank, as if it were empty,
which it was not. It was Indian land, much of it belonging to the Cherokee.

To explain the change of sovereignty, the Continental Congress summoned the Cherokee leaders to the wealthy Hopewell Plantation on the
Seneca River in South Carolina's present-day Pickens County, just across the
Tennessee border. Refusing to hear any talk of peace, Dragging Canoe did
not show up. The leadership fell instead to a grandee called Old Tassel, the
revered First Beloved Man of the so-called Overhill Towns of the higher elevations that had been decimated in the war. He was desperate for peace in his
old age. Almost 1,000 other Cherokee attended, including thirty-six chiefs.

Old Tassel produced a map of the Cherokee Nation that included the lands passed to the Transylvania Company in 1775, and pleaded that there had been a terrible misunderstanding. The land was never intended to be sold; it was only to be leased, and it needed now to be returned to the nation. The commissioners must have snickered at his naïveté. The land was now the state of Kentucky, and its residents were not about to leave. However it was come by, the agreement would be honored forever.

The three American commissioners assured the Indians that their government did not seek any more Cherokee land, and solemnly promised to enforce the existing boundaries of the Cherokee Nation against further encroachment. They agreed to remove any white settlers who had already gone over the line. But the Americans did insist that their traders be given free access to the territory, and promised to prosecute, in American courts, any crimes committed by whites. To all this, the Cherokee chiefs could only bow their heads in agreement.

It was a historic treaty between two sovereign nations, and it did not last. When he learned the details, Dragging Canoe reluctantly deferred to the Cherokee Nation's acceptance of the new territory of Kentucky on its ancestral lands. But he refused to acknowledge the new State of Franklin founded the following year, 1786, by the headstrong militia commander John Sevier— appropriately pronounced *severe*—and William Campbell, a former captive of the Indians. They carved it out of northeastern Tennessee, hoping to make it the new nation's fourteenth state, with Sevier as its governor. Sevier was a handsome and dashing hero of the frontier to his many followers, who hailed him as Nolichucky Jack. To the Cherokee, on the receiving end of his exploits, he was a remorseless brute who would stop at nothing. When Sevier was outraged that the Cherokee would not be brought to heel, Dragging Canoe vowed to burn the whole State of Franklin to the ground and trample on the ashes. And then he started in on just that, waging a war of terror everywhere. "Every spring, every ford, every path, every farm, every trail, every house nearby, in its first settlement, was once the scene of danger, exposure, attack, exploit, achievement, death," wrote one contemporary historian.

When Dragging Canoe's warriors swarmed a settlement of ex-Franklinites near his home base of Chickamauga, they slaughtered a close friend of Sevier's, Colonel William Christian. Although Old Tassel had nothing to do with it, Sevier held him responsible as the signer of the treaty. As it happened, the genial Old Tassel had known Christian and was sorry to learn of his death. "I loved Colonel Christian and he loved me," he wrote to Sevier. No matter. In May 1788, after some of Dragging Canoe's Cherokee butchered all but one member of a family called Kirk by the Little River outside present-day Knoxville, Sevier burned the town of Hiwassee in a frenzy of retaliation. Then he summoned Old Tassel with some other Cherokee chiefs to talk peace under a flag of truce. During the parley, Sevier stepped outside the meeting room just long enough for the only surviving Kirk, the wrathful John Jr., to burst inside and lay a tomahawk into the side of Old Tassel's head. Seeing Old Tassel crash to the floor, blood pouring from him, the other chiefs froze, and then bowed their heads to the inevitable.

Dragging Canoe was apoplectic at such a dastardly trick—how could Sevier, how could *anyone*, kill any Cherokee chiefs under the flag of truce, let alone a revered figure like Old Tassel? He roused warriors in outrage. All along the shores of the Tennessee, the Clinch, the French Broad, the Hiwassee, the Nolichucky, the Powell, and the other Long Men that had nurtured Cherokee for generations, and from there up into the more remote settlements in the mountains, the drums of war pounded as warriors donned face paint and gathered about fires. In tiny, secluded Sequatchie, too, warriors stripped to breechclouts; painted their faces vermilion, one eye circled in spooky white, the other in deadly black; and seized hefty war clubs to dance the war dance, first the slow stomping that pounded the earth, and then the brisker hacking gestures of blind rage, before easing back once more into the glorious calm of victory.

One of the youngest warriors was The Ridge. He was now a solid, strapping seventeen, deep-voiced and rock-steady, and ready to prove himself. He'd shaved his head clean, except for a scalp lock adorned with a sprig of red feathers tipped with white, and he'd stripped down, his body and face painted like the others'. He would enter the forest with the other men, but move like a hunter, silent on his moccasins, hidden among the shadows, until he struck with a roar. As the youngest, he was given only a spear; bullets and powder were for the older men, as were arrows. But The Ridge had practiced thrusting his spear deep into a tree. He was ready.

"In this expedition," wrote an admiring McKenney, "he endured, without a murmur, great hardship and dangers." The Ridge brought with him only a single cup of corn mush, tucked into a pouch about his waist. No one ate on the first day, and then each day afterward each man limited himself to a single, sparing portion of the mush, washed down with stream water. As The Ridge's band moved through the forest in search of American militiamen to kill, other Cherokee from other villages joined in to swell the war party to 200. They set their sights on Houston's Station, a small fortified settlement of maybe a half dozen families not far from White's Fort, now Knoxville, where the French Broad joins the Holston in eastern Tennessee. A small force led by Major Thomas Stewart was garrisoned there. Aware of the rising tension, Stewart sent scouts into the forest to listen for approaching Indians.

But the Cherokee had scouts of their own, far stealthier ones, and intercepted the white scouts and slit their throats before they could sound any warning. Then they spied some militia soldiers rushing on horseback to Stewart's defense. A band of Cherokee peeled off from the rest to ambush them as they passed nearby Setico, ten miles from the North Carolina border. The whites had abandoned the town amid all the talk of war, but an orchard outside its walls was heavy with glistening ripe apples that the Cherokee knew the militiamen would crave after a hard march in the summer heat. They hid in the shadowy woods just back from the orchard and waited.

It wasn't long before a small mounted detachment of perhaps two dozen soldiers came galloping up. Sure enough, the leader called a halt by the orchard and let his men dismount. Leaving their horses, the men splashed across a stream. They carried their rifles over their heads, but chucked them away when they reached the far side and dashed hungrily for the fruit. They were reaching up into the branches when the Indians charged at them from the trees with terrifying war whoops. A flight of arrows immediately dropped six of the soldiers, and then four more fell screaming to tomahawk blades. The rest dashed to save themselves, only to be hacked at by waiting Cherokee.

Holding himself back from the action, The Ridge saw a Cherokee haul one soldier off his horse as he tried to gallop away. Grappling, the two fell to the ground, where the Cherokee tried to work a bowie knife into the enemy's chest. But the soldier shoved the Cherokee off and was digging out his pistol to finish him when The Ridge roared in with a spear. He caught the soldier just as he turned toward the sound. The Ridge crashed the iron tip into his chest, then rammed the spear clear through. It's an intimate death, a spearing, and Ridge could watch his victim's face dissolve as the life fled from him. The Ridge stepped on the dead man's chest to jerk the spear free, and then drew out a knife to hack off the scalp, his first trophy. He was an Outacite now, a Mankiller.

The enemy routed, the Cherokee ripped open the uniforms of the dead to carve out their bowels and chuck them into the water, which turned a hideous scarlet. Raising high a tomahawk, one infuriated warrior hacked off the head of one soldier, then ripped out his pulpy heart and coiled entrails to splatter them onto the ground and stamp on them. If The Ridge was not one of the frenzied, he was one who watched. When the Cherokee returned gaily home, they held high plenty of scalps on pine branches, The Ridge's trophy was among them.

He found Tar-chee had fallen sick, making The Ridge fear for his family with the war closing in around them. The Ridge moved everyone on from little Sequatchie to Pine Log, a larger, more secure Cherokee village of about twenty huts well away from the action, thirty miles into present-day Georgia, along a creek by 2,300-foot Pine Log Mountain, near what is now the modest town of Waleska, halfway to Atlanta.

A symbol of Franklinite arrogance, White's Fort preyed on the minds of the Cherokee. It was a nearly impregnable fortress of malignancy, bordered by an eight-foot stockade fence, with indestructible corner blockhouses that had plenty of rifle portholes. Inside, the evil whites had created a tree-shaded village square that made an infuriating little piece of America inside the Cherokee Nation. It projected insolence, but was scented with genteel serenity—"an air of enchanting coolness and rural retirement and seclusion" said one early historian. Settlers had come to this walled-in paradise in droves, and put up shops all around, as if it were New York.

The Ridge joined an army of warriors raised by the Cherokee chieftains Little Turkey and White Dog to waste the place. But the various chiefs soon fell to squabbling, an all too common hazard of the Cherokees' otherwise commendable lack of rank. The Americans conducted their wars the way they ran their businesses, with a strict hierarchy that descended through the troops from a single leader with a sensible strategy and the means to enact it. Too often, a band of Cherokee warriors was little more than a posse of overheated individuals, with no line of command, and rarely a battle plan beyond terrifying chaos. Stymied by disagreement, the Cherokee this time withdrew without firing a shot and had to clobber a tiny garrison in Maryville, just south of Knoxville, to come home with any scalps.

Back from battle, The Ridge realized that local game had grown so scarce he'd have to roam farther afield to get meat for the winter. With his father sick, it was up to him to feed the family. Abandoning the war, The Ridge joined a hunting party to hike over the central Cumberlands and up into their old lands in Kentucky that proved to be good hunting. On the way back, the men came upon some settlers working in their fields. The Cherokee would have left the whites alone but for the heady fragrance of pipe smoke that blew on the wind. The Cherokee slaughtered them all for their tobacco. The Ridge had been in camp, and McKenney claims that he was "mortified" when he learned the men had killed for so little. But he'd soon do worse.

Back at Pine Log, The Ridge joined a new chief, John Watts, sometimes known as Young Tassel because he was the nephew of his foully murdered older namesake. Unusually portly for a Cherokee, Watts was a warrior of some ambition, and he was keen to take another crack at White's Fort and strike a mighty blow against the Americans' wilderness empire. But once again, the Cherokee leaders fell to bickering, and White's Fort didn't fall to Watts, either. To salvage his pride, Watts took aim at Captain John Gillespie's station, a lesser prize on the French Broad River, which joins with Holston to drain into the Tennessee from the east. His men charged out from the trees to hack some unsuspecting farmers to pieces, and then swarmed the station with blood-curdling shrieks. When the defenders ran out of ammunition and their guns fell silent, the Cherokee scrambled over the outer fence and dashed across rooftops to drop down inside the yard. "Great was the horror of the scene that then ensued," declared the *South Carolina Gazette*. The Ridge joined in that slaughter. The white men dispatched, the Cherokees roped together the women and children, twenty-eight in all, and led them away to slavery and worse.

John Watts blamed Sevier for the brutality. "You began [the bloodshed] and this is what you get for it," he declared. When Sevier offered no reply, Watts took yet another futile run at White's Fort. By now, winter was coming on, and the Cherokee were far from home. Watts led his men into the mountains to hunker down in some huts they threw up along Flint Creek. The Ridge among them, they hid there, shivering, from Sevier's men.

But Sevier had his nose up. The freezing Cherokee awoke one morning to the crunching sounds of Sevier's weather-beaten soldiers surrounding them from everywhere, rifles at the ready. At the first volleys, the Cherokee dashed down the valley. But Sevier had hidden his men all along the one trail out, and a horrendous turkey shoot followed. "We have buried 145 of their dead," Sevier wrote later, "and by the blood we have traced for miles all over the woods, it is supposed the greater part of them retreated with wounds."* The Ridge was one of the few who slipped away. And he stayed away, perhaps nursing his wounds, or perhaps just sick of death, for seven months.

When he finally returned to Pine Log, he found both his parents dead, not just his ailing father. Gone, their bodies anointed with oil and buried with all their belongings under the spot where they'd perished, implanted in the earth that the water beetle had made. The women of the village had filled the air with lamentations; the men had dabbed themselves with ashes and worn tattered clothes in tribute. So he came to know. The Ridge had not been there to see.

He had another brother now besides David Oo-watie and a sister. As the oldest son, The Ridge was their father now. In caring for them, he fell into what McKenney terms some "obscurity," as he engaged in only occasional "predatory excursions" against the whites that would win him attention. Instead, The Ridge took to the mountains on long, solitary hunts for elk, bear, or deer, all of them now so scarce he had to roam for weeks at a time, sometimes venturing far onto the upland prairies of the Cumberlands, or along the slender traces that wove between the trees into the contested lands of Kentucky, to fill his meat pouch. His family was counting on him now.

---

* Sevier did not escape unscathed. His longtime political rival, North Carolina's Governor Johnson, took advantage of the uproar to jail Sevier on trumped-up charges of treason, seize his State of Franklin for North Carolina, and present it to the federal government as payment for the state's war debt. Franklinites could then become North Carolinians only if they pledged allegiance to the state, as Sevier was ultimately obliged to do, too.

5

FOREIGN RELATIONS

fter Washington's inauguration in April 1789, his beefy secretary of war,
General Henry Knox, the hero who'd broken the British siege of Boston,
alerted him to a danger he'd probably not considered: the "disgraceful
violation" of the Treaty of Hopewell. Under it, the Americans had guaranteed
the Cherokee borders, but they were being breached on all sides, not just by
individual settlers, but by entire states, such as Georgia, that were selling off
Cherokee land several million acres at a time. To Knox, this not only was
unfair to the Cherokee but ran against the interests of the United States, as
such unlawful moves demonstrated "manifest contempt" for the federal government that was struggling to assert itself under its bold new Constitution.

Washington had appointed the airy, highborn William Blount the first
governor of the loosely organized Southwest Territory, soon to be forged into
the state of Tennessee. It now consisted largely of Indian lands in which Blount
illegally speculated, a blatant conflict of interest that did much to undermine

his gentlemanly demeanor. To work out relations with the foreign nation in the midst of America, he convened a meeting with some tribal leaders at White's Fort, which was not a good start. Long a target of Cherokee wrath, it had now spawned a thriving town, named Knoxville after the very secretary of war who was supposedly defending their interests. Blount had made it the capital of his territory, erecting for himself a fine mansion overlooking the Holston River. The town also boasted a fledgling college, a log courthouse, a jail, a barracks, and grand plans for a grid of streets with sixty-four house lots.

For the discussions Governor Blount attired himself in military dress complete with an absurd ceremonial sword, and, flanked by several deputies, he seated himself on a kind of throne under the tall trees. The Cherokee sent a delegation of forty-one chiefs, the younger ones with chests bared, their shaved heads adorned with eagle feathers. More than 1,200 other Indians came to watch the spectacle, humbled by the realization that their Great Spirit had proved no match for the Christian God of these white dignitaries— and the possibility that their ancient ways were simply unsuited to these new times. The American president was their Great Father now. Roundly defeated with their British allies in battle, the Cherokee could hope only for pity, a terrible comedown for a proud people.

Governor Blount grandly affirmed the right of the Cherokee Nation to exist, but alas, not with its earlier borders, as he had to recognize the rights of the pioneers who had so courageously settled in the Cumberland valley, and he would require from the Cherokee yet another cession to accommodate them. Just as his predecessors at Sycamore Shoals had done, Blount pledged to remove any settlers who pushed even an inch farther onto Cherokee soil. In fact, the treaty would require Americans to carry a passport to enter the Cherokee Nation, as if it were Canada. But the United States would reserve the right to set the terms for trade with the Cherokee, and it would forbid their government from engaging in any foreign diplomacy on its own. That authority would belong solely to the United States government.

Was the Cherokee Nation a nation, or not? This was a question that would prove convulsive in the years ahead. To seal the deal, the United States offered cash for the lands it was now acquiring, in the form of an annuity—$1,000 annually to be distributed to all the Cherokee, later increased to $5,000. Not entirely a kindness, the arrangement would make the Cherokee dependent on an American government that might prove capricious. The United States would also greatly enhance the power of the Cherokee authority it selected to make the distribution. The money, in short, made the Cherokee Nation less sovereign.

As did an article, XIV, supposedly requested by Washington himself, by which the Cherokee were to aspire to "a greater degree of civilization," that is, something more to the liking of the white world. The Cherokee were to be less dependent on hunting, and more on farming. While this was presented as a boon to the Cherokee, the true intent was not so magnanimous. Farming used less land than hunting, freeing the remainder for whites. The transformation would upend Cherokee life. Farming, after all, had always been women's work ever since the days of Selu, the "Corn Mother" who was the Cherokee Eve, and her husband, the hunter Kanáti, the Cherokee Adam. Men were hunters, simple as that. *Women* were farmers. No matter. The U.S. government would provide the Cherokee with "useful implements of husbandry" like plows and hoes, and send a few interpreters to explain the basics of farming.

After Old Tassel, Little Turkey had taken over as the White Chief, with the fearsome Dragging Canoe as the Red Chief. Seeing no good alternative, Little Turkey had persuaded a retinue of local chiefs including John Watts, Bloody Fellow, Lying Fawn, and Doublehead to sign this Holston Treaty on July 2, 1791. It was a lousy deal, but it would bring peace with the Americans who had conquered them.

When the Cherokee heard about what their chiefs had given up, outrage spread like wildfire across the land, and warriors formed into roving bands of fury, sending arrows thudding into the backs of settlers who ranged too far from their homes or stations, and taking their scalps to adorn a hemlock branch. Cherokee fighters picked off a couple of boys outside a small farm in Hunt's Valley up by the Kentucky border; four adults near there at Zeigler's Station off the Cumberland River; two on the Kentucky Road that sweeps north; and one by lonesome Pistol Creek. Shocked by this uprising, Governor Blount was obliged by the treaty to protect the Cherokee from the settlers, not the reverse. So settlers hunkered down to protect themselves, strengthening their fortifications with thicker logs, more portholes, and more guns to fill them.

Of all the Cherokee leaders, Dragging Canoe, now in his early seventies, was the one who had been most loath to surrender the tribe's age-old customs and any more of its land to these upstart Americans. Spoiling for war, Dragging Canoe turned to the Creeks and the Choctaw for warriors to create an Indian army to strike at their American overlords. He had just the target: the smug, Scottish-born General Arthur St. Clair, who had lost Ticonderoga for the Americans in their Revolution, and whose 1,400-man army camped by the Wabash seemed ripe for the plucking. They were there to watch over the settlers who'd pushed onto the Indian land in the Northwest Territory of present-day Ohio, but Dragging Canoe had heard that the men had grown lazy with such a tedious assignment. Many of them spent their nights getting drunk, and their days sleeping it off.

Dragging Canoe's men, 1,000 strong, saw their chance when they spotted the tipsy, caterwauling American soldiers loll about. In the half-light of an early November morning, amid falling snow, they struck. Shrieking Indians in war paint charged into the camp from every direction to shower the drowsy troops with arrows, then bring down the tomahawks. Many of the soldiers ran for their lives, stopping only when their commanders screamed they'd kill them otherwise, then turning tail once more. Six hundred soldiers fell to the Indians' assault, and uncounted more received horrific wounds. When the battle was done, and the Indians had finally left, military investigators found the bodies of the American dead littering roads for miles all around, many of them with their uniforms ripped off, their flesh ripped up as if by wild animals, and their scalps missing. It was the worst defeat ever suffered by Americans in their long war against the Indians. General St. Clair was one of just two dozen soldiers to survive. Outraged by his ineptitude, President Washington demanded his resignation.

All across the nation, Cherokee celebrated around roaring fires, especially at Chickamauga, where Dragging Canoe exulted, his eyes blazing, his blood up. When a couple of warriors brought the scalp of an American trader named Mims, they shredded it with their teeth while Dragging Canoe watched delightedly. Then, eagle feathers poking up off the back of his head, he joined in the scalp dance, stomping the earth to the beat of the drum in an all-night frenzy. All the excitement proved too much for the aging chief. When the sun climbed up into the sky the next morning, he did not rise with it.

Dragging Canoe may have dreamed of a vast Indian uprising against their

American oppressors, but when John Watts succeeded him as Red Chief, he was more realistic. He preferred to go after the immediate targets of Cherokee wrath, hoping to frighten the encroaching settlers away from their nation, not from all the Indian nations, and to intimidate the federal government that was supporting the settlers. To improve his chances, Watts won the secret support of the Spanish governor of Florida, who was willing to back the Cherokee against the Americans with money and munitions if there would be land in it for the Spanish. It was a reprise of the Cherokees' ill-fated alliance with the British against the Americans just over a decade before. Even with Spanish backing, the Cherokee Nation was not designed to mobilize for full-scale war; it could organize only for fleet raiding parties intended to scare off motley groups of settlers.

Nonetheless, The Ridge got caught up in all the excited plans to evict the Americans. Leaving Oo-watie to look after their siblings, he came from Pine Log, his body smeared with war paint, to join Watts's attack on Nashville. But the old chaos plagued them, as Watts's Creek ally, Talotiskee, insisted on going after John Buchanan's station first. An uneasy lowing of a herd of cows gave away their plan; the settlers hurried inside the station, shut the stockade gates, sealed the hatches, and, through the portholes, fired at the Cherokee with everything they had, including a blunderbuss that shot hunks of lead and even bits of cutlery.

Dozens of Indians were hit as they charged. John Watts himself was struck by a bullet in the chest, and pleaded with a warrior to hack off his head if he died so no white man could claim his scalp. Others fell back into the trees as their bullets and arrows banged uselessly against the station's thick walls. Talotiskee hid in the woods until a Cherokee called him out for his cowardice. Just then, another Creek burst into the open to try to torch the station, only to be shot dead before he'd taken more than a few steps. With that, Talotiskee haltingly came forth as well—and was killed by a single rifle shot. Four other chiefs tumbled dead before the Indians retreated and the Buchanan guns finally fell silent.

His force decimated, a chastened Watts retreated to Willstown, sixty miles into what's now Alabama, to heal. But The Ridge did not go with him. Watts's uncle, the notorious Doublehead, had noticed the young warrior's skill with a bow and his coolness under fire, and invited The Ridge to continue

on with him. Not tall but twisted in ways that suggested height, Doublehead
was unusually dark, almost black, fiercely energetic, quick to anger, and giddy
with violence. His most unforgettable feature was his eyes, which gleamed
like black diamonds, people said, crystallized darkness. After the ill-fated
Nashville venture, he'd gathered a band of about sixty warriors to avenge the
humiliation. The Ridge could not say no. He would soon wish it had been
otherwise.

Doublehead's war party was lumbering north through the snowy barrens
of Kentucky when he heard a jangling of some packhorses in the distance.
Whites, Doublehead was sure, making their way to a watering hole nearby.
Doublehead hid his men in the trees, well away from the trail. Sure enough,
they soon spotted a militia captain named Overall and a trader, Burnett,
headed to Nashville with a load of salt, whiskey, and other goods. Doublehead
and another grisly young chief he favored, his nephew Bob Bench, waited
until the two men had dismounted and were dipping their cups into the watering hole. Then a cry from Doublehead brought the Indians shrieking with
tomahawks. The two men fought desperately but they soon fell to the slashing
blades. Someone took the dead Overall as a spy for the hated Sevier, and this
may account for the horror that followed.

Doublehead ordered his men to get a cooking fire going and, when the
flames were high and the coals glowing, to drag over the two corpses. Doublehead scalped them and sliced off the men's clothes with his hunting knife. It
was the tradition of their Iroquois ancestors, he grunted, to eat their enemies.
Yes, to chew and swallow them. To draw from them their strength—and then
to shit them out. These men would make them stronger!

Were the warriors horrified by the vulgar ravings of a madman—or awed
by a staggering display of nearly supernatural power? What did The Ridge
think? All that is known is that no one tried to stop Doublehead as he pressed
the knife blade down on the tender white flesh and peeled the skin off in long
bloody strips. Then he found some sticks, whittled their tips to sharp points
for skewers, and roasted this delicacy over an open fire. When the flesh was
grilled, oozing fat, burned at the fringes, he slid the pieces off and handed
them out to his men to eat like bacon.

The Ridge—did he take one? Did he eat?

Then Doublehead slammed his tomahawk into the ravaged chests of the dead men to pluck out their dripping hearts, and, with a whack to their skulls, scooped out their brains, too. He slopped them all into a pan and set them sizzling. Once these organs were panfried, Doublehead ate heartily. Bench did, too.

Did The Ridge?

Roaring with excitement, Doublehead took the scalps of the two white men and did a merry war dance with them.

When he led his men back to the nation, he bore the two scalps aloft to display to everyone. Not just at Watts's camp in Willstown, but at Turnip Town due east in the lee of Turnip Mountain, by today's Rome, Georgia; and at Coosawattee farther east still, by today's Calhoun. He regaled them all with the gory tale of what he'd done, sure that it would excite warriors everywhere to dream again of war. "We have eaten a great quantity of the white men's flesh," he declared, "but have had so much of it we are tired of it, and think it too salty." The Cherokee didn't know what to make of that, but the Chickasaw were sickened. "We have eaten weeds and grass, but it will be a long time before we think of eating Virginians' flesh," one chief replied scornfully.

The Ridge had left Doublehead by then, peeling off with a band of about thirty Indians to take his own route home to Pine Log. That suggests disgust. But there was more to it, for he then did something that Doublehead would have done, and it tormented him forever.

The Ridge's band was making its slow way south when, a few miles outside freshly fortified Knoxville in a hollow called Raccoon Valley, they came upon a tiny log home owned by a settler named Thomas Gillum and his young son James. The two were out in a field when The Ridge's Cherokee appeared. The Gillums made a dash for the cabin, but some Cherokee arrows found them first. It must have troubled The Ridge to kill the defenseless, reminding him of the settlers dispatched for their tobacco. After his men finished off father and son with tomahawks and then clipped off the scalps, they stole a dozen horses from the corral, and then did the thing The Ridge would forever regret. They left behind a pair of war clubs painted in the distinctive colors of another tribe to deflect any blame from The Ridge and his men for what they had done. Doublehead's crony, Bob Bench, had told The Ridge he'd engaged in such a deception once.

At that point, a number of chiefs had gathered not far away at Coyatee, home of the Cherokee chieftain Hanging Maw, just north of Chota on the Little Tennessee, to talk strategy before a big meeting in Philadelphia with the new American government. Doublehead was there, as was Governor Blount, but they'd both left early. Still, Otter Lifter, Scantee, Fool Charlie, and several other full-blood dignitaries remained when The Ridge's company passed through, staying just long enough, before they continued on to Pine Log, to sell a couple of the stolen horses to Hanging Maw's son, who tied them up outside the house.

When Governor Blount heard about the Gillum murders, he told the militia captain John Beard to arrest the killers. Cherokee, he was sure. No one had been fooled by the war clubs. Still, Blount insisted that Beard not cross the so-called Hawkins Line by the Little Tennessee River that marked the official border into the Cherokee Nation, lest he provoke Doublehead or some other hot-blooded chief into retaliating. Blount didn't want an insurrection on his hands. But Beard was not a man of restraint. He charged across the Little Tennessee with a few dozen men and roared into Coyatee, just to the south. When they spotted the distinctive Gillum markings on the two horses, they started ripping up the town. Whooping, firing off guns, they kicked in doors, and aimed for anything that moved. Defenseless Indians jumped out windows, dashed upstairs, hid under beds. But Beard's men gunned down Scantee, Fool Charlie, the old chief Kitegista's daughter, and many others, leaving their bodies sprawled where they fell. They shot up the revered Hanging Maw and his wife, although both somehow survived. Nine Indians were killed in cold blood, all of them gathered under a flag of truce. It was Old Tassel all over again. "Governor Blount always told me that nothing should happen to me as long as I did live," the wounded Hanging Maw wrote to Blount's secretary, since the governor himself had left for Philadelphia, "but he scarcely got out of sight when I like to have been killed."

Doublehead roared: "I am still among my people living in gores of blood. We have lost nine of our people that we must have satisfaction for. Some of the first and principal people of our Nation fell here. This is the third time we have been so served when we were talking peace, and they fell on us and killed us."

Blount could not have mistaken the threat.

The Ridge must have hoped that the horror of the massacre would distract attention from his own role in it. But at Pine Log his party of warriors was "coolly received," McKenney wrote. In particular, the families of the dead were "incensed," he added, and ready to kill The Ridge for his role in the disaster. The Ridge tried to distract the families from their wrath by boasting of his triumph, and then summoning them to the warpath against Beard's men. This time, no one joined in. Instead, the mourners scowled at him and the elders refused to allow the usual celebrations.

"The young aggressors," McKenney concluded, "so far from being joined by others in a new expedition, fell back abashed by the chilling and contemptuous reception which they met." A shocking reversal for a rising young warrior. But a conjurer came to The Ridge's aid. He cited his prophecy that The Ridge's warriors would return with scalps mounted high, and he persuaded everyone that this whole unhappy incident could not have gone otherwise. It had been fated. With that, the village chief solemnly invoked blood law, the ancient Cherokee edict that punished such blood crimes with equal retaliation. Death for death. The whites must not have the last kill. When the chief started in on the low rumble of the war chant, The Ridge was the first to join, in a voice that had deepened by now into a bass, and this time other warriors followed.

With the whole nation roused in fury, John Watts gathered 1,000 warriors to march on Knoxville, as White's Fort had formally become known, and The Ridge and his men joined in. Doublehead rarely missed out on a chance for killing, and he pressed Watts to burn to the ground every last white settlement they passed. No one would be spared. Remembering the previous blunder when the Cherokee had been distracted, Watts refused to be delayed, but Doublehead exploded into a shrieking, stomping fury. A young chief, James Vann, had brought along a younger Cherokee, barely a teenager, who shook in terror at Doublehead's wrath. Doublehead rode up to the boy, raised his tomahawk high over him, and with a roar, brought it down on the boy's skull, splitting it open, the blood bursting everywhere. The company halted, speechless, as the boy tumbled to the ground. Watts said nothing; he simply told everyone to keep on to reach Knoxville before sunup.

It was already evening, but the men continued on through the woods by moonlight, a long trail of somber warriors. They were about ten miles from Knoxville when dawn broke to reveal a clearing where stood Cavett's Station, a stout log cabin along the Holston where a settler named Alexander Cavett lived with his wife and eleven children.

Despite Watts's insistence that everyone keep going, Doublehead took The Ridge and two dozen other men to surround the house. Doublehead would have his scalps. At Doublehead's signal, the Indians let fly with arrows and bullets. The Cavetts clamped shutters over the windows, braced the doors, and fired back through portholes. They struck five braves, but Doublehead would not relent. Inside, three Cavetts lay dead, but the rest kept firing through the morning until their guns finally faltered. Bench was there, and he spoke a little English. Over Doublehead's objections, Watts had him shout to the Cavetts that if they surrendered, he'd let them all leave freely. He gave his word: he only wanted them gone, not dead.

Silence from inside the cabin, and then the thump of the front door being unbraced, and a squeak of balky hinges, and eight surviving Cavetts ventured out, obviously terrified, their hands lifted into the air in anxious surrender.

Doublehead gave out a terrifying whoop and charged at them. Before they could scatter, he hacked one of them dead, then whipped around to slash two more as the rest froze. Other warriors joined in the frenzy, hacking and stabbing amid shrieks and wailing, and soon Cavetts lay dead everywhere. Doublehead went about "mutilating and abusing the bodies of the women and children especially in the most barbarous and indelicate manner possible." The Ridge was appalled, but powerless to stop the slaughter. Finally, only the youngest, the five-year-old Alexander Cavett Jr., stood quivering before them. Doublehead was poised to dispatch him, too, but Watts scooped him up and handed him off to some Creek warriors, who bore him away, while Doublehead fumed. Years later, The Ridge related the tale of the "foul deed" to McKenney with "abhorrence." He insisted that he had turned away from the hideous slaughter, "unwilling," said McKenney, "to witness that which he could not prevent."

At the news, John Sevier took 700 men to chase Watts south to the Hiwassee. The Indians commanded a height above the river, but Sevier sent his men charging up on horseback, even though the going was so steep that some of the horses tumbled down the slope into the river, tossing their riders. But a Sevier man reached the top and grappled there with a Cherokee chief, Kingfisher. When the American plunged in his blade, the Indians fled, leaderless.

Sevier gave chase, destroyed several Cherokee villages, and took prisoners beyond number.

For Watts, that was the end; he gave up all hope. It was time for peace. Now a man to be reckoned with, Doublehead was one of the chiefs summoned to discuss terms with President Washington and Secretary Knox in Philadelphia. There, he claimed to speak for the Cherokee Nation.

> We mean now to bury deep and forever, the red hatchet of war. Let us therefore forget past events. Let us endeavor to find the means by which the path between us may be kept open and secure from all harm.

Doublehead returned to the nation aboard an American warship as if he were a head of state. There, he wrote to remind Governor Blount that the fall harvest might be coming on, but farming was not the Cherokee way. "My people are now wanting to go hunting, and you will know it is high time to be out." And one thing more. "You know very well where our hunting grounds are, and we hope you will keep the white people from coming to hunt the hunters." No one could mistake the threat, least of all Blount.

6

A BIRTH ON THE COOSA

ocated on a broad plain, rich with crops and dotted with wildflowers, beside the snaking Coosa River, Turkeytown stood not far from John Watts's Willstown in what would be northeastern Alabama, a world away from the Smoky Mountains that rose into the clouds well to the east. In 1790, the town still had the vestiges of the traditional Cherokee settlements—the council house, the ceremonial square. But the crude huts had yielded to finer wooden houses that reflected the new prosperity borne in by the well-laden trading ships that plied the river. Up from the Gulf of Mexico they'd come, riding the Mississippi to the Alabama River, before fanning out to tributaries like the Coosa.

The Coosa was alive with sturgeon, darters, shiners, and freshwater mussels. It brought health, stirred crops, and gleamed silver in the moonlight. Still, few would have thought of it as the Tall Man. Turkeytown was not a spiritual but a mercantile place, a trading center on the border between white and red. If the mountains along the Hiwassee secreted the Cherokee from whites, the flatland of Turkeytown joined them in prosperity.

Here lived the Rosses. A bluff and ruddy Scotsman, with the natural over-confidence of his native clan, Daniel Ross was one of the slicker traders in the nation, and he'd made himself rich. He'd married the daughter of another rich Scottish trader, the imposing John McDonald, and with his father-in-law created a small trading empire. With the spoils he built one of the grand-est homes in the region, an edifice that inspired wonder. In contrast to Tar-chee's one-room hut, Daniel Ross's house rose two stories, solidly built in the British fashion, with bedrooms above, a parlor and dining room below, all with swinging, latched doors. It had a proper chimney; smooth walls; glass windows, an extraordinary luxury that kept out the cold but admitted light; bookcases filled with the works of Shakespeare and the English poets as well as the requisite Holy Bible; shining mahogany furniture shipped from Edin-burgh; and a tiger maple dining table stacked with Scottish newspapers that were only a month or two out of date.

While The Ridge was roaming the far mountains for game to feed his family, John Ross was born here in an upstairs bedroom. No shaman was present for his birth, and there were no auguries. It was a matter for a Chero-kee midwife and plenty of hot water. At first, the little boy was given the In-dian name Tsan Usdi, but everyone called him Little John. His mother did her best to raise him like a proper, God-fearing little Scot. While the full-blood Cherokee boys dashed about town naked, their slick little copper bod-ies topped with jet-black hair that flopped behind them, Mollie made sure her son was dressed like a tiny gentleman, often in a pale-yellow nankeen suit, with cuffed trousers and a trim jacket, until the taunts of the Cherokee boys made him toss off his fine clothes and go naked like the rest of them. Of course, his stubby, fish-white body revealed the deeper truth. Genetically, he was white almost to the core.

Ironically, the high-minded Mollie brought John Ross the only Cherokee blood he possessed. Her father's mother was a Cherokee of the Bird Clan, the product of a liaison like that of The Ridge's mother. But, for Ross, his Cherokee great-grandmother was the exception. All seven of his other great-grandparents were Scottish. They would have made a remarkable set of por-traits in the parlor. His ancestry accounted for John Ross's paper-white skin, which turned pink in the sun but was otherwise ghostly amid the bronzed features of his fellow tribesmen. More strikingly, perhaps: Little John never entirely shed his nickname, as he was never more than a stubby five-five. That left him the smallest man in almost any room and, to judge by appearance, one of the less prepossessing. He did have a pair of remarkable china-blue eyes that were capable of the kind of eternal gaze rendered in a Byzantine mosaic. His hair was so thick it needed to be oil-slicked to hold a part. He was a man for English leather shoes, a well-tailored jacket, and a cravat. It was impossible to see him doing a war dance in a loincloth and moccasins, his head shaved, with a pair of eagle feathers behind. Instead of a tomahawk or bow and arrow, he was completed by pen and paper. He never learned more than a few words of Cherokee, spoken haltingly. English suited him, the more ornate the better. The son and grandson of traders at a trading post, soon to be a trader himself, he was a border person, and no one could be sure which side he was on, or why. Traders, of course, never enjoyed the best reputations. "Villains and horse thieves," British Indian agent Alexander Cameron called them. They "will invent and tell a thousand lies." And Cameron said this as a close friend of John McDonald, Ross's grandfather, one of the greatest traders of them all.

McDonald had come from Inverness at nineteen to clerk for a trading company in Georgia in 1766, and then found himself in the thick of the Tennessee wilderness, running the firm's trade with the Cherokee a year later, swapping guns, cloth, and liquor for animal skins. He was a natural. To McDonald, the fog-shrouded Smokies might have been the misty Scottish Highlands, and he had a feeling for the Cherokee with their clannish ways. But for safety's sake he lived close by heavily garrisoned Fort Loudon by Chota to the east, where he could repair if the Indians came screaming through. In 1769, he married a half-blood, Anne Shorey, just seventeen, the fetching niece of the translator Timberlake had brought to London, only for the man to die of drink en route. McDonald settled with her by the long ridge called Lookout Mountain, just south of today's Chattanooga, and gradually went native, wearing Cherokee buskins and speaking the language with some authority. Seeing how easily McDonald passed for red, Captain John Stuart, the canny confidant of Attakullakulla, made McDonald his man in the mountains—a spy, really, to keep watch on these savages. When the Revolution came, McDonald sided with the British against the Americans; and the British, in return, made him their commissary agent, providing the Cherokee with food and supplies to ensure their loyalty to the crown. For a fee, of course. After the war, McDonald was that rare emigrant who remained British, but imported trade goods despite the laws that reserved such trading privileges for Americans. Covetous of his intimacy with the Cherokee, the United States, Spain, and England all sought to make McDonald their secret agent, and McDonald obliged them all, each one on an exclusive basis. It was McDonald who had delivered Spanish might to John Watts, even as the Americans paid him to put their interests first. Asked about his loyalties by a suddenly suspicious Tennessee governor, McDonald turned indignant. "Believe me Sir I shall never turn *Spaniard.*" Nevertheless, he took Spain's money until the end of the century.

John Ross's father, Daniel, might have been McDonald's son. Born on Scotland's raw northern Atlantic coast, Daniel Ross crossed the seas with his parents, only to be orphaned in Baltimore after the American Revolution. He took to the rigors of the backwoods trading life, teaming up with an older partner, Francis Mayberry, to trade with the Chickasaw in Indian territory. They'd float salable goods up and down the Tennessee, occasionally offering rides on their flatboat. One day, they brought along the Chickasaw chief, Mountain Leader. When they stopped at the Setico trading post along the shore, Bloody Fellow—a prominent signer of the Holston Treaty known for his hotheadedness—stormed aboard with some imposing Cherokee warriors, furious that Ross had brought such a villain into their territory. They pulled out long knives to be done with him, and possibly with Ross and Mayberry, too. But the imposing John McDonald had a trading post there, and he suddenly came aboard, drawn by the commotion. Everyone froze, if only in wonderment at this forceful Scot in Indian dress. In fluent Cherokee, McDonald explained to his friend Bloody Fellow that this was all a misunderstanding. No one had meant any harm. McDonald persuaded Mountain Leader to say a few respectful words to Bloody Fellow, and for Bloody Fellow to reciprocate. Things loosened up so considerably that Bloody Fellow invited the two young traders to open a trading post right there in Setico, too. With McDonald's help, Daniel Ross did just that. With such backing, the business soon thrived, and Daniel Ross solidified the partnership by marrying McDonald's daughter Mollie. Not long afterward, Ross and McDonald moved together to Turkey-town.

Daniel Ross was not about to give his Little John an education in the mountains as Tar-chee had done for The Ridge. Eventually, he moved the family from Turkeytown to Maryville, a pleasant town not far from White's Fort, site of the rising Knoxville, that John Watts had twice tried to storm. There he sought to bring in an itinerant schoolteacher, George Barbee Davis, to tutor his children. The national council was loath to bring white ways into the nation, but it made an exception for the wealthy Daniel Ross. Once Little John hit his teens, however, his father had created something entirely new for him: a boarding school overseen by Gideon Blackburn, a Presbyterian minister with long, flowing hair and a silky manner to match. He was, said one commentator, "uniformly followed by weeping, wondering, admiring audiences wherever he went."

Blackburn's Chickamauga school consisted of a one-room schoolhouse, a boys' dormitory, a dining hall, and a master's quarters where the few girls would be housed. Proper clothes were required, all the classes were taught in English, and the curriculum was heavy on Presbyterianism. "The moment we open our eyes in the morning we bless and thank God we did not open them in that hell which we now read of in the Bible." Any student who took his eyes off a book in class would be whipped.

It took four years for most Cherokee to speak even the most rudimentary English, and few lasted that long. Blackburn didn't last much longer. In 1809, he was found to have personally distilled 2,226 gallons of whiskey for illegal sale to the Creeks. His brother was caught ferrying the tremendous load of liquor down the Tombigbee River that ultimately empties into the Mobile River in southern Alabama. The Cherokee were not sorry to see the sanctimonious Blackburn disgraced, and his school shuttered.

By then Daniel Ross switched the boys to a religion-free academy called South West Point near Kingston, a trading center that John Ross found far more educational than any school. He boarded with a merchant friend of his father's, Thomas N. Clark, who taught Ross the rudiments of the trade. After graduating, Ross joined the Kingston trading firm of Neilson, King and Smith. Whatever Cherokee qualities he'd been born with, he had fewer of them now, as he stood every day behind a counter, bartering, always looking up to the powerful dark-skinned Cherokee men who came to trade. No storyteller, no drinker, unimposing, able to say hardly anything in Cherokee, he must have been taken for what he was—a sharp, hardworking Scottish trader, here to make a fortune off the Indians, nothing more.

7

A DEATH FOR A DEATH

D espite the inglorious incident involving the faked war clubs, The Ridge had distinguished himself in battle, won the admiration of powerful men like John Watts and the terrifying Doublehead, and embodied the "martial virtue" that (as Adair saw) the Cherokee prized. Every inch the warrior, he stood a good six two or three, solid and muscular, with a thick chest, a piercing gaze under a heavy brow, and a voice of command. In a language that could not then be written, speaking was everything, and The Ridge had a reverberant bass voice that, when he was roused, could shake the leaves off the trees. He used words that made simple even the most complicated things, and brought murmurs of agreement from nearly everyone who heard them.

This did not escape the notice of the members of the tribal council at the Oostanaula River, south of the Coosawattee in northwest Georgia. In 1796, when The Ridge was just twenty-one and struggling to make a living as a farmer, with three siblings to support, they asked him to join. This was unexpected, but he accepted. He did not make the best impression when he rode in for his first council meeting on a mangy off-white pony. His moccasins were scuffed, and he was cloaked in well-worn animal skins, not the colorful ceremonial garb expected for such an honor. Some of the younger men on the council couldn't keep from snickering at this bedraggled youth coming from nowhere.

But The Ridge had a sturdy manner that immediately impressed his elders on the council. "They invited him to a seat near them," McKenney noted, "and shook him by the hand." As a rule, only the oldest members spoke at these conclaves, often delivering speeches that might last an hour or more.

The Ridge did not say a word at that first session, but he did at the second a few months later, much to the derision of his young peers. As surprising as it was that he said anything, it was astounding what he spoke *about*, for he went at a matter of clan loyalty, morality, and tribal justice fundamental to Cherokee life. His speech amounted to an attack on the essential organizing principle of Cherokee society and the source of the animus behind the Cherokees' futile wars against the settlers, to say nothing of their earlier battles with rival tribes. It was as if The Ridge had suggested that the sun replace the moon. For he challenged blood law, that long-standing Cherokee decree by which anyone who killed should *be* killed in return by a member of his victim's family, and if the actual killer had fled, a clan relative of his must be killed in his place. It didn't matter if the death was an accident. Someone must die for it. That squared things, canceled a debt, restored order.

Blood law was simple, but its implications were vast, as it inspired a code of vengeance that could potentially lead to further cycles of retaliation. The issue was never how or why you killed, only that you had. To the Cherokee, Western notions of culpability were beside the point, if they were even comprehensible, for they sought motivations that could probably never be determined, and, to the Cherokee, weren't especially relevant. In Cherokee justice, only two things mattered after a murder: that the actual killer be identified, and that he—or a tribesman—die for his crime. Only a second death would cancel the first.

While blood law lay behind the retaliatory raids against more powerful states—raids that had proved so self-destructive to the Cherokee Nation—it also provided the basis for any number of private killings that only worsened the mayhem in the name of relieving it. The Ridge's friend James Vann had been slated to die for a murder by a fellow clan member who was deemed too eminent to be slain for his crime. At first, Vann had numbly accepted his fate. When he learned that a gang planned to ambush him as he rode home one evening, he decided simply to let them do it. He reconsidered only when he survived the attack because of their poor marksmanship. To avoid paying for the murder Vann sacrificed his uncle instead—shot him dead at a party, in front of everyone. The Ridge was determined to end the cycle of violence that was all too widespread in the nation. Drinking started fights, fights brought deaths, and deaths yielded more deaths.

So, now, in council The Ridge spoke up. Too many good men have been sacrificed to this ancient principle, he declared, either in war or at home. The assembled council must have listened in stunned silence as he raised such a sacred topic. But The Ridge knew his subject too well. He'd been a warrior; he had killed. But this made him value life all the more. He went even further to declare that he admired the legal principles of the whites. For them, a jury—not just tribal custom—decided who should die for a murder, and its decision was based on evidence, sworn testimony, and established procedure, all conducted in the open, for anyone to see.

After much deliberation, the council agreed that The Ridge was right, and decided unanimously to eliminate blood law. If the council had decreed that the Tennessee River was now to run uphill, that edict would not have been more astounding. After that, the younger council members still did not speak to The Ridge, but they took note.

To make sure the change took hold, The Ridge visited every chief in the nation, securing his promise to obey the council and abandon blood law, even though it was not yet clear what penalty would replace it. By this means, The Ridge also let everyone know he was the man behind this development. He could see that politics would be the means by which the Cherokee people would adapt to a rapidly changing world. He could also see that he was good at persuasion.

Soon enough, the question of blood law was put to the test. A murderer took flight, leaving his clansmen to atone for his crime. Frenzied with outrage, the families of the victims spoiled for the usual revenge. But The Ridge got wind of their plans and dispatched a rider to tell them to abandon any thought of fresh murder. He would slaughter anyone who disobeyed.

That ended all talk of blood vengeance. With such acts, The Ridge's name spread.

Then he fell in love—if love is the term for a society and culture that largely segregated the sexes, had few romantic traditions, and offered scant privacy. With Susanna Wickett, whose last name was sometimes spelled Wicked, which couldn't have been more wrong for a good-hearted woman of such frail tenderness. She was known to the Cherokee as Sehoya, but The Ridge, in his growing admiration for white society, called her Susanna. McKenney termed her "handsome and sensible," a "fine person" with an "engaging countenance" and "excellent character." But other accounts hinted at a woman more slyly seductive. When, after a courtship that almost surely included no intimate conversation, or even a touch, The Ridge approached her in a way that made clear his desire for her, she tipped her head down "like a drooping leaf" to accept this obvious proposition in the Cherokee way. This is according to a white trader, General Sam Dale, who then turns unexpectedly lyrical. "It is only in the deepest recesses, when no others are near, that her lover sees the luster of her eyes, or even the blushes that mantle her cheeks."

Before any marriage, however, a shaman had to consult the auguries. The Ridge invited the shaman into his hut, built of wattles and clay, with a square hole in the ceiling for the smoke, like the one in which he was born. Chanting, the shaman drew out a pouch of tobacco, just as a predecessor had at The Ridge's birth, and set it smoldering on a plate, its penetrating fragrance filling the hut. But this time, instead of studying the smoke as it rose, he attended to the puffs of ash left behind as the tobacco burned down. He lifted his head with a smile.

To secure the permission of Susanna's parents, The Ridge took his rifle into the forest. When he had a deer in his sights, he offered the time-honored prayer of gratitude to the animal for giving up its life, then caught it square on. He hoisted the deer onto his shoulders, carried it back down into the village, and butchered it himself. He reserved some of the meat for his siblings, but wrapped up the choicest parts in deer hide to present to Susanna's parents.

When he showed up at their door, smelling of delectable meat, they guessed his intentions. To show their approval, they let Susanna grill the venison for dinner, and ate with them.

The wedding ceremony itself involved a great banquet for the entire village of Pine Log, the men and women eating separately at two long tables. The feast culminated in an offering of beautiful, freshly woven blankets from each half of the bridal couple. The Ridge rose up from among the men, Susanna from the women, to present a blanket to the tribal chief, who took the two blankets in his arms and lifted them high in tribute to the Great Spirit. Then he set them down to unfold them, and lay one on top of the other. With that, a cry of joy rose up all around, for the couple were joined.

Afterward, Susanna and The Ridge returned to his cabin. They brought some venison and corn, and the two blankets. He set a fire roaring, and, when the hut was warm, they laid the blankets down side by side on the earthen floor before the blaze, and then closed the door behind them.

For some time, federal agents had been fanning out through the territory to instruct nascent Cherokee farmers in the finer points of agriculture. The Ridge was proving an avid pupil, adept in all the aspects of farm management, from soil quality to pest control, and he expanded his operation so much that he soon ran out of arable land in Pine Log. He secured permission to farm a bigger spread along Oothcaloga Creek, named for its beaver dams. There he laid larger fields for more profitable crops—not just the usual corn, but cotton, barley, and wheat, too—and then added pens for lucrative livestock. As wives were displaced by farming husbands, the government agents shifted them to the domestic arts, making them weavers and spinners of the cotton being grown by their husbands. Susanna "learned after her marriage the domestic arts appertaining to good housewifery," said McKenney with obvious approval.

"Industrious" was McKenney's primary description of The Ridge in this period. That and "persevering" in the face of such a radical shift from old to new. But The Ridge himself was surprisingly matter-of-fact about it all, as he seconded the appraisal of the tribal council. "The hunting is almost done & we must now live by farming, raising corn & cotton & horses & hogs & sheep," he said, shrugging. "We see that those Cherokees who do this live well." Together, the couple seemed to their white neighbors the picture of canny Yankee adaptability, quick to abandon "the habits of their race" and take up "Christian employments." And their efforts were rewarded, as The Ridge was soon able to build them one of the finest houses around, with a proper chimney, slender roof beams, and solid walls.

Oothcaloga was fast becoming the place to be, attracting the Cherokee elite: the Adair family, formidable descendants of the ethnologically inclined James Adair; the savvy chieftain William Hicks, who would rise to principal chief; and Hicks's brilliant son Charles, whose library of English books had made him the most knowledgeable Cherokee in the nation. With The Ridge, they made up a cadre of forward-thinking men to push the Cherokee into the modern age.

The Ridge children came along swiftly, starting in 1801 with Nancy, who quickly grew into a bright, hardworking girl. John came two years after her. He proved a brilliant, mesmerizing child, even though he'd been crippled from birth by scrofula, a debilitating lymph infection akin to tuberculosis that made it hard for him to walk. Rife in the nation, scrofula probably spread through the unpasteurized milk that was now a staple of the Cherokee diet. Charles Hicks also suffered from it, as did Susanna's mother. The first two Ridge children proved the stars of the family, John especially. A third child died in infancy; a fourth, the boy Watty, proved feebleminded; and finally Sarah, named for her mother, was born about 1810 and proved an active, impetuous child. Along with English given names, they all bore the surname of their father in the modern manner. By birth, they belonged to their mother's Wild Potato Clan, but (unlike their parents) they wouldn't be defined by their clan. Still, only Cherokee was spoken in the house, and The Ridge retained many of his ancient spiritual beliefs, although these were now cast as a great battle between good and evil, in which good had a slight but precarious edge, to reflect the rising Christian doctrines spread everywhere by the missionaries who were flooding into the nation in search of fresh souls to save. Tellingly, the paradise promised to good Christians after death looked a lot like the world in which The Ridge had grown up. Years later, his son John Ridge explained his beliefs in a letter to Albert Gallatin, the former secretary of the treasury who founded the American Ethnological Society of New York:

They believed in a great first cause or Spirit of all Good & in a great being the author of all evil. These were at variance and at war with each other, but the good Spirit was supposed to be superior to the bad one. These immortal beings had on both sides numerous intelligent beings of analogous dispositions to their chieftains. They had a heaven, which consisted of a visible world to those who had undergone a change after death. This heaven was adorned with all the beauties which the savage imagination could conceive. An open forest, yet various, giving shade and fruit of every kind. Flowers of various hues & pleasant to the Smell—Game of all kinds in great abundance—enough of feasts and plenty of dances, & to crown the whole the most beautiful women, prepared and adorned by the Great Spirit, for every individual that by wisdom, hospitality & Bravery was introduced to this happy & immortal region. The Bad place was the reverse of this & in the vicinity of the good place, where the wretched, compelled to live in hunger, hostility & darkness, could hear the rejoicings of the happy, without the possibility of reaching its shores.

In The Ridge's mind, Oothcaloga was a place where the good was advancing. But elsewhere in the Cherokee Nation, he could see that evil was taking hold. Nowhere was this more true than in the Five Lower Towns collectively known as Chickamauga, where Dragging Canoe had struck back so fiercely against the encroaching white settlers. In the late 1790s, the diabolical Doublehead had seized the leadership, setting himself up there in a small southern village called, aptly, Doublehead's Town, where he intimidated local villagers and the federal government alike.

By 1796, Doublehead had bullied his way into becoming speaker of the nation, the second-highest national post, after the principal chief, Little Turkey, a meek figure Doublehead tended to overlook. When the federal government sought more of Tennessee, it turned to Doublehead for the acquisition.

It was still sacred policy that Cherokee land was owned collectively, to be ceded only by the nation at large, but Doublehead never made a clear distinction between the nation's interest and his own. After one cession of land to the United States in 1798, Doublehead came away with a stable of fine horses and two dozen slaves. After that, he did increasingly better for himself, and in 1805, after he gave away Cherokee land to the United States, he received a good stretch of the Hiwassee shore for himself, and then some more for his cousin. Such "gifts" for facilitating land transactions weren't without precedent, but it was a flagrant abuse for Doublehead to take land privately, and then, all the worse, to kick the Cherokee off the property and lease it to white settlers instead. But such was Doublehead's reputation for horror that no one dared question his actions. "The chiefs and the people began alike to fear him," writes McKenney.

Doublehead was like Dragging Canoe, except that he fought only for his own personal interests, as if he were a state all his own. He was a formidable businessman, buying flour at $2 a barrel and selling it at $8, and he quickly accumulated an impressive array of ferries, mills, roads, even houses of prostitution, by one account, most likely offering services to settlers. But his capitalistic fervor had a merciless edge, and he engaged in a campaign of intimidation throughout Tennessee and well up into Kentucky. He left one woman pinned shrieking to the outside of her house by a heavy nail driven into her palm, her husband dead at her feet. He killed freely, and collected as many as a hundred scalps; his close ally Bob Bench took forty-five. He built a vast boat, complete with cannon, to patrol the Tennessee River and scare off any villages tempted to rise up against him. The Americans decided it was best not to provoke this monster they'd created. The new secretary of war, Henry Dearborn, directed his agents to give Doublehead whatever he wanted—cash, gold, cotton fields, cropland. Anything to avoid a confrontation. Even President Jefferson openly bribed him to win his favor. The Indian agent Return J. Meigs was a highly dubious moral commodity anyway, equally comfortable serving the Cherokee and exploiting them. They called him the White Fox for his silver hair, but the term hints at their mistrust. Only Doublehead was able to play Meigs as Meigs played everyone else, leaving Meigs thinking that he had gotten something for his bribes. "As he sought office with selfish views," McKenney summed up Doublehead, "he very naturally abused it, and made himself odious by his arbitrary conduct. He not only executed the laws according to his own pleasure, but caused innocent men to be put to death who thwarted his views."

Doublehead's land thefts were no secret. James Vann, for one, was only too well aware of them. Two decades before, he had been the timid, aimless boy of the Wild Potato Clan targeted for murder by another clan. But by

now he'd inherited his father's estate, and showed considerable entrepreneurial vigor to turn it into a vast and thriving enterprise of his own. He had a
gristmill, a ferry, a commercial license on the federal road he ran through his
property, a magnificent Federal-style hilltop mansion called Diamond Hill,
and an 800-acre farm worked by 100 slaves. He'd provided land for the pio-
neering Moravian missionary school at Spring Place, and he'd become a pillar
of the nation, serving on the national council.

To Vann, Doublehead was not just detestable, but a hazard to everything
he was trying to create for his nation. And he expected that his enterprising
near neighbor, The Ridge, would agree. But Vann was bonded by marriage
to this horror. He and Doublehead had married sisters, and Doublehead was
proving a diabolical brother-in-law. Prone to fury even in the best of circumstances, Doublehead was wrath itself when drunk. Fully loaded one night, he
decided he could no longer abide his pregnant wife, Vann's wife's sister, and
kicked her so hard in her midsection that she doubled over, gasping in pain.
The baby died inside her. Seeing his wife wailing with pain and grief, Doublehead repeatedly cracked a club over her head and shoulders until she fell dead
to the floor.

When he discovered what had happened, Vann decided Doublehead
must die. It was not blood law, but simple necessity. The nation must be rid of
this ogre. Vann might have wielded a pistol once, but he was years away from
being any sort of warrior now. He was a man of some refinement, a wearer
of cravats. He could never handle such a grisly job. The Ridge, however, was
a different story. He was the only man Vann knew who could possibly think
of slaying a powerhouse like Doublehead, and face the consequences. When
Vann quietly raised the matter, The Ridge recognized the grim necessity of
the job, and agreed to take it on, despite its obvious hazards. It was for the
good of the nation, if not for goodness itself. Doublehead should not be allowed to take public land for his private use and silence everyone who thought
otherwise.

The Ridge could see that Vann was not likely to be much help in carrying
out such a plot. He turned instead to his friend Alex Saunders, a mixed-blood
who kept a cool head. This was the summer of 1807, and The Ridge and Saunders quickly came up with their scheme. On the afternoon of August 9, there
would be a ball game outside town. It always attracted an immense throng,

heavy on gamblers who would bet on the outcome. Doublehead was sure to be one of them; he never shied away from laying out a little money in hopes of making a lot more. And he was likely to sample some of the whiskey that whites liked to put out for the pleasure of seeing the Cherokee go legless. Doublehead was sure to ride on light-headed from there to McIntosh's tavern in Hiwassee for some more whiskey afterward, since that was his custom.

It was perfect. The Ridge and Saunders would wait for Doublehead at the tavern, let him drink himself further into a stupor, and blast him.

As expected, Doublehead appeared for the game, watching from the tall grass past one end of the field. And, after collecting on a bet, he did indeed have a celebratory taste of the whiskey the whites had put out for fun. But unlike the others, he showed few ill effects of the liquor as he climbed onto his horse to head into McIntosh's tavern for his usual. But before he left, a drunken half-wit named Bone Polisher lurched toward him, grabbed the bridle of his horse to hold him up, and then laced into him with a stream of invective for his land deals. When Doublehead gave it right back to him, Bone Polisher slammed his tomahawk down on Doublehead's thumb where it was splayed across the saddle. The blow nearly sliced it clean off, but Doublehead gave out no cry, just yanked out his pistol with his other hand and shot Bone Polisher in the chest, then cracked the pistol butt down on the top of his head to be done with him. When Bone Polisher fell dead, Doublehead continued on into town without a backward glance, just wrapping some cloth around his bloody hand before he reached the tavern.

Vann was supposed to be outside, ready to give the alert. But he'd sought the bravery that comes out of a glass, and overdone it. He was nowhere to be found when Doublehead pulled up and dismounted. Saunders and The Ridge were alone at a table inside the tavern when the door opened, and Doublehead filled the doorway. After a quick glance about, he moved uneasily to a small table by the wall; it was lit by a single, flickering candle. He took a seat and then eased his bloody hand down, and shouted for whiskey. When it came, a drunk from across the room mouthed off at him, but Doublehead did not lift his eyes from his drink.

The Ridge let Doublehead go two rounds, and then crept along the wall to Doublehead's table. There, he bent down quickly to blow out Doublehead's candle and hide his own identity, shoved a gun into Doublehead's face, and pulled the trigger. The sound exploded in the tavern, and blood sprayed everywhere. The Ridge hurried out the back door. Saunders found him outside, and the two men jumped onto their horses and galloped off. The plan was to hide in the next town until they knew how Doublehead's death played out. Would everyone be overjoyed—or would someone now come gunning for *them*?

While they were lying low, they received the stunning word: Doublehead had survived the blast. In the darkness, The Ridge had somehow sent the bullet straight through both of Doublehead's cheeks without killing him. Shocked, the two men galloped back to finish the job.

They made their way to the tavern and checked around inside it. The table where The Ridge had shot Doublehead was splattered with blood, as was the wall beside it. The tavern itself was nearly empty. Anyone left must have been startled to see Saunders and The Ridge come back; by then, despite The Ridge's precautions, everyone knew what had happened. There was no sign of Doublehead. The Ridge and Saunders climbed back onto their horses and cantered through the town, but Doublehead was nowhere to be found. They doubled back to the tavern—and this time noticed a slender trail of bloody drool leading away from the tavern door. They tracked it to some outdoor stairs that led up to a large room under the eaves leased by a Mr. Blacke—the teacher, as it happened, of the young John Ross at Gideon Blackburn's school. He lived up there, where he gave private classes. The Ridge and Saunders quietly climbed the stairs, following the line of blood up to a shut door on the landing. A feeble light filtered out around the edges. The Ridge pressed an ear against the door. Silence inside.

Was Doublehead there? Was he still alive? Alone? Badly hurt? There was no way to know.

The Ridge gestured. He'd burst in first; Saunders was to follow. Both men drew their guns and cocked them. Then The Ridge yanked open the door and the two charged inside with a war cry. They found Doublehead alone, slumped in a chair nursing his wounds at the far end of the room. But the powerful little man leaped up at the sound and let fly a dagger from his belt. It whistled past The Ridge's head and cracked against a far wall. With a growl, he charged at The Ridge, his mouth spewing blood that spilled down his shirt onto the floor, his eyes wild. The Ridge and Saunders both fired their pistols at this ball of rage, but didn't stop him. With a roar, Doublehead closed on The Ridge, and wrapped his meaty arms around him. He pushed him backward onto the floor, reaching with his good hand for an eye to puncture, or flesh to claw, lifting his knee into The Ridge hoping to jam it into a soft place. Doublehead smeared The Ridge everywhere with his hot blood. As the two men churned about, Saunders managed to fire again, catching Doublehead on the hip. He gave out a cry, twisted around to find the source of the bullet, and locked an eye on Saunders. Saunders tossed his gun aside, drew back his tomahawk, and crashed it down on Doublehead's forehead. The blow struck straight up from his nose, and split the skull down the middle, releasing a torrent of blood. Doublehead lost his grip on The Ridge as he slipped down to the floor, the tomahawk still jammed in his forehead, cleaving his head in two, his dead eyes staring up.

The blade was in so deep that Saunders couldn't free it even when he jammed his foot down on Doublehead's face to get leverage. The Ridge had to help him work it loose. Doublehead's blood blackened his face and drenched the floor.

The fight had raised such a racket that it wasn't long before the room was full of Cherokee coming to see what had happened. They were silent at first, staring at the dead Cherokee chief. But one of them had brought a shovel, which he raised high, and then slammed the flat of it down on Doublehead's face, over and over, until his features were oozing pulp.

More Cherokee tried to jam into the room, all of them talking excitedly. Finally, they were coaxed back down the stairs, but they milled about the yard, waiting for what would happen next. Exhausted and bloody as he was, The Ridge knew he should address them, reassure them that all would be well. Everyone hushed when he stepped out onto the landing to address the crowd below. He hated Doublehead, he told them in his deep, penetrating voice, hated everything he'd done. But he hadn't done this for himself. He'd done it for the nation. No tribe should be led by a man who stole the nation's land, lied about it, and killed indiscriminately, terrifying everyone. He'd killed Doublehead for the sake of the Cherokee people. It wasn't personal. It was right.

As he spoke, he held everyone in thrall. When he was done and tried to leave, the crowd of Cherokee trailed him down the street. They'd follow this man wherever he went.

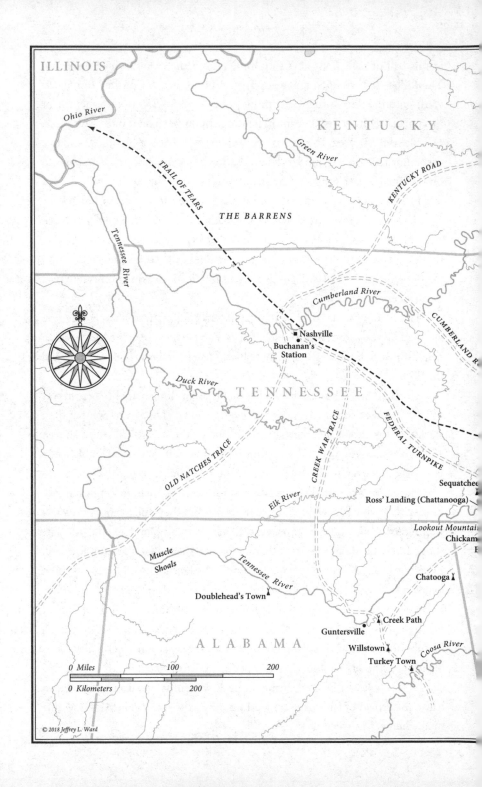

ILLINOIS

Ohio River

KENTUCKY

Green River

KENTUCKY ROAD

TRAIL OF TEARS

THE BARRENS

Tennessee River

Cumberland River

CUMBERLAND R

■ Nashville
Buchanan's
Station

Duck River

TENNESSEE

FEDERAL TURNPIKE

OLD NATCHEZ TRACE

CREEK WAR TRACE

Sequatche

Elk River

Ross' Landing (Chattanooga)

Lookout Mountai
Chickam

Muscle
Shoals

Tennessee River

Chatooga ▲

Doublehead's Town ▲

Guntersville ● ▲ Creek Path

Willstown ▲

ALABAMA

Coosa River

Turkey Town ▲

0 *Miles*   100   200

0 *Kilometers*   200

© 2018 Jeffrey L. Ward

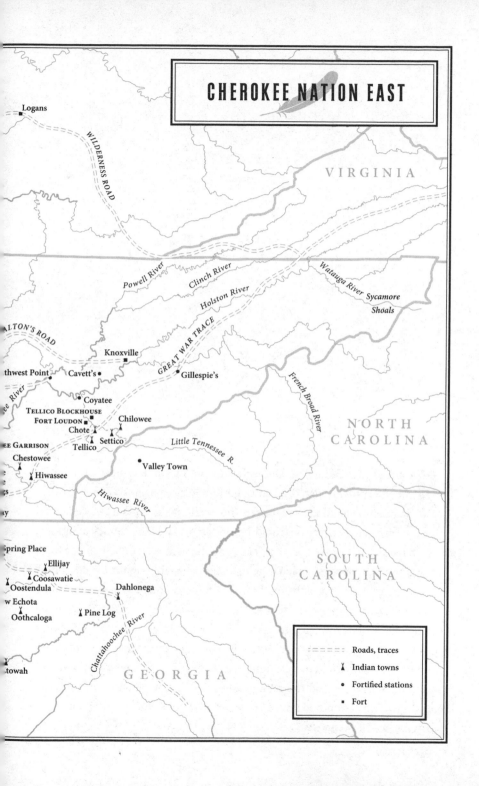

CHEROKEE NATION EAST

Logans

WILDERNESS ROAD

VIRGINIA

Powell River

Clinch River

Holston River

Watauga River

Sycamore
Shoals

ALTON'S ROAD

Knoxville

GREAT WAR TRACE

thwest Point   Cavett's

Gillespie's

French Broad River

ee River

Coyatee

TELLICO BLOCKHOUSE
FORT LOUDON   Chilowee
          Chote
EE GARRISON   Settico   Little Tennessee R.
Chestowee   Tellico

NORTH
CAROLINA

Hiwassee

Valley Town

Hiwassee River

pring Place
        Ellijay
      Coosawatie
Oostendula   Dahlonega

SOUTH
CAROLINA

w Echota
Oothcaloga   Pine Log

Chattahoochee River

towah   GEORGIA

| Roads, traces |
| Indian towns |
| Fortified stations |
| Fort |

8

PROSPERITY

B y the ancient blood law, Doublehead would soon have been avenged by members of his clan. But no one lifted a hand against The Ridge and Saunders. The Ridge had indeed ended all that, even as he had enforced the *other* ancient edict, against holding land in private. The council at Brooms Town made that one part of an official code the next year, in September 1808. It was the first law ever enacted by the Cherokee, although it would not officially enter the books of the modern nation for another twenty years. Still, it was the first stirring of the Cherokee to create a system of laws administered by the nation, not by clans. To enforce it, the nation established a lighthorse guard, replacing what had amounted to clan vigilantes. An uneasy combination of police force and mobile judiciary, the guard consisted of two six-man companies who roamed the nation, administering justice to horse thieves, primarily, with a hundred lashes as the penalty. But a stolen cow would incur fifty, and a hog twenty-five.

Such a system of justice had to be headed up by a man of utter probity and impeccable judgment, as he would hold virtually unlimited power over everyone.

The Ridge was chosen, and anecdotes prove his fitness for the task: According to one, the Ridge was out in the woods when he saw that a certain Colonel Blair had waylaid two men who'd stopped by a spring for a drink. The Ridge knew them—a pair of lawbreakers, Wiley Hyde and Tom Philips. As The Ridge watched, the two men aimed rifles at Blair, who backed away, his hands in the air, loudly offering them whiskey if they didn't shoot. Hyde pressed his rifle tip into Blair's chest, and cocked the hammer, but the blast that followed didn't come from Hyde. It was from The Ridge, shooting Hyde with his rifle from his hiding place in the woods. Colonel Blair then pointed a gun at the startled Philips, who tossed his own rifle to the ground.

Colonel Blair must have been relieved by this remarkable turn of events. It turned out that he had been tracking a pair of horse thieves all the way from North Carolina. He'd gotten the idea that Hyde and Philips were his men, but approached them a shade too casually. The Ridge and Blair buried Hyde, and tied Philips to his horse for the long ride back to Blair's quarters at Onachee Station. There, The Ridge appointed Blair to give Philips his 100 lashes.

As justice spread, so did Cherokee confidence, and a general prosperity rose with it to the point where, in 1809, the agent Return J. Meigs thought it time to compile some boastful statistics. He conducted a census of the nation to reveal a population of 12,395, less than half the 25,000 at the tribe's height a hundred years before. But they possessed 19,778 pigs; 19,165 black cattle; 6,519 horses; and 1,037 sheep, revealing the shift to farming—plus 429 looms and 1,572 spinning wheels for the women's new work turning cotton into cloth. There were thirteen gristmills, three sawmills, and a single power mill. All of these possessions together came to just $571,300. Meager numbers, perhaps, but they would establish a benchmark for the progress to come. For now, they revealed something more potent: that, as the nation's economy rose, most of the wealth was going to a small percentage of the population, roughly a tenth. Most of them were the mixed-bloods whose white lineage had left them with aspirations—for education, and for the wealth it was likely to produce—that were not widely shared among the full-bloods. Slowly, the Cherokee Nation was dividing in two.

The Ridge was typical of the rising class of mixed-bloods, as his fortunes rose in the new economy. Farming might have been women's work, but he threw himself into it. Other Cherokee men raised livestock like the game of old, letting their cows and pigs roam freely and then hunting them down like bear and deer. The Ridge fenced his in, and bought African slaves to tend them. No simple country farmer, he sought to become a planter like the refined white gentlemen in light cotton suits he'd seen sipping lemonade on front porches at their plantations farther to the south in Georgia. Like them, he shifted to cotton, a more valuable crop, and then bought yet more slaves to raise it. When he outgrew his original parcel of new lands on the Oostanaula River, he acquired more, and then more after that. Before long, he would turn his log cabin into the finest house around—a true mansion of two stories, pitched-roofed, clapboard-sided, with glass windows and doors that closed, and all the refinements, such as genuine silverware and fine china, of a plantation grandee. And he would ride about town in an unimaginable conveyance for that part of the world: a cream-colored coach drawn by four gleaming horses and driven by a liveried Negro if he didn't take the reins himself. In society, he would deck himself out in a frock coat, ruffled cravat, and fine derby hat. Everything about him declared that The Ridge had arrived, and he intended to stay.

For Susanna, the change was no less dramatic. Silent and deferential as a bride, she was the one to milk the cows, to learn the arts of animal husbandry, to manage the slaves, to spin the cotton to weave into cloth for market, and to prove her mettle as a capitalist. "Females have made much greater advances in industry," Ross's grandfather John McDonald declared with a hint of disapproval when he first surveyed these enterprising women. The government cleverly offered to pay the Cherokee annuities due from the land sales in fine goods that were likely to catch a Cherokee woman's eye, like silk stockings, gold lace, damask tablecloths, and fancy "morocco" shoes, at exaggerated prices. Susanna took hers in cash.

Considering the value of the land they supposedly paid for, those annuities were a pittance, about $10,000. Distributed to all the Cherokee people, they amounted to less than $1 each. Unfortunately, without a proper system of government that spread through the nation, much of the money that wasn't siphoned off in federal graft went disproportionately to the more politically united Upper Towns of the northeast rather than to the scattered Lower Towns of the southwest. By 1808, the discrepancy was reaching such crisis proportions that The Ridge's ally Alexander Saunders journeyed to Washington to complain to President Jefferson, and to propose a radical solution. The Cherokee Nation should be divided in two.

To Jefferson, this was the chance he'd been waiting for. Tall and lanky, with a persistent air of blowsy detachment, Thomas Jefferson was many things to many people, and few of them combined easily with the rest. Shrewd politician and airy aesthete, frugal in disposition while spendthrift in act, a tribune of liberty who held slaves, Jefferson took an equally contradictory attitude toward the Indians that could not be easily summarized, or contained. While he claimed to have their best interests at heart in urging them to join the ranks of the yeoman farmers he professed to revere, he was not unmindful that the switch to agriculture would free up the hunting land for the white settlers who were clamoring for it. While George Washington had believed that the two races could coexist once the Indians turned to farming, Jefferson thought white society would be better off if the Indians moved elsewhere, and he'd imagined that his vast Louisiana Purchase might be just the dumping ground, oblivious to the fact that countless tribes of Indians already lived there. He answered Saunders with a sly proposal. If the Cherokee of the Lower Towns became farmers as Washington had recommended, he offered them full citizenship as Americans. But if they persisted in this archaic habit of hunting, they should relocate west, past the Alleghenies, in the new lands. It was classic Jefferson—crude self-interest disguised as magnanimity. Whether they went west as Indians or stayed east as Americans, they would not remain in Tennessee as Indians. Problem solved.

In the sweet but perfidious Indian agent Meigs, Jefferson found the perfect henchman for his plot. He put Meigs to talking up western migration with Black Fox, the new principal chief of the Cherokee, who was willing to listen to this proposition. It was just as the conjurers had feared. The Cherokees' feet would indeed be turned westward, to the sunset.

"Our game has disappeared," Black Fox told Jefferson, his simple words disguising the lament within them, "and we wish to follow it to the West." Speaking of the Great Father in the respectful third person, he went on: "We are his friends, and we hope he will grant our petition, which is to remove our people toward the setting sun. But we shall give up a fine country, fertile in soil, abounding in water-courses, and well-adapted for the residence of a white people. For all this we must have a good price."

By the new laws, however, Black Fox would need the approval of the national council, and by now The Ridge had joined it with Saunders and Vann. Together, they were the "young chiefs," eager to see the last of sellouts like Black Fox. When Black Fox raised the prospect of going west at a council meeting in the fall of 1808, most of his fellow chiefs listened silently, "apparently awed or cajoled into compliance," according to McKenney.

But not The Ridge. Craftily, he began by pointing out that Black Fox had every right to his opinion, but then he twisted the knife. His opinion was his alone. "It was not formed in the council in the light of day, but was made up in a corner—to drag this people, without their consent, from their own country, to the dark land of the setting sun." To this, The Ridge would never agree. His voice echoed throughout the council house. "I resist it here in my place as a man, as a chief, as a Cherokee, having the right to be consulted in a matter of such importance." He demanded: "What are your heads placed on your bodies for, but to think, and if to think, why should you not be consulted?" And more: "I scorn this movement of a few men to unsettle the nation and trifle with our attachment to the land of our forefathers! Look abroad over the face of this country—along the rivers, the creeks, and their branches, and you beyond the dwellings of the people who repose in content and security. Why is this grand scheme projected to lead away to another country the people who are happy here? I, for one, abandon my respect for the will of a chief, and regard only the will of thousands of our people."

He put it to the men of the council. "Do I speak without the response of any heart in this assembly, or do I speak as a free man to men who are free and know their rights?" He waited, dramatically. "I pause to hear."

There was silence, and then roars, stamping. The chiefs were with him.

Black Fox remained silent, shamed, "broken on the spot," by a later account. He and two close allies in this perfidy, the Glass and Tahlonteeskee, were summarily cast out of the council, although Black Fox was later reinstated. None of them ever lived down the ignominy.

While he had won the council, The Ridge had not won the towns, and, to his distress, thousands left for a tract along the Arkansas river that Jefferson dangled before them, the distant hills of the west that were supposed to be rich in bear and deer, where the men could continue to hunt as always, or so it was claimed.

While the Lower Towns continued to look to the west, the Upper Towns sought to consolidate their hold in the east with a far bolder government than they currently possessed, a truly democratic one, elected, in the manner of the United States itself. To discuss that idea with this mysterious President Jefferson, they dispatched six prominent men to Washington. The Ridge would lead them.

They started that November, just as winter was setting in. It was an arduous journey on horseback up the Georgia Road to Greenville, South Carolina; then on to the Moravian settlement founded by the German-born Bishop August Gottlieb Spangenberg in Salem, now Winston-Salem, North Carolina; and finally, in mid-December, to the capital, which was that winter, just a few years after its founding, little more than a chilly swamp up from the Potomac. Rows of meager boardinghouses and shabby storefronts were interrupted by an occasional state building, of which the grandest were the still unfinished Capitol, not yet domed over, and the pink-plastered Executive Building. Still, as The Ridge rode up wide, muddy Pennsylvania Avenue the city was the grandest thing he'd ever seen.

Upon arrival, the delegates sent an obsequious message to Jefferson thanking their "Great Father" for "his protecting and fostering hand" that had taught them some of the "useful facts of english education" and had encouraged "agriculture & domestic manufactures" to do "the desirable work of civilization." Jefferson responded graciously, offering a personal meeting with the six in his executive office. Even if his deeds did not exactly match his politesse, the memory of the shy, urbane president, his reddish hair going gray, stayed with The Ridge for a long time. The president had obviously been worn down by the cares of his office, but seemingly also ennobled by them, and The Ridge was moved by his evident concern for his Cherokee "children," not yet aware that such American gods could be skilled at deception. The Ridge was always inclined to be respectful of American power, perhaps too much so, and this meeting established a tone of obeisance that would not serve him well.

Jefferson followed the meeting with a letter, always the more comfortable form for him, in which he applauded the Cherokee for their efforts to pursue a "civilized life" by becoming a nation of laws. He wondered, though, how they would draw the line between the towns whose people wished to become an independent nation and the ones whose people expressed a hankering to go west. Perhaps American surveyors could help with that? Hardly an innocent suggestion, as Jefferson well knew. The bigger the Lower Towns, the more land to sell to settlers. Still, assuming that a democratic northeast could be detached from a westbound southwest, Jefferson offered a sensible caution. "Who," he asked, "is to determine which of our laws suit your condition, and shall be in force with you?" He recommended that each town send delegates by majority vote to a central council, replacing the national council, whose members currently chose their successors.

All of this was eminently sensible, but it did not come to pass, at least not then, and not in that form. For the residents of the Lower Towns realized they would much rather stay where they were than leave for a distant, unknown west. And a constitution, everyone soon realized, would take a little doing. But The Ridge came back to the Oostanaula a bigger man. "The advantage of traveling through the United States was not thrown away upon this intelligent and liberal-minded Indian," McKenney wrote. "He returned with a mind enlarged by travel, and with a renewed ardour in the cause of civilization."

Still, his faith that the Cherokee might become civilized anytime soon took a blow when The Ridge learned that James Vann had been shot to death—and probably by his friend Saunders, shattering the tight threesome The Ridge was hoping would lead the nation forward. Vann had been found slumped over in a tavern, a glass in one hand, a bottle of whiskey in the other, and a bullet in his head.

Wealthy, powerful, and dignified as he was, Vann had been undone by the vice that was an increasing temptation for the Cherokee, who had no history of it until the white men came. Whiskey had left Vann indisposed the night of

Doublehead's death, and lately it had turned him into a monster who himself rivaled Doublehead. Vann had served with The Ridge in the lighthorse guard, and Saunders had been disgusted to see how brutally Vann had abused the privilege, convicting fine men on scanty evidence and then whipping them until their skin was ripped off the bone.

But even before this, Vann had been prone to terrifying rages that he took out on his slaves, reserving his harshest punishments for those who dared to defy him. In 1805, while Vann was off on business in Tellico, just outside Chota, three slaves sneaked into his bedroom, where his wife Peggy and another woman were sleeping, and made off with a steamer trunk in which Vann had hidden $3,600 in cash and gold beneath several layers of silk. The plan was to buy their freedom, but once they had the money, they decided to be free of their hated master forever. A tragic mistake. Vann got wind of their scheme, and when he arrived home he burned dozens of his slaves with branding irons to get the details of the plot. In a drunken fit, he hung one slave by her thumbs, and when she still would not confess, by her toes. With a band of slave catchers, plus bloodhounds, he rooted out the scattered conspirators; he then whipped them savagely until they confessed all. Vann dispatched one with a pistol shot, another by a noose, but saved the harshest death for a house slave known as Isaac. By far the cleverest of the slaves, Isaac knew enough English to read Shakespeare, and he played the fiddle at Vann's parties. He'd tried to escape three times before, each time, such were his charms, winning his way back into his master's good graces. This time, though, Vann's mercy ended. He gathered all the slaves, piled high the logs and branches, lashed Isaac to a stake, and set the bonfire blazing, Isaac's cries filling the valley.

But it was the bottle that did him in. Sober, he'd helped found the Moravian school on his property, built the grandest home in the Cherokee Nation, and silenced the room when he spoke up in councils. Drunk, he'd hog-tied a stranger who'd made eyes at his unmarried daughter and given him seventy lashes on his bare back while he screamed for mercy.

The transformation was not simply a matter of a good man going bad, but may have been a reflection of the fierce forces of "progress" that were worming their way inside. That year of the slave rebellion, 1805, he told some Moravian missionaries nearby that he was in unbearable pain. "A live creature had gotten into his ear," and he hoped that the missionaries could somehow draw it out. He was being gnawed from the inside. The outward aristocrat did not match the inner Cherokee; he could not fit his soul to the responsibilities of the new nation. Was that it? Was it that simple? Whatever the cause, Vann became another Doublehead.

And Saunders had shot him, or so it appeared, although he was never charged with the crime. The Ridge must have been horrified, but he refused to be set back. He turned to his neighbor, the learned Charles Hicks, who'd recently been discharged as the official translator for the Indian agency for calling out Meigs on another of his boondoggles. Hicks would take over for Vann, and the nation would go forward.

Ever ambitious for their children, the Ridges sent their two oldest, Nancy and John, to a Moravian school, Spring Place, just north of the Oostanaula by today's Chatsworth, to be educated. Ironically, this improving institution was located on property provided by the decaying James Vann before his death. It was run by an austere missionary couple, Anna and John Gambold, of the sort that were now descending on the nation from all sides, bent on saving these tender souls from heathenish error by providing an education that would show them the way to God's glory. Nancy came first, at age eight. Susanna had developed into something of a worrier where her children were concerned, and she had apprehensions about sending little Nancy off to a boarding school mostly for boys a full day's ride away. There was no proper girls' dorm, since there were only three girls, but Vann's pious widow, Peggy, had moved out of the mansion, with all its hideous memories, to a blacksmith's cottage by the school and agreed to take in Nancy if she helped with the housework—as Peggy explained, "to wash, milk, churn & do other work early in the morn, at evenings & on Saturday when we have no school." Hardly light chores.

A squared-off property with a schoolhouse, dorm, and other modest buildings at the corners, Spring Place might have been a military fort designed to protect a fragile outpost of Christianity. It had a splendid herb garden inside the cloister, while outside were peach and apple orchards, leafy catalpa and shaggy chinaberry trees, broad crop fields, and a big bárn, all of this beside the trickling spring that gave the mission its name. "A bright light in a dark, very dark place," a Congregationalist missionary called it. He did not mean just religiously; the Gambolds took their roles as surrogate parents for these little godless wayfarers seriously. The prim Sister Anna handled all the academics and proved a niggling teacher of the sort that could recite the Latin name of every one of the 1,600 herb specimens in her garden. The more outgoing Brother John took charge of the religion. Childless themselves, in the Moravian belief that missionary wives should remain chaste for Christ, they were surrogate parents for the "*brown* ones," as Anna once termed them, with proud italics, whom they sought to improve in manners, English, work ethic, morals, farming techniques, Bible study, the classics, and much more. The Gambolds knew no Cherokee, and spoke English with a gruff Germanic intonation. But language was not the only barrier between them and their charges, who could be a mystery. The full-bloods among the children proved they could be a trial, as they were slower than the others and were always throwing off their clothes to play, much to the Gambolds' horror. But the mixed-bloods like the Ridge children were far more open to the Gambolds' firm-handed instruction. If Meigs had ever sought to understand the widening economic divide between the full-bloods and the rest, he needed only come here to see that the difference in outcomes probably reflected the difference in disposition. The full-bloods weren't particularly interested in the "enlightened" definition of success.

While young Nancy found it exhausting to keep up with all of Peggy Vann's housework and her own studies, she did well enough that The Ridge decided to send John there too, a year later, when he was just seven. Black-haired but slight, just a sliver of a thing, he had such light skin—a legacy of his Scottish great-grandfather—that he might have passed as white. This may have reflected his father's intentions for him. By now, his scrofula had twisted his hip and run purplish bruises down his legs, leaving him, for long intervals when he was under stress, unable to walk unassisted.* Such a disability must have disturbed a vigorous man like The Ridge, as there would be no tramping through the forest with his son, guns in hand. But young John's mind was alert and nimble, curious about every last thing, and he seemed determined to make the most of it.

---

* In England, scrofula was called the king's evil, since the king was thought to be able to cure it with his touch, and it was sometimes manifest in hideous goiters that bulged out from a neck or shoulder, although not in John Ridge's case.

The Ridge must have thought that young John was his only chance, now that Watty had turned five and made clear he would never live up to his last name. Unfailingly pleasant and cheerful, he could not hold a thought in his head. Once, such a hapless child might have been left to die on a mountaintop, but The Ridge attributed his infirmity to the Christian God he was struggling to understand. "If the child were to blame for his lack of intelligence," he acknowledged, "I would be very ill-tempered with him, and could hardly love him; but since it is God's doing, I must have great patience with his weakness."

If Watty made The Ridge all the more determined to make the most of his older son, he made Susanna more protective, afraid something awful might happen to John, too. John's legs were not his only infirmity. His eyes turned an angry bloodred when he concentrated too long on anything close up. That might be a tadpole at the Oostanaula, but Susanna feared what might happen at Spring Place. The Ridge would not hear of any doubts. John Ridge would be educated, and in November 1810, he drove John to Spring Place himself.

Always an imposing presence, The Ridge must have turned heads when he drove his fine carriage into the little cloister, the horses' hooves clattering on the stone drive. Shy anyway, John was even more abashed as he stood before the Gambolds in a hunting shirt woven by his mother, and tight breeches, when he was used to running about gloriously naked. Speaking even less English than his father, he relied on Peggy Vann, who knew some Cherokee, to make the introductions to these nodding Germans who would now run his life.

The Gambolds took to John, albeit with some reservations, as they took to most of their charges, and in a few weeks they were reporting to John's parents that he was "quite happy with them, and doing well in school." And John warmed to them, too, seeing the kindly devotion in hearts that must have seemed hard at first. "The venerable Rev. John Gambold & his amiable lady were a standing monument of Industry, Goodness & friendship," he later declared. They made "the 'Wilderness blossom as the Rose.'"

Daybreak brought a round of prayer from Brother John, followed by lessons led by Sister Anna, and then work in the fields, which the unsteady young John Ridge must have found arduous. His Christianity came along haltingly, its saints and miracles a mystery. But academically he caught fire.

He spoke marvelously fluent English before the first year was out, and he was soon tearing through the hundred or so volumes in the library, including the poems of Robert Burns and Milton's *Paradise Lost*. Not bad for an eight-year-old Cherokee who'd never held a book in his hands before he arrived. "My heart received the rays of civilization & my intellect expanded & took a wider range," he later rhapsodized.

The whole thing went so well that The Ridge persuaded his brother David Oo-watie, now called just Watie, to send his son, Gallegina, better known as Buck. Much darker-skinned than John, and pudgier, with lanky black hair, Buck was much more the Indian than his light-skinned cousin, but he took to John like a brother, and the two were soon almost inseparable at the little school. Brighter and quicker than Buck, John could be impatient, and the Gambolds learned to brace themselves for questions that could sound impertinent. But Buck was a total joy. His soft eyes radiated sympathy, and something about his gentle, quiet manner melted Sister Anna, who favored him shamelessly with cookies and sweetmeats.

The Ridge dropped in occasionally for lunch, and he was pleased to find the boys deep in their religious lessons, and penetrating mysteries that were well beyond him. The Ridge admitted to some jealousy that he was not "still their age so that he could have a chance to gain understanding." Susanna never did make her peace with a remote place dedicated to learning she couldn't quite fathom. Alarmed by reports that John was suffering from eyestrain, she insisted that her husband drive her there to check on him immediately. By the time they arrived, though, the strain had eased and, as the Gambolds recorded, "they went away much soothed."

While Christianity was taking hold of the mixed-blood elite, eager to get ahead in the world, the old beliefs still captivated everyone else. Many were disturbed by the modern ideas that seemed to be rushing into the nation like an ill wind. Practically everyone shook with the frightening news of the Cherokee couple who'd taken shelter in an abandoned Georgia cabin—and there had seen a vision that lit up the nation. One night, they'd been jolted awake by thunder and lightning, but when they went to the window they found, instead of rain falling from heavy clouds, hundreds of Indians in war paint galloping across the night sky on black horses all to the terrible pounding of unseen drums. And these Indians were shouting themselves hoarse, saying that the Great Spirit was enraged because the Cherokee had let the whites overrun their country and change its ways.

So began the Ghost Dance movement. If the missionaries were pulling the nation one way, the Ghost Dance movement was yanking it back. It drew on loss and longing to rouse the bygone spirit of the Cherokee to cast off all things white. It had many seers, but one above all—a one-eyed Shawnee dubbed the Prophet. His blind eye revealed an inward vision of a land cleansed of marauding whites and restored as the paradise the Great Spirit had bestowed upon the Cherokee. Such a vision would not have been nearly so captivating if the Prophet hadn't had a powerful brother, the Shawnee chief Tecumseh, to make it real. Nearly godlike, Tecumseh had a giant-size personality that made others chiefs seem puny. "About six feet high, straight, with large, fine feathers, and altogether a daring bold-looking fellow," one American captain described him. Tecumseh was determined to win back Indian land. To do it, he sought to fulfill Dragging Canoe's dream of uniting all the Indian tribes into a single confederation to take on the Americans in the ultimate conflict, a kind of Indian Armageddon.

The Ridge met him in September 1811 at the Creek capital, Tuckabatchee, on the banks of the Tallapoosa, well to the south in Georgia. The Ridge had arrived quietly with his men when Tecumseh marched in like a Roman emperor as part of a grand procession of forty foot soldiers, all of them dressed for war, with silver bands about the biceps, circles of fire around the eyes, streaks of bloodred down the chest, their hair plaited in long black strands. Tecumseh himself bore a pair of tall crane feathers, one white, one a dazzling vermilion.

If that weren't awesome enough, a comet appeared in the sky for several nights, as if to celebrate Tecumseh's arrival. The first night, a wild-eyed Tecumseh led a rousing, stomping Dance of the Lakes about a raging fire that reddened the skin of his warriors and threw their shadows to the trees.

All the tribes, it seemed, were spoiling for war, all with a common refrain. It was time to rise up! This was 1812, the year for which the famous war with Britain was named, although it actually ran through early 1815. It was not confined to one year, just as it was not confined to one set of antagonists. The war was ostensibly fought over the impressment of American seamen by a

PROSPERITY   91

high handed British navy, which aggravated tensions already caused by trade restrictions. But it also involved other fights that had been brewing. One had to do with the long-standing American desire to seize Canada. Another came from America's history of cruelty toward the Indians. The Cherokee wanted no part of this aspect of the larger war. In their desire for "civilization," they were not inclined to turn against their American mentors. But plenty of other tribes thought differently. Just as John Watts had once looked to the Spanish for help against the Americans, now the other tribes looked to an aroused Britain to help them push American settlers back into the sea. At the great gathering with Tecumseh, speaker after speaker rose to address the council on this theme. Tecumseh himself was among the last, and his message was apocalyptic. As one startled white attendee summarized it later:

> Kill the old chiefs, friends to peace; kill the cattle, the hogs and fowls; do not work, destroy the wheels and looms, throw away your ploughs and everything used by the Americans. Sing the song of the Indians of the Northern lakes and dance their dance. Shake your war clubs, shake yourselves, you will frighten the Americans; their arms will drop from their hands, the ground will become a bog and mire them, and you may knock them on the head with your war clubs. I will be with you my Shawnees, as soon as our friends the British are ready for us. Lift up the war club with your right hand; be strong, and I will come and show you how to use it.

When an immense Creek, Great Warrior, dared question Tecumseh about the wisdom of such a holy war, Tecumseh fairly shrieked with fury and declared that Great Warrior must have white blood to be so cowardly. If anyone doubted him, Tecumseh shrieked that he would stamp the earth so hard that he would level every house in Tuckabatchee.

Ridge had his doubts about that, but he said nothing, and soon assured the new American president, the quizzical James Madison, that Tecumseh's rhetoric had done nothing for the Cherokee delegation. "We turned away our ears and never listened a moment to the orations of the enemies of our father."

But then something alarming happened. On December 16, when The Ridge was back at the Oostanaula, the earth did indeed shake, delivering itself of deep rumblings that rattled even The Ridge's house, easily the tightest in the village; scattered the birds into the air until their shadows darkened the ground; and spooked all the livestock so much that the horses nearly knocked over the fence posts of their corrals.

It was Tecumseh's doing. He did have supernatural powers. He had to! It was a terrifying thought, but almost impossible to deny. First the comet, then this, the ultimate Ghost Dance, a rattling of the whole cosmos. And the tremors kept on. For weeks, as if the world might burst apart.

Unnerved, The Ridge galloped to Spring Hill to seek guidance from John Gambold as to the meaning of all this terrible shaking. Gambold must have smiled benignly as he explained to The Ridge about these seismic events called earthquakes. He did not know exactly what caused them, but he assured The Ridge that they were a natural phenomenon, like floods or tornadoes, and were well beyond the powers of Tecumseh. Rather, they were the province of Gambold's God, the Christian God, and they were God's way of sending a message that the Indians must abandon their wickedness and follow the Lord. The Ridge listened to this advice in a "meditative silence," Gambold wrote in his diary. Then The Ridge gave out a moan from deep in his chest. Cessions, war, earthquakes, God. "We are just too worthless," he said despairingly. Gambold must have been pleased, as this was exactly the Christian message. As Gambold put it, "This afforded us the occasion for further conversation."

Reassured that Tecumseh was not behind the earth's shudders, The Ridge tried to tamp down his talk of war, letting the Indian agent Meigs know that the Cherokee would never fight the United States, and dispatching Charles Hicks to discourage the neighboring Creeks from such ambitions, too. If they had to fight, they should fight with the United States *against* Britain, not with Britain against the United States, and in that way win the gratitude of the country within which their own nation so uneasily resided.

But others were not so easily swayed. As if powered by these supernatural forces, the Ghost Dance fervor roared through the nation like an earthquake of its own. Thoughts of Indians battling the cruel agents of "civilization" pestered the dreams of the Cherokee, and chants went up everywhere extolling the old glories. Women started dancing wildly, wearing around their ankles tortoise shells filled with pebbles that cracked to the beat of "wild uncouth sounds." Others tossed their European clothes into the fire to cavort naked. Crazed full-bloods claimed they could summon a deadly hurricane or fierce lightning, or turn dry land into a bog that could swallow their enemies. After Tecumseh's earthquake, who was to say they couldn't?

Around then, some of the old-timers staged a great medicine dance at The Ridge's own Oostanaula, and an old conjurer known only as Charley came down from the mountains to participate. He claimed to have been escorted by a pair of demons in the shape of ferocious black wolves, but The Ridge never saw them, nor did anyone else. He told an outdoor Cherokee assembly that the Great Spirit was furious to see the Cherokee with the whites' gristmills, cotton clothes, liquor, featherbeds, and house cats. The Great Spirit had sent those terrifying horsemen across the sky to shock that Cherokee couple into sense. Heed their message! Go back to the old ways—cast off the European clothes, abandon the crops, stop drinking, kill the cats. Observe the feast days, paint yourselves. If not, Charley warned, the Great Spirit will kill you all. And then he paused dramatically, gazed upward, and added, "If you don't believe me, look at the sky." Just then, the clouds parted to reveal a radiance shining forth from "brilliant houses," Charley said, and the rays would incinerate any white men who helped them.

It was quite a performance. The fiery language, the vision. Nearly everyone fell speechless with dread. But not The Ridge. He'd had enough of this nonsense. He saw no houses in the sky, and he thought that the thing most likely to spell the Cherokees' doom was war, not any flouting of bygone traditions. He rose, waited for the crowd to quiet, then told everyone to stop listening to this absurd Charley and his foolish talk. "It would lead us into war with the United States, and we should suffer. It is false; it is not talk from the Great Spirit. I stand here and defy the threat that he who disbelieves shall die. Let the death come upon me. I offer to test this scheme of imposters."

Furious, several Cherokee jumped up from their seats, ran over to The Ridge, lit into him for saying such terrible things about a prophet, and then tore at him with their fists. The assailants surged at him from everywhere, so many he could not fight them all off. The Ridge shoved them, mashed at their faces, anything to push them away, but there were too many, and they kept coming. They pinned him to the ground, held a knife over him, and pressed it against his throat. As others held The Ridge down, one stabbed a friend, John Harris, who'd come to The Ridge's aid and dropped him to the ground, blood pooling beneath him. But several others led by Jess Vann, son of the late

James, managed to haul The Ridge's attackers off him. The Ridge jumped to his feet, and dared anyone to stick him. But then another chief intervened to calm the surging crowd, and The Ridge's enemies dispersed.

Defiant, Charley prophesied that the Great Spirit would send down hailstones the size of cannonballs to kill anyone who didn't save himself by fleeing into the Smoky Mountains and climbing Clingmans Dome, the highest peak, just over the North Carolina line. Sure enough, hundreds of Cherokee abandoned their homes—even their "orchards and bees" by one account—and climbed up to the sacred mountaintop, but the hailstorm never came. That dimmed Charley's influence. The Ridge's rose.

9

INTO THE WILD

By 1812, almost 2,000 Cherokee had followed Jefferson's advice to go west. They settled on the far border of what would soon be the state of Arkansas, much to the consternation of the Cherokee who stayed behind. Their removal posed a problem for the Indian agent Meigs, whose job it was to maintain commercial contact with all the Cherokee, including these new western ones. If he let them feel ignored, he was afraid the British might try to take advantage of the coming war to win them over. He needed to send a trusted emissary to the western band to let them know that he had not forgotten them. But who?

Such an assignment would mean taking the same miserable route west as the emigrants: slogging through bogs, wading across streams, hacking through thickets, trudging through an uncharted territory thick with hostile Indians, prickly settlers, brigands, and snakes.

For this, Meigs thought he had just the man: John Ross, the small but enterprising son of Meigs's good friend Daniel Ross. When Ross's mother had died suddenly in 1808, Ross left Neilson, King and Smith and returned home to the handsome log house by Lookout Mountain to live with his McDonald grandparents. The rest of the Cherokee Nation might have been in turmoil, with Tecumseh's cries echoing through every valley, but Ross spent a quiet four years learning the trading business with his grandfather. Although he considered himself a Cherokee, he was an unusual-looking one, with a clerk's inexpressive face, eastern dress, and skin as white as a doily.

Ross had thought of taking charge of a western "factory," a federal agency designed to regularize the fur trade to the Americans' advantage, going so far as to begin negotiations with Meigs, who controlled such positions, as he did so many things, for a salary of $1,000 a year, plus $1 a day in expenses. Officials in Washington weren't unwilling, but they preferred to see if this Ross could actually get himself out into the mountains first. Once Ross agreed to check on the western Cherokee for him, Meigs staked Ross with $1,000 worth of goods to sell them, from calico to beaver traps, and they were on— mixing business with business, another of Meigs's specialties. For the journey, Ross enlisted a mixed-blood, John Spears, as his translator; and a Spaniard, Peter Esquebell, as his manservant. To establish his bona fides in a backwoods where he might easily be mistaken for white, Ross added a husky full-blood, Kalsatee.

In Chickamauga, the men boarded a flat-bottomed boat, heaped with Meigs's trading goods, for the passage down the Tennessee, looping northwest. It was early December, and very raw. A freeze had left a film of ice along the water's edge and now reddened the men's hands on the oars. Their first stop would be Fort Massac, a stockade-fenced outpost high above where the Tennessee dumps into the Ohio in present-day Metropolis, Illinois. From there, they'd ride the Mississippi down to the Arkansas for the long hike into the western settlement.

But a flatboat proved a poor choice for a surging river, especially when weighed down by supplies, and after a "very disagreeable voyage" down the twisting Tennessee Ross switched to a keelboat. Things turned worse when some "Banditts" spotted them from the shore, leveled their rifles, and demanded that Ross pull his boat to shore. "I was not disposed to go to them," Ross wrote to Meigs. The men said they were under orders to scour the river for Indians, and it looked to them as though Ross had two Indians on board. The leader shouted that he'd send soldiers "to persue & kill us." An anxious Ross shouted back that the men were not Indians but Spaniards. Let's hear some Spanish then, the bandits demanded. When Esquebell obliged, he "confounded their apprehension of it being an Indian boat," Ross chortled. Ross himself was sure no one would mistake *him* for an Indian.

Not really "bandits," the gunmen were probably freelance vigilantes operating under General Jonathan Ramsey to rid the area of Indians, regardless of any treaties that had made the *whites* the illegal settlers. The vigilantes would dress as Indians to steal valuable pelts from whites, and rake their settlements with rifle fire—and then round up innocent Indians to gratify the whites' demands for justice. Under the circumstances, Ross told Meigs, it would be "quite imprudent & unsafe for Indians to attempt to descend the river." Except for an Indian like himself.

Fort Massac had always been a Gibraltar up on its cliff over the Tennessee, offering views out over the wooded plains of Arkansas it was intended to oversee. But Ross found its stockade fences still all twisted up and its roofs buckled from the earthquakes Tecumseh had claimed credit for the previous year. They had actually followed a fault line that ran through New Madrid eighty miles down the twisting Mississippi into today's Missouri. The crunch of shifting plates had sent out shocks through the underlying granite for hundreds of miles around, toppling church steeples up and down the Ohio River valley. Ross stayed long enough to pick up some more goods that Meigs's associate, Samuel Ripley, had left for him. Turmeric and chile peppers, leather straps, twine, several colors of dye, Scotch whiskey, and other oddments. Then they were off again into the vast emptiness to the west.

It must not have made for a joyful New Year's Day, 1813, to return to the icy river, faces burning from the winter wind, fingers uncooperative. An hour or two into it, the skies darkened, the wind kicked up, and the overloaded keelboat started tipping wildly this way and that. As river water sloshed over the gunwales, they continued gamely on down the Ohio. But when they hit the inrushing waters of the Mississippi, the unwieldy boat tipped and failed to tip back, pitching everyone into the icy drink. Unable to swim, dragged down by heavy clothes, Ross floundered in the swift current until Kalsatee swam him safely to shore, where he gathered with the others before a warming fire.

Eventually, they were able to press on down the Mississippi to the Arkansas shore, and there they hoisted their sopping trading goods onto their backs to lug them two hundred miles to the western settlement. The woods were thick with heavy snow, the trail was unmarked and crisscrossed with tumbling streams, but the real hazards were the scattered bands of whites and Indians who lived among the trees. For Ross, it was the bandits all over again, as he had to pass as white with the whites and then as Indian among the Indians. His heart had to be in his throat either way. Who was he? That was the question, over and over. And it remained the question after he finally reached the Arkansas River on the far side of the state, two full miserable months later. Tramping along the shore, they found the settlement. Did he deliver his goods as a fellow Indian, or as a white representative of the Indian agent?

Whichever, he abandoned the idea of a western factory and instead set up a trading post with Meigs's son Timothy on little Tallapoosa Island on the Tennessee River, a property Ross had inherited from his great-uncle, the other Scottish trader, William Shorey. The trading post led to a ferry, and to a wife, Elizabeth Brown Henley, known as Quatie, a recent widow with a daughter. No image of Quatie survives, and scarcely a detail. She and Ross were married in 1813 at Quatie's family home in Ooltewah, just east of Chickamauga, near the Alabama state line, in a traditional Cherokee ceremony performed by her father. Ross brought her to live with him at his grandfather's place in Rossville. Neither spouse spoke the other's language, or learned it. Quatie bore Ross five children, but the marriage otherwise seems not to have been meaningful to her husband. In his enormous two-volume collection of correspondence, Quatie is not once mentioned by him or anyone else. As a full-blood, however, she did much to bolster his tribal credentials, which were a key to his trading career, and indispensable to the political life that followed. She made John Ross something he had never been before. A Cherokee.

Busy staying alive, Ross and everyone else in the Cherokee Nation gave little thought to the growing tension on the high seas between the British and the Americans that would erupt in the War of 1812. To the Cherokee, if they were aware of it at all, the war occurred solely in its western theater, past the Ohio and up to the Canadian border, where the Americans were pushing against the Indians of the Northwest Territory as part of a march on British

Canada. All in the name of what would be termed "manifest destiny," which to the Americans was their birthright, as glorious and inevitable as sunrise. Not to the Indians, of course. And many of them, like the Winnebago, Shawnee, Fox, Kickapoo, and Delaware, were heeding Tecumseh's call to band together against this latest American assault. They would again be backed by the British Empire, this time determined to keep hold of its vast Canadian territory, and avoid the insults of the Revolution.

The Ridge was not inclined to join them. In the tense months of anticipation before President Madison finally declared war on Britain on June 1, 1812, The Ridge had joined with two other chiefs—John Walker and John Lowrey—to reassure an anxious Meigs that the Cherokee would never join a pan-Indian army of Tecumseh's, but stick with the Americans in any conflict. To The Ridge and the other enlightened Cherokee, America was their future. Any identification with their fellow Indians was long past. Yes, America may have oppressed them, but that was behind them now as they marched ahead to fulfill what they saw as their own manifest destiny as a thriving people, fully the equal of the Americans they had every reason to despise, but didn't. Meigs was not just relieved, but heartened that his efforts were paying off: he was turning the Cherokee.

The Cherokees' immediate neighbors to the southwest, the Creeks, were not all of this persuasion, however. Some stoutly resisted the idea of any kind of affinity with the hated Americans who had abused them for so long. These Creeks were the Red Sticks, so named by Tecumseh himself when he came around to recruit warriors for his war on America. To demonstrate the value of Indian unity, Tecumseh had gathered up some red sticks and snapped them one by one. But when he bunched a handful of the sticks tightly together, he could not break them in two, no matter how hard he tried. You must be Red Sticks, he said, and so they were.

The following summer, in 1813, about 1,000 of these fearsome Red Sticks gathered in the woods outside Fort Mims, a thinly defended federal outpost just up from the Gulf Coast near Mobile, Alabama, where a few hundred settlers had taken refuge. Imagining themselves well protected by a federal battalion behind a stockade fence, they soon grew casual about security precautions. Spying from the distant trees, the hostile Creeks noticed that the gates often stood open well after the noontime dinner drum sounded to draw everyone from the fields into the mess hall. This was the Red Sticks' chance. Their bodies slathered with the war paint of old, their faces colored ghoulishly, they surged several hundred strong across the field to pour through the open gate, filling the air with their frenzied war cries. With a rain of bullets and arrows, they slaughtered soldiers and settlers alike, and then swarmed howling over the open fort and surrounding grounds, crazed for the tender flesh of any survivors. Men, women, children—it didn't matter; the Red Sticks hacked and hacked at them until the fort was silent except for the moans of the dying, the light scuffing of men in moccasins prowling for anyone left in hiding, and the wind.

There had been 553 in the fort: 100 men and the others women and children. Only thirteen escaped the slaughter. When a federal investigator named Thomas Holmes arrived a few days afterward, the stinking, mangled corpses of all the rest made a grisly feast for buzzards and stray dogs. "Indians, negroes, white men, women, and children lay in one promiscuous ruin," he reported. "All were scalped, and the females of every age were butchered in a manner which neither decency nor language will permit me to describe." The fetuses of the pregnant women had been hacked from the womb and dropped on the bare, blood-drenched chests of the mothers. "The main building was burned to ashes, which were filled with bones," Holmes concluded. "The plains and woods around were covered with dead bodies."

The job of protecting Americans of the southwest from such horrific onslaughts fell to General Andrew Jackson, a Tennessee plantation owner whose innate belligerence was perfectly suited to war. Elected major general of the 2,000-man Tennessee militia in 1802, he was thrilled when the War of 1812 offered him a chance to make his post more than an honorific, and, in the bargain, to take out his ire against the two classes of humanity he most reviled— the British and any Indians who collaborated with them. Soon to be dubbed Old Hickory, Jackson might well have been made out of this iron-hard wood that encases a sweet sap. Born fatherless in North Carolina, the young Jackson had run messages for the colonial forces in the Revolutionary War, was taken prisoner by the British at fourteen, and then clapped in a smallpox-infested shipboard prison where an English officer slashed him across the face with a sword after Jackson refused to clean the officer's boots. This left a scar, both physical and metaphorical, that never fully healed. Jackson well remembered that the Cherokee had fought with the English to put down the Americans' quest for freedom—and then massacred the intrepid pioneers along the Tennessee where Jackson now had his home. That was the 1,000-acre plantation he called the Hermitage, with a graceful mansion where he lived with his beloved Rachel, the sensual daughter of one of the settlers who'd dared to infiltrate Muscle Shoals, where Dragging Canoe lurked. Tall, rugged, and leonine, Jackson required enemies to defy. By the summer of 1813, when he learned of the horrors of Fort Mims, he already bore a bullet in his chest from a duel over his status as a gentleman. (Jackson put the questioner in his grave.) That fall, he took two more bullets when he confronted Thomas Benton, the future senator from Missouri, over other aspersions on his character. The two met unexpectedly in the doorway of a Nashville hotel. Benton was there with his brother Jesse, and Jackson with Colonel John Coffee. Everyone reached for a pistol, but it was Jesse who fired first. One bullet struck Jackson in the left shoulder, cracking bone and slicing an artery; a second shattered his left arm. Jackson fired uselessly as he went down. A frenzy of gunfire and daggers followed, but Jackson remained the only one seriously hit.

Carried to an upstairs bedroom, the future president drenched two mattresses with his blood. Doctors decided to amputate Jackson's left arm to save him, but the delirious patient refused to allow them to do any such thing. Jackson rallied and restored himself, but he ached from his wounds for the rest of his life. And he was not in the best shape when the war he craved was at last upon him.

The Ridge learned of the attack on Fort Mims from the Creek leader William McIntosh, an impressive mixed-blood who gloried in his Scottish ancestry. No loyalist of Tecumseh, McIntosh had come to recruit The Ridge's help in resisting those rampaging Creek dissidents, the Red Sticks. Together, McIntosh and The Ridge went on to the Creek capital, Tuckabatchee, to see the Creeks' principal chief, Great Warrior, who'd dared stand up to Tecumseh the year before. Great Warrior greeted The Ridge warmly with a sheaf of tobacco to be smoked, for its fragrance of harmony, at the meeting of the tribe's national council.

After Fort Mims, The Ridge could see that the Indians' war, which was sweeping across the continent, did more than just pit one band of Creeks against another, or even pit the Americans against British; for him as an aspiring Cherokee, it involved something larger still. It set the dream of civilization—*his* dream now—against the forces of disorder. It was a war between those who stood for something and those who stood for nothing. That was how The Ridge saw it, and he stood for something. He was a builder—of families, of plantations, of nations. He would not abandon that ambition now. He must have poured his heart out to McKenney, who put it starkly later: "If the Creeks were permitted to put down their chiefs, and be ruled by the prophets," he wrote, summarizing The Ridge's views, "the work of civilization would be subverted, and the Red Sticks, in their efforts to re-establish a state of barbarism, would destroy all the southern tribes," the Cherokee among them.

Great Warrior and McIntosh saw it the same way as The Ridge, but the other Creek and Cherokee chiefs were afraid to take on Tecumseh, with all his frenzied oratory and nearly mystical powers, especially if he was backed by the vast power of the British Empire. When The Ridge returned to the nation, he discovered that the Cherokee council members could not bring themselves to fight for the Americans.

It should have been understandable, given everything the Cherokee had suffered at American hands, but The Ridge would have none of it. He declared that if the Cherokee would not provide warriors for this great war, then he would collect his own. "I will act with volunteers," he declared, and asked his "friends" on the council to join him, turning to enlightened younger men, such as his new ally Charles Hicks. When these rising chiefs proved receptive, the principal chief, Pathkiller, grew fearful that he would face the humiliation The Ridge had dealt Black Fox just five years before. And so Pathkiller relented, and declared war on the Red Sticks after all.

The Ridge collected several hundred warriors at Hiwassee garrison, and, knowing their value to the Americans, he prevailed upon Meigs to persuade the War Office to outfit them all with regulation army rifles and ammunition, and to accord them standard pay, plus benefits to the families of any warriors killed or wounded in battle. In this war, they would be treated like Americans.

One of the enlisted soldiers was that scrappy young man Meigs had sent west, John Ross. No warrior, small, unprepossessing, and remarkably white, he would have attracted The Ridge's attention only as an oddity. He'd joined up with his brother Lewis and a brother-in-law, John Golden Ross, all three of them in civilian clothes. Now forty-two, his own fighting days well past, The Ridge himself still wore a warrior's loincloth and knee-high leggings despite the October chill, and he rode out of the garrison high on a fine horse, equipped with rifle, powder horn, hunting knife, tobacco pouch, and bedroll. He was no John Ross.

The Cherokee were there to serve under Jackson, but Jackson did not cotton to the idea of using Indian soldiers. Nevertheless, the disaster at Fort Mims affected him much as it had The Ridge. In the North, Indians may have been roused as one, but the enemy down in the South was not *all* Indians, but *these* Indians, the Red Sticks bent on annihilating decent people guilty only of being white. When Jackson sensed that the Cherokee would stand with him against the Red Sticks, he realized he could use *these* savages to fight *those* savages. The Cherokee would bolster the ranks of his Tennessee volunteers, and give his men a touch of the ferocity that, to Jackson at least, only Indians could provide.

The Cherokee could not have been completely enthusiastic about the assignment, for Jackson's soldiers were the sons of the settlers—or perhaps the settlers themselves—who had shoved the Cherokee off their lands. More gallingly, many of them were dressed for the backwoods, in buckskins and coonskins, in twisted imitation of the Cherokee they professed to detest. But of course, The Ridge was imitating them, too, by joining their ranks as a fellow soldier.

The Cherokee would march with these hardy volunteers, on foot or horseback, under the command of General White, who deferred only to General Jackson. White selected the up-and-coming half-blood Gideon Morgan to take command of the Cherokee regiment as a full colonel, with Lieutenant George Lowrey as his second. Principal Chief Pathkiller was made a colonel too, but that was largely an honorific, since he was far too old to fight. The Ridge's good friend Alexander Saunders was made a captain; The Ridge was merely a first lieutenant, a lesser rank. Since he was a leader of the nation, the senior man, and a person of considerable pride, this had to have been a blow. But The Ridge had no English, the language of the army, and so was not fit for higher command.

John Ross, a boy, really, of twenty-three, would be an adjutant, or staff officer, for a company of mounted Cherokee under Captain Sekekee. That may have won him notice from The Ridge. Ross was clearly a fellow of some use. It fell to Meigs to tutor the Cherokee in the rules of American warfare: follow orders; respect rank; no killing of defenseless prisoners, women, or children. And please, for God's sake, try not to take scalps.

Jackson's plan was simple: destroy the Red Sticks wherever he could find them. To do just that, on November 4, 1813, Colonel Morgan led his Cherokee troops out to the village of Talleshatchee, which was just south of John Ross's Coosa, and was thought to be a Red Stick enclave. But they arrived only to find that the troops of General Coffee—the ally who had saved Jackson's life at the Nashville hotel—had beaten them to it. They'd reduced the once thriving town to a hell of charred, blood-smeared Red Stick bodies, limbs off, stinking of death, amid a terrible wailing from widows grieving over the dead. General Coffee's 1,000-man cavalry brigade had swooped in to slaughter them, first with slow deliberation, and then in a frenzy of retribution after a Creek woman, sprawled out half-dead before her hut, had let fly an arrow to kill a young lieutenant as he approached to offer her aid. Davy Crockett, a young soldier attached to the cavalry, told what happened next. The soldiers were so infuriated that they fired on her from all sides, putting, he said, at least twenty balls into her; then shot every Creek they could see; and then set fire to a house harboring forty-six warriors. That created such a furnace that a twelve-year-old boy who lay prostrate just outside it, his arm and thigh blasted, started literally to sizzle from "the grease . . . stewing out of him." Even so, Crockett noted that "not a murmur escaped him" as he tried to crawl away. "So sullen is the Indian, when his dander is up, that he had sooner die than make a noise, or ask for quarter."

When the Cherokee came upon this charnel house, however, they did not recoil. Rather, despite Meigs's admonition, they dropped on the dead like furies and hacked off all the scalps they could find.

Jackson himself went after the Red Sticks at Talladega, fifty miles east of today's Birmingham, advancing on them in a long, thick line, its two arms closing to crush them in a lethal embrace. When the Red Sticks fled into the mountains, Jackson sent his cavalry on a rampage after them. Wildly outnumbered, the surviving Red Sticks gathered at Hillabee, just south of

Talleshatchee, to talk peace. But General John Cocke was peeved to have been left out of these spoils, and charged in to dispatch sixty Red Sticks as they tried to surrender. It was the murder of Old Tassel times sixty, and it would not be forgotten by the Red Sticks, who now vowed to fight to the last man, dragging into the underworld as many of the enemy as they could.

Finally, winter came, and the war had to be suspended. Temporarily released from service, The Ridge was rewarded with a pretty Creek girl to take back to the Oostanaula as a house slave, a gift for Susanna. She'd taken sick in The Ridge's absence and could use an extra pair of hands for the younger two children, the helpless Watty and his little sister Sarah, still at home. As it was, The Ridge had had to pull young John home from school to help out.

It's not clear what Susanna's ailment was. It may be that she'd simply given in to the chaos mounting around her, with her grand protector away. She refused to have anything to do with any cure from what she called the "Indian sorcery" of the conjurers her husband recommended. She would be treated only by Sister Anna's medicinal herbs, and she enlisted their aging neighbor William Hicks to bring them. More frighteningly, Susanna's mother's scrofula had flared up in the long drenching rains that fall, and the infection had spread throughout her body. Shortly after John returned, the disease had finally stopped her mother's heart. At that, John's own pains roared to life; his legs had never been so useless. Frantic with worry, Susanna tried to be his protector, even as he tried to be hers.

The reprieve was brief, and The Ridge was re-called to battle just a month later. When Meigs asked him to bring warriors with him, The Ridge replied with a request for ammunition. It's the first letter of his that survives. It was doubtless written for him by a translator, but if so, the translator knew only a little more English than he did himself, and it shows what The Ridge was up against, operating at two removes from English, as he tried to reveal his thoughts to Americans.

This is a phew words from your friend the Rige. Sir when eye saw you last fall eye had taken up my gunn against the hostile Creekes but itt was because the done bad and eye went agains them and taken a good maney and have taken up my gunn to gow against them again and expect to have a

lairg of my people with mee this time. We will gow with our oaldes brothers the whites like a band of brothers.

It is heartbreaking to see a great man so humbled by a language that would
always be foreign to him, no matter how hard he strived to be a full American.

Without the Indians, and without the volunteers who also returned to their
families, Jackson's army fell to just 130 men that winter, and many were on
the verge of starvation. The winter had been cold but dry, and the rivers
ran so low that boats could not make it down the Coosa to bring food. In
desperation, the men were reduced to foraging for acorns when neighboring
Cherokee offered them meat and corn, although they themselves had little
to spare.

Temporarily restored, Jackson took the fight to the Red Sticks at various
towns in Creek territory before retreating to Fort Armstrong, on the Mississippi at the foot of Rock Island near today's Quad Cities in Illinois and Iowa,
to receive the returning Cherokee in February. The Ridge rode in proudly
with several hundred warriors, many of them full-bloods bearing evocative
names like the Mouse, the Broom, Club Foot, Old Brains, Whiteman Killer,
and Shoe Boots. The last was a commander so exuberant he was known to tip
his head back and crow to the sun like a rooster. Seeing them all, a relieved
Jackson on the spot promoted The Ridge to major, a title he wore for the rest
of his life as if it were his first name.

John Ross had returned to his trading post in Chickamauga, and didn't
emerge until Meigs ordered him flat out to report to his regiment, and even
then, he delayed another two weeks before setting out for Fort Armstrong
with his brother Lewis. By the time they joined up, Jackson had gathered an
awesome force of 5,000 men for the final assault on the Red Sticks, huddled
along the Tallapoosa River at a place called Horseshoe Bend.

If a native people were ever to retreat, and then retreat again, and then
again and again, Horseshoe Bend, in today's Dadeville in mid-state Alabama,
was the kind of place where they might end up—on a green peninsula created
by a wild turn of the vigorous, wide-swinging river that had cut deep into the
forest all around it. The dashing Creek commander, William Weatherford,
had sheltered the last of his force, and their families, behind a stout fortifica-

tion of logs and earth that guarded the entrance to the peninsula, which was elsewhere protected by the brisk but dirty river that swerved around it.

To Weatherford, the promontory must have seemed not just safe, but somehow sacred, a place chosen by the Great Spirit for a valiant people. Weatherford himself was the sort of daredevil who trusted in fate. It was his idea to exterminate everyone at Fort Mims—only to arouse the concentrated fury of Jackson and the superior forces that had now chased him here to this potential Armageddon on the Tallapoosa. Weatherford had dash, no question. He'd survived one battle by plunging on horseback off a high cliff into the Arkansas River some eighty feet below. An enormous splash and then nothing but bubbles for several long moments—before Weatherford surged up to the surface still firmly in the saddle, clinging to the horse's mane with one hand and clutching his rifle with the other. Now, he'd found safety for his men behind the surging river and breastworks of fat logs he'd laid out, caulked with mud and placed over a long mound of dirt, with porthole openings for riflemen, that ran like the side of a log house across the only link to land.

"Nature furnishes few situations as eligible for defense; and barbarians have never rendered one more secure by art," Jackson declared later in his report, when he had reason to convey that he'd achieved the impossible. In fact, the position mostly offered false comfort to native warriors unversed in modern artillery and the wiles of a canny enemy. This fortress did not keep Jackson's forces out so much as keep the Creeks in—and in a highly precarious position. While the promontory loomed impressively over the river, it was actually slightly lower than the surrounding land, and lowest at the peninsula's neck, its point of entry. Worse, Weatherford was down to just 800 Red Sticks, only a third of them with guns. The rest had to make do with arrows or blades. Jackson had 5,000, all of them fully armed.

When Jackson looked down at the lowly Creek outpost, he saw an anthill fit for stomping. He'd ordered his artillery company to drag a pair of powerful cannons a hundred miles just for the purpose. They'd drop massive balls of lead on this feeble Creek outpost, crushing the fortifications, leaving Jackson to pick off any survivors at his leisure.

Shortly after dawn on March 17, 1814, Jackson signaled for his cannons to begin, and great booms echoed through the river canyon. Jackson had arrayed his men all around the lip of land enclosing the river, waiting for the cannonballs to shatter the Creek fortifications below. For hours, the cannons fired their heavy load, rocking with each blast, smoke rising from their iron mouths. But, incredibly, the Creek wall stood just as it had, and the brazen enemy was starting to shout up taunts at the Americans who were so useless in battle.

Then a few daring Cherokee warriors led by Major Ridge devised a new plan. With his in-law Charles Reese, and an immense full-blood aptly called the Whale and several other men he trusted, Major Ridge climbed down the face of the canyon wall to the riverbed. He set foot on a spot at the peninsula's watery tip, well away from the breastworks that were being so heavily pounded. Major Ridge had spotted a pair of canoes that the Creeks, never imagining an enemy might find them of use, had beached there. Wearing nothing but breechclotths, their heads adorned with twin eagle feathers to distinguish themselves from the enemy, Major Ridge and the others slipped quietly into the river and, with just their eyes above the water like crocodiles, swam smoothly to the far side. Once ashore, the Cherokee grabbed the canoes to swim them back and then ferry across a full contingent of fighters that had by now descended the canyon. Major Ridge took the first boat and, paddling from the stern, his head low, his rifle at his side, slipped the first contingent of warriors across.

The Creeks had thrown up some meager huts not far from the water's edge. Cherokee rifle fire shocked the Red Sticks huddled inside—mostly women and children—and sent them running for safety in the barricades. The Cherokee attackers then torched the empty dwellings, drawing attention from the warriors at the breastworks, who'd expected the enemy to attack from the other side. They rushed to fight off Ridge's men, whose eagle feathers let Jackson, watching from above, know they were *his* Indians. Jackson then ordered thousands more men to scramble down from the cliffs to pour into the breach left where its defenders were pulled away. Jackson sent many more soldiers splashing down into the river to attack from that side, too, catching the enemy in a deadly cross fire.

Furious Red Stick warriors, knives in hand, closed on Major Ridge and his men, but The Ridge dispatched six of them. The last died after a terrific hand-to-hand fight, the two combatants thrashing about in the water, each trying to force the other under. Finally, The Ridge pulled the Creek's own knife from his belt and thrust it into his belly, and then another Cherokee finished him with a spear. They left the Creek floating facedown, the water reddening around him.*

Attacked from the front and the back, hundreds more Creeks fell. "The carnage was dreadful," Jackson acknowledged later. In a rare attempt at mercy, he sent an emissary to the Creeks to talk peace, but after the Americans' murderous betrayal at Hillabee, the Red Sticks fired on the man and the slaughter continued. When the Red Sticks' guns finally fell silent, the last man dead, Jackson dispatched soldiers to nip off the noses of the fallen to make a count. On land, 557 had perished; the river had claimed at least 350 more.

John Ross prepared the Cherokee casualty report. "Capt. Ridge Company," as Ross termed it, was listed third, marking Major Ridge's official entry into Ross's awareness, although he mistakenly downgraded Ridge's rank. He lists the dead and injured—Katchee, Netwowwee, and Woyehahkeskee, among many others—and grades their wounds from slight to dangerous.

Ross's English defined him, as did his talent for bureaucracy, placing him at a desk at field headquarters, well away from the screams of battle. He was not a man to show up on a list of fallen Cherokee; he was a man to make one.

Once the Red Sticks were put to flight, Jackson dispatched his friend General Coffee to inventory the ghost towns they'd left behind. Huts, council houses, stables—they were all empty. The cattle were gone, the fields picked clean. A few grisly mementos turned up, like the collection of scalps from Fort Mims that hung off arrows on the central pole of one council house. They might have been fur hats, if they weren't so curled up and bloodstained.

After the sweeping defeat at Horseshoe Bend, Weatherford did not flee to parts unknown, but, astride the remarkable horse that had survived the plunge into the Arkansas, rode alone into the fort that Jackson was erecting to oversee his conquered territory. Fort Jackson, he called it. Of mixed blood,

---

* McKenney has Major Ridge equipped with a sword, but it is hard to imagine that he'd have brought one along for a sneak attack across a river, not if he also carried rifle, powder, bullets, and a knife, too. To the recently promoted major, the sword was probably more a symbol of his new rank than an actual weapon—and *that* was something Major Ridge would take with him everywhere.

Weatherford had a noble bearing—six feet tall, taut and tough, with a nose "like a hawk's beak," said an observer. He arrived in the pants and shirt of the American frontiersman, but added an Indian's colorful turban. Jackson was surprised to see him ride up. He'd expected to find Weatherford dead or a prisoner, if he found him at all.

"I am in your power," Weatherford told Jackson. "Do with me as you please." If he'd had an army, he'd have fought on, he said, but he could not "animate the dead." He'd come to seek peace for his people. He did not expect to find any for himself.

Under other circumstances, Jackson might have slapped Weatherford up against a wall and had him shot, but something about the man's manner made that impossible.

"On the miseries and misfortunes brought upon my country, I look back with deepest sorrow," Weatherford continued, adding that he wished to avoid further bloodshed. "You are a brave man and I rely upon your generosity. You will exact no terms of a conquered people but such as they can accede to. Whatever they may be, it would be madness and folly to oppose." Then he concluded: "I have told the truth. If you think I deserve death, do as you please."

If that was a ploy, it was clever. It left Jackson unsure of his ground. Was he being flattered, or challenged? While Jackson was quite familiar with straight-out aggression, he may not have known about the passive variety, especially when it was exhibited so artfully by a warrior Jackson couldn't help admiring. He told Weatherford to tell any remaining Red Sticks to stop their war against the Americans. Then, with a wave, he let him go.

With that, the war with the Red Sticks was over. The Indians of the western Plains would fight on for almost the rest of the century, but the peace with Weatherford ended the Americans' long war against the Indians of the East.

It did not bring peace to Major Ridge. He may have won Jackson's temporary respect for his bravery, but he left unsettled. When he arrived home, he assured Susanna that he would not leave for war ever again and, over her protests, returned his son John to his studies at Spring Place. For the next few months, Major Ridge often stopped in at the school, ostensibly to check on his son, but there may have been more to his visits. Whenever he came, the Gambolds read to the major from the Bible. At first, Ridge merely humored these missionaries to whom he'd entrusted two of his children. But soon he got interested in this remarkable story of what the Gambolds called "the fall and salvation of man." He'd never thought in moral terms. His reason for doing anything was never that it was right, but simply that it was necessary, and he assumed that *this* was right. "I myself would like to hear what is good," he told the Gambolds. Of course, the good was what was not evil, a concept that required guilt. This was an emotion that Major Ridge at first had found inconceivable. But he soon realized he'd felt it acutely. "When a young man, I killed a wicked Indian," he confessed to the missionaries, "and have often wondered since then whether God would not punish me for that deed one day." It was the murder of Doublehead that was weighing on him. Not because he'd been part of it, but because he'd failed to consult the proper authorities first. "I've resolved never to do such a thing again," he told the Gambolds, "unless the Council orders me to rid the world of a bad man."

Good and evil. They were emerging as the two poles of this strange new moral order Major Ridge was finding himself in. But which was which?

An 1886 political cartoon depicting the tragic subjugation of the Cherokee Nation.

PART TWO

THE
DESCENT
INTO HELL

1814–1837

1

THE PERILS OF PEACE

The treaty ended the war with the Creeks, but it did not bring peace to the Cherokee. When Ross returned to his grandparents' place near Lookout Mountain, and Major Ridge to his house on the Oostanaula—a slim tributary of the Coosa that ran through much of northwest Georgia—they were expecting a springtime of dogwood blossoms and wildflowers, of valleys greening with the first nubs of corn and beans, of lowing cattle and romping horses. Instead they found devastation through the valleys across to the foothills. While the Cherokee warriors were off fighting for Andrew Jackson, the Tennessee militia had thundered through the defenseless Cherokee Nation like an avenging army, stealing horses, slaughtering hogs and cattle, destroying corncribs, tearing down fences, seizing private stores of corn, maple sugar, and clothing and what few possessions the Cherokee could call their own. And brandishing weapons at anyone who dared defy them.

The devastation shocked Indian agent Meigs, not that it should have, given the history. But he was nearly breathless in his report to his superiors in the War Department. "The return of the Horse thro' the country has been marked by plunder & prodigal, unnecessary and wanton destruction of property: their stocks of cattle & hogs have been shot & suffered to rot untouched—their horses in some instances shared the same fate: their clothing intended to defend them from the wet & cold in the present campaign has been stolen and in some instances where they remonstrated their lives have been threatened."

All the more outrageously, the Tennessee militia was General Jackson's, with whom the Cherokee had fought so loyally, at such peril, against the Red Sticks. And this was how the Cherokee were repaid? And after their impoverished fellow tribesmen along the Coosa had given Jackson's troops corn and food to keep them from starving—now the troops trample the Cherokee fields for sport? How could they have been so heartless? No explanation was forthcoming, possibly because no one in authority imagined that any explanation was needed. At least, Meigs never received one to pass on to the Cherokee. The truth was that the Cherokee didn't particularly matter to the Americans. And so the best explanation is probably the cruelest one: they did it because they could.

When the Cherokee demanded payment for these "spoliations," Jackson dismissed their claims as "one complete tissue of groundless falsehood." Rather than concede anything, he widened the claims he'd made of Creek land in the peace settlement to include territory that had always been Cherokee, raising the natives' outrage to a point of desperation. In protest, the Cherokee dispatched a delegation to Washington to appeal to President James Madison in person. Despite everything, they still believed that their Great Father had their interests at heart. For the mission, the gruff half-blood Lieutenant Colonel Lowrey assembled a small group of Cherokee dignitaries that included Major Ridge. Ridge, in turn, added one more: John Ross, the young adjutant whose brisk efficiency and fluent English had impressed him in the war. Major Ridge knew that those qualities, plus Ross's city clothes and white skin, would be useful. Ross would serve as scribe and clerk—but not translator, of course, since he didn't know much more Cherokee than Madison did.

It was just before Christmas, 1815, when Major Ridge, accompanied by a Negro manservant, wended his way north on horseback, trailed by pack mules, through the chilly, snow-whitened Smoky Mountains, to Washington by way of Knoxville, a wearying journey of well over a month. When the view of the capital finally opened up, Ridge must have been staggered to see that the city, which had seemed full of promise a decade before, now lay in ruins, burned nearly to the ground by the retreating British, infuriated to have lost another war to their upstart cousins. Only torrential rains had saved the capital from a total conflagration. Still, the symbolism was dire: the Executive Mansion was reduced to smoldering rubble. And the ignominy: when the first bombs descended, Madison and his flamboyant wife, Dolley, had fled for their lives.*

Still, the burned-out capital had already sent up a few green shoots. Ramshackle storefronts and flimsy houses were rising from the mud amid the few state buildings that remained standing. As a major in Jackson's army, Ridge may have felt superior to his surroundings as he rode in so high in the saddle. Once he was situated, the city's leading citizens looked with some awe on this handsome, broad-shouldered Indian who strode manfully into their drawing rooms in a well-cut jacket and a fashionable cravat. The correspondent for the *National Intelligencer* was quite taken aback, for the Cherokee, all of them in civilian clothes issued by the War Department, did not look the part. "These are men of cultivation and understanding," he instructed his readers. "Their appearance and deportment are such as to entitle them to respect and attention."

Nonetheless, Major Ridge got into the carefree spirit in the after-hours. At one soiree, when he was invited to sing a little Indian music, he offered a lusty Cherokee song. Asked for a translation, he shrugged it off: "Oh, you don't want to know. It's just like a white man's song—all about love and whiskey." One of the ladies present declared that if she were an Indian, she'd marry a man like the major so he could bring her home a calico petticoat. It was a bit of a tease, and Ridge didn't bite. "Oh, Washington husbands are of no use to our women now. They can weave their own petticoats."

Ross wasn't one for such lighthearted parties. The industrious Scot, uncomfortable with any sort of joshing ribaldry, worked while others caroused.

The delegation had plenty to contend with. Andrew Jackson's star had

---

* The bombardment nonetheless inspired Francis Scott Key's hymn to endurance, "The Star-Spangled Banner," which improbably emerged as the national anthem over a century later.

ascended even higher after his smashing victory over the Creeks, for he had pressed on to defend New Orleans from a British assault by sea. After he drove the British off, a feat Napoleon himself had failed to achieve, Jackson became not just the savior of New Orleans but the greatest hero of the war, and he was eager to make use of his aura.

When Jackson learned that the Cherokee were coming to Washington to complain about the actions of his troops, and to try to undo the postwar borders he'd set, he saw his chance. He galloped ahead to let President Madison and the War Department know exactly where he stood. Madison, the smallest president ever, was such a remarkably little man that Jackson could have stuffed him into his coat pocket. Worse, he was touchy about his standing, so much so that when his presidency was over, he devoted himself to doctoring the record to improve on his accomplishments, rewriting whole paragraphs of his correspondence. Madison would listen to Jackson's case, but only up to a point. Unlike his mentor Jefferson, Madison was not Machiavellian when it came to the Indians. He always treated them with genuine consideration. And if he wavered, he had his secretary of war, William Crawford, to bolster him.

Brawny and solid-jawed, Crawford was too much like Jackson to indulge Jackson for long. As a hot-blooded young Georgian politician, Crawford had fought two duels of his own, shooting dead a member of a rival political faction in one, and in the other taking a bullet from its leader, the rabble-rousing John Clark, that shattered his wrist—much as Jackson had nearly lost his arm. With a long history in government behind him, Crawford was gunning for the presidency, just like Jackson, and this hardly bred amity. Although Georgia was notoriously hostile to the Cherokee, Crawford himself was personally sympathetic, possibly because that would irritate Jackson no end.

Once the Cherokee delegation was settled into its hotel, Colonel Lowrey submitted his credentials to his "Father," President Madison. Holding back any indignation, he appealed to Madison's loyalty by reminding him that the Cherokee had been compatriot soldiers in the American war against the Creeks. Or rather Ross did this for him, since Lowrey could not even write his name. The next memorandum ghostwritten by Ross got into it, as it inveighed against the devastation of Cherokee lands by the white militia "warriors" whose feelings of liberty "relaxed into licentiousness" and set them rampaging across the Cherokee Nation. Such wantonness, Ross wrote, stemmed from "prejudice founded only on the difference in shade of our complexion, proving that even in an enlightened country there are some men who are not worthy of being armed, and who are not worthy of being numbered amongst the great defenders of liberty."

It was all too true, as the sympathetic Madison must have recognized, and all the more pointed coming from an Indian who wrote with such eloquence. Ross begged the president to look at the mounds of evidence of this "licentiousness." For good measure, he demanded compensation for the families of the Cherokee warriors killed in the war, putting them "on the same footing as our white brothers."

Another Cherokee memorandum went straight at Jackson with such raw Cherokee fury that it was almost certainly not written by Ross.

> Father, you have with you, as with us red children, those who make crooked talks; they like the serpent, speak with a split tongue. Believe not their talks, for they are false; nor their actions, for they are deceitful. The spirit of gain urges them, the laurel of popularity prompts them, and we, your faithful children of the Cherokee nation, who expected nothing but justice, are to fall a sacrifice to their rapaciousness. We therefore pray, oh father, that you will interfere in our behalf, and use your powerful sword for our protection; that sword which is wielded by justice and tempered with humanity.

If this was Major Ridge, it was Major Ridge in a rare high fury, for he was not inclined to speak ill of the general who made him a major. Too high a fury, it was decided. That memo was never delivered.

On March 22, after weeks of edgy preliminaries, Madison agreed to meet the Cherokee delegation in person. By then, Madison had swung toward Crawford's position regarding the Cherokee claims, and away from Jackson, who had retired from the city in a quiet rage. With the president's Executive Mansion in ruins, Madison had relocated his office to the *second*-grandest residence in the city, the merchant James Tayloe's quirky Octagon House, a misnomer as there were actually just six walls, not eight, that rose up above its jumbled surroundings. Like so much of the high-principled young country, its majesty rested on shaky moral foundations: while the airy upper floors were as glorious as anything in Europe, the tight downstairs was jammed with the slaves who did all the work.

When Major Ridge laid eyes on the latest incarnation of the Cherokees' Great Father, he found a cerebral little man with whitening hair that drooped down the sides of his face as if it were rain-slickened and a face pinched from a lifetime of scrutinizing dense documents in dim light. For Madison's part, he must have been a little intimidated to find himself amid so many hulking Indians, all of them veterans of battle, to say nothing of the imperious, often scowling Major Ridge.

Then there was John Ross, the only one in the room who came anywhere close to straddling the two cultures. As the sole fluent English-speaker, the clerk made this into a private colloquy with an American president who might have been kin, he was so similar in height, build, and hue, giving Ross new ideas about his own place in the world.

"It makes my heart as glad to enter your house as it does when I enter my own house," Ross began.

"It always gives me pleasure to receive my friends in my house," Madison replied charitably, "especially my red Brethren the Cherokees, who have fought by the side of their white Brethren & spilt their blood together."

Clearly, Crawford had done his work. Absolutely, Madison went on, the Cherokee families of the slain and wounded should be compensated just like white families, and yes, of course he would pay for the spoliations—although only "as much as what is right," he cautiously added, without specifying what that might be.

Then Madison brought up the awkward question of some Cherokee land that the state of South Carolina would like to purchase. The Cherokee coolly replied they'd consider the offer when it came. With that, Madison brought the meeting to a close. He would save for another time the critical question regarding Jackson's attempt to change the Creek border.

That time, however, never came, for Jackson had gotten busy. While the delegation was still in Washington, he'd directed the survey commissioners back in Georgia to push the state border deep into land where the Cherokee had lived for generations, 2 million acres. It was like a reprise of what his militia had done while the Cherokee were off fighting the Creeks. Hearing the news, the Cherokee felt betrayed all over again, and angrily told Meigs to tell the president to forget about any land for South Carolina.

With that, the surveyors miraculously restored the line to the Cherokee position. But the damage was done. Their confidence in Jackson was broken, and it would never be healed. The Cherokee did accept South Carolina's offer of $5,000 for the land it sought, and were grateful for the $25,000 Crawford came up with for the grieving families of the Cherokee war dead. And they were touched by his presentation of a handsome silver-mounted rifle for the Whale, the Cherokee who'd daringly swum across to the Red Sticks' canoes, amid a hail of bullets, some of which had wounded him. But those offers only reminded the Cherokee of everything they had failed to receive from Jackson.

Major Ridge returned home to the Oostanaula on April 12. Even though Susanna was up to her elbows in children, and the plantation was desperate for his attention, he left again ten days later. He needed to make sure the land commissioners indeed observed the proper border. He was about the only one who knew where the ancient line went, as it was recorded only by vague landmarks like "Vann's store by the Ocmulgee" or "below Ten Islands" on the Coosa, spots not to be found on any map. From his years roaming the territory, Major Ridge had an uncanny sense of the curving, haphazard landscape, overlaid with a crazy quilt of farms tucked into narrow valleys and meandering roads built on hunting paths. Sure enough, he found the lonesome spot on Cedar Creek, below Ten Islands on the Coosa, where the line began, and traced it across to where the Chattahoochee waters "ran clear and deep," to the former site of the two-story log "Vann's store," now long gone, on Georgia's Ocmulgee. This was the border, he was sure.

Major Ridge's confident assertions did not sit well with whites, who saw millions of acres pass to an upstart Cherokee's hazy memory of a vanished past. Back at the Hermitage, Jackson was furious that Crawford would so easily hand back to the Cherokee what he'd won in war. "On the principle of right & justice," he thundered, "the surrender ought never to have been made." He declared it his "diplomatic ambition [to] restore to the U. States the territory fairly and justly ceded by the Creeks."

Few people ever stood up to Jackson when he was in high dudgeon, but Madison proved to be one of them. He would let General Jackson take the land back—but only by purchase. If he could persuade the Cherokee to sell the land, he could have it. Otherwise, no. Hearing that, Jackson dispatched his man General Coffee to set the price. Coffee asked Major Ridge to be his liaison to the Cherokee for the negotiation, but the major knew a suicide mission when he saw one. Indeed, the national council told Coffee to forget about it: the land was not for sale at any price.

Jackson would not be denied so easily. He said then he'd buy it from the Chickasaw instead, since they'd claimed at least part of the land to be theirs. When that bluff failed to move the chiefs, Jackson turned to a time-tested means of persuasion: bribes. He offered fifteen of them $5,000 to split if they'd hand over 1.3 million acres of disputed territory. Given what had happened to Doublehead after he'd pocketed such sums, and given the quantity of land involved, it is shocking that twelve of the fifteen chiefs revised their opinion, presumably on receipt, and, on behalf of the entire nation, duly ceded all that Cherokee land to the United States. Major Ridge was one of the three who flatly refused. To insulate themselves from the wrath of the Cherokee, and to avoid the terrible penalty of blood law, the twelve chiefs on the take sought the blessing of the full national council for the deal at their next meeting in Turkeytown. There, the blessing was granted, much to Major Ridge's vehement disgust.

As ever, that sale only whetted Jackson's hunger for more. Not quite knowing what else to do with this imperious "general of the South East District," his postwar title, who had such strong ideas about the Indians, President Madison appointed him an Indian commissioner to decide the Cherokee land claims. In accepting the appointment, Jackson predictably pushed his authority to the limit, addressing not just the border dispute but Cherokee rights to any eastern land at all. He wanted all of the Cherokee land, every last acre, even if that meant removing the Cherokee from it by force. He styled it as a kindness. The Cherokee should all leave *for their own good*. They had no future in the east, not with so many whites like Jackson himself menacing them, and they would only come to harm if they stayed. Indeed, a good number of Cherokee had come to the same conclusion, and already left. One of the first had been Chief Tahlonteeskee, a cousin of the devilish Doublehead; he'd left largely out of fear that he might be targeted for assassination next. In any case, he had relocated a contingent to the banks of Arkansas's White River, the place John

Ross had visited. Tahlonteeskee's close ally, his brother Chief Jolly, came in the next wave of emigrants, bringing with him a young runaway named Sam Houston, who'd fled his family to join the Cherokee, and now passed as one.

Those emigrants had come solely for the better life the Americans had advertised. But their promises about the west had proved as empty as their pledges in the east. To start with, the Cherokee hardly had this new land to themselves: other Indian tribes, like the Osages, not only claimed it, but lived on it. There was little game for hunting; the soil was lousy for farming; and they would never again feel as settled as they had back home.

Nevertheless, Jackson declared the west to be the perfect place for the Cherokee. He even had the audacity to charge Tahlonteeskee's band for the parcels accorded to them as new settlers, whether they had clear title or not, the bill to be paid in the land they'd vacated. When Tahlonteeskee had refused to pay up, Jackson enlisted Tennessee's governor, Joseph McMinn, to secure other land in payment, and to spread bribes around to silence any opposition. This was the first of a series of travesties that would blacken the name of the baby-faced governor, who was already embarrassed by a scandal regarding his failed attempt to divorce his wife, the former Nancy Glasgow. Her father was renowned for his illegal purchases of Cherokee land in the Glasgow Land Fraud. Jackson could not have been less interested in such moral quibbles. He would no longer pay cash for Cherokee land; now he would just take it.

The issue came to a head on June 20, 1817, when Jackson gathered a quorum of western chiefs to hear about the land exchanges with the western Cherokee he was planning, exchanges that went way beyond securing valuable eastern parcels for land given to Tahlonteeskee's band. He was done trying to acquire just bits and pieces of the Cherokee Nation. He'd evict every last Cherokee, and send them all to western lands paid for, even up, with the land they left. In a final insult, he'd give each "a rifle gun, ammunition, a blanket and a brass kettle or in lieu of that a Beaver trap." And, presumably, a hearty *Good luck.*

If the Cherokee insisted on staying, they could do so only as citizens of the United States, Jackson declared, for the Cherokee Nation would be no more. It was an imperious position for an unelected official to take, and it said a lot about Jackson's high regard for himself and his low regard for Indians. It was the same raw deal that Jefferson had offered. Leave as Cherokee, or stay as Americans. The Cherokee would be gone either way. When the proposal was circulated to the eastern chiefs, sixty-one of them joined Major Ridge in rejecting it in the strongest terms. To leave, they said, meant to "return to the same savage state of life that we were in before." But to stay was to cease being Cherokee. No, they would continue on the present course, as Cherokee who were determined to prove themselves "civilized" in the eyes of the whites, by becoming educated, English-speaking, God-fearing farmers, just like them except for the color of their skin.

At that, an infuriated Jackson threatened to end federal guarantees of protection from white invasions, and cancel the roughly $10,000 yearly annuity payments left over from the many cessions to the government, even if they were legally required as federal treaty obligations. Jackson had already won over the western chiefs; bribes had worked on a good number of the eastern chiefs; and his bluster was causing many of the remainder to waver. And then it happened. Astonishingly, a vote revealed that a slim majority of the nation's chiefs would agree to the unthinkable. They had bowed to Jackson's plan to sell out their nation. All that was needed now was a census to determine exactly how many Cherokee were in Arkansas so they could tally up the eastern lands that were already owed and for the U.S. Congress to authorize payment for the rest. After that, the Cherokee Nation would be no more.

Utterly discouraged, several thousand Cherokee soon boarded boats that would carry them to new lives in the Arkansas wilderness. The very first of this latest wave was Chief Toochalar, Pathkiller's second in command, but the emigrants were heaped with such abuse from Cherokee who were determined to remain that few were willing to follow them. And by drawing off the most willing, Jackson made the remainder into the less willing, who would be harder to dislodge. To lure them, Governor McMinn offered whiskey and cash—$80,000 in total, paid from the U.S. Treasury. When the Cherokee council resisted such a measly sum, McMinn offered $100,000 for "an entire extinguishment" of the Cherokee presence east of the Mississippi. No, again.

Afraid that McMinn might bribe individual chiefs to make side deals, giving away Cherokee land on their own authority, Major Ridge persuaded the council to declare formally that anyone who sold land without the explicit approval of the full council would meet Doublehead's fate. It would be the new blood law and a core tenet of the nation inscribed in the Cherokee legal code. Unlike the other blood law that Ridge had revoked, this one promised, not a death for a death, but rather a death for something possibly worse: selling a piece of the Cherokee Nation for private benefit.

Seeing that McMinn was making no headway with the council, the War Department tried to work on a new member of the national committee who seemed to be increasingly influential, John Ross. Impressed with how Ross handled himself in Washington, Major Ridge had brought him in to join the committee. Perhaps, McMinn wondered, the young man could be bribed? Not with cash, but with an offer Meigs knew would be far more tantalizing— a government-backed fur-trading factory all his own. It had been a dream of Ross's to possess one since that perilous trip into Arkansas in 1812. To Meigs's disappointment, however, Ross declined.

Jackson's deal all came down to price, and finding Cherokee chiefs who would accept it. When McMinn upped his offer for Cherokee removal to $200,000, Ross led the national committee's decision to say no. By now, the ambitious young man had risen to be its president. And then he did something quite unusual. He sent to the newspapers a full account—*his* account— of how he had stood up to Joseph McMinn.

Why? It's not known, but possibly rumors that John Ross could be bought were starting to dog him, and he needed to clear his name. This would be all the more necessary when McMinn added a further inducement to the mixed-blood elite that made up most of the Cherokee leadership. He offered each of them a parcel of 640 acres of Tennessee. It wasn't just land, but clear title to land. Land *ownership.* Private property that could be freely sold, since it had belonged to the United States, not the nation.

Ross accepted McMinn's gift. In his case, he received clear title to the "Big Island in Tennessee River being the first below Tellico" that he had always claimed had been willed to him by his great-uncle, William Shorey. That will had been oral, however, given only to John Ross himself when he was a teenager, or so he said. It had been a subject of controversy in the family, as his shortchanged relatives figured that Shorey had to have been drunk to do such a thing, if he did it at all. So the suspicions about John Ross started early. The first parcel of Ross's extensive landholdings, Big Island, would now be assigned to him free and clear by Joseph McMinn. As American land, it brought the chance to become an American citizen. He took the land, but declined citizenship. For Ross, there were limits.

That was not the only suspicious parcel dealt out by McMinn. At a meeting with the Cherokee leaders, McMinn awarded John Walker two 640-acre parcels—one for his home, another for his gristmill—whereupon Walker dared ask for a third. A half-blood who fought valiantly with Ridge against the Creeks, and had gone to Washington with him, Walker had a reputation far more dubious than Ross's, as he had been known to act as a spy for various Tennessee politicians, probably including McMinn.

Hearing about McMinn's offer, Ross demanded to know why Walker should be so deserving. Wasn't it enough to get the two other parcels, and a $500 bribe from McMinn on top of them? *Bribe?* When Ross mentioned that, the meeting turned into an uproar. Walker charged at the little Scot, ready to stab him with a knife. Fortunately for Ross, a couple of other Cherokee restrained Walker, who then stalked off, furious to have been so impugned.

How, one wonders, was Ross privy to such a secret? Bribery may have been rife in the nation, and many chiefs were on the take, but the information was closely held. Had Ross learned it from McMinn directly? Had the two men become . . . close?

Walker did not let it go. He still had sufficient standing to join with Ross in a twelve-man Cherokee delegation that traveled to Washington a short while later to protest a treaty that Jackson had struck with the Arkansas contingent. They persuaded the new President Monroe's secretary of war that Jackson had drastically overstepped. That secretary was not Crawford, but John C. Calhoun, the wild-haired former South Carolina congressman. As secretary of state, senator, and vice president under two presidents, Calhoun would loom over the nation for a half century. Despite this momentary kindness, he would bedevil the Cherokee for much of it.

Relieved by their victory, several members of the Cherokee delegation went off to the theater to celebrate. Ross remained in a hotel suite he shared with his brother Lewis and his brother-in-law Judge James Brown, who'd come along with the group. Ever-dutiful, he was attending to his correspondence when another delegate, John Martin, came in to regale him with a description of the play. Then the door burst open again, and this time Walker charged in, quite drunk, a jagged brickbat in one hand and a long dagger in the other. He hurled the brickbat at Ross, missing him, and then with the wild shout "I am come to whip you!" he charged at Ross with the knife. Ross pulled a knife of his own, and he managed to keep Walker at bay long enough for Martin and brother Lewis to pull Walker away, disarm him, and hustle him down the hall to his bed to sleep it off. Peace reigned in the morning, and no harm was visited on either of them. But that would not be the end of the matter.

The story has often been cited to demonstrate the little man's courage, but it seems more to be about his morals. It seems Walker was furious that Ross was shaming *him* for taking a bribe, when Ross had probably done the same himself. Unlike Walker, however, Ross had never been exposed. Ross always knew what to show, and what to hold back. He had a talent for deception.

Ross had survived, but the nation remained in peril.

2

DELIVERANCE

In 1817, when the Cherokee were faced with the bitter choice of leaving the nation as Cherokee or staying as Americans, they received help from an unlikely quarter, one that brought Ross and Major Ridge into a tighter alliance. Missionaries from the Northeast took up the Cherokee cause, not just bellowing from pulpits, but venturing out into the heathen lands to act on their beliefs, often at great cost to themselves. Those beliefs were simple: Cherokee were fully the equal of whites in God's eyes; they lacked only education and the Christian faith to prove it. The missionaries set out to deliver both. They weren't entirely selfless: by saving souls they would put themselves in better stead with God, and with their superiors. But in the main they were also compassionate and genuinely sought to ease the misery of a downtrodden people. At a time when Jackson presented the Cherokee with two bad choices—stay as Americans or leave as Cherokee—the missionaries supported a third, to remain as enlightened Cherokee, equals of any Americans, and worthy of deciding their own destiny.

The missionaries offered deliverance, in short, and it may have seemed as though Christ himself had come to the Cherokee Nation when thirty-one-year-old Reverend Cyrus Kingsbury, a sturdy Congregationalist from rocky New Hampshire, rode by wagon into Ross's Landing. Educated at Brown, ordained by the Andover Theological Seminary in Cambridge, backed by the august American Board of Commissioners for Foreign Missions, and filled with the nobility of high purpose, the enterprising Kingsbury had spent a year roaming about the Southeast, trying, as he'd told outgoing Secretary of War Crawford, to see how to "extend to the Indians, as far as is practicable, the distinguished advantages which we enjoy." Now he had come to the Cherokee.

A stiff character well suited to parson's black, his hair windswept in the one surviving photograph, Kingsbury was the rare sort of fellow who actually seems to enjoy suffering, and he found a lot of that in the hardscrabble outback, surrounded by forbidding natives who spoke none of his language and were threatened by his piety. Kingsbury's wife died two years into this hardship, but he would carry on and on, finally expiring in the western territories at eighty-five after a hard life of service to Indians who were not always appreciative. He could be judgmental about his charges in return, once complaining of their "deathlike stupidity." But he clearly felt something for a people "entirely destitute of instruction, and living without hope and without God in the world."

Neither Ross nor Ridge had made much progress with Christianity. Ross wouldn't become religious until years later when it suited him socially; and, despite his curiosity about good and evil, Ridge had trouble letting go of the comforting notion of a spirit world, free of moral conundrums. Besides, Christianity was so bizarre. How could a god allow himself to be nailed to a cross? Why did true happiness not come until after you were dead? Both Ross and Ridge would have agreed with Cherokee chief Drowning Bear's appraisal of the Book of Matthew: "It *seems* to be a good book. Strange that the white people are not better after having it so long."

It was good timing that, around the time Kingsbury arrived, Major Ridge had just pulled John and Nancy, and their cousin Buck, too, from the Moravians at Spring Place. The Gambolds had feared that the major was making such a drastic move *"because,"* as they wrote with dire emphasis, *"he is not treated well by us,"* but they received no explanation. When the Gambolds asked John Ridge about it, he "paled visibly," they recalled, "but confessed nothing of having made such a complaint against us."

Actually, Susanna simply could not bear to be away from her children, especially her crippled son John, another minute. Ever since the death of her mother, she'd been feeling a vague, persistent dread that some awful harm would come to John, too. Still, the Gambolds could not help feeling miffed. "Such is our thanks for . . . long faithful service and care, giving him of our best." All the same, the Gambolds had their three charges ready for the major when he came in his carriage to take them away. When he drew up, Major Ridge tried to assure the Gambolds that he "would always feel affection for us and come to our house as before whenever he came into the neighborhood," as they wrote.

The Gambolds solemnly took each child's hand in turn to bid farewell. Always the reserved one, John said little. The Gambolds took that as stoicism, since, as they said, he was "real proud to be a savage." But the sensitive Buck wept as he grasped Sister Anna's hand for the last time, and this pained both Gambolds. They were afraid "our promising little Buck" might prove too tender for his own good.

None of the three children were happy to come home, a situation not improved when Major Ridge's tutor for them proved a dim-witted drunkard who was soon sent packing. When the major could find no one better, he rode with some embarrassment back to Spring Place to tell the Gambolds he'd been forced to reconsider. He would keep charge of his own children, but could they please take Buck back?

"He seemed very low in spirits," Sister Anna remembered. When she said yes, Buck was so eager to return that he insisted his father, David Watie, drive the carriage straight through the night even if it meant arriving before dawn. It had been only a few weeks, but the Gambolds were thrilled to find the little boy still "childlike, warm and loving." John and Nancy, however, remained at home, continuing their education through books recommended by their father's friend, the learned chief Charles Hicks.

Then Cyrus Kingsbury arrived. He'd quickly secured permission from the

Cherokee council to build a missionary school. Now, where to put it? When the Moravians had been looking for a place, John Ross's grandfather, John McDonald, had offered some property, only to be outbid by James Vann. Determined to secure a worthy legacy, McDonald was not going to make that mistake again. He offered Kingsbury his entire twenty-five-acre estate near Ross's Landing, soon to be Chattanooga, for just $500. It was enough land for a proper campus with schoolhouse, dormitories, chapel, administrative buildings, pens for livestock, and extensive crop fields. It would be called Brainerd.

While the Moravians believed the Cherokee had to turn Christian before they could be educated, and the Presbyterians the reverse, Congregationalists like Kingsbury believed the two efforts had to go hand in hand, as if education itself was a kind of conversion, and vice versa. No one could be educated and still believe in any nonsense about the Great Spirit.

Major Ridge's children Nancy and John were the first to enroll, and the major proudly delivered them by carriage the day the school opened in May 1817. At Brainerd, they would be taught by the "Lancastrian method"—the more advanced students teaching the less advanced ones, the teachers supervising. The day started a half hour before sunrise with a horn blast, then ran through morning worship and farm chores—pounding corn, cleaning the fish trapped in weirs down at the creek—then more scripture, reading, catechism, and classwork until another horn blast ended the day at nine. John Ridge was frail, and the educational program arduous, but he quickly rose to the top of the class. Still, he was clearly under some strain, as he could not help making petulant remarks to teachers who were forcing him not just to learn, but to teach in their place. Once, when he was rebuked, one recounted, he "burst into a flood of tears—said he meant no harm and was sorry he had given us so much trouble & pain." Another such outburst brought a hasty visit from his father, who was mortified to learn that *both* his children were proving unmanageable. "If they misbehave," he told the missionaries, "it won't be good to keep them at school." He'd send his Creek slave girl instead. The missionaries assured him there was no need of *that*. The Ridge clapped his hands with relief. "Never was I so glad!" he exclaimed.

"Can it be that my children," he asked them, "after all the advice I have given them, could conduct themselves in such a manner?" Perhaps it was *because* of all the advice of a rather meddlesome father, even if he was only acting on the wishes of an anxious wife. But the mix of the school must have been stressful for two young members of the new Cherokee elite. It wasn't easy to be part of this ruling class; that was the short of it. The teachers caught glimpses of the class schism in student essays they assigned on social life in the nation. The mixed-bloods—or "Mbs" in the missionaries' code—lived in decent log houses, with flower gardens and crop fields. The full-bloods, or "Fbs," did not.

One mixed-blood was clearly mystified that her people could still be so backward as she described the primitive tribal dances, the women adorned with rattling shells, the crazy ball play, the conjurers' weird antics, and that horrific scratching ceremony, as if they were all products of an alien race. Of course, this was the very life that Major Ridge had lived—and intended his children to avoid by attending a school like this one.

Major Ridge was intrigued to learn that there might be a better school even than Brainerd. For, shortly after his children began there, in came yet another missionary, this one a handsome young Yale graduate, the Reverend Elias Cornelius, to reveal yet another educational opportunity for a few of the very best students. Cornelius had been instructed at divinity school by Yale's esteemed president Timothy Dwight IV himself. Freshly ordained, Cornelius was set to marry a prime catch for any Yale man, the daughter of a Hooker. As an official agent of the American Board of Commissioners for Foreign Missions, he'd come to make an important announcement about a new educational opportunity for suitable Cherokee, and The Ridge gathered with several other Cherokee fathers in the drawing room of The Ridge's friend Charles Hicks to hear all about it.

The mixed-bloods like Major Ridge bore a look "of utmost contentment" amid the fine furnishings of the Hicks home, Cornelius noticed—but not the full-bloods. The primary chief Pathkiller sat leaning up against the far wall, his back cushioned by blankets, a skeptical look on his face. Around him stood imposing full-bloods in "hunting shirt, vest, turban, deerskin leggings . . . their ears slitted after the Indian manner, with pieces of silver attached to them," all of them silent.

To everyone, Cornelius rhapsodized via Hicks's translation about how he'd been sent by "a society of great and good men at the North" to find the very best male students in the nation to attend a brand-new Foreign Mission School—a men's college, really, that the American Board had opened in Cornwall, Connecticut. It was little more than a schoolhouse right now, but it was still the finest institution of higher learning any Cherokee could hope to enter, an Indian Yale.

Having held out that tantalizing possibility, the earnest Cornelius withdrew to search for these paragons among all the so-called five civilized tribes of the region, among which the Cherokee now were universally recognized as ranking first. Sure enough, when Cornelius returned weeks later, he found the top two students in all five tribes very close by—at Brainerd and Spring Place. John Ridge and Buck Watie.

Buck's father, David Watie, accepted eagerly, but Susanna couldn't bear to send her son so far away, and the major had to say no to this great honor, at least for now. To the surprise of many, he'd agreed to join General Jackson's campaign against some remaining militant Creeks and their Seminole allies in Florida. Despite everything Jackson had done to the Cherokee people, there was something about the general that made it impossible for Major Ridge to say no to him. Young John would remain with his mother while the major was gone.

Reverend Elias Cornelius escorted Buck north, along with a promising Choctaw named Folsom; Charles Hicks's son Leonard; and Redbird, a brilliant Brainerd graduate whom Cornelius had picked to take John Ridge's place. The little group passed through Greenville, Tennessee, and up through the Great Smokies, Cornelius preaching at the occasional church along the way, clear to Monticello, Jefferson's hilltop shrine in the Blue Ridge Mountains, where they paid a call on the aging, soft-spoken former president.

When Cornelius's party arrived, Jefferson took an anthropological interest in these "aborigines," as he called them. Fascinated by the well-educated young specimens in proper clothes speaking proper English, he seemed to examine them under a magnifying glass. Perhaps his hopes for the natives were not exaggerated after all.

Then it was on to Montpelier to dine with Jefferson's protégé, the recently retired James Madison, in his sumptuous mansion, laden with oil portraits. A kinder soul than Jefferson, he was charmed to meet such a promising nephew of Major Ridge, whom he recalled from the Octagon House. Then it was on to Washington for some sightseeing before a visit to the new president, the lofty but rather vacant James Monroe, who greeted them hastily in his threadbare office—the product of a niggardly Congress—in the newly rebuilt Executive Mansion, which was now called the White House. He sent them on to his grim secretary of war, Calhoun, who'd studied law at Litchfield, Connecticut, not far from Cornwall. Calhoun had a gift for these Indian marvels: $100 a year each to help with expenses, drawn from the U.S. Treasury.

One last stop, in Burlington, New Jersey, to see one of the great benefactors of the American Board—the aged Elias Boudinot, early president of the Continental Congress, former head of the American Bible Society, and backer of all manner of worthy causes. When the four students gathered before him in his parlor, he lit on the gentle, soft-eyed Buck Watie, and soon made an unusual proposition. He had no son, he explained, and no one to carry on his lineage. Would Buck Watie be willing to change his name to Elias Boudinot?

That was quite a request. Buck Watie was a frisky native Cherokee, son of David Watie of the Deer Clan; Elias Boudinot was a doddering, plump, lily-white American statesman of French extraction. Could Buck Watie *really* become Elias Boudinot? Was that like casting off buskins for broadloom cloth, or a true translation of souls—or nothing at all, just words? Whatever it was, Buck had to feel he was moving up if he could be a Boudinot, and moving up was the whole idea.

His answer was—sure! And so Buck Watie became Elias Boudinot, the last syllable pronounced in the American manner, "not," which fitted, as he was indeed *not* Boudinot. But he was not Buck Watie, either, for Buck Watie was no more.

Cornwall proved a hilly farm town, quilted with rocky fields of wheat and corn, way up in Connecticut's northwestern corner, in a valley fringed with spruce and pine along the Housatonic River. Its dozen villages were spread out over almost thirty square miles; bore piquant names like Yelping Hill (a reference to baying coyotes); and had 1,600 inhabitants, most of them farmers, all of them with deep respect for the Lord, giving him tribute in white churches with high spires that pricked the sky. Connecticut was once all Indians, like everywhere else, but now only some Schaticokes were left in a few wigwams in Kent, one town over. Although it was too late to educate any local Indians, missionaries had chosen this remote spot to enlighten "foreign" ones in a Mission School, locally dubbed the Heathen School. It was off the village green at the center of town and was paid for by fervent locals eager to do their bit for Christian civilization.

The school wasn't much to look at, and after such a long journey, the newly minted Elias Boudinot, dusty and aching atop his weary horse, must have felt a surge of disappointment. It was no Brainerd; it was not even tight little Spring Place. The main school building was a big, white clapboard-sided box, twenty by forty feet, topped by a puffed-out gambrel roof with a bell tower. The nearby boardinghouse was a little less. Simple, functional, Puritan—those were the watchwords. By the time Buck's little party pulled in that September, there were about a dozen boys in residence, itchy in their proper clothes, many of them exotics: a Hindu; two Chinese; a Bengalese; a flamboyant Cherokee named Jim Fields who would later depart "in fine calf boots, blue cloth pantaloons, silk velvet vest, fine beaver hat, with silver band," a gown of "red flowered calico" and a cape "trimmed with a blue fringe"; plus several refugees from the Hawaiian Islands. One of them, Henry Obokiah, became a sainted figure for his piety when he expired from tuberculosis a year into his residency.

The school was presided over by Herman Daggett, a minister who doubled as a schoolteacher, with all the Puritan virtues that were so hard to distinguish from vices. He was strict, industrious, and uncharitable. Surveying the latest lot of students, Daggett had a bad feeling. These "heathen youths" were "not pious," he decided, "or even serious." He was worried about Boudinot in particular. "Elias, I fear, is also losing his hopeful impressions." Not so unreasonable for a sensitive boy under an assumed name in a chilly, gray autumn far from home, but Daggett probably meant he was losing his own hopeful impression of Boudinot as the boy wondered what he had gotten into.

Back home, though, Major Ridge was reconsidering about John. After Buck left, tragedy had struck the Ridge family. Ridge's studious daughter Nancy had married an Indian, gotten pregnant, and died in agony in childbirth. When the missionary Daniel Butrick came around to try to talk The Ridge into sending John to the Mission School, he found the whole family sitting by the door in mourning. Susanna was utterly inconsolable, but Major Ridge had Butrick come in to talk of the mission's work, and to shed more light on this perplexing Christianity of his. Major Ridge again asked Butrick about sin, clearly a preoccupation. After explaining, Butrick asked Major

Ridge to pray with him. Something lifted in the major, and, casting aside his wife's worries for young John, he agreed to let the boy go north to be educated at Cornwall.

John Ridge was escorted there by a Dr. Dempsey along with a full-blood named Darcheechee, and James Vann's grandson, George, both of whom would attend as well. Up the Georgia pike they went, and across to Salem, North Carolina, where a Moravian missionary, Brother David Steiner, bestowed his name on Darcheechee. At the Female Academy there, John Ridge swooned over some young ladies playing classical music on the piano, an unimaginable thrill to every sense. No visit to Jefferson or Madison was in the offing, but they did pop in to see Monroe in the White House.

When John finally arrived in Cornwall that November, Elias Boudinot was overjoyed. Everyone was. "A noble youth, beautiful in appearance, very graceful, a perfect gentleman everywhere," said one. He was "not dark and swarthy . . . [but] fine-looking." Whatever irritability John had displayed at Brainerd became an eagerness to please in Cornwall. He copied out inspirational hymns, and wrote charming, lightly confessional poems. One of them was a remarkable ode to a small round god, his pocket watch.

> *Little monitor, by thee,*
> *Let me learn what I should be:*
> *Learn the round of life to fill,*
> *Thou canst gentle hints impart,*
> *How to regulate the heart.*
> *When I wind thee up at night,*
> *Mark each fault and set thee right,*
> *Let me search my bosom, too,*
> *And my daily thoughts review,*
> *Mark the movements of my mind*
> *Nor be easy when I find*
> *Latent errors rise to view,*
> *Till all be regular and true.*

The work of the school was taxing, and all the harder for a boy with a crippling disease, but John bore up. The day started at six with a reading from the New Testament; then came an hour of labor in the fields or the blacksmith shop before the pupils settled down to a strict program of geography, rhetoric, surveying, ecclesiastical and common history, the *Aeneid*, the orations of Cicero, "Natural Philosophy," more prayer, and so on until nightfall.

John Ridge took easily to it, and was soon paired with Boudinot at the top of the class. Both of them were known for their sunny charm, too. That spring, they performed some Indian dances together and wrote the thank-you letters to the school's benefactors. Boudinot handled the one to the wealthy Baron de Campagne; John Ridge addressed former president Madison. John worked through two stiff paragraphs, gently arguing against a Cherokee removal to Arkansas, before ending with a boyish outburst: "My father and mother are both ignorant of the English language," he declared. "But it is astonishing to see them exert all their power to have children educated *just like the whites!*"

Gradually, life at the school proved hard on John. Lonely, far from home, and exhausted, he slept in a cramped space under the roof, hot and stuffy in summer, frigid and drafty in winter, and casket-tight all year round. He endured it for the first year and tolerated it for the second, but by the third its joys had started to wear very thin. That winter he had a nasty flare-up of his "scrofulous complaint"—detailed this time in a letter to the incumbent President Monroe. Soon he was in grinding pain, and scarcely able to stand.

That won him a lengthy stay in the school's one-bed sickroom and the close attention of the town physician, Dr. Samuel Gold, who finally wrote to tell his parents they should bring him home to recuperate, as he was getting no better there. Alarmed, Major Ridge rode to Cornwall at a full gallop, switching to a splendid coach and four at the end so he could make a memorable entrance. A "large tall man in white top boots," as one witness remembered him, wearing a "coat trimmed with gold lace" over his military uniform. To a breathless young lady, the major was "one of the princes of the forest."

The major found his son lying stoically in bed, his face twisted in pain, scarcely able to speak. Ridge stayed on for weeks, daily sitting at John's bedside, frowning with concern. Elsewhere, however, the major's presence created a daily sensation that was heightened on Sundays, when he visited the local tavern rather than attend church.

Truth was, John didn't much like having his father there hovering over him. It did not make his scrofula any better—although neither did it make it any worse. Finally, Major Ridge decided he'd done all he could, and returned home.

There was another factor in his son's convalescence, a secret one: Sarah Bird Northrup, better known as Sally, the sweet, soft, blue-eyed, auburn-haired fifteen-year-old daughter of the school's steward. Sally had been tending to the slender, pale John most afternoons, running a cool washcloth across his forehead and down the sides of his face.

Cherokee students had been encouraged to enter Cornwall "society," as the principal termed it, where "a keen eye will mark many facts respecting social life." One being "the situation and character of females in Christian society," which he termed "one important point of distinction between that and the society of heathen." Mixing should not have been a scandal, but there were natural limits to such intercourse. At first, the two young people spoke only of John's health, but soon the conversation must have roamed, for Dr. Gold noticed a surge in his young patient's health after Sally had been around. So much of a surge that Gold tapered off his medicine.

Doctor Gold noticed a strange unease in the boy, though, even as his vitality improved. He seemed to be in "some deep trouble" that he couldn't piece out, and Gold asked Sally's mother to have a talk with the lad.

A neighbor set down what happened:

Mrs. Northrup, taking her stockings to darn for the students, went in to sit with John. She said to him, "John, you have some trouble, and you must tell me; you know, you have no mother here, only me, and you have always confided in me, as you would your own mother."

He started up in wild amazement, and said, "I got trouble? No."

She replied, "I can not leave until you tell me all."

JOHN: "I do not want to tell you."

MRS. N.:   "You must tell me."

JOHN: "Well . . . if you must know, I love your Sally."

MRS. N.:   "You must not."

JOHN: "I know it . . . and that is the trouble."

MRS. N.:   "Have you ever mentioned it to her?"

JOHN: "No, we have not said one word to each other; I dare not, but
         how could I help loving her when she has taken such good
         care of me these two years?" When Sally returned home that
         evening, her mother was waiting for her.

MRS. N.: "Sally, do you love John Ridge?"

SARAH: "Yes, I do love John."

At that, Mrs. Northrup saw there was trouble in the sickroom.

It must have knocked the wind out of her. An Indian in love with her daughter? Mrs. Northrup herself had been the one to call John "beautiful in appearance." But when it came to it, even the most enlightened whites saw every Indian as a "dirty Indian," and a threat to the chastity of a white girl. Such a union presented a vile specter to Mrs. Northrup.

Did Sally love John Ridge? That was the essential question, and when Sally blushingly admitted that yes, it was true, she did, there was only one thing to do. Mrs. Northrup sent her daughter away.

To her own parents in New Haven, with instructions for them to introduce Sally to as many bachelors as it took to free her from this absurd preoccupation with a Cherokee. Sally duly went to her grandparents' house, but she rarely left it. She remained mostly in bed, and she stopped eating, determined to waste away. Her weight dropped; her skin turned sallow. She was soon almost all bone. When visitors came, she stared at the wall. After three months, her parents could bear it no longer, and brought their daughter home.

She was forbidden to see John Ridge. He was determined to marry her.

When Susanna and Major Ridge learned of their son's attachment to a white girl, even one with Sarah's lineage, they were not pleased, either. He could have done much better at home, married the daughter of a chief, and gained stature among his own people. How could this Sarah Bird Northrup ever manage in a faraway place like the Oostanaula? Susanna turned to the friendly missionary Daniel Butrick for guidance, and he confirmed her predisposition. "I told her that a white woman would be apt to feel above the common Cherokees," he related, "and that . . . her son would promise more usefulness for his people were he connected with them in marriage." He should marry a Cherokee. The

Ridges wrote to their son in Cornwall they would never allow any marriage with Sarah Bird Northrup.

Receiving the letter in Cornwall weeks later, John was devastated. How could his parents forbid him to marry the girl he loved? He had to wonder— did they even believe in love, his kind of love, romantic and passionate? Or was that some idea he'd picked up from the whites along with the value of money? Had his parents married for love, or simply out of custom or practicality? They never spoke of it. Perhaps they didn't know. Rather than acquiesce, John Ridge set down a letter of twelve effusive pages detailing all the ways he cherished Sally. Receiving it, Susanna was moved to tears; she knew his feelings, for, indeed, they had once been her own. She could not stand in the way of her son. She persuaded her husband not to, either. They sent John their blessing.

The Northrups came to see that it was unchristian to forbid their daughter's marriage to an Indian on religious grounds, even if she was only fifteen. They decided instead that it was simply impractical for her to marry a cripple. By now, John had risen off his sickbed to resume his studies with the other students, but he still needed crutches to walk. The Northrups told him they would let their daughter marry him only if he could walk unaided.

About then, the American Board told John to go home to recuperate. From his scrofula, ostensibly, but more likely his desire for Sally was the real illness. Either way, he yielded. His hip was now so inflamed that he could bear the bone-jostling stagecoach ride only to the Connecticut shore. From there, he continued down the coast by schooner with a party of schoolmates headed up by another missionary, named Reynolds, to Charleston, South Carolina.

By now, his cousin Elias was training for the ministry at Andover Theological Seminary in New Hampshire, fulfilling the ambition of the Mission School for its graduates. He had followed the story of John's romance with astonishment, but not gotten involved. Still, he himself had suffered, perhaps sympathetically, from a "bilious complaint." He decided to sail home via Charleston, too, leaving a few days after his cousin. John waited for him there, and Elias found him on the wharf one afternoon, reading a book under a sun umbrella.

Charleston was a lively city, but its citizens still enjoyed a good sermon. Backed by the missionary elite, the two handsome young Cherokee delivered to them some inspirational soliloquies on the fate of the Indian. John gave a stirring account of the rise of his people, which he perfectly demonstrated as a handsome, eloquent, learned young man with curiously white skin. From the pulpit, John Ridge decried the frenzied efforts of whites to hold Indians back, and he went straight at the foolish notion that the Indians might be better off if they stayed in the woods. "Will anyone believe that an Indian with his bow and quiver, who walks solitary in the mountains, exposed to cold and hunger, or the attacks of wild beasts, trembling at every unusual object, his fancy filled with agitating fears, actually possesses undisturbed contentment superior to a learned gentleman of this commercial city, who has every possible comfort at home?"

If the young Ridge had suffered by being rebuffed in his own recent attempt to be accepted as a "learned gentleman," he gave no hint of it. He made it clear in every utterance that he was no Indian, not anymore. All the fine phrases and high-toned argument told his listeners that he was at least their equal, if not their superior. It is a fair guess that no one in Charleston had ever heard or seen anything like it.

When the cousins finally returned to the Cherokee Nation in early December 1822, they were greeted like conquering heroes. John Ridge was declared "a leading man in the Nation . . . the idol of the half-breeds, and well respected by most intelligent Cherokees." Everyone turned out to catch a glimpse of them. They looked in on Spring Place and were saddened to see how much the Gambolds had aged. Sister Anna would be dead within a year. Then on to Brainerd to show the students—almost 100 now—what had become of them. John let nothing slip about his courtship of Sally. The news was kept quiet by the Ridges, and by the Northrups, too, like a terrible secret. John brooded over the unfairness that he would be scorned in Cornwall as an Indian, whatever he did. The Indian is "almost considered accursed," he complained, "frowned upon by the meanest peasant" and called "the scum of the earth." There was nothing he could do. No matter how "modest and polite," he went on, "yet he is an Indian, and the most stupid and illiterate white man will disdain and triumph over [him]."

3

A NATION OF VERBS

Yet the Cherokee everywhere were on the rise. That was ironic. With peace, the Cherokee had cleared farms, raised gristmills, and filled the countryside with the clanging of cowbells and the banging of hammers. And Christianity was spreading through the Cherokee Nation, although it was mostly the mixed-blood elite who had proved receptive, as the full-bloods continued to cling to their spirits. Charles Hicks had been the only professed Christian when John Ridge and Buck had left, but, despite Major Ridge's misgivings, now there were dozens, maybe hundreds of them, including the major's own Susanna, who'd been baptized at Spring Place and taken Catherine as her Christian name, not that she used it. Major Ridge professed to be admiring. "She has chosen the good part," he declared. "I am glad." He did not convert with her, however.

And a proper government was coming to a newly created town called

New Echota, a few miles from Major Ridge's home at the Oostanaula near what is now Calhoun, Georgia. The original Echota had been the closest thing in the nation to a capital city. In 1821, New Echota was just a pair of sheds, but they housed what had emerged as a bicameral legislature, as the national council and the national committee operated a bit like a house of representatives and a senate. All of it was overseen, at least ceremonially, by the elderly principal chief, Pathkiller, who now relied on the very capable John Ross to handle his correspondence and, increasingly, to offer advice. As speaker of the council, Major Ridge had been the one to mount a "splendid tall horse" to lead the initial ceremonial procession to the first council house on the new site.

This government was writing laws, with courts and judges and marshals to enforce them through the lighthorse brigade, now a mounted police force only. Until 1819, the Cherokee had gotten by with a total of only two laws— one governing the theft of livestock and the other Ridge's prohibition of the retaliatory killings of blood law. Now, the national committee had pushed through taxes on shopkeepers, restraints on the importation of liquor, and a daily stipend for the council president of $3.50. The courts, in turn, had established legal precedents with each decision, such as the awarding of a private turnpike to an individual, or the declaration of the true owner of a disputed piece of property.

In 1821, the same year that New Echota was founded, came the greatest triumph of all: a Cherokee written language. It used to be that words were lost in the wind if they weren't consigned to memory. Now they could be set down forever for anyone to see.

Of all the mysteries of the white settlers—their gunpowder, whiskey, diseases, and God, among many others—the most potent had been their "talking leaves," the papers lined with pen scratchings that held meaning *here* and then proclaimed it, verbatim, *there* and *there* and *there*. Now the Cherokee could set down immutable truth in Cherokee, and send it everywhere, too. And the whole thing was so easy to learn that even children could pick it up in a matter of days. Not like English, which took years and years of close study, with all its homonyms, diphthongs, irregularities, archaisms, silent *g*'s, and whatnot. It had come to the Cherokee Nation like a first spring, a national blooming.

Stranger still, this invention did not come from a brilliant missionary or an ingenious student or an enlightened half-blood. Rather, it came from a slender, gimpy-legged, illiterate blacksmith who'd been called George Guess after his father, an unlicensed German peddler, but who, after his invention, was given the far nobler name of Sequoyah. He'd grown up among the full-bloods in the Lower Towns; fought against the Creeks; and then, not knowing what else to do, fallen in with the chiefs who floated west in a train of keelboats to the wilds of remote Arkansas. Unknown and unaccomplished, he went unmissed. When John Ross pointed out George Guess's old cabin to Elias Boudinot shortly after he'd left, Boudinot had to say he'd never heard of him. More than Moytoy of old, or the warrior Dragging Canoe, or rising statesmen like John Ross and Major Ridge, Sequoyah would bind the Cherokee Nation together.

While most of the others found little on the far side of Arkansas except hardship, Sequoyah had devoted himself to the possibility of a written version of Cherokee. Like everyone, he'd thought that the printed words of the English were black magic, as though a tree could talk. Still, Sequoyah couldn't see why that power would be confined to English. Surely, Cherokee sounds could be set down on paper, too. Sequoyah liked to ponder such mysteries while smoking his pipe, letting them settle in his mind and then sorting them out at leisure, even if it took months, *years*, to the irritation of everyone around him.

Every invention is a fluke that matches a special talent to an unusual circumstance. Sequoyah was a singular character—dreamy but clever, idle but persistent—and his peculiar talents exactly suited the matter at hand. He was like a man who comes to a locked door, only to find he happens to have the key in his back pocket. With no knowledge of any language at all except Cherokee, and in fact no hard knowledge of much beyond practical things, Sequoyah had no idea what he was doing when he set out to invent written Cherokee. And Cherokee was a hard language to capture. Charles Hicks had tried for years to teach it to the Moravians, and failed utterly. They were daunted by all the weird sounds that seem to come from everywhere inside a Cherokee, from the belly up into the nose, and all of them so different and so foreign to their ears, from a kind of deep bass thrum through a range of chesty wails and rasps and singing to a breathy sort of snort. In the main, the sounds seemed to come from down deeper in the throat than English, as if from a secret place buried inside. And the words were nothing like English, and nothing like the German they favored, so the Moravians were flummoxed. The meaning had to be snagged from the air, and the Moravians could not catch it.

Strange as the sounds were, the syntax was far more complex. For Cherokee consists almost entirely of verbs, as befits, perhaps, a vigorous people. (Thus, the Great Spirit was a far more active presence, ever *doing*, than the Christian God, a relatively stately being who reposed in heaven.) Those Cherokee verbs were loaded up like pack trains to carry subject, object, and various qualifiers that indicated the substance involved—whether it was liquid or solid, for instance. And they took not just the six tenses of English, but seventeen tenses that allowed such fine distinctions as the one between an "I go" meaning *I am going* and an "I go" meaning *I customarily go*. Curiously, Cherokee pronouns don't distinguish gender—there is no "he" or "she," just "a person"—but they include an unusual "dual" subject that means "we two," suggesting a fundamental pairing in the culture. With all these expressive variations, a single verb might take an incredible 21,260 forms. Cherokee was like music that didn't stop at major and minor, or at the eighty-eight keys of the piano keyboard, or at the twelve key signatures, but included a whole universe of sounds too subtle to be detectable by non-Cherokee ears.

Paradoxically, Sequoyah's ignorance was his greatest good fortune, for he was free to approach the whole matter without preconceptions. Sequoyah first had to whittle his own sharp-tipped pen and make his own ink from tree bark, since the Cherokee did not stock writing implements. Then he set to it. Initially he thought each word in Cherokee should have its own symbol. But, contriving one for each, he found himself adding word after word after word, until he had several thousand, and he had come nowhere close to covering all the words he knew. Without realizing it, he was creating not a system of writing but something closer to a dictionary. Then he tried to break the sounds down to make a Cherokee alphabet, but that didn't go much better, since there were far too many of them. At some point in his mulling, Sequoyah noticed that the crisp individual sounds like *t* or *ck* did not recur nearly so often as the clumps of sound the English call syllables. No one had ever noticed it before, but those clumps repeated fairly frequently. It was as if the very word *alphabet* was recorded not as eight letters but as three: *al-pha-bet*. After much fiddling, he was able to identify eighty-six syllables that could render just about every utterance in the Cherokee language. Sequoyah knew not a word of English, and planned to leave it that way. But gawking at written English, he assigned its letters at random to his syllables, then added a raft of fanciful squiggles of his own to make the full complement.

Once he worked it all out, he taught a friend, who learned quite easily. Together, they made a public demonstration. He placed the friend in another room, well out of sight and hearing. Then Sequoyah took suggestions from curious onlookers for a message no one would ever guess, and set it down on paper using his syllabary—a wonder right there, all these strange symbols so carefully inscribed. The paper was then carried to the friend—or, in another version of the demonstration, to Sequoyah's young daughter, who'd been taught this great trick of reading and writing. In either case, the recipient had only to glance at it to recite the exact message Sequoyah had been asked to write, word for word. It was simply incredible, a magic trick, surely, and it had to be repeated many times in many places, with his daughter, and then with others nearby, and then still others farther away who were in on it, before the Cherokee began to conceive that, yes, they did indeed have a system of writing just like the Americans. Before long, messages were flying around everywhere in Arkansas and then across the continent to the eastern band back home. Written Cherokee started to appear everywhere, not just on notepaper, but painted on trees, or cut into them, splashed on fences and the sides of houses, in an outpouring of exuberance, all of which loudly declared, We are Cherokee! Cherokee! It was as if they finally had their own private code that only Cherokee knew, for few others could penetrate the language, and it forged an identity that was theirs alone. And it was so easy to learn that schools didn't bother to teach it, since children could pick it up on their own. Remember the eighty-six symbols, sound them out, and you had it.

More than a Gutenberg, Sequoyah was a Leonardo, an inventor who created not just an invention, but modernity. It is hard to find in all of recorded history as dramatic a transformation of a people in such a brief period of time. It unleashed an outpouring of notes, letters, essays, records, reports, newspapers, Bible translations, books. It was remarkable, a miracle. Yet all the excitement had little effect on Sequoyah, who continued to tend his small farm, with just a few cows, leaving only to tend his salt kettles at the lick near Lee's Creek, ten miles from home, in what is now called Sequoyah County, in his honor.

• • •

But when people first started to write, they had appallingly little knowledge to convey. By 1826 the number of Cherokee schools would triple to eighteen, but Ross admitted to President Monroe that his "red children" were still "ignorant and wretched." The census of 1826 would show that the number of swine had tripled to 46,000; spinning wheels had doubled to 2,488; and plows had increased almost sixfold to 2,500, but it still wasn't much of a nation. It had no army, hardly enough money to pay its bills, no colleges, and, for all the burgeoning economic activity among the mixed-bloods, a gross national product that hardly touched six figures.

What was more hazardous, the population had increased only slightly to just under 14,000, and they were surrounded by well over 1 million whites south of the Ohio and west of the Alleghenies crushing in from above, and hundreds of thousands of Georgians pressing up from below. In 1822, whites continued to pour in, defying the laws intended to keep them out. And they could be insidious, these insurgents. "Well armed," Meigs admitted, "some of them [of] shrewd & desperate character, have nothing to lose & hold barbarous sentiments towards Indians." Believing the Cherokee had more land than they knew what to do with, they simply took what they wanted, and would pay for it later only if they had to. Jackson was urging them on, but the state of Georgia was proving the real threat, all of it under the dubious authority of an egregious "Compact" it had signed with the United States back in 1802, and now was primed to enforce.

Of all the interlopers, the Georgians were the worst. Their low character stemmed in part from the state's peculiar history. The last of the colonies to be formed, Georgia had not been settled by hardy pilgrims and thrifty pioneers like the others; rather, it was founded from afar by a board of trustees in London headed by James Oglethorpe, who conceived of Georgia as a repository for the debtors who were overcrowding British prisons, rather like Australia for felons. That plan never materialized, but the high-handed attitude persisted even as cotton and rice plantations spread out from the coast. The colony was ruled by an imperious governor who proclaimed himself "His Excellency, Governor and Commander in Chief of the Army and Navy of this State and of the Militia thereof."

The original colony was bounded on only three sides. Its western border extended indefinitely all across the uncharted frontier to the Pacific. The early governors reluctantly acknowledged that American aborigines might have a claim to some of it, but this recognition evaporated with the 1783 Peace of Paris, in which the British formally ceded the territory inland all the way to the Mississippi, well beyond the presumed colonial borders. Speculators formed companies to acquire 35 million acres of Georgia's so-called "Yazoo Lands" to the west—named for the long river they contained—for $500,000. The transaction was greased by the usual lubricants to the influential—politicians, newspaper editors, et al. Even though the scheme was soon exposed as the Yazoo Land Fraud, the U.S. Congress shelled out $5 million for the land to create the new states of Alabama and Mississippi. As part of the deal, Georgia extracted a promise from the United States to cleanse Georgia of all its Indian residents as soon as their lands could be "peaceably obtained, on reasonable terms." It was one of the great scams. The Georgians sold something they had never actually possessed, winning valuable federal promises without cost. This was the Compact of 1802. The Cherokee were never a party to the agreement, but they would be bound by it.

Preoccupied with larger concerns, such as the British, the federal government put the Compact out of its mind, but the departures of Tahlonteeskee, Chief Jolly, and the others from the Cherokee Nation to the west set Georgians' minds afire with the idea of Indian removal. By 1822, the Cherokee had ceded away so much of Tennessee that half its population now resided in a northern strip of Georgia. As Georgia's plantations spread, equipped with slaves and Eli Whitney's cotton gin, the state population, compared with the number in 1800, doubled to more than 340,000. There were only 6,000 Cherokee in the state, but they occupied a quarter of the land. To the Georgians, this was not right.

In January 1822, Georgia persuaded President Monroe to install a pair of Georgian congressmen—Duncan J. Campbell and James Meriwether—as Indian commissioners to see what they could do about getting the Cherokee to leave the state. Ross, handling things for Pathkiller, refused to meet them. He knew perfectly well what they wanted: "More land, more land, the whole limit of our chartered limits," as he put it. He delayed as long as he could, but finally a meeting was set for October 6, 1823, at the spanking new capital, New Echota.

By now the two sheds of the national council and the national committee had been replaced by a two-story building with a podium at one end of a grand rectangular hall, and a huge fireplace at the other. The flames warmed the chiefs' backs as they welcomed the two commissioners, who must have been a little uneasy to discover that the Cherokee had created the beginnings of a proper modern government.

As council speaker, Major Ridge had enlisted his son John to be an official interpreter, giving him his first taste of council business—and a chance to provide his own meaning to communications that were "at once solemn and pregnant with conjectures." The meetings stretched over many days, with the negotiations all conducted in writing, since the Cherokee did not trust the commissioners to keep their word otherwise. Ostensibly, the commissioners had come only to secure a single square mile for a new Cherokee agency. But it turned out that the agency would house private taverns serving forbidden alcohol. To the suspicious Cherokee, that was probably just an opening wedge in a larger plan for dismemberment. To dismiss the question, Ross quoted the chiefs' letter to Meigs refusing such a privilege back in 1820. He then raised another: why wasn't the federal government removing the insurgent white intruders as required by the treaty of 1817? Simple, Campbell and Meriwether replied with unusual frankness: because the federal government wished to remove the Cherokee instead. The Lord would never have wanted so many Georgians to live on so little land, they explained, when the few Cherokee had so much. Ross's reply was arch, perhaps too much so. "The Cherokees do not know the intention of the Supreme Father in this particular," he wrote. "But it is evident that this principle has never been observed or respected by nations or by individuals."

Such cleverness must have been infuriating. Clearly, these Indians were not going to be easily defrauded. The commissioners tried money, whiskey, and flattery, but this time, none of these offers worked. The challenge brought out the best in Ross, as he rose to an unusual height of moral indignation. No deal, now or ever. Ross uttered a cry that echoed across the council grounds and down through the years: *"Not one foot of land in cession."*

Campbell and Meriwether might have retreated in embarrassment, the Rosencrantz and Guildenstern of America's Indian diplomacy. But on the Tennessee side, the Indian agent Meigs, whose sympathy for the Cherokee had risen over the years, had died that January, and the post had gone to the loathsome McMinn, formerly the governor of Tennessee, and he had a plan. He'd use a Creek to bring these Cherokee around: William McIntosh, the stouthearted Creek warrior who'd fought with Major Ridge against the Red Sticks. He was the Creek version of Ridge—the "Creek king," it was said, as Ridge was sometimes the "Cherokee king." Unlike Major Ridge, though, McIntosh had always been bendable on the subject of Creek land. He figured it was better to sell it now rather than see the white man simply take it later. Then, said McIntosh, "The little band of people, poor and despised, will be left to wander without homes and beaten like dogs."

All this is to say that McIntosh was amenable to a bribe, and indeed $7,000 did the trick. Now he was to buy off any of the Cherokee powers he in turn thought amenable. He started with John Ross. To McIntosh, Ross must have had a residual aura of corruptibility, despite his current posture. For the big meeting at the council house, Ross seated McIntosh on the "white bench," reserved for esteemed guests. While Ross was escorting him there, McIntosh slipped him a note written in clumsy English by his semiliterate son Chilly that nonetheless captures the right conspiratorial tone.

> If the chiefs feel disposed to let the United States to have the land part of it, I want you to let me know. I will make the United States commissioners give you two thousand dollars, A. McCoy [clerk of the national committee] the same and Charles Hicks $3000 for the present and nobody shall know it.

He added that he had another $12,000 for Ross to pass to any other chiefs willing to get in on a deal to sell out their country.

It's telling that McIntosh didn't go to Major Ridge, his close friend from the war, or directly to Hicks, either of whom was better positioned to pull off such a scheme. Why Ross? And why would he dare commit his request to writing—and without a word of justification, as if Ross would take the money instinctively? It is hard to escape the idea that McIntosh simply assumed that Ross's brave words about *not one foot* did not match his meaning. The high rhetoric was just for show. He was on the take. The drunken John Walker had come to the same conclusion.

John Ross had gotten rich quicker than most. Major Ridge was now, at fifty-two, one of the richest men in the nation, but John Ross, at thirty-four, was at least his equal. And, as with McIntosh, there was always the question of the true loyalty of mixed-bloods like Ross. Were they on the red side—or the white? Or simply on their own, like traders everywhere? And Ross's Cherokee blood was so thin. Without a common language, how could he really know a Cherokee, or how could a Cherokee know him? All of this fed suspicion. McIntosh assumed not only that his overture to Ross would work, but that it would work easily. A single sentence would be enough.

Unfortunately for McIntosh, he had misjudged his man, or perhaps just misjudged the occasion. Once Ross read the note, he said nothing to McIntosh. Instead, he pondered the matter and concluded that, right or wrong, the scheme was unworkable. Having spoken up so powerfully against a cession of any size, Ross could not recant now. He took the note to some "close associates," who recommended passing the matter to Major Ridge, who would know what to do. And he did. Bringing the national committee's clerk McCoy with him as a witness, Major Ridge met with McIntosh that evening to say he'd heard about his proposal. It must have been frightening for McIntosh to learn that his secret was out, but Major Ridge was an old friend. Ridge had only one question for him: had this come from Campbell and Meriwether, or was it his own idea? From the commissioners, McIntosh said. Marvelous, Ridge said. Would McIntosh be willing to lay out the rationale for the sale to the Cherokee council and national committee in the morning? That would help move things along. McIntosh had to agree. And so the trap was set.

At the council meeting, McIntosh was returned to his seat of honor, but he must have sensed a coldness in the room that was not due entirely to the fact that the council fire had not been lit in greeting. When Pathkiller turned to look at him, he held his gaze, but few others would look at him at all.

When everyone was settled, Ross rose to speak, his voice all ice. He reminded the hall that he'd served as national committee president for five years. "The trust which you have reposed in me has been sacredly maintained and shall ever be preserved," Ross said, then paused significantly. "A traitor, in all nations, is looked upon in the darkest color, and is more despicable than the meanest reptile that crawls upon the earth—an honorable and honest character is more valuable than the filthy lucre of the whole world—therefore I would prefer to live as poor as the worm that inhabits the earth, rather than to gain the world's wealth and have my reputation as an honest man tarnished by the acceptation of a pecuniary bribery for self-aggrandizement."

Strong words, obviously, and they must have made McIntosh acutely uncomfortable. But didn't they go without saying? Did the chiefs really need to be assured that Ross would never take a bribe? Or did Ross see his opportunity to make himself the hero of the piece, and burnish his credentials for probity, a helpful element in any political career? The oration went on for some time—an agonizing period for McIntosh, surely—and it culminated when Ross dramatically drew McIntosh's damning letter from his pocket and held it out for all to see. "It has now become my painful duty to inform you that a gross contempt is offered to my character as well as that of the General Council. The letter which I hold in my hand will speak for itself, but fortunately the author of it has mistaken my character and sense of honor."

His character and *his* sense of honor, note.

He had McCoy read it out, which he did slowly.

Aging, infirm, Pathkiller had not been informed of the full details of the perfidy, and he was shocked to hear them, as were the others, who gave out an anxious murmur. McIntosh had turned ashen and startled to tremble. As the highest officer of the council, Major Ridge declared the punishment. In his son's translation, he mourned that anyone could contrive such a plot against the nation, let alone someone he had regarded as a "brother" and a "standing guardian" of Cherokee interests for many years.

But now? Every chief leaned in to hear. Unlike Ross, Major Ridge felt no need to call bribery evil, or to assert his own innocence. He focused instead on his own grief for having been betrayed by such an esteemed friend. Said the Major:

A plain maxim of our Nation is, never to trust a man who goes astray from duty, or corrupts the obligation of sacred confidence—This has been observed in McIntosh's conduct.—He has stood erect, encircled with the generous confidence of the people and the authorities of his own Nation. I now depress him. I cast him behind my back. I now divest him of his trust, and put it firmly in my hand. . . . Money is out of the question. We are not to be purchased with money. The trust placed in our hands is a sacred trust. The most distinguished chief of the Nation is liable to be disgraced, as this man, when found deficient of patriotism, that precious standard of moral excellence and political virtue.

Major Ridge did not have McIntosh killed, as he might have. Instead, he banished him. "You have stained yourself with eternal infamy and disgrace," he concluded, turning at last to the disgraced Creek quaking before him. "Never raise your voice again in the council of the Cherokee Nation. Now go, and quit the White Bench forever."

Stoning, a blade, the whip, nothing could have been more hurtful. McIntosh left the council building a dead man. He staggered to his horse and, with a kick, had it bear him away at a full gallop. He kept on toward Creek Nation, lashing the horse in a fury until the exhausted animal's legs buckled and it tumbled dead to the ground. McIntosh was left to walk the rest of the way, the final insult.

McIntosh never returned to the Cherokee Nation, but he did not change his ways. Within a year, he was caught trying to sell Creek land to the state of Georgia. The Creeks were not so forgiving. At daybreak one morning in the spring of 1825, some 200 Creek warriors quietly surrounded McIntosh's home on the Chattahoochee River in northwest Georgia, placed stacks of dry kindling along each wall, and then lit them with torches. As the flames rose, McIntosh's wives (he had more than one) and children fled the house, screaming. McIntosh stayed inside, rifle in hand, as long as he could bear it. Then he made a run for it, too. He was hardly out the door before he was gunned down. But he was still alive when the men dragged him out into the yard, rolled him onto his back, and a warrior plunged a long knife into his heart. With that, the rest of the men emptied their rifles into his lifeless body. McIntosh's women were left to bury him, but they were forced to strip him first. He would greet his ancestors naked, to carry his shame to the next world, too.

4

"BARKS ON BARKS
OBLIQUELY LAID"

B y 1823, John Ridge had been away from New England's Cornwall, and from Sally Northrup, for nearly two years, but he had certainly not forgotten her, or her parents' challenge. Nor had his mother. Susanna had cooked him restorative meals from his favorite recipes, and spiced them with the healing herbs she'd gathered from Anna Gambold's garden of medicines. And he had worked to build up the strength in his legs. A month after the McIntosh affair, he could finally walk unaided—staggering, to be sure, but without crutches or anyone's arm to hold him up. He was now free to pursue Sally Northrup's hand in marriage, and in some ecstasy he wrote to let her know to expect him at her door.

Major Ridge brought him north this time, in late December 1823, but only as far as Washington, where he stopped off to meet with John Quincy Adams, the urbane, glisteningly bald son of America's second president. John

Quincy had served as Monroe's secretary of state en route to what he always imagined was his destiny, a presidency of his own. John Ridge might have been having trouble winning over the Northrups, but the major did just fine with the far snootier Adams. He immediately impressed Adams with an opening speech "in the figurative style of savage oratory, with frequent recurrence to the Great Spirit above." Secretary of War Calhoun and some Georgian representatives were there was well, and so was Ross, who pressed the key point. "The Cherokee Nation have now come to a decisive and unalterable conclusion not to cede away any more lands." Not one foot. When the headstrong Calhoun snapped that the United States could never tolerate a permanent, independent Cherokee Nation inside Georgia, Ross huffed that the Cherokee were "not foreigners, but original inhabitants of the United States." The *Americans* were the foreigners. At that, the Georgia representatives curtly informed Monroe that he should instruct these "misguided men . . . that there is no alternative [except] their removal beyond the limits of the State of Georgia and their extinction."

Bad move. Much as he agreed with the sentiment, the ever-prickly Calhoun was irked that the Georgians were lecturing the president. For his part, Adams was struck by the canny statesmenship of these supposed savages. "They write their own state papers, and reason as logically as white diplomats," he marveled. The Georgians sneered that these crafty Cherokee "memorials," or written statements to Congress, had to have been ghosted by white men. Ross was indignant, but it was flattery of a sort—proof that a Cherokee could, indeed, be fully the equal of a white. If Ross really was a Cherokee, of course.

Adams had the Cherokee come regularly to soirees, where he quite warmed to them, possibly to his own surprise. Far from being the uncouth primitives he'd expected, they had the manners of "well-bred country gentlemen." Watching everyone, punch cup in hand, Calhoun murmured his reluctant admiration for Major Ridge's "fine figure and handsome face." A correspondent for the *National Intelligencer* sniffed that by comparison most of the white dignitaries were "nothingarians," some "with powdered head, others frizzled and oiled, and some whose head a comb has never touched, half hid by dirty collars reaching far above their ears stiff as pasteboard."

In a rare bit of politesse, the Georgian representatives did join a few of the Cherokee for dinner at the Tennison House one evening. But one of them had slandered the Cherokee as "savages subsisting upon roots, wild herbs, [and] disgusting reptiles." At the dinner, the full-blood George Lowrey made a point of loudly asking the waiter for potatoes, or as he said, "some of those *roots*."

When John Ridge finally arrived at Cornwall, he walked with a limp, no question, but he walked unaided. The Northrups could do nothing about it. The Cherokee was free to marry their daughter, now seventeen.

When word of their permission got out, it spread like "wildfire," according to a neighbor, J. F. Wheeler. It was horrifying even to think that, as Wheeler put it, "an Indian should go to a civilized community of New England and marry and carry away one of the finest daughters in the land." Carry away— the implication was clear enough. A primitive had stolen out of the forest to seize a fair maiden and violate her unspeakably.

With opposition mounting, the wedding came in haste: on January 27, 1824, in the front parlor of the Northrups' house, with the local pastor, Reverend Walter Smith, presiding. A crowd was milling about outside during the hurried service, and it surged around the newly married couple when they left, terrifying them both so much that they boarded a stagecoach for Georgia without delay. Even so, they were hounded at every stop by "excited throngs denouncing [Ridge] for taking away as wife . . . a white girl"—so said a self-described "gentleman" from Litchfield. No matter that John Ridge was white-skinned, educated, articulate, and exquisitely mannered. To these hordes, he was a brazen savage.

The news spread like the wind, from town to town, catching up the newspapers along the way until it seemed that the entire East Coast was electrified by the tale of a fine white girl who was, according to Isaac Bunce, the rabble-rousing editor of the *Litchfield American Eagle*, "taken into the wilderness among savages." It wasn't matrimony—it was a kind of abduction. Sally had "made herself a squaw, and connected her ancestors to a race of Indians." *Squaw.* Bunce declared that "the girl ought to be publicly whipped, the Indian hung, and the mother drowned." Not everyone was appalled. A few saw in the tale a heartwarming romance with a tingle of the forbidden. Wrote the poet Silas H. McAlpine:

O, come with me, my white girl fair,
O, come where Mobile's sources flow:
With me my Indian blanket share,
And share with me my bark canoe:
We'll build our cabin in the wild,
Beneath the forest's lofty shade,
With logs on logs transversely piled
And barks on barks obliquely laid.

However sympathetic the verse, McAlpine's sexual theme was unmistakable.

The puritanical Bunce chased the scandal to its source—the wanton *"missionary spirit"* that had encouraged such dangerous liaisons by letting Indians think of themselves as fully the equal of whites.

> Have not the females in that place been seen to ride and walk out with
> them [the young men of the Mission School] arm in arm, by night and by
> day—spend evenings with them—invite them to tea-parties—correspond
> with them by letters—and this by some who there called themselves the
> first, in short receiving them as the most favored gallants, and beaux, and
> the topknot of the gentry?

He assailed the American Board of Commissioners for Foreign Missions for the whole misbegotten idea of a Mission School. What could it have been thinking? An educated Indian was a far greater menace than an ignorant one. So widespread and shrill was the outcry that the American Board didn't dare try to rebut the attacks for fear of inviting more. It claimed only that it had never meant to encourage *marriage*. This particular liaison, it insisted, stemmed only from "peculiar circumstances"—John Ridge's lengthy infirmary stay—"which can never again be expected to recur."

Some of the first citizens of Cornwall rose to defend the school against such bitter allegations of "improper intercourse" between its students and the fine young ladies of the town. One of these eminences was Colonel Benjamin Gold, so it was painfully ironic when John Ridge's cousin Elias Boudinot fell for the colonel's very own devout, sweet-natured daughter Harriet Ruggles Gold, at nineteen the youngest of his fourteen children.

The Golds were an illustrious family in Cornwall, even more than the Northrups. The colonel was an agent for the school, no less, and Harriet's uncle was the town physician who had treated John Ridge. Most of the other male Golds were prominent ministers, two of them Yale-educated, and none of them were keen on another scandal involving matrimony.

Initially, the attachment could not have been more innocent, as the two had met at the First Congregational Church they both attended—and it was then fostered at occasional teas at the Gold home. Once Boudinot returned home to Georgia with John Ridge in 1823 he and Harriet exchanged letters that for a long time were just newsy, but over the months became more personal, and finally, two years into the correspondence, positively breathless. Harriet received a letter from Boudinot containing "some things . . . that convinced her that she must stop short—or continue to correspond & be ready to meet the consequences." But she "knew that she should be unhappy if she stopped there." And she did not stop, nor did he.

In the winter of 1825, Harriet could bear it no longer. She told her parents that she loved Elias Boudinot and wished to marry him. After the Northrups' experience, the Golds were terrified that a sea of outrage was about to crash down on them.

The Golds wrote to Boudinot and said no—they refused to allow him to marry their daughter. When Harriet heard that, she fell into a stupor reminiscent of Sally's. Listless, wan, hardly able to eat, or to sleep for more than a few hours at a stretch. Panicked to see their daughter deteriorate, the Golds were forced to reconsider, just as Sally's parents had been. Colonel Gold told Boudinot that he would allow the marriage after all.

But there were other members of the family to contend with, and they proved less obliging. Of all her many siblings, Harriet was closest to her brother Stephen, just a year older. She knew that Stephen was not likely to agree with her, and that he was inclined to be severe. She needed to tell him herself, but also to take precautions. In early June, she decided to deliver her brother a letter that bore just one line. "I am engaged to Boudinot." Fearing his reaction, she gave it to him only when they were safely enclosed in the family parlor, behind two sound-insulating pairs of double doors. As she solemnly handed him the envelope, she asked him not to open it until she'd left the room, closed both sets of doors behind her, gone upstairs to her bedroom, and locked her door.

Once she was safely in her bedroom, she heard his screams from the parlor, but only faintly. *"Harriet! Harriet!"* over and over, great agonized shrieks that must have rocked the parlor walls. When the shouts subsided, she came down and shouted through the parlor doors that he was not to come out until he "promised to behave." He promised but he did not behave.

Instead, Stephen wrote outraged letters to all the Golds he could think of, and they in turn spread bilious word throughout Cornwall, and well beyond. On June 7, a disquieted brother-in-law, General Daniel Brinsmade, marched to the Cornwall school, where he too was an agent, and laid the matter before the board, who went "white as sheets" at the news. A minister sent Harriet a screed via her parents to deter her. Harriet would not be denied. When a number of other school agents pleaded with her to stop this nonsense, Harriet was unmoved. "They talked to her half a day, but she would argue them down. . . . She would say, 'We have vowed, and our vows are heard in Heaven; color is nothing to me; his soul is as white as mine.' "

Boudinot remained in Georgia for all of the drama. But when word of his impending marriage leaked out, several citizens sent him hateful anonymous letters threatening to kill him if he dared show himself in town, and he heard about the angry mobs swarming the Gold house. "Half the state would rise up against him," the American Board's missionary Daniel Butrick told Boudinot's old teacher John Gambold at Spring Place, if he dared to wed Harriet. "The hand of the assassinating murderer, upheld by ministers, and Christians, and the gathering mob, will take away his life! All will unite in the clamorous cry, 'Let him be put to death!' . . . Even the *heathen* world *blushes*, and humanity sickens at the thought." Gambold couldn't imagine why there was such a fuss. If he didn't already have Sister Anna, he'd be happy to marry a "Cherokee woman of suitable character & attainments."

The Cherokee were even more mystified. Weren't these northerners Boudinot's friends, teachers, townsmen, and fellow worshippers? Stunned by the reaction, Major Ridge asked a missionary to show him where was it written in the Scriptures that a Christian should hate two people whose only "sin" was that they loved each other? The editor of *Niles' Weekly Register*, a national journal, weighed in, professing to be mystified. "Why so much *sensibility* about an event of this sort?" he asked.

Boudinot never questioned his love for Harriet, or his determination to marry her. But there were moments when he wavered in his Christian faith. As the controversy neared its height, he confessed to the secretary of the American Board, Jeremiah Evarts, that he'd gone to watch some "ball play," the ancient Cherokee game, on the Sabbath. As Boudinot well knew, it was sinful enough to violate the Sabbath at all, let alone to do it for a raw heathen ritual that involved gambling, drinking, and frenzied dancing. Boudinot had been out at a mineral spring twenty miles from his father's house, not far from the game, and he simply couldn't stay away. "He was very wretched, & did not care what became of him," Evarts explained. Boudinot was past caring about sin, as he no longer knew what sin was.

In Cornwall, the town minister dutifully published the banns of marriage (public announcement), but he refused to perform the marriage itself. He said it would be "criminal" to back a union that so insulted the Christian community. That evening, a mob gathered with torches in front of the Gold house on the Cornwall village green by the Mission School, demanding to see the harlot. By then, Harriet had fled to a neighbor's house, where she locked herself in the basement. From there, through a blurry strip of window, she could see a large, painted effigy of her being solemnly placed on a funeral pyre consisting of a barrel of tar, and she could just make out the figure setting it ablaze. It was her brother Stephen, his face a ghastly orange in the flickering firelight. As the crowd roared its approval, the flames blackened Harriet's image, and then devoured it altogether—just as the flames of hell would soon do to her. "My heart truly stung with anguish at this terrible scene," Harriet wailed. There was talk that an even larger mob was marching in from surrounding towns to hack down the schoolhouse with axes, set the remaining students to flight, and come for her.

Once again, the newspapers weighed in, none more cruelly than the *American Eagle*, whose horrid Bunce scorned Harriet as a "lewd, graceless, God-forsaken, loathed, disgusting, filthy female" for loving an Indian. Once again, Bunce was a man obsessed. How could the founders of the Mission School have ever thought "these pupils . . . would lose all sexual feelings by coming here?" Didn't they know that "these youths . . . would never think of going back to marry their own dirty, ignorant, and uncouth females . . . after they had learned our habits and seen the attractions of our females?"

In the face of such horror, both parents rallied around their daughter. And gradually, many of the other Gold women did, too, seeing that their Christianity required sympathy, not its opposite. One of them, a cousin, saw something entirely different and almost appealing in Harriet: "She never seemed so interesting as she does at this moment," she declared in some wonder. But Stephen remained "strenuously opposed to the Indian."

The whole affair dragged on for months, with Boudinot hunkered down in Georgia, Harriet doing her best in Cornwall. Sometime in late February 1826, Boudinot decided he would wait no longer. At first, it seemed wisest to marry somewhere well outside Cornwall, but Harriet refused to slink off. She wanted to be wedded at home "like other folks." Boudinot duly came north, and, according to legend, donned a disguise when he came into Cornwall to avoid being lynched. The wedding took place in the Golds' front parlor the next afternoon. It was conducted by a minister from the next town. Only the Golds and a few married friends were present, none of the cantankerous children. An armed guard was stationed outside the house, but proved unneeded. The service was brief, and when it was over the couple left for Georgia, never to return.

So Boudinot left Cornwall, but Cornwall remained forever with him, as vivid, terrifying proof that the dream of inclusion, of equality, of acceptance in white society was worse than just folly, but a delusion that would mock anyone so stupid as to believe in it. Everything that he strove for, first at Spring Place, then at Brainerd, and finally at the Mission School, everything that his father and uncle had preached and the nation endorsed, had vanished like the wiliest prey, out of the range of his arrows. Not nearer, nearer, but farther, farther. The plain, undeniable facts crushed his dreams and broke his heart. And from that, there would be no recovering.

Once they had returned to the nation as married men, Boudinot and Ridge both embarked on the missionary work they'd been taught in Cornwall, with their wives joining in as they could. Harriet Boudinot and Sarah Ridge both believed strongly that the Cherokee needed church teaching, no matter what cruelties had been committed in God's name, and their husbands agreed. John Ridge translated the Bible into Cherokee, using Sequoyah's written version, and Boudinot would edit a new national newspaper, the *Cherokee Phoenix*. These acts would do what their weddings in Cornwall did not—bring whites and Indians together in shared understanding. Or so, in Christian charity, they hoped.

The following January 1825, Major Ridge led yet another delegation to Washington to plead the case for Cherokee lands once more. The presidential election had drawn as candidates not just Jackson against Secretary of State John Quincy Adams, as expected, but Henry Clay, John C. Calhoun, and Jackson's old War Department rival, William Crawford. When no one received a majority, the issue was thrown to the House of Representatives, where Adams would prevail, possibly benefiting from a corrupt bargain with Clay that gave him the post of secretary of state in exchange for his votes.

But that wrangling was still to come, and Jackson greeted Major Ridge warmly when he came by to pay his respects to his old general. Despite his profound misgivings about Jackson's policies toward the Cherokee, Ridge addressed him in magnanimous remarks he'd obviously been mulling for some time. "My heart is glad when I look on you," Ridge told Jackson in an account that got into the newspapers. "Our heads have become white. They are blossomed with age." At fifty-four, he was assuming the solemn bearing of a wise elder. "When first we met we were taking the red path"—of war—"we waded in blood until the murderers of our women and children had ceased." He went on:

In the land of our enemies we kindled our war fires. We sat by them until morning, when battle came with the yells of our enemies. We met them; they either fled or fell. War is no more heard in our land. The mountains speak peace. Joy is in our valleys. The warrior is careless and smokes the pipe of peace. His arms lay idle; he points to them, and speaks to his children of his valiant deeds; his glory will not depart with him, but remain with his sons. We have met near the house of our great father, the president. Friendship formed in danger will not be forgotten, nor will the hungry man forget who fed him. The meeting of friends gladdens the heart. Our countenances are bright as we look on each other. We rejoice that our father has been kind to us. The men of his house are friendly. Our hearts have been with *you* always, and we are happy again to take the great chief by the hand.

It was a moving reminiscence, and Major Ridge's tactful way of letting Jackson know that now it was time to say good-bye to a man he'd like to think of as a friend. If they had been joined in war, they were now to be separated in peace. Their political interests were now opposed, as Jackson would remain a man of Washington, and Major Ridge a representative of the Cherokee. They would not speak again for many years; and when they did, it would be under far different circumstances.

In Washington, Major Ridge detached himself from the rest of the Cherokee delegation so that he and his son John could serve as agents for the Creeks in recovering lands delivered to the Georgians by the perfidious McIntosh. In this, they were successful, and won President Adams's help to force the Georgians to relinquish it. When the Georgians turned militant, John Ridge counseled passive resistance, a new stance for a warrior people, or for any people at all. As Adams's chosen commander, General Edmund Gaines, summarized it, John Ridge had recommended that the Creeks should "make no sort of resistance, but will sit down quietly and be put to death where the bones of their ancestors are deposited; that the world shall know the Muscogee nation so loved their country that they were willing to die rather than sell it or leave it."

The Georgians did not hold back, however, and forced the Creeks to give up lands east of the Chattahoochee, setting up Georgia's current boundary with Alabama. While Major Ridge's reputation was undimmed by his work for the Creeks, his son's was tainted by what detractors saw as naked ambition. To them, John Ridge had none of his father's nobility, and little of his good sense.

Nevertheless, John Ross had reason to worry about this rising political star, and may have been behind a rumor designed to bring him down. It was said that John Ridge had struck Sally in anger, and took other women, leaving Sally so distraught she wanted to drown herself. After their blood-stirring romance, it was all nearly impossible to picture, but it made enough of an impression that the Brainerd missionary Butrick told the Northrups in Connecticut not to believe any of it. Their daughter looked "more like a lady, than when at Cornwall," and always seemed "cheerful and contented" whenever he had seen her.

The Creeks stuck by John Ridge in their effort to get what they could from the federal government for their Georgian land. With his father's help, he secured $217,000 in cash, plus a perpetual annuity of $20,000, half of it to go to the thirteen chiefs, with John Ridge taking $15,000 for his services, and his father $10,000. That would mark the end of the Creeks in the East, and prove a chilling harbinger of what was to come for the Cherokee, too. The deal was scarcely different from bribing McIntosh, but it was negotiated in the open, and approved by the Creeks' "great fire" council. Still, John Ridge took such criticism for his role that he rode to Washington to ask the War Department to clear his name. After an investigation, it found "nothing improper" in his conduct. But the damage was done.

Before he left Washington, John Ridge visited McKenney to take him up on his offer to do an official portrait to be hung with those of dozens of other Indian dignitaries in a long gallery at McKenney's Indian Office in George-town. It would be painted by the illustrious Charles Bird King, a white Rhode Islander whose father had been killed and scalped by Indians along the Ohio during the Revolution. King had studied in London with Benjamin West, and was known for sensitive oils that were both touching and true to life. For McKenney, he recorded these exotic Indian leaders for $20 a head. *Before they were all annihilated* was the unstated implication.

While McKenney was at it, he hired researchers to gather biographical sketches of all the participants in a two-volume *Indian Tribes of North America*, illustrated by King, which would deliver the only contemporaneous account of Major Ridge's life. The portraits proved a stunning depiction of a vanishing race—all these solemn, proud chiefs tragically unaware of their fate. Most of them were resplendent in their colorful native dress, noses and ears decorated with hoop rings, heads topped with bright turbans or gay feathers, and many of them displaying from their necks the large silver medallions they'd received from the government as symbols of permanent friendship that proved all too transient. Major Ridge and John Ross would soon be included, both in handsome business attire, sans medals, Ross stern in a suit and Ridge scowling over a cravat. The ill-fated McIntosh is there, too, in magnificent Scottish plaid, bearing a sword and a plume of ostrich feathers.

Now it was John Ridge's turn, and he sat serenely for King outside his Twelfth Street home, at a desk set out under a tree. A perfect gentleman, slim and stunningly handsome, Ridge wears a fashionably ruffled white shirt and a trim black jacket as he turns to gaze confidently at the portraitist, seemingly taking a moment from his labors over a quill pen on a sheet of parchment placed on the writing table before him. If the other chiefs represented the past, John Ridge would be the future.

Both Ridges would, in fact. Major Ridge used his Creek money to expand a ferry he owned and to build up his estate. He'd already redone his 1794 cabin and erected upon its stone foundation an "elegant painted mansion with porches on each side," according to General Daniel Brinsmade, Golds' once vitriolic relative who came south to see what these Cherokee were about. It was two stories of white clapboard, with chimneys at each end of a pitched roof; graceful verandas; a porched-over front door with turned columns; and eight generous rooms inside, four on each floor, with walls and ceilings of paneled hardwood and thirty glass windows, triple-hung, one of them arched. The house "would look well even in New England," John Ridge boasted to his father-in-law, Dr. Gold, needlessly adding that it "resembled in no respect the wigwam of an Indian." The house was furnished in mahogany, the dining room replete with English porcelain and engraved silverware, with a copy of Charles Bird King's portrait of John Ridge assuming a prominent place in the drawing room.

The place rose up amid a lush and romantic landscape of sky-high oaks, peeling sycamores, and dripping willows giving way to sun-sparkled roses and low, spreading woodbine, altogether a lazy paradise that inspired a gasp from a passing missionary, N. D. Scales. "If I were a poet, I would extend my hand and hit my harp from the flowing willows and sing of the elegant edifice on the opposite shore," he declared. "Down the bosom of the rolling Coosa with darkened shadows commingled with the paler rays of the moon I would send a note of praise and muse in expressive silence."

The grounds extended out from vast orchards of 1,141 peach trees, 418 apple, 11 quince, 21 cherry, and a few plum to include 280 acres of cleared fields, primarily for corn, but also cotton, tobacco, wheat, oats, indigo, and sweet and Irish potatoes. There was also a vineyard, nursery, and garden of ornamental shrubs; a cow pasture; and free-roaming hogs, plus sheep for Susanna's wool. Upstream stood a trading post in which the major partnered with George Lavender, a white who'd previously worked for John Ross's brother, Lewis. Major Ridge provided needed legitimacy, since whites were not allowed to own such enterprises, and Cherokee customers swarmed over the calicoes, silks, and cambrics, their cash payments stuffed into a keg on the premises. Add the thirty Negro slaves, and the holdings put Ridge, with John Ross, among the five richest men in the nation.

The son wasn't doing too badly, either. At first, he and Sally had lived with his parents, but by 1826 he'd built a handsome two-story house of his own some six miles away. Set atop a low hill, it was called Running Waters for the gentle stream that curled by below. He had ample orchards and crop fields, even a ferry of his own, which would soon come to rival his father's, as may have been the point.

By then, John Ross—now a regular point of comparison for the Ridges— had set to building an impressive house of his own on the Coosa. Wider than the major's, it presented a broader facade to the world, with a genteel porch across the front and topped with four brick chimneys that drew from as many fireplaces, and twenty windows that welcomed the light. The place was surrounded by smokehouses and workhouses, including one for a blacksmith. Its fields were less extensive than the major's, the orchards smaller. In this, at least, he was still the junior man. But in every other material respect, he had to be regarded a near equal.

But everywhere, Cherokee, the mixed-bloods especially, were astounding one another with how much they had come to possess. They'd traded land for peace, and when Elias Boudinot returned to the nation, settling in New Echota, with Harriet Gold, John Ridge took to the speaking circuit up and down the Atlantic coast to trumpet the Cherokees' progress. He gleefully recited the statistics: 22,000 cattle; 7,600 horses; 46,000 swine; 2,500 sheep; 762 looms; 2,488 spinning wheels; 172 wagons; 2,943 plows; 10 sawmills; 31 gristmills; 62 blacksmith shops; 8 cotton machines; 18 schools; 18 ferries. All of it was proof of the Cherokees' rapid evolution. As Boudinot declared to numerous eastern audiences:

> You behold an Indian; my kindred are Indians, and my fathers sleeping in the wilderness grave—they too were Indians. But I am not as my fathers were—broader means and nobler influences have fallen upon me. Yet I was not born as thousands are, in a stately dome and amid the congratulations of the great, for on a little hill, in a lonely cabin, overspread by the forest oak I first drew my breath; and in a language unknown to learned and polished nations, I learnt to lisp my fond mother's name. In after days, I have had greater advantages than most of my race; and I now stand before you delegated by my native country to see to her interest, to labour for her respectability, and by my public efforts to assist in raising her to an equal standing with the other nations of the earth.

To show off these triumphs, Elias Boudinot put out the Cherokee newspaper, the *Phoenix*, starting in February 1828. The Cherokee legislature provided $250 to get it going, and then the American Board of Commissioners for Foreign Missions kicked in $1,500 more for the printing press, with the newfangled type for the Cherokee syllabary forged at a Boston foundry. The whole contraption weighed a ton, literally, and was shipped by steamer to Augusta and then by wagon two hundred miles more to New Echota, an epic journey that took six months. For $2.50 a year—if paid in advance, $3.50 otherwise—the newspaper was available not just in the Cherokee Nation but elsewhere in the United States, and it even reached the noted explorer Baron Alexander von Humboldt in Berlin. Boudinot arranged for exchanges with more than a hundred other papers, extending the *Phoenix*'s reach, and its sources of news, to fill five long columns on four broadsheet pages every other week. Remarkably, it was printed in English and in Cherokee, the texts side by side, with the idea of introducing the Cherokee to the wider world and vice versa. Its columns were filled with a bit of everything—tales of Petrograd and Turkey; a heartrending suicide in France; anecdotes of George Washington; instructions on how to exterminate vermin; and the terrible story of a drunken Cherokee woman who set herself on fire.

It was printed in a little shop in New Echota, fragrant with printer's ink, a few steps away from the two-story log cabin Boudinot had built for himself, Harriet, and, as of 1828, their three little children: the quick-witted three-year-old Eleanor; her younger black-eyed sister Mary; and tiny William Penn, named for the nom de plume of the missionary Jeremiah Evarts, who pleaded the Cherokee cause.

Laid out on a grid for a hundred house lots, New Echota was on the verge of becoming a true capital at last. It already had four thriving stores, a few substantial houses, a charming if tiny supreme court house, and the grand council building. John Ridge was backing plans for a national academy to supersede Brainerd; a national museum devoted to the Cherokee heritage; and a Moral and Literary Society "for the suppression of vice, the encouragement of morality and the general improvement of society," according to its prospectus, with a grand library of books on "Morality, History, Religion, Jurisprudence, and general Literature."

The council house offered religious observances, and when, after one service, a minister named Chamberlin returned to his lodgings, his route was lit up with enchantment by torches. "I fancied myself in some of our larger towns to the north," he noted. The transformation of these once heathen people was remarkable, but he found the pace of it worrisome. "I cannot but exclaim, Lo, what hath God wrought?"

Behind it all stood a remarkable document, the Cherokee constitution, the first such from any Indian tribe. Presented as a group effort of the legislature, it was the product largely of John Ross and Major Ridge, who met almost daily in the parlor of one man or the other to create it. Modeled on the Constitution of the United States, it was intended to shame the Americans into recognizing the sovereignty of the Cherokee Nation. The preamble established the parallel between the two countries.

> We, the representatives of the people of the Cherokee Nation, in Convention assembled, in order to establish justice, ensure tranquility, promote the common welfare, and secure to ourselves and our posterity the blessings of liberty; acknowledging with humility and gratitude the goodness of the sovereign Ruler of the Universe, in offering us an opportunity so

favorable to the design, do ordain and establish this Constitution for the Government of the Cherokee Nation.

The rest was no less assertive, as it declared the geographical boundaries "solemnly guaranteed and reserved forever to the Cherokee Nation by the Treaties concluded with the United States" in exacting detail, as if they were as clear as the borders of a cornfield. It established an American-style government, with a chief executive, the principal chief; a single Cherokee council that subsumed the previous bicameral legislature; and a supreme court, the roles of each well specified. It detailed the rights of its citizens to a jury trial, to protection from unreasonable searches, and to elect their public officials by popular vote. While all citizens were free to practice whatever religion they favored, civil office would be denied to anyone "who denies the being of God," a provision that would, not accidentally, restrict the candidacy of heathen full-bloods.

It was signed into law with great fanfare at the end of July 1827, but by then the excitement was tinged with uncertainty. The aged Pathkiller had died in January, leaving the post to his second in command, Major Ridge's old friend the scholarly Charles Hicks; but Hicks had caught a chill in the woods and died just eight days after Pathkiller. It fell to his son William to serve as primary chief until a new one could be elected under the new constitution in the fall. But, young and inexperienced, William inspired little confidence, given the breadth of the demands upon him at such a tense time in his nation's history.

Now Georgia saw its chance. With the upstart Cherokee Nation saddled with novice and uncertain leadership, the state persuaded a reluctant President Adams to send three army generals to summarily fulfill the long-standing Compact of 1802 and send the Georgian Cherokee west. It was utterly peremptory, but the generals soon appeared, ready to execute their mission. The first to arrive was General John Cocke, late of the Creek War, appearing as the constitution was on the verge of being officially ratified on July 26. At first, Major Ridge greeted his old comrade with a "hand of friendship," but when Cocke explained why he'd come, Ridge abruptly turned away and refused to hear another word.

In filling out the leadership under the new constitution, Major Ridge said the Cherokee should "elect those who will be promoters of our national interests," but then added that it "would not be well" to choose "too speedy imitators of white people." Was this a dig at Ross? He signed the announcement, "Your friend, THE SPEAKER."

Not interested in becoming principal chief himself, Major Ridge thought his son John might be the man for the job. But John's reputation had been tarnished by his dealings with the Creeks, and, at twenty-five, he was a little young. That left John Ross as the only serious candidate to oppose William Hicks, who hoped to stay on. Ross trounced him, a blow that left Hicks, it was said, "bewildered, inconsistent and unaccountable in his conduct." He soon left for the west, where he emerged as principal chief of the western band—and an annoyance to the eastern leadership. As for Major Ridge, the Cherokee voters elected him first counselor to the principal chief, a post that made him, after Ross, the second most powerful man in the nation.

The two quickly forged a tight alliance of backslapping harmony, and were often seen out together, the very best of friends in the thriving new nation they'd jointly created and now ruled. It was a serious time, but they made room for laughter and stories, exchanged via translator, or "linkster," while Ross indulged in a few sips of the liquor he normally did not allow himself, and Major Ridge imbibed a bit more freely.

5

GOLD FEVER

Then gold was found in Cherokee Georgia, and that ruined everything.

By legend, it was Benjamin "Uncle Benny" Parks who first spotted something shiny. He'd lived easily among the Cherokee for years, often sharing their commy corn with them in their huts. But then, at the salt licklog by the Chestatee River in the Georgia Appalachians, he noticed that one of the pebbles underfoot was the shimmering yellow of egg yolk. He quietly leased the parcel from its owner, the pastor of his very own Yellow Creek Baptist Church, Reverend Robert O'Barr, and then got up a rig to mine it properly. Like everyone else, O'Barr found this hilarious—until he saw that some of the dirt brought up in buckets was speckled with "good color," and became, said a neighbor, "the maddest man in the country." Furious to have been duped, he demanded his lease back, claiming it had been secured on false pretenses. When Parks refused, the two got into such a fight that O'Barr's mother started hurtling rocks at Parks as he grabbed the pastor by the collar and threw him to the ground. Done brawling, O'Barr demanded Parks's arrest, but the Georgia police refused to get involved. The lease held for its full two-year term, when O'Barr leased the parcel to another gold digger for $1,600, sixteen times what he'd gotten from Parks. Ultimately, the deed fell into the hands of none other than John C. Calhoun, the former secretary of war who'd been so hard on the Cherokee. He pulled $24,000 worth of gold from the site, and it made him one of the richest profiteers in what became the Georgia gold rush.

Word of the gold strike did not get out formally until August 1, 1829, when the *Georgia Journal* reprinted a notice of just one sentence: "Two gold mines have just been discovered in this county, and preparations are making to bring these hidden treasures to us." If it had been announced that the Cherokee hills were made of cash, the effect could not have been more uproarious. "Such excitement you never saw," one prospector recalled years later. "It seemed within a few days as if the whole world must have heard of it, for men came from every state I had ever heard of. They came afoot, on horseback and in wagons, acting more like crazy people than anything else. All the way from where Dahlonega now stands to Nuckollsville there were men panning out of the branches and making holes in the hillsides."

Once the gold appeared, the Cherokee hills of northern Georgia no longer belonged to the Cherokee; they belonged to just about anyone with a shovel. No law, no religion, no morality could ever hold back gold fever. Gold prospectors swarmed over Indian lands to wade crazily into creeks with their pans, to float down rivers in flatboats and dredge the bottoms, or just to plunge shovels into the earth about anywhere. Four thousand miners clogged Yahoola Creek after someone saw a speck of yellow; more created a boomtown called Auraria after a few colorful nuggets showed up; still others turned humble Licklog into a mining metropolis, Dahlonega, named for the Cherokee word for "golden," which the prospectors stole along with everything else.

When he realized he'd started a great, squabbling landgrab, Uncle Benny Parks felt bad. "We always treated them right and they did the same by us," he said of the Cherokee, remembering the chummy meals they'd shared. He'd even fallen in love with the daughter of a Cherokee chief, and wished to marry her. But when the Cherokee were pushed out of their homeland by the intruders, she'd left with them. "The Cherokees would have gotten on all right if they had been left alone," he told the *Atlanta Constitution*, years later. And then, according to the reporter, "his eyes wandered in their gaze toward the tall tree tops."

The Great Intrusion, as the gold rush was called, upended everything, for it made Cherokee land, already an object of desire, into an object of mass hysteria. It made all too real a notion that the Cherokee had found inconceivable, that land itself, the soil, the earth, the *fundament*, could indeed be bought and held by a single person on the strength of a piece of paper. Plus, the Cherokee had never found gold all that valuable; it was pretty, but lots of things were prettier, like wildflowers or the sunset, and nobody thought to own *them*. But gold was different: you could hold it in your hand, close your fingers over it, touch its cool softness, and sell it for cash that could make you feel better about everything.

This whole outlandish notion of getting rich quick made an impression on the Cherokee, who left their crops to pan for gold themselves, standing guard over promising deposits, fighting off interlopers, and doing other things they'd never considered before. It taught them greed. But it also inspired some of them to take their gold profits, go west, and be done with these despicable Georgians forever.

None other than Alexander McCoy, the former clerk of the national committee, had tried to sell off the rights to any gold on his property and do just that. Hearing about McCoy, Major Ridge demanded an end to a vile practice that was all too reminiscent of what Doublehead had done. He stood up at council, waited for silence, and then asserted the eternal Cherokee truth in resounding tones that must have reverberated for days afterward: death to anyone who sells Cherokee land without authorization. This new blood law was written up by his son John Ridge, passed by the new Cherokee council, and printed in the *Cherokee Phoenix* of October 24, 1829:

If any citizen or citizens of this nation should treat and dispose of any lands belonging to this nation without special permission from the national authorities, he or they will suffer death.

What's more, if a seller somehow escaped trial, he would be deemed an "outlaw," and anyone was then free to kill him "in any manner most convenient."

It was that simple. After the repeal of revenge killing, this was the only blood law. Obey it, or die.

• • •

Of all the many enemies of the Cherokee people that year, Georgia's new governor, George Rockingham Gilmer, was probably the cruelest. He became governor by accident. A self-styled Southern gentleman with the requisite military background, he was elected a state congressman the year before, in 1828; but he never got around to formally acknowledging his acceptance of the election results in the allotted time, and a new election had to be called. Irked, Gilmer ran for governor instead, and he won the next year, just in time for the gold rush that turned the state upside down. In his memoir, *Sketches of Some of the First Settlers of Upper Georgia, of the Cherokees, and the Author,* not always in that order, he interrupts his account of the most calamitous event in Georgia history to praise his wife's feet. "My wife had the prettiest feet in the world, such as a Chinese lady would envy," he coos. "They were small, delicate and symmetrical. I have threatened a thousand times to kiss them, and as often expressed a wish to have them painted as a model for painters and sculptors in our country." He then lovingly details his efforts to enlist a Washington friend to hire the city's finest shoemaker to make a dozen pairs of shoes in the French fashion to show off these prized wifely feet to their best advantage, and have them all hand-delivered by a certain "French gentleman" to the governor in his private quarters.

An odd detail, but revealing of his gross obliviousness. For this occurred in the midst of his seizing all of the Cherokee Nation for its gold as if it, too, were merely a set of French heels he fancied. That, of course, had long been Georgia's position, ever since the Compact of 1802: the king of England had bestowed the land on Georgia, and the state governor could do with it as he pleased.

On December 19, 1829, Gilmer delivered a decree that, although it would not be ratified by the legislature for six months, had the immediate force of law: not only did all the gold in the Cherokee Nation belong to Georgia, but all the land did, too. It was the imperiousness of Oglethorpe all over again. The Georgian portion of the Cherokee Nation would now be Georgian, simple as that, consisting of four new counties, no different from all the others in the state, except that Cherokee residents would possess none of the rights and privileges accorded to virtually everyone else. Instead, they were to be treated like free blacks, about the lowest of the low, forbidden to own property, to seek justice in the courts, or to testify, even in a trial brought against them. So it came down to this: the whites were free to steal from the Cherokee, abuse them, even kill them, with impunity. The Cherokee would have no legal recourse. They could not invoke Cherokee law, either, because Georgia refused to recognize it as any law at all. Georgia's own law, meanwhile, was a matter of very rough justice, which by one account often consisted of a plump judge on a felled log "paring his fingernails" while the accused were gathered nine at a time "tied with hickory wyths." The national council was no longer permitted to convene in New Echota, since that was now Georgian soil; any members who tried would be arrested on sight and sentenced to four years at hard labor. As far as Georgia was concerned, the Cherokee Nation was finished, and the Cherokee with it.

When the neighboring states of Alabama, Tennessee, and North Carolina saw Georgia cancel Cherokee laws, they moved to seize Cherokee property, too, although a bit less ruthlessly.

If the gold diggers had showed any restraint before, they showed none now, for Cherokee gold was theirs for the taking. Georgians of every stripe stormed onto Cherokee land in their mad quest for gold and more gold. They trampled fields, slaughtered any livestock they didn't seize, rousted Cherokee out of their homes to take them over, or just torched them for the joy of seeing them burn. The Georgians started "pony clubs" to roam the Cherokee countryside in packs and bring more misery to the Cherokee.

From the Oostanaula, Major Ridge watched all this until he could bear it no longer. While Ross fired off indignant letters to Washington demanding protection, the major took matters into his own hands. White-haired at sixty, he was nevertheless determined to strike back. On the frozen night of January 4, 1830, a light snow drifting across the fields, he pulled a buffalo headdress over his head, angry horns rising up on either side, and then gathered a posse of thirty more Cherokee all in war paint to charge, hooves flying, at the Georgian squatters along Cedar Creek, just inside the border with Alabama. Unlike the whites, the Cherokee gave their enemies a chance to flee before burning their huts to the ground. Eighteen huts were set ablaze, the black smoke rising into the dark sky, as their owners fled in terror to the woods.

When their fury was spent, the major led all the men home in triumph. But four of the warriors peeled off to celebrate with whiskey on their own, and were soon reduced to a merry stupor.

When Boudinot heard of this lightning strike, he was afraid it would give the Georgians an excuse to retaliate all the more fiercely, just as the Cherokee strikes against Sevier's men long ago had led to far more vicious counterstrikes. Sure enough, Gilmer decried the attacks in apocalyptic terms, claiming that the Cherokee had turned the settlers out into the snow to freeze to death. As for Ridge, the *Savannah Georgian* proposed its own idea of a portrait for McKenney's famous gallery: "Dressed in his Buffalo's head and horns, brandishing his tomahawk over suffering females and children."

The settlers were in a vengeful mood when they returned to their homes and found the four drunken Cherokee stumbling about. They bound them, beat them senseless, and threw them across their horses to take to jail. Three of the prisoners made it; the fourth had toppled off his horse, smashing his skull.

Although Boudinot had been apprehensive about the raid, he regarded the four wayward Cherokee as martyrs. "A Cherokee has, at last, been killed by the intruders, and three more taken bound for the Georgia!" he exclaimed, whipping up popular sentiment. But this did nothing to stop hundreds of self-righteous Georgians from galloping into the Cherokee Nation to destroy Cherokee dwellings in vengeance. They made for the houses of Ridge and Ross, only to be warded off by dozens of well-armed Cherokee who loyally stood guard around both.

In the *Phoenix*, Boudinot preached biblical restraint: "If our word will have any weight with our countrymen in this very trying time, we would say, forbear, forbear—revenge not, but leave vengeance to him 'to whom vengeance belongeth.'"

A noble, Christian sentiment, surely—and more evidence, if any more was needed, of the progress of the Cherokee. Who were the savages now?

Although no federal troops came to the aid of the Cherokee targeted by wrathful Georgians, their travails did not pass unnoticed in Washington. For over a year, the missionary Jeremiah Evarts had been firing off pro-Cherokee articles under the pseudonym William Penn (the name that Elias Boudinot had taken for his son), inspiring the messianic, perpetually frowning Reverend Lyman Beecher to ring out a gospel of respect for the Cherokee people from his Brooklyn pulpit. The antislavery evangelist William Lloyd Garrison had taken up the cause, creating a political furor that caught up the sagacious

Massachusetts congressman Edward Everett—the future Harvard president, and the orator who would deliver the *other* address at Gettysburg—who declared the issue of Cherokee removal "the greatest question which ever came before Congress, short of the question of peace and war." He bewailed the plight of the Cherokee, prostrate before a merciless Georgia, in the most heartfelt terms.

But Andrew Jackson was president now, and he could not have been less sympathetic. He had pressed his Indian Removal Act on Congress in early December, and Georgia's mendacity had done nothing to change his mind. "Progress requires moving forward," he said. He was not insensible to the miseries of the Indians who "have been made to retire from river to river and from mountain to mountain." But that was in the past. All of the five civilized tribes of the Southeast must leave, Cherokee included. That was all there was to it.

There were larger national forces at work, too. The great divide over slavery was splitting the country in two. Any sympathy for the Cherokee might require a consideration for the slaves that half the country depended on for its livelihood—and the other half was coming to decry as morally abhorrent. Who knew where that might lead? As a hardy Tennessean with his own slave-run plantation, Jackson relied politically upon Southerners' sympathy, and he was irritated by the bleats of northerners like Everett and the New Jersey abolitionist, the "Christian senator" Theodore Frelinghuysen, who declared that "where the Indian always *has been*, he enjoys an absolute right *still to be*." For Jackson, the matter was not so much moral as it was political. He was wary of ambitious men like Senator Henry Clay, ever-thirsting for the presidency, who might summon northerners' sentiment to unseat him. Nonetheless, Jackson would brook no compromise. The Cherokee must go. He made it a matter of personal loyalty. If a congressman expected ever to be with Jackson, he needed to be with him on this. The emotional heat rose with the temperature, and when the bill finally came to a vote on May 26, loyalty to Jackson overrode other considerations, and it passed by a scant five votes, 102–97.

The Cherokees' last hope was the United States Supreme Court, presided over by the pragmatic liberal John Marshall, now a fiery seventy-five. After three decades of furious legal battles, he had secured for his court the last word on constitutional issues, infuriating nearly every president since 1801, when

Adams appointed him Chief Justice. If Jackson had turned populist with a monarchical streak, the federalist Marshall retained considerable fellow feeling. As a younger man, he'd worked hard to get the bold new Constitution ratified, with all its federal power, and he remained convinced that it was the Supreme Court's job to hold the government to it. The Supreme Court alone could determine that "an act of the legislature repugnant to the Constitution is void." And this Indian Removal Act? Where, the advocates for the Cherokee wanted to know, did the Constitution say it was legal for the United States to evict foreign nationals from their homeland?

The American Board and other missionary groups had pooled funds for the Cherokee defense, and they secured the services of William Wirt, the long-serving attorney general under both Monroe and Adams, now in private practice. The son of a Swiss-born tavern keeper, and a sometime author, Wirt was a shrewd lawyer known for grandiloquence that had won him the title "Whip Syllabub Genius" from his detractors but could be useful in advancing a moral cause like the Cherokees' determination to remain on the land of their ancestors.

As a tactical matter, Wirt recommended that the Cherokee set aside their outrage over the Indian Removal Act and focus on the narrower question of whether Georgia had a right to push its laws on the Cherokee Nation. That hinged on the age-old matter of Cherokee sovereignty. If the Cherokee Nation was indeed sovereign, Georgia could no more impose its laws on the Cherokee than it could on the French. But if the nation was just a stateless collection of indigenous people, that was a different matter. To Wirt, the long history of treaties between the United States and the Cherokee argued for sovereignty, since treaties dealt with agreements between independent nations. If the United States had considered the Cherokee Nation subordinate, it would have made the nation subject to American law. How could Georgia now declare that it ruled the Cherokee?

Wirt needed a test case to determine the principle, and he quickly found one in the matter of George "Corn" Tassel, whom the Georgia state guard had arrested for the murder of another Cherokee on Cherokee soil, and the Georgia superior court had then tried, convicted, and sentenced to hang under Georgia law. How could this possibly be just? Why shouldn't Cherokee law prevail in the Cherokee Nation? Wirt was determined to find out.

Wirt appealed the Tassel verdict, and asked John Marshall as Chief Justice to order Georgia to explain why a "writ of error"—an admission of a legal mistake—should not be issued for such obvious malfeasance. When Marshall put the question to Georgia, the state did not reply. Instead, it hanged Tassel, and then refused to send a lawyer to the Supreme Court to explain why.

Surprisingly, Marshall did not take this usurpation as a mortal affront. For all his talk of the supremacy of the Supreme Court, Marshall was indeed a practical man, and he knew there were other considerations. A newly elected president, backed by Congress, had signed into law the Indian Removal Act that legitimized Georgia's move against the Cherokee, amid a hardening stance against according new rights to America's oppressed people, be they black or red. That was not to be challenged lightly. The Cherokee Nation could claim to be a sovereign nation like France, and subject to its own laws, but, unlike France, it was surrounded by a larger and infinitely more powerful nation that it depended on for protection from invaders, such as these Georgians. If the Cherokee Nation was indeed sovereign, then Georgia had no right to invade it—but neither was the U.S. government obliged to intercede. And Marshall had to know that, law or no, might can make right, especially if the might was being wielded by a rampaging governor backed by masses of Georgians mad with gold fever in an America that was about an inch away from warfare over slavery.

Ross and both Ridges had come to Washington with some other Cherokee to try to limit the effects of the Indian Removal Act, as well as to support Wirt in his battle with the Supreme Court. Some Cherokee had crowded into the gallery to hear Senator Everett deliver another of his earnest stemwinders in favor of the Cherokee. One of the newspapermen there was suddenly startled. "I heard something like a drop of rain fall upon the cope [sic] of my cloak near to my ear," he wrote. "I looked up, and the head of one of the Cherokees had fallen upon his hand, and he was endeavoring to conceal his tears." The reporter went on: "An Indian bending over me in tears! I knew him—had talked with him sympathetically. I loved him. But now he asked no sympathy. He was overtaken in an unexpected moment. And he sought to hide his grief—and in that very effort his grief was betrayed."

Everett's motion did not carry, and that night the Cherokee withdrew to join other Indian deputations who had come to the capital in protest—

Iroquois, Quapaws, Choctaw, and Creeks among them—for a private day of "humiliation" marked by fasting and prayer. Mourning, really, in the manner of people too much accustomed to sorrow.

On the heels of the disappointments in Congress, Wirt pressed his case in the Supreme Court, with oral arguments on March 12 and 14. To address the central issue of the Cherokees' standing as a foreign nation, he recounted the history of their remarkable efforts to "civilize" themselves. Didn't that obligate *other* civilizations to treat them with kindness, if not admiration? "Our wish has become their law," Wirt said of the Cherokee. "We asked them to become civilized and they became so." He gave a nod to Major Ridge as the very best of them—a "'lion,' who, in their own language, 'walks upon mountain tops.'"

The delegates had to wait four long months in the sweltering capital to hear John Marshall's decision—which he finally revealed in his court on July 18 in a tired, rasping voice worn down by years of impassioned argument. As he spoke, he made it clear his sympathy lay with the Indians, but there were limits to how far that could take him. The Cherokee Nation was not a foreign nation, he decided, but neither was it part of the United States. Instead, it occupied an awkward, in-between position that lacked the full benefits of either. The Cherokee Nation was, in a phrase that revealed the difficulty of finding the right words for this strange hybrid, "a domestic, dependent nation . . . in a state of pupilage." A student nation, in other words, a ward of America, and thus a country not fully on its own, at least not yet. And the Supreme Court, sadly, was powerless to intervene in such a matter.

It was a terrible defeat, but, led by John Ridge, the Cherokee refused to see it that way. They took comfort in the description of their country as one that was learning its way in the world. For his part, Jackson exulted that he'd been right all along. But John Ridge wrote to Boudinot that Jackson was wrong to make any "inferences of desponding humiliation in the minds of the Delegation.—We felt none, and therefore could not exhibit any." When Ridge saw that a Georgia paper claimed the delegates were afraid they had angered Jackson by going to the Supreme Court in the first place, he was wildly indignant. "Sooner than ask the President *if he was angry with me*, I would cut my tongue out of my mouth.—I could not, unless the independence of my mind had been metamorphosed to the mentality of his 'palace slaves.'" No, John Ridge would cherish his anger, and never apologize for it.

Nonetheless, the younger Ridge and the rest of the Cherokee delegation paid a call on Jackson after the decision. Jackson said he'd never doubted that Marshall would see things his way, and he was sorry that the Cherokee were now stuck with steep legal fees for thinking otherwise. "Fleeced" was his word. He chuckled to think that, as a country lawyer, he'd been in the business of doing the fleecing. For all the high-handedness, Jackson insisted that he was a friend to the Cherokee, with whom he'd fought "defending the United States," and always would be. When the delegates pressed him about his understanding of their "abstract rights of justice," he reminded them of the once mighty Catawba, who'd defeated the Cherokee in battle and then gloried in devouring their barbecued intestines, much as Doublehead had with the two traders, but now were "poor and miserable." So would the Cherokee be, he warned, if they continued to oppose the United States. He wished to save them from that. The message was heartfelt, but also perverse, since in effect he *was* the United States in this matter.

With that, a representative from Georgia appeared in the doorway, and the delegation withdrew rather than spend a moment in such vile company. Before leaving, each member shook Jackson's hand. The eldest, Richard Taylor, was the last of them, and he held Jackson's hand longest. "You can live on your lands in Georgia if you choose," Jackson told him, "but I cannot interfere with the laws of the state to protect you." He sounded sympathetic.

Desperate for hope, Major Ridge clung to Marshall's description of the nation as "a domestic dependent nation," even though that fitted no sovereign category and made it vulnerable to powers far greater than its own. Still, he carried John Marshall's words to local tribal councils all over Tennessee—pointedly staying out of Georgia—to assure the Cherokee people that outside Georgia they were safe from the Georgians' demands to move west. For his part, Ross was sure that time was on the Cherokees' side. He was convinced that Jackson had proved so high-handed he would yield the presidency after just one term, and no successor would be as hostile to the Cherokee. But that, of course, required two eventualities to break his way. Still, this was the message of Major Ridge to his people, too: stay put, forbear, and wait for better times.

6

THE IMPRISONMENT OF REVEREND SAMUEL WORCESTER

To the Georgians, however, Marshall's ruling meant the federal government would not restrain them whatever they did, and they ran wild, their quest for Cherokee gold turning into a lust for everything of the Cherokees'—horses, cattle, houses, you name it. When temporarily sated, they left behind dozens of barrels of whiskey to dull the natives' fury. Any Cherokee who dared resist were sentenced by Georgian judges to be flogged or to serve years of hard labor in fetid prisons.

The missionaries—not just Congregationalists and Moravians, but Baptists, Presbyterians, and Methodists—all rose up as one in support of the Cherokee, and so brought Georgians' ire down on themselves. Convinced that the Cherokee could never advance their own interests, the Georgia legislature decided that the missionaries had to be behind them and went after these provocateurs by requiring all white men who sought to live in Cherokee Georgia to secure a permit, signed by Governor Gilmer, by March 1, 1831. The targeted missionaries, needless to say, were all white men.

Initially, the missionaries were defiant, and the American Board, safe in Boston, agreed that they should stay where they were, since the image of Georgia rounding up God's humble emissaries was sure to rouse other Americans' sympathies for the Cherokee. To frighten the missionaries into acquiescing, the Georgians started arresting innocent Cherokee on trumped-up charges and sentencing them to lengthy prison terms. The message: the missionaries would be next.

In the pages of the *Phoenix*, Elias Boudinot expressed his disgust that these Georgian "intruders" were allowed to burst into the nation but the missionaries were forced to leave. That sentiment won him a visit from the Georgia state guard, whose commandant, Colonel C. H. Nelson, demanded he answer for his "abusive and slanderous articles," or face a whipping. Boudinot coolly dared Nelson to disprove a single fact he cited in the newspaper. When Nelson was unable to do so, Boudinot was duly released. But he got that message: *We can do what we like with you.*

Many of the missionaries bowed to the rising threats and meekly left the state, but a dozen courageously stayed on. By far the most prominent was the Reverend Samuel A. Worcester, a seventh-generation minister from tiny Peacham, Vermont, then in his early thirties, who'd been with the Cherokee since 1825. In a daguerreotype from those years, he looks like a man who has no idea what is coming and is utterly unprepared for it. He poses boyishly— tousle-haired, soft-faced, with a loopy bow tie—but the apparent softness concealed an iron will the photographer could not capture. He'd befriended Boudinot at the Andover Theological Seminary. But when the American Board sent Worcester as a missionary to the Cherokee, it might as well have dispatched him to the South Seas for all he cared about the Indians' unique plight. With his wife Ann, "a woman of uncommon vivacity, and wit," who doubled as his assistant minister, he rode a horse-drawn buggy to the Hiwassee River. He lost his hat somewhere en route, but otherwise the couple arrived intact, his health "perfect," his wife's "nearly so." Ann admitted to some discomfort when she had to sit in church with Laughing Mush, Big Bear, and Long Hair; skimp on coffee, soap, and nice linen; rely on donated clothes; comb nits out of children's hair; and accept the infernal slowness of the Cherokee.

But Worcester never minded. With Boudinot as his sole contact, he built a two-story house for himself and his wife next door to the Boudinots in New Echota. Drawn to Boudinot's cause of publishing a newspaper in English and Cherokee, Worcester was the one to persuade the American Board to fund that expensive and fiendishly heavy printing press. Worcester tried to learn the language, but all those verb tenses defeated him. Instead, he enlisted Boudinot to translate the Bible into Cherokee, starting with the Gospel of Saint Matthew, and composed some inspiring English hymns and a tract on temperance. Without a proper chapel, Worcester preached on Sundays in the open air, and he also helped out as a blacksmith, postmaster, and sometime doctor.

Both Worcesters were close to both Boudinots, and their families expanded together. Ann Worcester and Harriet Boudinot found common cause, as they were both drawn to an alien race by passionate, charismatic men. And both of them were prone to ill health in a faraway place fraught with hazards. But Worcester clearly loved the brilliant, softhearted Elias, and would have done anything for him, and for the people he cherished.

This roused dark suspicions in Governor Gilmer. He saw Worcester as the secret power behind Boudinot; no Cherokee could possibly be so clever. When Gilmer singled out white males for expulsion, it was Worcester he most sought to banish. To him, Worcester was a "noxious presence." It was to eradicate this Cherokee scourge at its source that he required all the missionaries to take an oath of allegiance to the state, and intended to expel any of them who refused. He expected Worcester to be among them.

Worcester held firm, and early Sunday morning, March 13, 1831, Gilmer sent the Georgia guard to arrest him. While Gilmer was at it, he rounded up a few other whites, such as the *Phoenix*'s printer John Wheeler, to show that the loyalty oath was not intended just for Worcester, although it obviously was, and sent them all on to the state capital, Lawrenceville, now a suburb of Atlanta, for trial. There, to Gilmer's frustration, the superior court of Gwinnett County discovered that Worcester was above this sudden Georgia law as a federal postmaster and was obliged to release him.

An appeal to President Jackson soon brought an end to Worcester's postal duties. By then, he'd returned home to his family in New Echota to wait for the Georgia guard to return. "I am willing to bear the burden alone," he wrote to his advisers at the American Board. "Only let not God forsake me." Adding to his woes, his wife Ann had recently given birth to a sickly baby, Jerusha, her third, and she herself was down with a fever. Worcester wrote a long letter to Gilmer appealing to his sympathy, if not his reason, but it was no use. On July 7, the Georgia guard again stormed the house and hauled Worcester away, leaving his still stricken wife with their now desperately ill baby, sobbing behind him.

They arrested with him Dr. Elizur Butler, a proud, angular figure almost a decade older. The two men were "received like felons," John Ridge reported. The guard let Worcester ride, but clamped a leather collar about Butler's neck and chained him to a guardsman's horse to trudge on foot nearly a hundred miles to a stinking Lawrenceville jail that offered no bed or chair to keep them off the earthen floor. "This is where all the enemies of Georgia have to land," the sergeant declared, pointing. "There and in hell."

In all, eleven missionaries were arrested, and when they were brought once more before the Georgia superior court, an obscure Vermonter, Elisha Chester, who happened to be practicing law in Lawrenceville, stepped forward to represent the careworn missionary who commanded all the attention. Chester had previously come out in favor of Georgia's right to seize its Cherokee territory, but now he argued the opposite. That was hardly propitious, but Worcester had little choice. A nebulous, ambitious figure became a leader of the Cherokee resistance campaign, to Worcester's later regret. The trial came in September, a month after Worcester's little Jerusha died. Her own illness compounded by grief, Ann was in such a terrible state that Worcester begged Colonel Sanford, head of the Georgia guard, to allow him to leave to nurse her until her health improved. He promised he would return for trial, but the request was denied. This time, justice was swift and unremitting. All the missionaries were convicted and sentenced to four years of hard labor. Nine of the missionaries could not bear the prospect, and secured pardons from Gilmer when they agreed to leave the state for good.

Only Worcester and Butler held out. They were thrown into the state penitentiary at Milledgeville, by today's Macon, then the Georgia capital, within sight of the governor's executive mansion. It hadn't been long since convicts there were whipped at their own expense. Now, the punishment was mindless, endless drudgery—donning black-and-white garb to build rude cabinets ten hours a day, with a splatter of "Indian meal" and a scrap of meat eaten straight off the table for sustenance. It was meant, in the words of the principal keeper, Charles Mills, to send the inmates to "the lowest depths of degradation." But Worcester and Butler seemed to draw strength from their deprivations. Mills proved to be a pious Presbyterian, and he allowed the two to lead services every Sunday. Many months into the ordeal, Worcester professed himself "not cast down, but habitually cheerful."

In the martyrdom of these missionary saints, John Ross saw opportunity. Ever since the bitter Tassel decision, Ross knew that Wirt had been looking for a better case to put before the U.S. Supreme Court on the critical matter of Cherokee sovereignty. Might not Worcester and Butler provide it? If Marshall had been sympathetic to a murderer, he would surely be moved by these missionaries whose only crime was living among their heathen charges. It would require the men to hold resolute, but, as an enticement, Ross offered to contribute to a fund to bring their wives to them for occasional visits.

It wasn't much, but it was enough, and the case of *Worcester v. Georgia* was soon on its way to the Supreme Court, carried in the saddlebags of the indefatigable William Wirt, who had himself recently suffered the death of his sixteen-year-old daughter. He bore the document to John Marshall. The punctilious Marshall, shaken by the recent loss of his wife of nearly half a century, now sometimes appeared in court ill-shaven, and once bore "a quantity of egg on his underlip and chin."

Irked, Gilmer went after Ross and demanded to know if this so-called Cherokee actually had any Cherokee blood in his veins at all. He was worse than the missionaries, Gilmer sneered, since they at least never claimed to be Cherokee themselves. Gilmer dispatched the Georgia guard's Colonel Sanford to ask nosy questions about Ross's ancestry, as if he were a racehorse of unknown provenance. Ross had never claimed to be more that what he was, but the questions were reasonable, if irksome. How could a man who looked so white represent the Cherokee as if he were one of them?

Never the swiftest body, the Supreme Court did not move with alacrity now. The issue went well beyond the fate of two missionaries, not that the

Cherokee fully realized it, for forces were rising up in America that would ultimately be resolved by war. The coming election was likely to pit Henry Clay against Jackson after all. A towering figure in the Senate, and a longtime House speaker before that, Clay was a friend to the Cherokee largely because Jackson was not. A slaveholder himself, Clay believed that the issue of slavery would be the end of the American union. Rather than free the slaves, he preferred to return them to Africa. Determined to keep America whole, he had engineered the Missouri Compromise of 1820 that placed pro- and anti-slavery states in a tenuous balance, at sixteen apiece, and extended the border between them west to divide the Louisiana Purchase into equal pro- and anti-slavery territories. Of late, though, the friction between them was threatening to cause flames. The crusading William Lloyd Garrison had just founded his abolitionist newspaper, the *Liberator*, in Boston, rousing the North to new heights of indignation over the issue, and politicians everywhere were getting edgy. Amid all the agitation, John Marshall feared the consequences if he brought the federal government down on Georgia.

His ominous delay made for an uneasy time at the annual council meeting of the Cherokee that fall, as they could not help feeling they'd been abandoned. The meeting was supposed to be held in New Echota, but Georgia had declared that off-limits. After Worcester's arrest, the town seemed emptier than it actually was, with Boudinot providing the only discernible activity as he continued to push the cause of Cherokee emancipation in the *Phoenix*, as if to prove that Worcester had not been the driving force behind the paper. It seemed there was little left in town to stop the cool fall breeze as it blew through.

As principal chief, Ross was determined to hold the meeting at New Echota anyway, but the Ridges found few chiefs willing to risk it. If the Georgia guard didn't send them to Milledgeville, the "pony club" brigands would surely gallop through to crack heads and fire off rifles, and who knew how many would be killed? Perhaps everyone should meet at Ross's house in Coosa instead? That would at least be in accordance with the letter of the new law, but the council didn't dare, and ended up meeting in Chatooga just over the Georgia border in Alabama. It was a sad comedown, as the chiefs sat uneasily on long wooden planks outdoors in the chilly fall air under leafless trees. Nothing came of the meeting except a decision to send another delegation, this one headed by the rising John Ridge, to the president to say again that the Cherokee people would never leave Georgia whatever the Georgians did. But, of course, the council just had left.

And then John Ross was almost murdered. It made a complicated tale, described in breathless detail by Ross himself in the *Phoenix*, and its significance was hard to discern in an outback where power politics blurred with common criminality. When he and his brother Andrew were heading home one evening, they had swung by Major Ridge's house for a chat by the fire, just like old times. But they were interrupted by an urgent pounding at the door. Ross got up to answer it and found before him a "tall, gaunt person," in his description, who'd come asking for the principal chief. The gaunt man was named Harris, and he was hunting for a thief who'd made off with a horse of his, an all too common crime in the nation. The scamp had last been seen on his way to Ross's ferry across the Coosa. Had Ross by any chance seen a stranger on horseback?

Ross said no, and that might have been the end of it, except that Ross and his brother later caught up to this Harris again at the ferry port on their way home. Harris had enlisted a Cherokee—an obliging full-blood named Oonehutty—to help with the search, and they'd just reached the far shore of the Coosa when a horseman was spotted atop a far hill. The thief! Harris and Onehutty raced after him, and the Ross brothers followed once they got ashore but didn't catch up to Harris and the Indian until they were well down the trail. By then, Harris had captured his man. "A chubbed, grim-looking fellow," Ross reported, "with a pair of large reddish mustaches that curled at the corners of his mouth." Looney by name. He was unbound, Ross noticed, but Harris told him not to worry: he'd shoot this horse thief if he tried to get away.

The Rosses went off separately, but came upon Harris one last time a few miles on, after John Ross decided to turn off the main trail to pay a visit to an influential nephew, William Shorey Coody, before leaving for Washington with John Ridge's delegation. This time, Ross couldn't help noticing that Harris and the horse thief were ambling along contentedly together as if they were old friends. Ross demanded to know why Harris was so chatty with a horse thief.

Harris wheeled on him: "Ross, I've wanted to kill you for a long time, and I'll be damned if I don't now do it." With that he leaped down from his horse and pulled out his pistol. But Ross bolted away before Harris could shoot him. Harris turned the gun toward Andrew, who'd also taken off, and he was too late there, too. Oonehutty then knocked the pistol out of Harris's hand, leaped off his horse, and spun Harris down to the dirt. Harris cracked a rock down on Oonehutty's hand when he reached for the fallen gun, and then smacked him with it on the side of the head. But Oonehutty somehow yanked out Harris's own "French dirk"—a dagger—from his belt, and jammed it into his back just inside the shoulder blade. Harris screamed with pain, but twisted away, and, despite a ghastly wound, managed to throw himself onto his horse and take off at a gallop with Looney, who was clearly no horse thief at all.

In the *Phoenix*, Ross didn't come right out and call it an assassination attempt, but he made it clear that Harris had known exactly who he was and had intended to kill him, letting readers draw their own conclusion. Boudinot, in some editorial remarks at the end of Ross's story, was the one to use the word "assassination," calling it "a premeditated plot of rapine and murder," with Ross the "object" of "mercenary executions."

Ross had to have been pleased. Boudinot had Harris pegged as another member of a pony club, out to steal horses by whatever ruse he could muster. To Harris, it was nothing to murder anyone who got in his way, even a principal chief. But the grand word "assassination" served Ross's purposes, as it made him a target of the highest value, and all the better if Elias Boudinot, a Ridge, was the one to say so. It put him smack at the center of things. It made him a man worth killing—and a man who had heroically dodged that fate.

In Washington, John Ridge arrived to find President Jackson basking in the glory of having crushed South Carolina's "nullification" campaign, a brazen assertion of a state's supposed right to ignore any federal laws it disliked, and an obvious threat to the union. South Carolina had sought to disregard a federal tariff Washington had imposed to protect northern interests in Southern textiles, much to the irritation of Jackson's own vice president, John C. Calhoun. As a South Carolinian himself, he raised a fuss that Jackson had then had to quash by jettisoning Calhoun as his vice president before tossing over the bulk of his cabinet for good measure. But even as Jackson was standing up to South Carolina, he was giving in to Georgia on exactly the same point, allowing it to blithely ignore a series of federal treaties with the Cherokee.

A man who'd shown nothing but fierce resolution where the Indians were concerned, Jackson had reason to be selective here. While South Carolina's position was largely theoretical, Georgia was boldly acting on its assertions— and Jackson might need to call out the military to persuade the Georgians to desist. This was not the best time for John Ridge's delegation to remind him of his treaty obligations to the Cherokee.

Still, John Ridge managed to win an audience with the new secretary of war, the pudgy former governor of the Michigan Territory, Lewis Cass, who'd had his own battles against the Indians. He had taken over from Major John Eaton after Eaton was bounced in Jackson's cabinet purge. (In his case, it wasn't nullification that did it, but a romantic scandal.)* While Cass was a man of considerable rectitude, he was no more sympathetic to the Cherokee than was Jackson, for he too had gotten caught up in the convulsions over slavery on the pro-slavery side and would eventually run for president as a pro-slavery candidate. Cass could hardly have been more frank: he said that it was lamentable but the Cherokee were powerless "to resist the operation of those causes which have produced incalculable injury." They should "abandon [their] place of residence," and go west forever.

At that, John Ridge decided to take the Cherokee case to the American people. He and Elias Boudinot would hit the lecture circuit, just as they had with such fanfare a decade before. They'd start in Philadelphia and work their way up to New York City to rouse America against the cruelties of its president toward the Cherokee. They'd collect signatures for a vast "memorial" of protest against the many wrongs done to their tribe, and to them personally. An endless scroll of names—that was the idea. It was one thing to ignore the Cherokee; it was another to ignore Americans.

In Philadelphia, the two cousins won an influential friend in the publisher Matthew Carey, who invited the handsome, erudite pair to a nice dinner, but kicked in only $10 for the Cherokee. John Ridge was once again pursued by

---

* It appeared that the dashing major had impregnated his bride, the fetching former Margaret Timberlake, well before their wedding and while she was still married to her previous husband, navy purser John Timberlake. When he died shortly afterward, rumors swirled that he'd killed himself over her infidelity, although pneumonia was the more likely cause. Nonetheless, this "Petticoat Affair" created a social uproar that quickly became, for President Jackson, a political one.

the entrepreneurial Colonel Thomas McKenney, who had by now run afoul of Jackson for his Indian sympathies. McKenney's latest scheme was to cash in on the Indians by publishing an expensive lithograph of those portraits of Indian chiefs he'd commissioned from Charles Bird King. He wished now to add some biographical sketches, and hoped that John Ridge could persuade Ross himself to write up the remarkable Sequoyah. In exchange, McKenney pledged to press the Cherokee cause.

"He is apparently as strong a friend as we have," Ridge wrote to John Ross in passing along the request. "He desires to publish in this city short letters addressed to the President which shall strike him as the lightning strikes the branchless pine." He added a trumpet blast. "Onward in the path of duty is my motto. Strongly opposed to surrender our national existence I shall never give it up even unto death." But, despite such bravura, his heart wasn't fully in it, and he ended on a quieter and more realistic note. "I do hope that our people as usual remain united and continue to depend upon the advice of their chiefs—it is the only way to preserve them and their rights."

In New York, the cousins staged a couple of loud rallies at Clinton Hall and won over a standing committee that included a host of dignitaries, including the eminent law chancellor James Kent, the antislavery crusader General James Tallbright, the political satirist Theodore Dwight, and ex-mayor Philip Hone. They netted $8,000, and pushed the list of supporters toward its final total of 6,000.

From there to New Haven, and finally Boston, where the stalwart Brooklyn abolitionist Lyman Beecher greeted them with a flight of oratory at the Old North Church made famous by Paul Revere. The cousins were in Boston when they heard that Marshall's decision on the Worcester case was imminent. For days they waited anxiously, and then a friend, John Tappan, burst into the American Board offices in Pemberton Square to tell the two he'd just come from Washington with the news. Then he turned grave. "Are you prepared for the worst?" he asked.

At that, the two Cherokee slumped. "No, we are not," John Ridge replied weakly.

Then Tappan brightened, slapped the two men on their backs, and said he'd been joking. Marshall had struck down the law that had imprisoned Worcester and demanded that he and Butler be freed immediately.

If Christ himself had climbed down from his cross to bless John Ridge and Elias Boudinot, the effect could not have been more dramatic. It wasn't just the ruling, but the unexpectedness of it. Just when it looked as though nothing would ever go right for the Cherokee, something did. And it went so right as to make it seem that nothing would ever go wrong again. Georgia could *not* require a loyalty oath of white males who wanted to live within its borders. Its laws did *not* supersede the laws of the Cherokee. It could *not* incarcerate anyone who refused to sign a loyalty oath. On further reflection, the Cherokee Nation may have been a "ward state" after all—and that was not such a bad thing if it won the protection of the United States government. As Ridge and Boudinot scanned the ruling, they must have wondered if they were dreaming. "The Cherokee Nation then is a distinct community, occupying its own territory. . . . The laws of Georgia can have no force and . . . the citizens of George have no right to enter but with the assent of the Cherokees. . . . The Act of the state of Georgia is subsequently null and void . . . repugnant to the constitution, laws and treaties of the United States."

It was a joy almost beyond comprehending, and John Ridge and Boudinot were nearly overcome as they were embraced by Tappan and then swarmed with jubilant well-wishers. Beecher himself rushed in to find out what the fuss was all about. When Boudinot told him, the great divine clapped his hands and shouted "God be praised!"

To John Ridge, Marshall's decision could not have been clearer. Georgia could not take the law into its own hands any more than South Carolina could. There would be no nullification in this instance, either. Marshall had "forever settled as to who was right and who is wrong," Ridge wrote excitedly. Only the details were left, such as exactly how Jackson would carry out the Supreme Court's edict. After all, as thirty years of Marshall's decisions had demonstrated, the Supreme Court *always* prevailed. It determined the law in a nation of laws. At his inauguration, Jackson had sworn to uphold the law in *his* loyalty oath, to the Constitution, with his hand on the Bible. Worcester and Butler would immediately be freed, and the United States would require Georgia to remove itself from the Cherokee Nation, at gunpoint if necessary. It was all too joyous.

While the ruling was greeted with glee almost everywhere, there was ominous silence in the White House. The days ticked by without any public reaction from Jackson at all. Finally, troubling reports started to leach out from Jackson's intimates. Here is one: "A gentleman who dined with General Jackson heard him say he thought the decision of the Supreme Court erroneous on the Cherokee Case and tis doubted here whether he would see it executed—a pretty thing indeed, for him to give such an opinion of the highest tribunal and to hesitate about executing its decrees."

Was that possible? Could a man whom so many had derided as a brute who cared nothing for reason, custom, rules, or common civility—could he now dismiss the law, too? Incredible as it seemed to Ridge and Boudinot, Jackson had indeed decided that this epic Supreme Court ruling was merely John Marshall's opinion, nothing more. "John Marshall has made his decision," Jackson was said to have declared, and rather idly. "Let him enforce it." With that, he let the superior court of Georgia ignore the U.S. Supreme Court's ruling altogether. Rather than send in the army to force Georgia to obey the law, Jackson simply let the matter go.

In his defense, Jackson may have ignored the interests of the Cherokee because he was attending to the higher interests of the nation. The case was called *Worcester v. Georgia*, but it was really "Georgia v. the United States of America." For if the United States was obligated to enforce Worcester's victory, it would quickly turn a speck of trouble over a missionary or two into a colossal war between the federal government and the recalcitrant South. Georgia had too much invested in its land policy, outrageous as that policy may have been, to acquiesce without a fight. Neighboring South Carolina would probably have rushed to its defense, and who knew how many other Southern states, likewise committed to defend slavery and passionate in their convictions about states' rights, would have followed suit? Jackson would have had quite a fight on his hands, and for what?

Horrified at what they saw as Jackson's intransigence, Ridge and Boudinot broke off their lectures to hurry to Washington to plead with him to reconsider. Jackson agreed to see them, but his removal policy was still in effect, and would always remain so. Period. Georgia could do what it wanted with the Cherokee Nation.

Remarkably, he insisted once again that he did this out of his enduring friendship with the Cherokee, and in fact with John Ridge himself. Perhaps it was flattery, but he made it clear he had no use for John Ross anymore. Pushy, self-important windbags like Ross had been anathema to Jackson all his life. John Ridge was a cloth of another cut altogether. Whatever the intent, John Ridge must have taken these words from the Great Father as earnest praise, for he went so far as to name his next son after the president: Andrew Jackson Ridge. Perhaps this was an inheritance from his father. But John Ridge accepted it as truth: Jackson was a friend of the Cherokee, and it was as a friend that he wished the Cherokee would leave.

Jackson had already hired a federal agent to oversee, and hasten, their exodus. Major Benjamin Currey, a crisp Tennessean not known for his love of Indians. But he too was there for the Cherokees' own good.

John Ridge maintained a public face of stoic resistance in his letters to Ross, in his remarks to the newspapers, and even to his stalwart, rough-hewn cousin Stand Watie, son of Major Ridge's brother Watie. Stand Watie was filling in as editor of the *Phoenix* while his brother Elias was away. But others who saw John Ridge when he left Jackson's office saw the look of bitter defeat. One of Jackson's close advisers, Amos Kendall, saw the normally upthrust young man after that last, pivotal meeting. He must have sagged, for Kendall saw him weighed down with "the melancholy feeling that he had heard the truth." Jackson's truth, to be sure, but that was all the truth there was right now. "He was convinced that the only alternative to save his people from moral and physical death was to make the best terms they could with the government, and remove out of the limits of the state."

It was hopeless. The Cherokee had done everything to better themselves, but they were still to be removed like the bearers of contagion. The whites had promised to treat them better, and instead had treated them worse. A cripple who had willed himself to walk, who had faced down humiliations in Cornwall, who had become more white than white, John Ridge had now taken a boot in the face. His father's massive pride would never accept such humiliation; and his cousin Boudinot seemed oblivious to slights. But, for all the force of his rhetoric and the majesty of his exquisite tailoring, John Ridge was not so unreachable. Treated with such frankness by Jackson, he did not glower with indignation, or deliver a blast of fury, but went ice cold, taking Jackson's grim words for harsh truth. But he resolved that, while his people might be crushed, he never would be.

The Cherokee had always been embattled; that was the nature of tribal life. Their boundaries were never fixed by a shoreline, let alone a surveyor's pole; these boundaries depended on a loose understanding that was always subject to revision. Their historic willingness to cede vast tracts of land reflected their lack of fixed points. Ross may have drawn a line in the sand—*not another foot!*—but Jackson and the Georgians had stepped over it with a sneer. The whole Cherokee idea had been a fantasy. There was no Cherokee Nation. Without a vast ocean or impassable mountains for protection, it lacked the resources any nation needs to assert and defend itself. It had no military worth the name, just a few thousand aging warriors who were no match for a modern fighting force. When Major Ridge had led a bunch of warriors in face paint against the pony club, the results could hardly have been more disastrous. The Cherokee government had been outlawed, its laws suspended, its treasury depleted. It had few roads, a smattering of one-room missionary schools. While the elite had advanced, the vast majority of Cherokee continued to live as they always had lived, with little concept of life past the horizon.

John Ridge had to think that John Marshall had it right the first time. This was a ward state, and it was a pathetic one, dependent on a vastly larger and more powerful nation that was proving indifferent to it, and powerless to hold off the mounting cruelties of Georgia on its own. The crisis had become existential. All or nothing. The Cherokee were being told to give up *everything*, and they had no choice but to agree. There was no way around it. The Ridges' magnificent dreams for their people were over.

When he finally returned home to the Oostanaula in midsummer, after so many months away, John Ridge must have feared the reaction of his proud, imperious, often snarling father. He'd think John a traitor or, worse, a coward to talk of surrender, of selling out his people. The son was braced for that, surely. A man of great intellect and immense feeling, but physically frail and now spent, John Ridge was now about to tell his aging warrior father that he was accepting defeat.

But Major Ridge had not been idle while his son was away. He had been out in the countryside to see for himself the state of the Cherokee people. And he'd seen how broken they were. Their lands trampled, their homes in jeopardy, hounded on every side. He could see they no longer had a place in the nation. It was tragic, but he could see it was hopeless. The Cherokee had to go.

It is doubtful that the Ridges embraced over that, but they might have, since their feelings were so much as one. More likely, they simply spoke to each other in the solemn tones by which Cherokee had always related the truth. And the talk might well have been brief, for once they agreed—*yes, we must all go*—there was little left to say. The Ridges, father and son, would lead the Cherokee to a promised land, whether they wanted to go or not.

7

THE TERRIBLE TRUTH

Meanwhile, Jackson's emigration agent Major Currey had gone at his rude task with cruel efficiency. He'd encouraged Georgian interlopers to steal Cherokee horses and livestock, knowing that it would dispirit the Cherokee and encourage their evacuation, as well as to leave kegs of whiskey about to lure drunken Cherokee into jail or debt, and therefore make them vulnerable to deportation. And he hired some unscrupulous full-bloods to whisper about dire consequences to their brethren if they didn't leave, too.

Currey patched together a small flotilla of sixteen barely river-worthy flatboats and offered a 50-cent annuity for anyone willing to go—and took down the names. Although this was a federal operation, any émigrés who tried to slip west on boats of their own faced seizure of all their belongings by Georgian sheriffs, plus hefty fees to allow them to proceed on unencumbered. Currey offered the only legal water passage west. He'd hoped to sign up 1,000 refugees, but, despite all his efforts, he got only about half that. He gathered them in ramshackle huts on the banks of Major Ridge's old Hiwassee, before cramming them onto teetering, overweighted boats for a three-week river passage that must have been terrifying. The swift Tennessee had to descend the notorious rapids at Muscle Shoals, where the drops had frightening names like the Suck, the Boiling Pot, the Frying Pan, and the Skillet. From there, the emigrants would take the aging, belching steamer *Thomas Yeatman* down the Ohio to the Mississippi and finally to the Arkansas; it would deliver them to the Cherokee agency near the border of Indian Territory at Fort Smith, a thick-walled, star-shaped federal fortress that was attempting to allay but surely only evoked the fears of an ungovernable territory.

There, the southeastern tribes were to be laid out in wide swaths of the wild foothills of the Ozarks on the far shore of the Arkansas: Cherokee, then Creeks, then Choctaw. Of course such federal boundary lines didn't mean much to Indians eager for the best hunting, fishing, and farming in the region. Yet it was here, on 7 million acres that were supposedly reserved by the American government exclusively for the Cherokee but were actually alien lands filled with rival tribes and jealous neighbors, that the Cherokee were expected to start afresh—friendless, without shelter or food or money.

Worse for Currey, every Cherokee he sent west made it harder for him to find the next one. The tales sent back were accounts of hunger, fights, poverty, and endless roaming. Each émigré made for one less person in the east who wanted to go.

Once the full Cherokee delegation had returned from Washington after the Worcester ruling in the summer of 1832, Ross called a meeting of a special council of elders and dignitaries to decide what to do. Ross had sent out runners carrying the joyous news of Marshall's miracle to every corner of the nation; and Secretary Cass was told, there was "rejoicing, yelling and whooping in every direction." Not to mention dancing, frolics, and whiskey. Ross, however, sent no runners afterward to reveal the terrible truth that the glorious Worcester decision had come to nothing.

Ross refused even to think about going west, and officially John Ridge deferred to him as "chief of the whole Cherokee Nation, upon whom rests under Heaven, the highest responsibility and well being of the whole people." But secretly Ridge had his own ideas. He had taken to heart the view of U.S.

Supreme Court justice John McLean, to whom he'd made quiet inquiries: prepare to leave *right now* on the best possible terms; the terms would only worsen hereafter.

The terms that Elisha Chester had brought back from Secretary of War Cass are an example. The meddlesome Chester, Worcester's self-appointed attorney, had taken it upon himself to negotiate departure terms for the nation, a wild overreach. But he'd come back with a seventeen-point proposal that could not be dismissed out of hand. It guaranteed the Cherokee ample land outside any existing state or territory, complete self-government, full transportation costs, fair compensation for their "improvements"—buildings and fields—on their eastern land, subsistence pay the first year, and annuities thereafter. Whether they were realistic or not, Ross was determined to give them no consideration whatsoever. But the Ridges persisted, and won the backing of the half-blood elite to force a meeting of the entire nation on July 23, 1832, to discuss the matter.

It was held at the campground at Red Clay, now in Cleveland, Tennessee. Red Clay was then a narrow valley between forested hills, tucked safely inside the Tennessee border, beyond the reach of Georgian law. Its only building was a rickety council house with a shed roof that left it open to the hot, dusty wind blowing through the valley. After New Echota, it was lonesome and dreary. But here the chiefs would deliberate amid breezes of pipe smoke, while a couple of thousand Cherokee gathered quietly around to follow what they could of the proceedings.

An English traveler, George William Featherstonhaugh, attended a later, similar meeting, and remarked that for all the Cherokees' "Arcadian" nature, as he put it, most of the attendees might have been taken for "decently dressed" Americans; even the full-bloods in turbans and deerskin leggings were not at all "the wild savages of the West." And Featherstonhaugh found that, momentous as the occasion was, the Cherokee maintained remarkable order, recognizing this as a time for cool reflection, not hot anger.

Now that four years had passed since Ross and the members of the council had first been voted in, the Cherokee constitution required fresh elections. This was essential for a democracy, needless to say, but Ross shocked the assemblage by decreeing that this year no vote would be held after all, and he persuaded the council to go along. That left all the incumbents, Ross included, in place until Ross deemed the nation ready to resume the democratic process. In the current crisis, Ross declared, the nation simply could not risk further discord.

To the Ridges and their backers, this was the very reason to have an election—to give the people a voice in charting the nation's course at such an uncertain time. Besides, Major Ridge had the idea that his son John, handsome, worldly and well-spoken, might now lead them as principal chief himself. The major was not alone in this. Even the sleepy-eyed Governor Lumpkin, the former congressman who'd taken over from Gilmer, believed that John Ridge made John Ross "a mere pygmy," but then, Lumpkin had ample reason to favor John Ridge's openness to removal.

Ross, always attuned to threats to his own power, could not have helped noticing the flash in John Ridge's eyes, the sharp way Ridge handled himself. Ridge made Ross seem plain and his speeches tedious, the drone of a mosquito in the ear. But Ross did know politics. The Ridges might have the mixed-bloods, but he had the full-bloods, who were still far more numerous and still—whether out of belief or ignorance—committed to the old ways. Hunting was scarce, but the spirits still abounded in the woods, and so did the joy that these gaily dressed traditionalists took in the land of their forefathers. The exuberance was almost as palpable as the earth itself, evident in every giddy stomp of the Green Corn dance, in every flavorful kernel of the corn that grew from the soil. Exactly how this virtual Scot captured the enduring devotion of the full-bloods is a mystery; they may have trusted him to handle the alien powers in Washington and Georgia because he was one with them. For whatever reason, Ross did hold the full-bloods, and he quickly stamped out all this foolish talk of needing an election before dismissing this absurd overture by a nonentity like Chester, who'd made a "rather uncouth" visit with his proposal to the nation. No full-blood would ever question him.

All would have been well for the principal chief except that, to Ross's irritation, Elias Boudinot had gone ahead and printed Chester's proposal in the *Phoenix*, needlessly arousing people, not the least of them the Georgian congressman General Daniel Newman, who took the publication to mean that the Cherokee were ready to make a deal. Boudinot himself had made no such admission, but there was little doubt he was open to the idea.

At Red Clay, the possibility that the Cherokees might reconsider their commitment to the east was electrifying, but as a political matter, it was also preposterous. If nothing else, Ross always knew where his votes were, once he decided to seek them. They were with the full-bloods, who weren't for removal. Why would they want to leave if they didn't absolutely have to? And who knew if they really had to? Henry Clay might well turn Jackson out of office in the presidential election that fall, ending the federal hostility to the Cherokee. And the western lands were hardly blessed with milk and honey. No, Ross declared them nothing but "extensive prairie badly watered," adorned here and there with "only corpses of wood." And as long as there was a particle of hope that the Cherokee did not need to go, the Cherokee would stay. That was John Ross's view.

To rout his opponents, he took a copy of a letter of Newman's expressing his interest in a deal and had it nailed to a tree at Red Clay for all to see. The implication was clear: someone in the delegation must have been bribed if a Georgia congressman thought that the Cherokee Nation was for sale. Bribery, of course, was Ross's signature accusation. Anyone who preached removal had to be on the take. And if a sympathizer's motives could be questioned, his ideas could be ignored. "The clamor raised upon the subject," Chester later acknowledged, "was well calculated to prevent all calm reflection upon the real situation and interest of their nation." Chester demanded a public inquiry to give the treaty's backers—meaning the Ridges—a chance to address such inflammatory charges, but, knowing he held the advantage, Ross wouldn't give them the chance. "No opportunity was conceded them for making their defense," Chester complained. A defense was probably useless anyway. As Chester said, it was nearly impossible "to press the subject of a treaty upon a people who have long been accustomed to regard the advocating a sale of their country as the blackest crime."

Ross forbade Boudinot to print another word about Chester's treaty proposal in the *Phoenix*. Boudinot was shocked: did Ross mean to silence the nation's sole newspaper? Did he intend to make it his house organ, promoting his ideas alone? Surely, the *Phoenix* had to present the other side if the nation was to understand the issues it faced. But to Ross, the nation needed unity of view above all else. Just as there would be no election, there would be no dissent. Dissent would only produce needless "fermentation and confusion."

Boudinot replied with his resignation. "Were I to continue as editor," he wrote to Ross, "I should feel myself in a most peculiar and delicate position." The principal chief might deem him "an enemy to the interests of my country and my people." And that would be more than intolerable—it would be dangerous. Still, the move would cost him, as Ross convinced the people that Boudinot had betrayed them, and besides, it deprived him of his editor's salary of $300 a year, the bulk of his income.

Boudinot had cultivated twenty-five acres, but most of them had turned to dust in a recent drought, and many of the rest had been trampled by a neighbor's wild hogs. Harriet, never the most robust, had fallen sick again, and he had five children to support. Fortunately, Worcester, still languishing in prison after Georgia refused to heed the U.S. Supreme Court, heard of his difficulties, and persuaded the American Board to restore his $300 salary for his work as a translator.

Ross accepted Boudinot's resignation without regret and named as his replacement his brother-in-law, Elijah Hicks, who shifted the attention of the *Phoenix* from tumultuous domestic politics to soothing religious matters, and gradually phased out the Cherokee translation of what had always been intended to be a bilingual newspaper.

Despite these two defeats on the election and on Boudinot's editorship, the Ridges insisted that the Red Clay council follow through on Ross's promise to consider Chester's treaty proposal. But Ross stoked the opposition to a fury, and the motion was voted down so resoundingly that the Ridges were obliged to recant their heresy by making the rejection of their own motion unanimous. They mournfully added their names to a letter to the secretary of war on August 8 reiterating the Cherokees' "true sentiments" against any treaty at all.

The Ridges were now under assault. In the *Phoenix*, Elijah Hicks devoted the few nonreligious column inches to attacking the patriotism of his predecessor. John Ross started to recast his followers not merely as a faction, but as a true party, the Patriot Party, sometimes the National Party. Their opponents, led now by the Ridges, would form into the Treaty Party, but to the Ross men, they were simply traitors. The nation was splitting in two.

In an essay the *Phoenix* refused to publish, Boudinot declared that he himself was the true patriot, for his patriotism consisted of "the love of the country, *and the love of the people*." To Boudinot, any claim by Ross to the first denied the second, for Ross's commitment to the land would only bring pain to the people he professed to love. "Our lands, or a large part of them, are about to be seized and taken from us," Boudinot cried. "Now, as a friend of my people, I cannot say *peace, peace,* when there is no peace. I cannot ease their minds with any expectation of a calm, when the vessel is already tossed to and fro, and threatened to be shattered to pieces by an approaching tempest." Given what he knew, he had no choice. "If I really believe there is danger, I must act consistently, and give alarm; tell our countrymen our true, or what I believe our true, situation. In the case under consideration, I am induced to believe there is danger, 'immediate and appalling,' and it becomes the people of this country to weigh the matter rightly, ask wisely, not rashly, and choose a course that will come nearest [to] benefiting the nation."

It was the clairvoyant's dilemma, as old as Cassandra. How to make a dire prediction without being dismissed as a crackpot—or an enemy? Just to identify a problem can make a seer the source of it—and then an object of scorn if the solution means that people must abandon their homes, their heritage, and the bones of their ancestors, and journey to a distant land that could be harsher than the one they'd left. And no glory would ever come to those who counseled removal, for no one would ever be able to say for sure that it wouldn't have been better to stay. No, the sensible position for a politician was to preach staying—and, later, if necessary, leave with the utmost reluctance, blaming those who had actively pushed removal for its hazards, and taking no responsibility for the consequences.

By that standard, only a fool would openly advocate going, and Ross was no fool. Always the more astute politician, Ross never got too far ahead of his supporters, those full-bloods who hung on the Cherokee translation of his every word, only too happy to be shielded from reality. At the full council meeting at Red Clay in October, Ross made the prospect of removal the sole subject, and saw it rejected by overwhelming numbers. Chester was allowed to lay out his proposal, but no one listened, even when he told how Georgia lands would be ripped from the Cherokee any day now. John Ridge hoped to add a note of reason, but he did no better, and his plan to send to Washington a delegation armed with a treaty proposal was voted down. He would go to Washington by himself to declare his views.

By then, the Cherokee stood virtually alone among the five civilized tribes in holding off removal. The Choctaw had sold all their land in 1830 in the Treaty of the Dancing Rabbit Creek, and had gone west a year later. The French traveler Alexis de Tocqueville was in Memphis to watch the Choctaw leave: "In the whole scene," he wrote, "there was an air of ruin and destruction, something which betrayed a final and irrevocable adieu; one couldn't watch without feeling one's heart wrung. The Indians were tranquil, but sombre and taciturn. There was one who could speak English and of whom I asked why the Chactas were leaving their country. 'To be free,' he answered, and I could never get any other reason out of him." The Ridges might have said something similar. The Creeks and Chickasaw would shortly follow, although the Seminoles would fight removal until 1839, when they were largely eradicated by the forces of General Zachary Taylor. By then, all the eastern Indians had been either removed, assimilated, or exterminated. Only the Cherokee would be left.

The end was coming for them; the signs were everywhere. Since 1805, Georgia had relied on a lottery system to apportion available land, and now Governor Lumpkin thought that this would be the best way to distribute Cherokee land, too. It would be fair, at least in his mind, and if it passed the job of extracting the Indians from their homes to individual Georgians, well, so much the better.

When Lumpkin floated the idea of giving away all the Cherokee property in Georgia by lottery, the Cherokee couldn't imagine that even a Georgian would do such a thing. But in the spring of 1832, Lumpkin started in. He recruited 550 surveyors—many of them destitute Cherokee, some heartless Baptist missionaries, and the rest energetic Georgians—to divide all of the Cherokee Nation into four equal "sections," each with hundreds of nine-mile-square "districts" that would, in turn, be subdivided into thousands of 140-acre house lots. As the surveyors scrambled across the nation, they emblazoned trees with strange numerical codes that assigned Cartesian coordinates to the vast, rambling world of the Cherokee, giving every house lot a numerical address such as Section 3, District 14, Lot 137. More than 35,000 of these addresses, all of them written down on slips of paper in the exquisite handwriting of a debutante, would be dropped like a pile of leaves into a large rotating drum, creating such a weight that it was not easily turned, even by a beefy associate straining on a hand crank. A companion drum would be filled

The Spanish conquistadors under Hernando de Soto were the first Europeans to lay eyes on the Cherokee. De Soto's men enslaved hundreds and tortured to death any they deemed unhelpful.

This three-chief Cherokee delegation met Britain's King George III in 1762. When Chief Ostenaco, pictured in the middle, encountered the novelist Oliver Goldsmith at a social gathering, he gave the writer a tight embrace that left his face smeared with face paint.

An evening primrose done in watercolor by the British naturalist William Bartram on his visit to the Cherokee Nation in the 1770s. His rapturous descriptions of the Smoky Mountains inspired Coleridge's phantasmagoric "Kubla Khan."

The Virginia militia commander John Sevier was hailed as "Nolichucky Jack" by followers who saw him as a dashing hero of the frontier. To the Cherokee, he was a remorseless brute who would stop at nothing.

The sole portrait of Major Ridge. It was done by the Rhode Island artist Charles Bird King, whose father, as it happened, had been killed and scalped by Indians during the Revolution.

Major Ridge's mansion by the Oostanaula River, one of the most impressive in the nation.

A society portrait of John Ross at fifty-eight. Seven-eighths Scottish, habitually attired in European clothes, the longtime Cherokee principal chief would not have looked out of place at a dinner party in Edinburgh.

John Ross lived in his grandfather's house in Rossville, Georgia, with his first wife, the full-blood Quatie, and their five children. Neither spouse spoke the other's language.

Left: Of Scottish descent, the Creek warrior William McIntosh tried to bribe the Cherokee leadership into selling Cherokee land for a pittance. Outraged Creeks stabbed him to death, and then had him buried naked to carry his shame into the next world. *Center:* An eccentric loner, Sequoyah invented a written version of Cherokee in 1821 that was so easy to learn that it transformed the nation in weeks. *Right:* Chief George Lowrey wears the traditional silver earrings and nose ring—and, around his neck, a presidential medallion given to Indian leaders as a symbol of permanent American friendship, but which in reality would prove all too transitory.

Written in English and in Cherokee, the *Cherokee Phoenix* was distributed throughout the eastern United States and to several cities overseas. It was read by the explorer Baron Alexander von Humboldt in Berlin.

This classical sculpture of the dying Shawnee chief Tecumseh was done in 1856 by Ferdinand Pettrich, court sculptor to the Brazilian emperor Dom Pedro II, who saw tragic grandeur in Tecumseh's unfulfilled dream of a confederated Indian nation.

Left: The famous Supreme Court chief justice John Marshall affirmed the Cherokee Nation's status as an independent sovereign state in 1832. But President Andrew Jackson refused to enforce the decision, freeing land-hungry Georgians to devour the Cherokee tribal lands. *Right:* Cruelly imprisoned by the Georgia governor, the missionary Samuel Worcester became the subject of an epic legal battle over the Cherokee Nation's constitutional status. Photographed in his early twenties, he looks utterly unprepared for his fate.

Two Ridge children along with their cousin Elias Boudinot attended this missionary school founded by the Yale graduate Cyrus Kingsbury. Intended to turn the Cherokee into educated Christians, the teaching was done by the "Lancastrian method," the quicker students like the Ridges and Boudinot teaching the slower ones.

Left: John Ridge had difficulty walking from scrofula, a scourge of the Cherokee, but he rose to become one of the most erudite and eloquent men in the Cherokee Nation. As this Charles Bird King portrait suggests, he strived for cultivation in dress, too. *Center*: Buck Watie took the name of the former president of the Continental Congress to become Elias Boudinot. He edited the *Cherokee Phoenix*, translated the Bible into Cherokee, and became a leader of the Ridge Party. *Right*: When the high-born Harriet Gold fell in love with Elias Boudinot, her outraged brother Stephen burned her likeness in effigy. She married Boudinot anyway and moved back with him to New Echota. There, she bore him three children before dying at thirty-one.

Left: Major Ridge wore a mask from the forest Buffalo Dance to scare off some Georgian homesteaders who had encroached on Cherokee territory. *Right:* This 1858 Thomas Sully portrait of Andrew Jackson suggests a more benign personality than the one the Cherokee saw in a man who was hell-bent on driving them out of their homes.

Left: A career soldier, General Winfield Scott was charged with removing the Cherokee by force. He displays here a characteristic note of indignant superiority. *Right:* A modern reconstruction of the Cherokee supreme court building that had been destroyed after removal. It was a feature of the 1827 Cherokee Constitution—crafted by John Ross and Major Ridge and modeled on the American one—that did much to establish the Cherokee reputation as the most "civilized" tribe in America.

Starting with George Washington, the Cherokee saluted the American president as their Great Father. This cartoon reveals the infantilizing aspects of the relationship.

Negotiated by just twenty Cherokee leaders, the controversial New Echota Treaty sold all the eastern lands of the Cherokee Nation to the United States for $5 million. Major Ridge signed his name with an *X*.

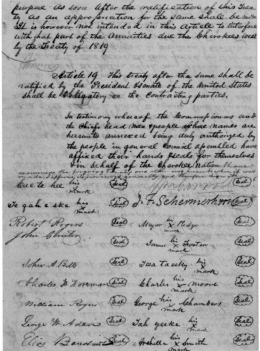

with the names of the Georgians keen to take Cherokee property for an $18 entrance fee and take on the job of removing its owners by force if necessary. The lucky winners were termed "fortunate drawers." When the drum started to whirl on October 22, 1832, the world of the Georgia Cherokee would be reduced to a big batch of chits to be plucked out, one by one, before a jostling crowd of greedy onlookers, and awarded to individual Georgians who yelped with joy at their luck.

It took some time for the truth about the Georgia Land Lottery to reach the Cherokee, and to sink in. The first public notice in the nation was a brief announcement in the *Phoenix*, almost three weeks later, on November 11.

> Our papers from Georgia bring us accounts of the operations of the lottery at Milledgeville, and the drawing of the lands, and gold mines of the Cherokee Nation . . . the magnitude of this atrocity on our property has created feelings of astonishment.

By then, the fortunate drawers had already started to fan out into the nation to lay claim to their property. One of the first parcels to be seized was Spring Place, the Moravian missionary school founded by the Gambolds. It was run now by the Reverend H. G. Clauder, who had been struggling for two years to convert Major Ridge—a plum for any missionary—but without success. It was Christmas Eve at the mission after a warm fall that left the roses in the garden still blooming when Brother Clauder, busy with a sermon in his study, was interrupted by an insistent knock at the door. In moments, several strangers, all white men, crowded in before him. "I represent the fortunate drawer of this place," one of the men declared. "He has given me power of attorney. You will pay your rent to me."

Word of the lottery had not reached Brother Clauder, and he was flabbergasted. Fortunate drawer? Rent? Surely there was some mistake. This was Spring Place, owned by the Moravian missionaries for the past thirty-one years.

No, the man replied, looking about. This land belonged to a Georgian now. But he might be glad to rent it out to Brother Clauder for $150 a year.

Pay rent for the Moravians' own mission? Even for a Christian required to be hospitable to strangers, this was too much. He told the men he was grateful for the information, but he'd have to see about such a request. With that, he ushered them out and bolted the door behind them. He dashed off an appeal to Governor Lumpkin himself, demanding an explanation. He'd received no reply by New Year's Eve when a covered wagon arrived in the drive by the herb garden. It was driven by the fortunate drawer himself, Abner E. Holliday, and was bearing his furniture. Brother Clauder refused to unbolt the door for him, and hoped to wait the man out. But in the morning, a posse of eighteen well-armed men galloped in, burst open the door, and forced Clauder and his family into two rooms upstairs while they stripped the rest of the house bare, replacing the churchly furnishings with Holliday's possessions. He converted the missionary house into a rollicking tavern and used the chapel as a courthouse to handle the other dispossessions in the area.

Brother Clauder was not alone in his misery. Hundreds of Georgians flooded in to seize their property in those first days, and thousands more would follow. John Ridge's house, built by his own hands, became merely the dwelling on No. 67 of the 23rd Division of the 3rd Section, which now belonged to a certain Griffin Mathis. Major Ridge's house—the finest in the nation, surely—was No. 196 of the same division. It was drawn by Rachel Ferguson, said to be a Revolutionary War widow. Their names were just two on what would ultimately be a seemingly endless roll that, when officially published by Harper and Brothers of New York as the *Georgia Land Lottery*, ran more than six hundred pages, all the names of the fortunate drawers in long, neutral columns, like an address book, without any reference to the original owners. It was a triumph of statistics, a lesson in the cold precision of numbers, a vanquishing of sentiment.

Because the two Ridges, and Boudinot, too, were considered by Governor Lumpkin to favor a general removal, the three men were allowed to remain with their families on their properties for now. Lumpkin portrayed this as the personal kindness of a good-hearted governor, but politically it just added to the Ridges' troubles. For their dispossessed neighbors were not pleased to see that an exception was made for that uppity family. Their displeasure worsened when Lumpkin placed a protective armed guard around the Ridge properties, making the Ridges into the obvious pets of a detested governor, and traitors to their people.

Nothing held the Georgians out. They flooded in, by one account, "single and in companies . . . in search of the splendid lots which the rolling wheel had pictured to their imaginations. Ho, sir! Where is the nearest line to this place, what district, number, corner, lot station, etc., and the impertinent questions forced upon us. When we see the palefaces again they are closely viewing the marked trees and carved posts."

Meanwhile, Samuel Worcester remained in prison, agonized about what to do. Since Georgia refused to follow the Supreme Court ruling, he would have to beg Governor Lumpkin for clemency to gain his freedom. Otherwise he would continue to rot in prison. Abolitionists wanted him to remain there as a symbol of defiance, but other Northerners wanted him free to reduce secessionist pressures on the union, and Southerners had always been sick of him. By now Elizur Butler had grown so enfeebled by his imprisonment that he left the matter to Worcester to decide.

After months of letters to the American Board beseeching it for guidance, Worcester finally received a reply on January 7 of the new year, 1833. Preserve the union and give up your case. Worcester agreed, informed Wirt of his decision, and then he and Butler wrote to Governor Lumpkin to ask for a pardon, saying they did so out of concern for "our beloved country." Lumpkin found this insufficiently obsequious, as it made no appeal "to the justice and magnanimity of the state," meaning to himself. The two refused to concede that Lumpkin offered "justice" but reluctantly acknowledged "magnanimity." That was enough. On January 14, 1833, after having confined the two men for sixteen months, Lumpkin let them go.

As they returned to New Echota, the worn-out missionaries were stunned by the ruins they saw all around them. The rampant seizures of the land and homes of the Cherokee, the ragged drifters dragging themselves down the road or milling aimlessly about the fields—these were distressing enough. But the public drunkenness was worse. They never could have imagined that the Cherokee would respond to such adversity by numbing themselves to it, staggering about, whiskey bottles in hand. The liquor was pressed on them by Georgian shopkeepers, who professed sympathy even as they extracted payment. The whiskey led to dissolution, disorder, and mayhem that left corpses unburied where they fell. Worcester recorded that a Cherokee was knifed, or shot, or bludgeoned to death every few days, and no one seemed to notice.

Worcester was overjoyed to return to the Boudinots, although he was distressed to find the ex-editor a dangerously thin and wan version of his former hale self. Boudinot was one of the few who welcomed him back. Elsewhere, when Worcester's old parishioners saw him, they did not rush to greet him as he had hoped, but pulled away, their eyes cast down, as if the very sight of him was noxious. Ross had turned the Cherokee against him by playing up Worcester's friendship with Elias Boudinot, that notorious treaty backer, and he'd started a rumor that the missionaries had won their freedom by taking an oath to Georgia after all. Some drunks even tried to kill his interpreter since they were convinced that Worcester was encouraging people to go to Arkansas. What did Worcester say to that? "I told them that there was nothing about Arkansas in the Bible, and that I came to deal with their souls." Leery of further emigration, the Cherokee vowed not to have anything further to do with any missionaries unless John Ross told them to. "Some said they would believe the Gospel if Mr. Ross would tell them to do it," Worcester reported, irritably. He was starting to detest John Ross.

That winter, the Georgians turned on the Cherokee with unspeakable malice. "The usual scenes which our afflicted people experience are dreadful," John Ridge declared. "They are robbed & whipped by the whites almost every day." As spring came on, the Cherokee who could hold off intruders from their grounds didn't dare plant their crops for fear the Georgians would reap the harvest in the fall. But if the Cherokee left their lands fallow, they'd risk starvation.

Would they stay or go? This became the central, dividing issue. To go was to fall in with the Ridges' Treaty Party; to stay was to ally with the Patriot Party of John Ross. It was the first divide in the nation since the Cherokee constitution, and it was probably as inevitable as the one that had split the United States into the opposing camps of Federalists and Republicans. But this fight wasn't just ideological. It was existential. It could not have been more profound, or irreconcilable. Stay or go left no room for compromise. No words from John Ross or any of the Ridges could ever bridge the gap. They remained at opposite poles, with nothing in between.

8

"A CONSUMMATE ACT
OF TREACHERY"

What worked for Ross in the nation did not help him in Washington, however. There, he was losing support by the day. Ross's determination to stay received a blow when Senator Theodore Frelinghuysen, one of the Cherokees' staunchest supporters, came out in favor of removal, following the American Board. Pressing his advantage, Jackson finally came up with a price for the Cherokee land in the east that could not be dismissed out of hand. He offered Ross $2.5 million for all of the Cherokee Nation. Ross rejected the offer, claiming that Cherokee gold alone was worth far more. Back in the nation, Ross told everyone that he had heroically refused a bribe by Jackson of $50,000 to say yes, a highly dubious assertion that may have reflected his anxiety about whether he would be seen in the right.

Ross trumpeted a letter he'd received from Elbert Herring, the latest commissioner of Indian Affairs, promising to dispatch a military force "to the assailed part of your country for the purpose of expelling and keeping out

intruders." Ross hailed this as proof that he'd shamed the American government into repelling the Georgians after all. Skeptical of such a turnabout, John
Ridge told Ross he doubted that Jackson would ever "exercise those paternal
feelings which some of the undersigned have often heard him express toward
the Cherokees." Sure enough, Secretary of War Cass soon directed Herring to
send John Ridge a clarification declaring that "no change whatever [had]
taken place in the opinions of the President." The Cherokee must go. The only
question was the terms. That proved no victory for Ridge, however, because
Ross's forces made it look as if he'd betrayed the nation by pushing Cass to
take a hard line against the Cherokee. "A consummate act of treachery," Elijah
Hicks called that.

Anger rose and spread on both sides. A treaty man, John Fields, fell to
quarreling with an anti-treaty full-blood during a game of ball play. Quarreling had always been a standard feature of these games, when passions
were stirred by gambling and drink. But this was political, and the full-blood
shouted that Fields should die as a traitor until an ally of Fields shut the man
up with his fists. Thinking that this was the end of it, Fields and his friend went
on to George Lavender's store for a look at the merchandise. But some of the
full-blood's friends caught up to the two there, and one of them cracked a ball
stick down on the head of Fields's friend, while another slashed at Fields with
a long-bladed knife, cutting him "nearly to pieces." Major Ridge's black slave,
Peter, tried to yank the assailant off Fields, only to get struck with the knife
himself. Finally, Jackson's man, Major Currey, rushed in to bring order. But he
arrested only the anti-treaty contingent of full-bloods, leaving the hacked-up
Fields and his friend to go scot-free. This did not sit well with the Ross men.

Hearing about such fights, Jackson asked General R. G. Dunlap of Tennessee to do some reconnaissance in the nation, and Dunlap reported what
everyone knew—there was mounting friction between the two parties. "Each
are catching at everything to weaken the other," Dunlap said, "and gain or
keep the ascendancy, for the furtherance of their ends."

John Ridge thought it might help if Jackson sent an exploratory party
west to see what Cherokee life there was actually like. All the talk of the problems out there made the prospect of removal even worse. In the meantime, he
begged General Dunlap to slow Currey down with regard to the emigrations,
which were draining away the Treaty Party's support, boat by boat. And he

pressed Ross to send to Washington a delegation that would be empowered to negotiate a genuine removal treaty, so the nation could at least consider the terms. Ross refused, but he did agree to let a delegation go and seek "a favorable Resolution for the relief of our afflicted Nation." To Ridge, that was a pointless deception if Ross would not allow the delegation to discuss a sale of the eastern lands, which remained off-limits. To dissemble just created needless hostility—and further delay. The delegation never materialized, and any hope for negotiation disappeared with it.

And then the heavens let loose with a dazzling meteor shower that sent streaks of white zinging across the midnight sky, as if, the *Phoenix* declared, "the world was literally striped with fire." The sight left the nation agog, everyone staring up in wonder. As with Tecumseh's earthquake at New Madrid, such a cosmic display had to mean something. Despite its new religious bent, the *Phoenix* left the explanation to astronomers, but the full-bloods knew a dire portent when they saw one. It was a sickening of the sacred Sun-Fire. There was treachery in heaven, too.

Ignoring John Ridge's plea to wait, Currey assembled another batch of emigrants on the banks of the Hiwassee for the perilous journey west in February 1834. They waited in rough-hewn barracks that had been thrown up by government contractors, crammed in twelve to a cabin, with their livestock— a smattering of horses, cows, sheep, and goats—roaming about outside, further befouling what was already just a big patch of mud. In midwinter, it was chilly enough moving about during the day, but it was bitter at night, since the emigrants' flimsy bedrolls did little to keep out the icy cold that seeped through cracks in the barrack walls. Seeing all the hungry Indians there, white traders flooded in to sell them pies, cakes, fruits, cider, and, of course, barrels of whiskey for the long journey, at extortionate prices that often took the last of their money. Predictably, the Cherokee turned early to the whiskey, making the settlements into scenes of drunkenness, wild frolics, and fights. Woozy with alcohol and sweets, the Cherokee fell victim to outbreaks of measles, which spread especially to children, and their numbers dwindled daily; the dead were buried in the forest.

Eventually, six steamers came to take the Cherokee off. All of the vessels were turned into "floating doggeries"—arks, really—loaded up with livestock, plus packs stuffed with meager possessions like a teapot, a few shirts, and a pair of moccasins, topped off with a heap of cakes and pies. Down the Hiwassee they went, a plume of stinking steamer smoke trailing behind, to the Tennessee, and then over the raging rapids of Muscle Shoals, stopping only to bury yet more Cherokee claimed by disease. A keelboat bearing sixty-seven Cherokee overturned on the Tennessee, dumping all of them overboard and sinking all their belongings. The passengers were rescued, but their extra weight made the remaining boats sag lower into the water. One Cherokee woman, Anna Reynolds, was pitched into the river when she lost her balance cooking some pork over a small fire on the afterdeck. She was never seen again.

Late leaving, the heavy boats moved slowly down the freezing water, and it took them well over a month to reach the Arkansas. A lack of snow and of rain had lowered the river alarmingly, and in early April, the boats had to be beached before they ran aground. Then cholera struck, bringing down the émigrés' sole doctor. The Cherokee scattered into the woods to limit the spread of the disease. The mixed-bloods, and the few whites who came along with them, tended toward loud grieving as family members took sick and died. The full-bloods were more stoic, quietly burying their dead while tending to the living. "The grief of the whites in my party," wrote Lieutenant Harris, the put-upon commander of the expedition, "is louder and more distressing, yet less touching than the untold sorrow of the poor Indians."

The cholera crisis had passed by the end of the month, and Harris was able to summon fourteen wagons to carry the sick on to Fort Smith, the standard terminus of the western-bound. The rest trudged along beside, many of them barefoot. They had to leave behind everything they couldn't carry on their backs, reducing their property to bare essentials like blankets and cooking pots. They finally reached their new country on May 8, but the sickness came with them, and half the survivors perished within a year.

The *Phoenix*, which was friendly to Ross, made much of the tale of the ill-fated doggeries. John Ridge, however, played it as a triumph of Cherokee will, as he told the American Board that, while the Cherokee had suffered some discomforts along the way, cholera included, they were greeted warmly by the western band and soon settled happily into their new lives. An émigré, William Bolling, wrote home the grim truth that the emigrants were everywhere being struck down by plagues and agues. "You can go to no place hardly but what you see tolerably large graveyards," he wrote, adding a plea for the federal agents to come through with the promised stipends for the trip. "If the government keeps payment back much longer we shall have no use for it, for the people generally are dying very fast."

Angered by the *Phoenix*'s skeptical coverage, Georgia officials arrested Elijah Hicks. He was able to scrounge the $1,000 bond for his release, and he returned to his post, where he wrote a scathing article about the threats employed by emigration agents to force Cherokee to leave. To him, the agents were like wild pigs foraging among the crops. "It is our desire that these pests shall be withdrawn," he declared.

In fact, not all the migrants were coerced into going. But even government officials like the ubiquitous Chester could see that these piecemeal departures were not helpful to the cause. Poorly planned and overcrowded, they were destined to failure. Only universal removal could possibly succeed. There would be safety in numbers.

By now, Ross had returned to Washington, where a western band of more contented settlers had sent their own delegation headed by William Hicks, the turncoat western principal chief. He made it clear that the western Cherokee were not just a rival faction, but a rival nation, splitting the Cherokee into three. Hicks hoped the three might unite to negotiate "a general arrangement or treaty" with the United States that would be good for everyone. It was a tall order anyway, and Ross immediately put a stop to it. "In the face of Heaven and earth, before God and man, I most solemnly protest against any treaty being entered into with those of whom you say one is in progress so as to affect the rights and interests of the Cherokee Nation East of the Mississippi River." He then lodged a formal protest signed by 13,000 Cherokee. Although many of the signatures proved fictitious, the point was made. There would be no treaty.

One of the Cherokee westerners, remarkably, was John Ross's younger brother Andrew. John Ross had always scorned him as a ne'er-do-well and had spent years bailing him out of one financial jam or another. But Andrew hoped he might be able to make something of himself in the west, and he didn't mind sticking it to his brother to do it. Jackson could see that Andrew might be useful, and invited him in for some preliminary discussions. Andrew brought along Major Ridge, Elias Boudinot, and James Starr, another of the rising half-bloods who would emerge in the Treaty Party leadership.

"Kitchen chiefs," Elijah Hicks scoffed in the *Phoenix*, and he demanded that they be arrested before they left for Washington. But it was too late for that. For by then the Treaty Party delegation was already being received in the capital by none other than former governor Gilmer, now a senator from Georgia. He was especially impressed with Major Ridge, whom he had never met, now, at sixty-two, a stout, white-haired, imposing presence. "A very large man with features indicative of clear perceptions," Gilmer appraised him. "His conduct was dignified, and his whole demeanor distinguished for propriety. He was the noblest specimen I ever saw of an Indian uncrossed with the blood of whites." Actually, of course, Major Ridge's blood was not entirely uncrossed, but it says something that Gilmer would take him for pure Cherokee, and extol him for it.

Colonel McKenney sniffed out Major Ridge's presence in Washington and descended on him to sit for a portrait before it was too late. And so Charles Bird King set to canvas the sole image of the great Cherokee leader. It was the major as he wished to be seen: a prosperous plantation owner in a smart blue coat, buff vest, and gentlemanly high-collared shirt. The nation was on the verge of disaster, but, in every aspect of his demeanor, the major displayed not just indifference to the monstrous hazards rising up all around him, but active defiance; his thick, wavy hair, like silver flames, was brushed back to reveal his hard-fixed eyes, set jaw, and glistening forehead. It is an image of solidity, of resolution—a towering rock in a thrashing sea. Riveting in itself, it is striking in the context of virtually all the other Indian chiefs in what amounted to a gallery of savages, as so many showed themselves off in their traditional feathers, face paint, and gay colors, proudly wearing those presidential medallions that only confirmed their status as perpetual supplicants.

Unnerved by word of his brother's negotiations, Ross hurried to Washington with a few loyalists and did the unthinkable. He offered to sell some Cherokee land after all. But just some—and then no more. This cession would be the last, creating a glowing borderline that would be forever inviolable. In a meeting with Secretary of War Cass, Ross inquired, hypothetically: if the nation were to cede this final piece of land, could it win federal protection for the rest? No, said Cass bluntly. Even if the Cherokee accepted American citizenship? No again. Even if the Cherokee surrendered their sovereignty? Might they then be allowed to remain in the east?

Now, that was a possibility, Cass had to admit, but he could make no promises.

Indeed, it was a stunning offer—the end of the Cherokee as a separate people, the dream of presidents since Jefferson. To Cass, it was the perfect solution. But to John Ridge, it was an outrage. How could Ross assail him for trying for a treaty he'd submit to a popular referendum, while Ross privately proposed ending the very idea of the Cherokee all on his own?

Desperate for stature, heedless of its consequences for his brother, Andrew Ross was willing to sign almost any treaty the Americans put before him. But in their negotiations with Jackson, the Ridges and Boudinot were infinitely more thoughtful than either Ross. Having long since given up the possibility of staying east as Americans, they focused entirely on going west as Cherokee. But for that, they insisted on securing more western land than Jackson's negotiators were inclined to give; a higher price for the land they'd leave behind; and funds for schools, "the promotion of Christianity for our nation," and ample annuity payments. In this, they were joined by David Vann, grandson of the long-dead James, and the renegade John Walker Jr.

When no agreement was struck, Andrew Ross went ahead and cut his own deal with the United States to sell out and go west. The Ridges quickly disavowed it as "made at loose ends, and containing no national privileges" and it proved such a shabby document that even the Senate rejected it as unworkable.

So nothing came of all the fevered negotiations for either delegation. Stay or go—the matter was still unresolved. After three months of useless effort, John Ross must have felt weary and rather hopeless when he rode back alone from Washington. And it could not have improved his spirits to finally turn onto the drive that led to his imposing house at the head of the Coosa and discover that a fortunate drawer had taken it over. Not only that, he'd seized Ross's ferry and even rounded up the flocks of peacocks that had always paraded about the grounds, and cooked and eaten them. Ross's wife, Quatie, had fallen sick and was probably powerless to resist anyway. She and the children had been shunted into a pair of small rooms upstairs while the interlopers made free everywhere else.

To add to the indignity, the new owners said that, given the hour, they would allow Ross to stay the night with his family—but only for a fee, with a surcharge to stable his horse. Ross had no choice but to pay up. In the morning, he packed up his family and as many belongings as he could carry, stacked them on a borrowed wagon, and made his slow, miserable way across the border into Tennessee, where he'd be safe from these Georgian ruffians. There he found a simple, rather pathetic cabin near the campgrounds of Red Clay, the temporary Cherokee capital, and called it home.

The council met there on August 18, 1834, to talk over his brother Andrew's treaty. The attendees rose up as one to reject it, just as the U.S. Senate had—and added the fillip that they would treat any other treaty the same, for all time to come. Ross didn't mention his conversation with Cass about one last land sale.

Instead, the councillors' fury was directed at the Ridges' Treaty Party sellouts, several of whom, including Major Ridge and John Ridge, were in attendance. And much of it came from the hot-blooded Tom Foreman, an anti-treaty diehard Ross had appointed sheriff of the nation. After Andrew's treaty was shouted down, Foreman drew an angry gang around him to assail Major Ridge as a selfish elitist who'd drained the nation to deck himself out in "good clothes," and all that that implied. A traitor. And that went for the other Ridges, and all their pro-treaty partisans, too. "These men," Foreman declared, "might as well carry a poisoned cup to your mouths and say, 'drink this and I will give you so much money'! or, 'let me give you money to allow me to kill you.' "

At that, the crowd erupted in scorn, and all eyes swiveled to Major Ridge, who listened intently, his face tightening. Then Foreman heaped it on, claiming that Ridge traveled about the country urging people to "love their land, and in his earnestness stamped the ground." Like Tecumseh, he meant. And what was the result? "The ground was yet sunk where he stamped and now he was talking another way."

At that, one of the full-bloods, Parch Corn, screamed, "Let's kill them!"

Appalled, John Ridge stood up for his father and shouted out that he had done nothing but serve his country loyally at every turn, from taking on the rampaging Sevier to battling the Creeks to trying to save his people now. He cared only for the nation. "He saw that it was on the precipice of ruin, ready to tumble down," the son declared. "He told [the people] of their danger. Did he tell the truth or not?" He added: "If a man saw a cloud charged with rain, thunder and storm . . . & urged the people to take care . . . is that man to be hated . . . or respected?"

Hated, it seemed, from the angry noises of the crowd.

Then the mighty Major Ridge himself rose to speak in his own defense. Despite the viciousness of the charges, he replied with firm, calm, unyielding dignity. He began by saying he was not in this fight for any personal glory. He "had not the vanity to hope for honors in his declining years," John Ridge later summarized. "His sun of existence was going down. It was low. He had only a short time to live." Now, when he saw the future, he felt only melancholy that the great Cherokee experiment had come to this. "It may be that Foreman has better expectations & that he should in slandering men establish his fame among you," the major declared. "But I have no expectation that he will enjoy it long, for we have no government. It is entirely suppressed." Then his voice swelled as he summoned the plight the Cherokee now found themselves in. "Where are your laws! The seats of your judges are overturned. When I look upon you all, I hear you laugh at me. When harsh words are uttered by men who know better . . . I feel on your account oppressed with sorrow. I mourn over your calamity."

But to Foreman, these were just pretty words. If these Treaty Party men didn't give in, he would have them all shot, the major included.

Then the *Phoenix*'s Elijah Hicks presented a petition signed by 144 Cherokee demanding that the two Ridges and David Vann be impeached and removed from their posts in the council for "maintaining opinions and a policy to terminate the existence of the Cherokee community on the lands of [their] fathers." That number of Cherokee was hardly a fair sample, but, at Ross's urging, the council duly stripped the men of their offices and then demanded they be tried for treason, a hanging offense, at the full meeting at Red Clay in October. Until then, the Ridges were allowed to go free.

But peace hardly reigned. The staunch treaty man John Walker Jr. and his friend Dick Johnson had left Red Clay the day before and, unaware of the frenzy behind them, were idly cantering along Spring Place Road, which led to the old Moravian school, now a Georgia courthouse. They'd just passed quiet Muskrat Springs, the two of them chatting, when a rifle shot rang out and Walker toppled off his horse, a bullet in his back. As he fell, Johnson saw Tom Foreman's brother James and his half brother Anderson Springston race off, rifles in hand.

Walker could barely move, but Johnson got him back onto his horse. Despite his agony, Walker somehow stayed upright in the saddle to get home, where he collapsed into bed. The bullet had passed clean through him, miraculously sparing any vital organs, but the bleeding could not be stanched, and it seemed that all his lifeblood was draining out of him. His closest friends gathered around him in a grim deathwatch; others ringed the cabin to protect him from anyone coming to finish him off.

His father, John Walker Sr., accused John Ross—never a friend—of the shooting and threatened to kill him in vengeance. At that, Ross's supporters ringed his little cabin in Red Clay, and some thought they spotted the senior Walker skulking about the trees, but no shots rang out from the shadows. Ross himself had remained at the Red Clay campgrounds a few miles distant, finishing up business. It wasn't until he came home a day or two later that he learned of the attack on the younger Walker, or so he claimed. He left the house immediately, and hid himself so well that Elijah Hicks was sure he'd been murdered and spent some time hunting for Ross's corpse in the woods.

As for the two Ridges, their supporters banded to them, too, to make a military escort as they took a more circuitous route home. There, the Georgia guard would protect the two leaders in whom Governor Lumpkin was so invested.

It seemed that everyone in the nation was on edge. No one was safe. "John Ross is under serious apprehension for his life," John Ridge reported. "And as for us we know we are in danger."

John Walker Jr. lasted three agonizing weeks before he finally bled to death. Hearing the bitter news at the Hermitage, his Tennessee home, Jackson was furious. Slashing at a sheet of pea-green stationary, he ordered the Indian agent Ben Currey to protect the Ridges at all costs. "The Government of the U.S. has provided them protection," he wrote. "*It will perform its obligations to a tittle.*" He made no such provision for Ross. He told Currey to let

Ross know that he held "Ross and his council . . . answerable for every murder committed on the emigrating party." Currey soon arrested Foreman and
Springston for the crime. The Ross Party raised a fund for the men's defense,
which only confirmed Jackson's suspicions. But Ross didn't care anymore how
things looked.

Because the Cherokee laws had been suspended by Georgia, legal proceedings dragged on for a year as lawyers wrangled over jurisdiction issues.
Then a "silver key"—outright bribery—freed the two men. No one doubted
their guilt; Foreman and Springston themselves never claimed innocence.
While the crime was obviously political, it probably had a personal angle,
too. One winter a decade before, Walker as a local constable had broken up
a whiskey-smuggling operation Foreman ran on the Conasauga River from
Tennessee across to Georgia. Walker had stormed the flatboat Foreman had
deployed, seized $1,000 worth of illegal liquor, then smacked Foreman upside
the head with pistol and pitched him into the icy water.

As for the Ridges, Ross never did bring them to trial, leaving the treason
charges neither proved nor dispelled. But the two men knew better than to
try to reclaim their positions on the national council. Instead, they created a
council all of their own, one that amounted to a rival government in opposition to Ross's. It was presided over by John Ridge as its principal chief, with
Elias Boudinot and others as chief associates. The nation was officially ripped
in two.

The first meeting of the new treaty council was at Running Waters on
November 27, 1834. It attracted nearly 100 supporters, enough to empower
a delegation to go to Congress at the beginning of the year to secure a proper
removal treaty at last. Headed by John Ridge, it left two months later in a
fiercely cold January—a "Lapland winter," the missionaries called it—that
seemed to encase the entire nation in ice. Not even the hardiest Cherokee
ventured into the hills to hunt, and children were kept home from school to
shiver by the fire. But John Ridge wrapped himself in blankets and set out
alone from Running Waters through wastes of snow to Washington.

From his home on the Coosa, John Ross did the same, not wanting John
Ridge to have the only word.

The two men kept their distance from each other in Washington. Jackson
agreed to meet with Ross, but only for the sake of appearance. He no longer

had any use for this principal chief if he had another who was more amenable, a prejudice confirmed when Ross arrived in his office with a long list of grievances. Jackson would talk only about removal with Ross, nothing else. But removal was not a subject that Ross cared to discuss.

To Jackson, John Ridge was the far more attractive character. Even if he was the leader only of his own party, and not of the nation, Jackson was glad to hear him out. Ridge was only too happy to be received by a man he still regarded, despite everything, as a friend to the Cherokee and to himself.

But first, Ridge would make an appeal to Congress, and for this he had brought all his words with him, evoking the history of Cherokee suffering in images that not only moved sympathizers like Edward Everett and Theodore Frelinghuysen but won a remarkable outpouring from the usually reticent Henry Clay, who declared that "it is impossible to conceive of a community more miserable, more wretched. Even the lot of the African slave is preferable." After all, a slave owner tries to preserve his property, as Clay well knew as a slaveholder himself. "What mortal will care for, [or] protect the suffering injured Indian, shut out from the family of man?" he asked.

Everyone in Washington, it seemed, was in love with this learned, eloquent John Ridge of the Treaty Party, who could not have been more alluring if he had come bearing diamonds for the ladies and cash for the men. To them, as to Jackson, John Ridge was offering to find a permanent solution to the Cherokee problem. All that was left, it seemed, was to find the terms. For that, Jackson came up with an unlikely negotiator—the long-bearded Reverend John F. Schermerhorn. A former missionary, he'd been enlisted by Jackson in 1832 as an Indian commissioner to oversee the Cherokee removal, in which office he'd acquired a deed of dubious legality to 400,000 acres of Virginia. Schermerhorn was a Jackson man, eager to serve, and to harvest any proceeds. Whatever reputation for piety he once enjoyed, it was long gone now, and he was admired in Washington only as a snake might be, for a slithery kind of flexibility. "Crafty and subtle," went one account, like the "wily prelates" of Rome. That was perfect for Jackson. He wanted a price for the Cherokee departure, and Schermerhorn would set it. For that, he was directed to deal with Ridge and Boudinot alone, Ross be damned.

And then it was done, just by the three of them, over a table. For all the eastern lands of the nation: $4.5 million.

When word of that got back to Ross across town, he demanded $20 million instead. To Jackson, such an exorbitant price was just another delaying tactic. He decried it as a "filibuster" and refused to talk further. But delay was Ross's only hope. He offered to let the Senate set the price, hoping that this great body would move at its usual elephantine pace. But the Senate reported back just a month later with an even $5 million.

Although he had pledged to abide by the Senate's decision, Ross dismissed that figure as preposterously low. He'd let the Cherokee people decide the terms, as that would surely take an eternity, and he would be able to control the outcome.

Jackson was aware that time was passing, and he'd had it with Ross. He directed Schermerhorn to talk only to John Ridge's Treaty Party, ignoring Ross's opinion, to round out the deal. Afraid for their lives, the Ridges were not inclined to hold out. Along with a dozen members of his Treaty Party, John Ridge met with Schermerhorn in New Echota over candlelight in his cousin Boudinot's log home to set the final terms. They followed the broad outlines that Chester had brought back from Secretary of War Cass two years before: Putting aside the Senate offer, the United States would give the Indians the agreed-upon $4.5 million for all of their lands in the east, and provide them a new home on 13 million acres of the Indian Territory of the west, past the Arkansas River, roughly equal to their eastern territory. The government would cover the value of improvements to individual proper ties; pay the Cherokees' travel expenses, including a stipend to tide them over on arrival; reimburse them for Georgian spoliations; and dispense the annuities individually. All of the terms, however, were subject to a vote by all the Cherokee. John Ridge was enthusiastic as he described the deal to his father back home:

> It is very liberal in its terms—an equal measure is given to all. The poor Indian enjoys the same rights as the rich [Indian]—there is no distinction. We are allowed to enjoy our own laws in the west. Subsistence for one, $25 for each soul for transportation, fair valuation, fair ferries & Improvements, $150 for each individual, more than forty thousand dollars perpetual annuity in the west, & a large sum of money to pay for the losses of the Cherokees against the white people. In fact—we get four millions & half

in money to meet all expenses & a large addition in land to that already possessed by our brethren in the west.

One can almost hear his relief at having a solution in hand. But, in truth, the solution remained almost as remote as ever. For ratification could come only from a people in thrall to John Ross, who was not about to release them.

Ross must have gotten the message, too, for he embarked on an unexpected gambit. In Washington, he'd become acquainted with the Prussian chargé d'affaires, Baron Friedrich Ludwig von Roenne, who introduced Ross to his Mexican equivalent, J. M. del Castilla y Lanzas. To Castilla, Ross made an unlikely request. Might Ross be allowed "to explore some of the provinces of Mexico . . . for settling a Colony within its sovereign jurisdiction"? It was an outlandish question, but Ross met Castilla in Philadelphia to show him the Cherokee constitution and other documents indicating that, whatever Castilla might have thought, the Cherokee Nation was a competent, modern state worthy of Mexico's respect. Nothing came of the overture, but it demonstrated that, despite Ross's unrelenting public opposition to removal, secretly he recognized its necessity. But he would do it his way, not the Ridges'.

9

SPECTERS IN THE SHADOWS

In April 1835, John Ridge returned from Washington with a load of presents—books for his oldest son, John Rollin, a clever boy of eight; clothes for his wife, Sarah; and books for the puritanical teacher Miss Sophia Sawyer, who'd moved her religious classes to Running Waters after Spring Place was seized by the Georgian squatter. She'd set up shop in the Ridges' front parlor, and the Ridge family put her up along with some of the schoolchildren who'd come from far away. Harriet Boudinot joined in to help with singing lessons, making Sawyer's efforts very much a family affair. Steady and industrious, if sometimes harsh in her judgments, Sawyer had grown so attached to the Cherokee, and particularly to the Ridges, that she planned to accompany them to the Indian Territory, if it came to that.

John Ridge termed her "a lady of fine feelings and susceptibility of mind," which suggests some mixed feelings, but he considered her essential if he was to win over the Cherokee. As it was, anti-treaty full-bloods were pulling their children from the school lest they be contaminated by the Ridges' pro-treaty atmosphere. The ones who remained could not help feeling the anxieties of a house that might at any moment be overrun by enemies wielding rifles or tomahawks. As it was, dozens of full-bloods had drifted through the trees at Running Waters to sit motionless in the tall grass on the edge of the field, wrapped in blankets that left slits for their eyes to gaze out eerily at the Ridge house.

John Ridge steeled himself to face such threats, but his wife, Sarah, did not have his constitution and was consumed with fear. Sophia Sawyer greeted these specters with indignation that anyone would deliberately spook small children, who sometimes fell into fits of tears when these motionless Indians hovered in the distance. To John Ridge's irritation, there were too many of these still, silent, haunting figures to fight off. So they remained there like so many of the Cherokee, beyond his reach.

Ridge had also brought back with him from Washington the Reverend John Schermerhorn, bearing the treaty they'd negotiated, and a letter from Jackson urging the Cherokee to ratify it. When Ridge summoned a council of his government at Running Waters to talk it over, Ross drew the men of his own government to his ally George Lowrey's house. There, they ignored the treaty and denounced John Ridge and his adherents personally. Major Currey later reported that he'd heard Ross make statements "of a character inconsistent with the facts," calculated to create "unmerited prejudice against the Ridge delegation." In the record, Ross never explicitly advocated violence against the Ridge men, but he didn't have to be explicit. The Ridge men remembered what had happened to John Walker Jr.

John Ridge wanted to present Schermerhorn's treaty to the nation to be voted up or down; Ross wanted to bury it. "Ross has failed before the Senate, before the Secretary of War & before the President," Ridge wrote in some exasperation. "He tried hard to cheat you & his people, but he has been prevented. In a day or two he goes home no doubt to tell lies. But we will bring all his papers & the people shall see him as he is."

It was personal. John Ridge versus John Ross. The son was taking up where the aging father had left off. "The issue is now fairly made up between us," Ridge told his cousin Stand Watie, as he girded himself for what he imagined would be the final confrontation. It might have been the campaign for principal chief that never happened in 1832. An earnest young man of thirty-seven against a grizzled elder of fifty-one. While John Ridge was still the dazzler with darting eyes and suave manner, Ross was the aging Scotsman, dressed with an elder's formality, in a funereally dark jacket and vest, sometimes brightened with a pocket watch, the whole array often topped with a stovepipe hat of the sort that Lincoln would make famous. Perhaps intended to make him taller, it made him more hat than human to his detractors. Despite his infirmity, Ridge had a brightness, although it was dimming now as his anxieties mounted; Ross was more lumpen, his face creased with concern around the eyes and disapproval below. Well-educated and well-read, Ridge had a literary gift that made his sentences fly like hawks; Ross's pedestrian prose trudged on like overburdened soldiers. It was Ross's good luck that most of his followers could not understand his English; the linkster could always liven him up a little.

But if the loyalty that Ridge inspired ran deep, it also was narrow, and barely reached beyond the literate few who made up the true believers. Ross commanded thousands, but they commanded him, too, as he was obliged to conform to the unfounded hopes of the ill-informed. As the overture to Mexico revealed, he must have known that the official course he'd set would lead nowhere good. It may have been his own misfortune that Ross had not stood for election in 1832. Unsure of his public support, he may have overpromised for it, locking himself into an unreasonable position that, ultimately, he could defend only with violence. For his part, Ridge's erudition and his brilliance may have proved a hindrance that won him those few powerful allies at the cost of more humble followers. He imagined that he alone could see the peril, and this blinded him to the fact that his remedy had its perils, too. Ever since Cornwall, he'd felt persecuted, not unreasonably, and that gave a cold edge to his missionary self-righteousness. He needed patience and sympathy to warm the people to an unwelcome message, but instead he pushed it on them, and when they resisted, he pushed it on them harder. He'd decide what was good for them, as he knew better. And he probably did know better. But that was not the way to win them.

In short, Ridge might have been the better seer, but Ross was the better politician. The Cherokee had to choose between them.

• • •

That May, Ridge called for a meeting later to unveil the treaty, and Colonel Currey thought he'd swell the turnout by joining to it a vote on his new plan for dispensing the federal annuity payments. That was bound to attract interest. Rather than award a lump sum to the Ross government to distribute after it took its cut, he thought he might offer to give each Cherokee his share directly. Who wouldn't want that? If this bankrupted the Ross government, so much the better.

Despite these two appeals, however, scarcely a hundred people turned out for the meeting, and many of those were white Georgians curious to see how things stood. Ridge claimed that heavy rains had pushed back the Cherokees' spring planting and kept them home, but he had to have been alarmed by the lack of interest. He put off the vote until July.

Disturbed by the idea of the federal government tampering with the annuities, Ross summoned a meeting of his own at Red Clay to take his own vote on the distribution question, and on the idea of a treaty behind it. The Cherokee flocked in as they always did for Ross. He easily roused sentiment against the treaty, and he secured the backing for the customary handling of the federal payment, too. But when Ross rode to the federal agency to collect the money, Currey refused to hand it over until after the Ridge vote in July.

It was then that the devilish Reverend John Schermerhorn paid Ross a visit. In Ross's financial problems, he saw political opportunity. "I would deem myself extremely fortunate if I could in any way be the means of bringing together and to a general close by a treaty the unhappy difficulties existing between you and the United States," he declared, every word dripping with lubricant. But not at Red Clay, where Ross reigned supreme—at John Ridge's Running Waters, where the pro-treaty forces were entrenched. Not only would this be Ridge territory, but it would be in Georgia, where many chiefs were reluctant to go for fear of being arrested under Georgia law. To Schermerhorn, that was all to the good: the Georgians rarely troubled pro-treaty men. This posed a serious problem for Ross. If Ridge won the annuity vote, he could bankrupt Ross's government. And it wouldn't matter how few people turned out. Currey had made clear that so long as Ridge won a majority, there could be just ten people voting, or just one.

Ross agreed, but he would not come to Running Waters alone. He would send out runners to every hill and valley of the nation to draw out his people and drown Ridge in Cherokee. They'd kill off any thought of changing the annuity payments—and drive a stake into Ridge's precious treaty, too. That would clear the field for Ross to rule on both topics at *his* annual meeting in October.

John Ridge had to feel that grim forces were closing in all around him. The silent Cherokee in his field, all the Ross men everywhere. Ridge asked Governor Lumpkin to deliver the Georgia guard for his protection. The treaty was at stake, Ridge reminded him, if nothing else. It was "a treaty of great liberality," Ridge emphasized, "the result of our most solemn consideration," and sanctioned by Jackson, Congress, and the American people, too. And don't get him started on the methods of the Ross Party. "They are, by means of falsehoods, in the field, valley & mountain opposing the ratification of it." And what, he went on, do these so-called Patriots propose? Only "procrastination—to outlive Jackson's administration or to compel it to abandon the rights of the Indians into their own keeping and management." And to keep hold of the federal money. "Five millions of dollars, managed and disbursed by a few of the Halfbreed race & Georgia-Lawyers, would be a speculation which the Rothschilds of Europe would be glad to obtain."

No matter. Ridge added that Ross had ridden on horseback to Washington to void Schermerhorn's treaty, but he asked Lumpkin to ignore whatever happened there. Jackson had "ceased to recognize them as representative of the Cherokee tribe," Ridge declared, referring to the Patriots. In fact, as Ridge thought yet more of the silent full-bloods huddled in his fields, Governor Lumpkin should not just forget Ross, but *end* him. Wasn't Ross bent on eliminating Ridge? Let him face death himself. "The last hold & retreat of this unholy Indian aristocracy is the *banded outlaws* who are harbored by the Ross party for the purposes of intimidation or assassination. Richard the Third never had better instruments to promote tyranny." Then he turned to the evils of the broader opposition. "Have you not heard of the armed outlaws harbored by the Ross party . . . ? Here is a band, a well organized power against the lives of the friendly Indians, the lives of the whites, & their property which sets at defiance your constables & sheriffs & laughs at your Judges & Jurors. And to cap the climax of this league the ablest lawyers of your own state are retained to defend them."

To Ridge, the Ross men had taken over from the fortunate drawers as the enemies of the Cherokee. And he asked Lumpkin to deal with them accordingly. "Organize a guard of thirty men placed under the command of Col. Bishop to scour and range in their fastnesses & to search for them in their caves, and to suppress their secret meetings close to all-night dances where the leaders of the Ross party usually meet with them for consultation. . . . These outlaws are fearfully increasing in the chartered limits of the state." Kill them! "Break up this incubus or nightmare which sets so heavily upon the breasts of the ignorant Indians." In sum: "Dissipate the mists which now blind the eyes of some of our people. John Ross is unhorsed in Washington and you must unhorse him here."

It was a stunning reversal. If once Ridge had advocated nonviolence to appeal to the conscience of a nation—well, no more. He'd suffered enough. The pain had bred anger, and the anger would out. Blinded, he'd mistaken Jackson for a friend. He did the same with Lumpkin now. He was no longer the mastermind of the cruel dispossession of the Cherokee. That role had been taken by Ross. He'd use Lumpkin to strike at him. A foul bargain, to contract with his oppressor, but his rage demanded it now.

Lumpkin must have stared at his letter for some time, wondering. He did not want to be drawn into a blood feud between rival chiefs. But he couldn't let the men of the Ridge Party be slaughtered, either. He promised that he would "protect and defend them, in their persons and property, from the violence and outrage of their enemies." He told Colonel Bishop, commander of the Georgia guard, to be "vigilant and watchful" in protecting the Ridges. But protecting only. He would bring no violence to Ross or Ross's party. To do otherwise would only drag Georgia into a three-way war with two parties who'd evolved into rival nations that were bent on destroying each other.

A heavy rain was falling on July 18 when the Cherokee descended on Running Waters for the great convocation, and it would continue to fall, swamping the meadows, turning the loose red dirt to ankle-deep slop, and causing the trees to droop, their leaves slick with rainwater. The heavy clouds sank low over the mountains and darkened the broad valley that was normally bright with wildflowers. It seemed like a miracle when the Cherokee emerged from the shadowy woods on every side. Mostly, they came in clumps of a dozen or so, but sometimes there were far more, as whole villages emptied to send emissaries. Most of them were full-bloods, their colorful dress a sopping gray in the rain. Ross's full-bloods. Many had come by way of his house, where Ross extended a hand in greeting, and then they sat "Turk fashion," as it was termed, on the ground with their backs against trees, on logs, or atop the rail fence.

Speaking via linkster, Ross turned them against the treaty, saying better terms would come if they held off. Afterward, the men circled around the speaker, exclaiming in the Cherokee language Ross could not understand. Then an old man shouted out a farewell, and the men grabbed their packs and continued on to the council grounds.

The Ridges, father and son, tried to be welcoming. They put up as many Cherokee as they could in their two homes, covering their floors with sleeping Indians, as well as white men whom they charged a hefty $1.10 apiece since their own funds were so tight. The Indian agent Major Currey bunked with the Ridges, as did Schermerhorn. The Ridge sent word to John Ross that he was welcome to stay. It was important to keep up appearances of comity, but Ross preferred to sleep on the wet ground with his people.

The rain cleared off sometime after dawn, and, in the sparkling sunlight, the Ridges—and Ross, too—must have been astounded to see the throng that had gathered there during the night. Bands of Cherokee had kept coming and coming, swelling to a vast horde of more than 4,000, from the doddering old down to the freshest of newborns, by far the largest number of Cherokee ever assembled. "Some starving, some half clad, some armed, and scarcely any with provisions for more than one or two days," wrote Currey in some wonderment—and in some distress, surely, as he peered out. For they'd come for Ross, responding to the runners he'd sent throughout the nation. When Ross had sent word earlier to boycott the Ridges' previous gathering, they had stayed away. Now, when he'd asked everyone to come, they'd come, some trudging on foot for well more than a hundred miles. And they spread out now across the valley, clear to the far trees, where, to the Ridges peering out from the council building, they were just specks of festive colors that caught the sun.

Governor Lumpkin had delivered on his promise to allow the meeting, and to keep the Ridges safe. He'd sent a detachment of the Georgia guard, a few dozen men, well armed but no match for a swarm of Cherokee if they turned wrathful. So the guard kept its distance. To lighten the atmosphere, the guardsmen had brought along a small regimental band of fifes and drums that performed a spritely military tune in the morning. It wafted in the breeze and lent some discordant notes to an ancient Cherokee ceremony.

Officially, the meeting was intended solely to consider the annuities. Should they be handed over to the Ross government, or go to the people directly? But this was not just a matter of procedure. This was a referendum on Ross himself. Was he to be trusted with the federal money? Without it, his government would surely wither and die. With it, he could carry on indefinitely. But the treaty hung over this decision as the rain clouds had hung over the valley. A vote for giving the annuity directly to the people would end resistance to the treaty, for it would bring an end to Ross politically. That is why Ross shook the earth to bring the Cherokee in such vast numbers to Running Waters.

David Watie, Ridge's brother, opened with a Christian prayer; he was followed by an invocation of the Great Spirit by a native preacher. The vast congregation listened in respectful silence to both. Whatever the political divisions, the Cherokee people astonished the whites from Georgia and from Washington with their solemnity and forbearance. Hungry, hot, and exhausted from their long travels, they nonetheless were models of restraint.

Seeing the overwhelming numbers that had turned out for Ross across the valley, Currey tried to pry the faithful loose from their leader. He frankly told them that Ross and his men had lied to them, "counselled in the bushes," as he put it, and left them to "ruin."

When it was his turn, Ross replied with calm indignation. He was, he said, "not disposed to quarrel with any man for an honest expression of his opinion." His magnanimous tone had its effect on John Ridge, who asserted that he himself would never treat in "sinister motives," either. No, he had pressed for a treaty "from an honest conviction that it was the only way in which the integrity and political salvation of the Cherokee people could be preserved." How could John Ross quarrel with that? Yes, Ridge had withdrawn his support for Ross as principal chief, but only because Ross offered no plan for dealing with the reality that was settling in all around them. If he had a plan,

Ridge would be with him. But he did not, and until he did, Ridge would resist his leadership with all his might.

But as he was speaking, he noticed something ominous—Ross's men were moving the Cherokee back from the speaker's box, ten, twenty, fifty yards, far enough that, no matter how loudly Ridge bellowed, none but the scant few at the front could possibly hear him. If Ross was sincere in being open to all points of view, why, Ridge asked, were his followers "not permitted to hear"? And how could Ridge's backers now sway them?

Schermerhorn then rose to address the convention. Even if he could have been heard, he was in no position to persuade anyone. Just a few months into his tenure as Jackson's chief negotiator, he had shifted from deceitful to menacing, a onetime preacher now ignoring God's interests to brazenly promote his own. "The Devil's Horn," his many enemies now dubbed him—Satan's own agent, sent to the Cherokee to bring trouble. Oblivious to the loathing, Schermerhorn spoke now of the treaty, that other great issue before the nation. He reminded everyone that Jackson had sent him to obtain a treaty, and a treaty he would get. This could not have sat well with the attendees in hearing range, but he charged ahead to discuss arrangements for a full treaty convention later in the year as if that were as inevitable as the dawn. As for the treaty provisions he had already negotiated with Ridge, he would discuss them in detail in the morning.

Ross had no plans to let anyone hear a word about any treaty and told Schermerhorn that, regrettably, few Cherokee would be able to stay through the next morning, since most had come without provisions. Well then, Schermerhorn replied, he'd see to it that the attendees got all the food they needed at Lavender's store, courtesy of the United States government. Ross had no good reply. Schermerhorn would speak to them at nine a.m. sharp.

Before the meeting adjourned, however, the tall, gangly Archilla Smith, a rare full-blood in the Ridge alliance, stepped forward in his customary red leggings and bright tunic to request the vote on the proposition at hand—that the government's current offer of a $6,666.67 annuity be divided among the people, rather than given to the Ross government. John Ridge seconded the resolution, and Major Ridge added a vigorous speech of his own. It went well beyond the annuity issue to push the treaty as the nation's salvation. The oration was as lengthy as it was impassioned, although precious little of it could be heard by the crowd. The sun was setting as he finished, engulfing the Cherokee faithful in a soft darkness that seemed all too metaphorical. The vote on annuities would have to wait until tomorrow.

When dawn broke on the meeting, Ross was distressed to see that overnight Schermerhorn had erected a stand that stood like a scaffold a good ten feet off the ground right in front. As before, the enormous crowd was set well back from the council house, but Schermerhorn, and any pro-treaty speakers who followed, would more easily reach the bulk of the crowd. As Schermerhorn started to climb up to address the crowd at the appointed hour, nine, Ross grabbed his arm to stop him and demanded he not say a word about the treaty until after the vote. Schermerhorn shook him off. By then, Schermerhorn had come to see John Ross as Ross probably did him, as the devil himself.

From his high perch, Schermerhorn shouted out a sermon that promoted the treaty by extolling Jackson as the Cherokees' savior as well as his own. He himself found it meaningful that when he recently visited Jackson's Hermitage and his horse had died there, the president had "sent him on his way rejoicing on a better steed." He was offering the Cherokee the chance for no less. He urged them to "take warning from the fate of the tribes of the North and emigrate and live; not like them remain and rot." Accept the offer of $4.5 million. What choice did they have? "If you do not the bordering states will forthwith turn the screw tighter and tighter till you are ground to powder." Don't hope for anything better from the next president, either. "The measures of the present ruler of America will not change with his successor." Act now! "Do you complain of wrongs? Remove and you can retaliate. If the white man here oppresses you, there you can oppress him. If he sticks you here, you can stick him there." That's how Schermerhorn would do it.

He went on like that for more than three hours. Currey claimed the Cherokee listened with "great gravity and serious attention." But they were not moved. The vote on Archilla Smith's resolution to return the money to the people was taken one person at a time, out loud. It would take courage to defy Ross amid so many supporters. And just a paltry 114 were willing to buck him. More than 2,000 went the other way before the Ridges conceded the issue to avoid further humiliation. Afterward, they tried to dismiss the result as the foolishness of the ignorant: most Cherokee simply voted for Ross. But the result stood, regardless.

When Ross's supporter Edward Gunter offered a vote on the obvious alternative—to place the entire annuity in the Cherokee treasury—the Ridges had to go along, but they offered a canny amendment, requiring that none of the money be placed in the hands of a lawyer. That brought chuckles of appreciation; no one liked lawyers. When the motion was entertained, it gave the Ridges another chance to defend the treaty, this time by rendering the nation in "a most pathetic description of national distress and individual oppression," as Major Currey summarized their argument later. "If there were any who preferred to endure misery, and wed themselves to slavery," they were free to remain where they were. Otherwise, they should follow the Ridges west. As the two men spoke, the father in his deep Cherokee, the son in eloquent English, Currey saw the crowd closing in toward them "as if attracted by the power of magnetism to the stand, and when they could get no nearer they reached their heads forward in anxiety to hear the truth."

But they would never vote against Ross. When the Ridges were done, they withdrew the motion as hopeless and the Gunter amendment was duly voted upon. It passed overwhelmingly. The Ridges had gone up against John Ross and lost. It was his nation after all, not theirs. When the vote was complete, Lieutenant M. W. Bateman of the Cherokee agency formally delivered the annuity funds to Ross's exclusive control.

With that, the convention broke up, and most of the attendees melted back into the forest. But a number of them slipped off to nearby fields to engage in the ceremonial ball play that had long accompanied such tribal gatherings. Usually expressions of zest and ferocity, with gouged eyes and cracked bones to show for it, the games this time were oddly subdued, a little sad, almost as if both sides were resigned to losing. The Georgians sent women into the stands with whiskey to stir up trouble, but few of the spectators could even bring themselves to drink.

The overwhelming defeat left the treaty forces in a bind. How to bring Ross around? Schermerhorn was determined to get at least some discussion going, so he invited both sides to meet him at the Cherokee agency a week later, on July 29. The Ridges showed up with about two dozen of their supporters.

But—no Ross. In some desperation, the Ridges waited through the night, and into the next morning, when a lone horseman rode up bearing a message from Ross. The principal chief wished Schermerhorn and the Ridges to know that he had come down with a terrible case of diarrhea, and would not be able to attend. The Ridges had to have wondered about that. Diarrhea? What kind of an excuse was that? It seemed . . . dismissive somehow. Still, Ross offered to have his man George Lowrey arrange another conference for the two sides to meet and "promote the common good of the Cherokee." The Ridges were puzzled but amenable. They wrote out a note to convey their acceptance, and then, accompanied by their two dozen followers, decided to drop it off at Ross's cabin in person, since they'd pass by the place on their way home.

They found Ross settling down to breakfast with a hearty appetite, whatever the state of his digestion. Hailing the two Ridges, Ross gaily invited them to come in to join him, and to bring in their colleagues. He cheerfully provided feed for their horses, too. Perhaps it was the smashing victory, but Ross was in an unusually good mood. The Ridges didn't raise the matter of the conference until it was nearly time to go. John Ridge offered any day for the rest of the summer except August 24, which was reserved for the annual celebration of the Green Corn dance. Ross said he would get back to them about the date. The two sides parted warmly as if somehow, despite everything, order had been restored.

But Ross never did suggest a date, and the conference never took place, as the division between the two groups soon widened again. It wasn't the surrounding states that turned the screws; the Cherokee agent Currey did. He was determined to send the Cherokee west, if he had to do it himself. His favorite ploy was to get Cherokee so drunk they'd sign anything, and then abduct them, claiming that he was simply making sure they followed through on their obligations. Atahlah Anosta, a full-blood, was fairly addled when Currey persuaded him to sign the roll to leave. When the time came, he fled, so the guards grabbed his wife and children and hauled them away instead. It went worse for the ancient chief Sconatachee. When he failed to show up on the departure date he'd drunkenly agreed to, Currey came for him with a revolver and had him bound hand and foot and carried by wagon to the embarkation place "like a hog to market" by one account.

This did not sit well with the Cherokee, and, afraid to strike back at Currey, they took out their ire on the Treaty Party. A treaty partisan named Hammer was beaten to death. Then a Ross man surged from the crowd at a frolic, pulled a knife on another treaty backer, named Crow, and stabbed him in sixteen places. A former Cherokee judge, James Martin, loudly threatened the life of John Ridge, but later claimed that he was so drunk he didn't know what he was saying. "The Ross Party," John Ridge said later, "tried hard to counteract the growth of our party by murders—it is dreadful to reflect on the amount of blood which has been shed by the savages on those who have only exercised the right of opinion."

Despite the violence, the Ridges held their Green Corn dance at Running Waters on August 24 as scheduled. It was to be a festive affair, and the Ridges wanted to show they were still on top of things. Major Ridge, never shy about expenditures, went so far as to buy a splendid new coach from New York City to deliver his son John and John's wife Sarah to the ceremony in high style. It was an odd purchase for such a time. The coach had the very latest suspension system of "C" springs and leather "swings," with the driver's seat on top, not in front of the carriage as usual. When it was delivered, "Chief Ridge inspected the outfit, even shaking the wheels to be sure they would stand up," an observer recounted. On the day of the festival, the major helped Sarah, resplendent in "silks and feathers," into the carriage, while his son climbed in on the other side. Then he dismissed the Negro driver and climbed up to take the reins and drive his son and daughter-in-law to the dance himself. It made for quite an entrance. The Ridges were indeed in charge.

At Running Waters, hundreds swarmed in for four days of dancing and debauchery. The dancers had stuffed pebbles into the mussel shells they tied to their ankles, to emphasize each wild, prancing step as they cavorted about. But wild dancing was just a lure to draw everyone in to hear yet more impassioned treaty talk from the Ridges and Schermerhorn. When he discovered what was up, Ross staged his own dances until the Georgia guard rushed in to disband them, steering everyone back to the Ridges' amusement—and to their speeches. Seeing everyone, John Ridge felt a surge of confidence. "Our cause prospers," he wrote, "& I believe will result in the general cession of the Nation." He went on: "John Ross and his party will try to outlive the administration of Genl. Jackson if they are not forced into the treaty, & it now depends upon the treaty party to take a bold and decided stand."

Ridge believed that any delay was pointless. Jackson's second term was blessedly drawing to a close, but his successor, whether it was Henry Clay or Jackson's vice president Martin Van Buren or anyone else, would be bound by the same political forces that constrained Jackson. And removal was already under way, as the Georgians continued to flood in, and Cherokee continued to leave, whatever Ross hoped.

In the meantime, John Ridge would take more immediate measures to ensure the desired outcome. He dispatched his burly cousin Stand Watie to do to Ross what Ross had done to Boudinot: take away the power of the press. In the middle of September, Watie teamed up with Colonel Bishop of the Georgia guard—an unholy alliance, surely—to break into Elijah Hicks's house and make off with the *Phoenix*'s printing press and all its type. John Ridge insisted that the Ridges were only taking back what was theirs, as Boudinot had helped raise the money from Worcester for the initial purchase. By then, the *Phoenix* had long since succumbed to irrelevance and had published its last issue back in the summer of 1834.

It had the look of a last straw, but it wasn't. Neither side would let the other go. Schermerhorn and Currey were able to draw the two back together into a treaty conference in late October. They were hoping to peel off just enough support from Ross's National Party that, when it was joined to the Ridge faction, Schermerhorn could claim the two sides were at last involved in a joint effort. For a few moments, it looked as if even John Ross himself might go along. Cleverly, John Ridge offered to reject the treaty they'd negotiated that spring and start afresh and thus play to Ross's raging hatred of Schermerhorn—and of the émigré-snatching Currey, for that matter. Just as a politician, Ross had to smile at that. Schermerhorn's treaty was summarily rejected. Both sides scorned the onetime pastor, and it seemed that John Ridge was done battling with Ross. He needed peace. Schermerhorn claimed to take this rebuff with Christian grace. "The Lord is able to overrule all things for good," he intoned, even as he secretly hoped the surrounding states would pound these uppity Cherokee into submission.

In the new spirit of harmony, the council asked for a committee of twenty to go to Washington to work out a treaty that both sides could endorse. John Ridge and Elias Boudinot were two. But in the next few days, the Ridges came to fear that Ross held too much power; the two sides fell to the usual bickering; and the peace was over. John Ridge resigned, and then Boudinot followed, and, since there was no point of contact with Ross's government, there was nothing left for the Treaty Party but to deal with Schermerhorn by itself on behalf of the entire nation.

When Ross held his October council a day or two later at Red Clay, it was only a formality. He had all the support he needed for any position he wished to take. As the Indians streamed in from the woods, they approached Ross reverently, like pilgrims, from an endless double line, to shake his hand.

10

A FINAL RECKONING

A t Red Clay, "the woods echoed with the trampling of many feet: a long and orderly procession emerged from among the trees, the gorgeous autumnal tints of whose departing foliage seemed in sad harmony with the noble spirit now beaming in this departing race," went one elegiac account. "Most of the train was on foot. There were a few aged men, and some few women, on horseback."

This came from a startling new visitor, John Howard Payne, who would be the latest eastern interloper to meddle with the fate of the Cherokee. Of them all, Payne was the least likely. Just five two, he was a peppery little man with tousled hair, a Van Dyke beard, and a knowing, cosmopolitan air. He was best known for writing the lyrics of "Home, Sweet Home," first sung in his opera *Clari, or the Maid of Milan*, which had played in London and created a sensation. A combustible mixture of ambition and sentimentality, Payne had gone through many careers, a few poetic, most theatrical, and, when all had foundered, he'd taken flight to Europe to escape his creditors. Now he was back in the United States with a magazine he'd founded called *Jam Jehan Nima*, the "World from Inside a Bowl"—an unpromising title he'd taken from Old Persian—to be published in London for subscribers keen to hear about the wild life in the American outback. Payne would be the storyteller. By 1835, he'd roamed over several midwestern American states before he came to the southeastern Indians, who held him spellbound. Solemn, exotic, and remote, they made for a nearly spiritual discovery, as he told his sister in a long letter about his picaresque travels that made its way into the *Knoxville Register*:

> I cannot describe to you my feelings as I first found myself in the Indian county. We rode miles after miles in the native forest, neither habitation nor inhabitant to disturb the solitude and majesty of the wilderness. At length we met a native in his native land. He was galloping on horseback. His air was Oriental; he had a turban, a robe of fringed and gaudily-figured calico, scarlet leggings, and beaded belts and garters and pouch.

He continued on for pages with colorful journalistic details, such as Indian women who referred to whites as "sneezer-muches" for their constant snuffling, an American flag floating incongruously over the huts of a local settlement, and a pile of ashes from a century of ceremonial fires.

This tribe proved to be the Creeks, but they led him to the more illustrious Cherokee, whose tragic saga would overleap the pages of *Jam Jeham Nima*. This was a book, one that would make Payne's name as not just the playwright of this drama, but an actor, too.

A good journalist, he immediately paid calls on the leadership of both parties to develop inside sources. He started with the Ridges and Boudinots. Elias charmed him particularly, what with his lovely Connecticut wife, Harriet. "A very intelligent and amiable couple," Payne called them. But he would be more beholden to Ross, who, as principal chief, had inherited the sweeping historical records of his predecessor Charles Hicks that would be essential. "Mild, intelligent, and entirely unaffected," Payne deemed Ross. He left out useful. He attached himself to John Ross and never let go.

By a quirk, Payne had been a schoolmate of Schermerhorn's, and he paid him a call, too. The talk quickly turned to the prospects for Cherokee removal.

True to form, Schermerhorn grandly assured Payne he'd "have a treaty in a week." But Payne knew enough by then to discount that. When Schermerhorn sensed Payne's doubts, he combined them with his dangerous affinity to Ross, and concluded that Payne was "very busy meddling with Cherokee affairs" and had to be stopped.

Schermerhorn relayed his suspicions to Currey, who asked Governor Lumpkin to send out the Georgia guard to teach this intrusive easterner a lesson. Late on the night of November 7, when Payne and Ross were busy examining a mass of historical papers in Ross's little cabin outside Red Clay, Payne suddenly heard "a loud barking of dogs, then the quick tramp of galloping horses, then the march of many feet," and then dozens of armed men burst in the door, "their bayonets fixed." When a guardsman started poking into his luggage, Payne loudly protested.

"Hold your damn tongue," the guard shouted, and smacked Payne across the face.

The guard arrested both Payne and Ross, seized Ross's papers, and hustled the two of them out onto horses for a long ride through a pelting, wintry rainstorm to a makeshift jail in Spring Place—not the former mission, which had been made a courthouse, but in the basement of the once princely Vann mansion adjoining it. That, too, had been claimed by a Georgian. By Payne's later account, a decaying Cherokee corpse was left dangling from a noose over his and Ross's heads in their dungeon, just to get on their nerves, but Payne was not above inventing such melodramatic details to enhance a scene.

When John Ridge got word of the arrests, he rushed to Ross's aid, probably moved less by altruism than by calculation—the idea that Ross might now owe *him* something. He demanded to see Colonel Bishop, who'd recently joined with his cousin in purloining the *Phoenix* printing press. When Ridge asked about the charges against these two men, Bishop stammered that it was his information that Ross and Payne were abolitionist agents of presidential candidate Henry Clay, plotting to enlist Negro slaves to overthrow slavery across the South. Under other circumstances, Ridge might have laughed. Agents of Henry Clay? To do what, exactly? More likely, Jackson had simply decided that Ross and Payne were holding up his treaty, and that Payne was nosy, besides.

Eventually, Bishop conceded he had no legal reason to keep the principal chief in custody, especially if Ridge was going to make an issue of it. The deal was clinched when Ross promised Governor Lumpkin he'd back a joint treaty delegation to Washington after all. Inviting the two rivals to dinner, Bishop agreed to discharge Ross and give him back his papers. As for Payne, Bishop was convinced he was a French spy after all his time in Europe. But he let Payne go, too, a few days later.

That was not the end of it, though. John Ridge happened upon a copy of the *Knoxville Register* with Payne's dramatic account of his arrest. It commanded the Cherokee people never to leave their homeland, and accused the Treaty Party of having been "seduced" by the U.S. government to betray its own people. How dare he? Ridge fired off an angry letter to Ross, sure that he was behind Payne's article. "That address unfolds to me your views of policy diametrically opposed to mine [and those] of my friends, who will never consent to be citizens of the United States, or receive money to buy land in a foreign country." This last was a dig at Ross's bizarre overture to Mexico.

In Ridge's outrage, Schermerhorn saw opportunity. If the Cherokee could not take a treaty to Washington, or make one there, they could negotiate one with him in New Echota. And if both factions would not come, well, he would happily deal with just one—and assume that any absentees were in full agreement. By now, Ridge felt no obligation to be inclusive. If Ross's men were afraid to gather in Georgian New Echota, so much the better. Jackson and his secretary of war agreed that this was a fine idea. Enough was enough. Schermerhorn set the date for the New Echota enclave, December 22.

This was a drastic measure, without question. For just the Ridges and a handful of their people to decide the fate of the entire nation? Could so few possibly speak for so many? Was it enough to say, as the Ridges did, We know and you don't? Weren't they obliged to follow the will of the people in a democracy, wherever it might lead?

To John Ridge, the answers were clear. A crisis of this magnitude, with anxieties rising by the day, demanded a response, even if it came from just a few. He'd been leaning this way ever since that meeting with Cass. His father quickly followed suit, and then Boudinot came along, and Stand Watie, too. All the Treaty Party leaders were convinced that they must act for the good of the nation. There was no more time to lose. And they blamed Ross for their desperation. As an angry Boudinot wrote to Ross later, "It was not until that hope was eradicated by your continued evasive and non-commital policy, and the refusal of the Government to negociate with you, that [John Ridge] broke his connexion with you, to do the best the times and circumstances presented." What else could he do? "He stuck with you as long as there was a bare probability of your doing what the compromise called for, and he left you as soon as he was satisfied that bare probability did not exist."

Schermerhorn expressed no qualms whatsoever. This was right and necessary. God was on his side.

When Schermerhorn put out the call for backers of the Treaty Party to assemble in New Echota for a final reckoning, only a few hundred came, most of them the educated mixed-bloods who had always made up the bulk of that slender group, plus some white men who'd married in. John Ridge and Stand Watie were not among them, as they were in Washington to counter Ross's last entreaties to Jackson. Ross would not deign to dignify such a shabby proceeding. And he sent out runners across the nation to tell his followers to stay away, too.

The Treaty Party men arrived in a somber mood, fully aware of the hazards of the crisis. They all crowded into Boudinot's house, many of them smoking long pipes as they "plunged into deep mediation and reflection," as one visitor recalled. A thoughtful silence would be broken by an observation that was usually greeted with appreciative grunts before the room descended into silence again amid the clouds of pipe smoke. "If the affairs of Europe had been under settlement, they could not have been more deliberate."

The council itself took place in New Echota's once stately town house, which had fallen into sad disrepair after Ross moved the capital to the safety of Red Clay. As a representative of the federal government, charged with encouraging the emigration of the Cherokee, Schermerhorn should not by rights have been the one to lead the assembly, but he was long past observing such niceties. Inclined toward the brusque, he was, said one viewer, "in his usual style, only a little more so."

The treaty under discussion was based on the one that the Ridge Party had negotiated in Washington some months before, but with the Senate price of $5 million. Major Currey read it out, with a linkster to translate, and the terms were discussed at some length, but ultimately all were acceptable.

At one point, someone outside shouted "Fire!" A thick haze of smoke was rising off the roof of the council house. Preoccupied, perhaps, with the higher matter at hand, the Cherokee all filed out calmly. An attempt at arson by the outraged Ross men, most likely. The blaze was quickly extinguished, and everyone returned to his seat inside.

When Currey finished his reading, a meditative silence followed, and then, finally, Major Ridge rose to speak. Sensitive to the moment, his speech was grave, as he recounted once again how the nation could have come to a point where it could no longer stay where it had always been.

"I am one of the native sons of these wild woods," he began, evoking a past that they all knew but that Ross had never spoken of with such obvious feeling. By saying where he was from, Major Ridge was claiming the right to say where the nation should go. "I have hunted the deer and turkey here, more than fifty years. I have fought your battles, have defended your truth and honesty, and fair trading." He was, he said, a "friend of honest white men," but he inveighed against the Georgians' "grasping spirit," extending their laws onto Cherokee lands, to "harass our braves and make the children suffer and cry." Who were they to do such things? By what right? "We obtained the land from the living God above. They got their title from the British." But the facts were plain. "They are strong and we are weak. We are few, they are many."

And now the bitter truth about where such facts must lead: "We cannot remain here in safety and comfort." It would be a grievous parting to leave their forefathers' graves and to leave their homes. "But an unbending, iron necessity tells us we must leave them." It was all too clear: "There is but one path of safety, one road to future existence as a Nation. That path is open before you. Make a treaty of cession. Give up these lands and go over beyond the great Father of Waters."

Across the Mississippi, he meant, into the unknown. It was an ending, no question, but also a beginning. After a pause to let the listeners take that in, there was grunting of approval, and many men, older ones especially, came up to him, their eyes welling with tears, to grasp his hand and pledge to follow him to the new lands.

It fell to Elias Boudinot, the softest and kindest of the three leading Ridge men, to speak of the dangers they were in. Tom Foreman had killed John Walker Jr. and was still at large, as were all the Ross men who had scuttled this treaty at Red Clay. They were not about to permit it now. They may have stayed home, but the fire was a warning. "They will come again. I know I take my life in my hand, as our fathers have also done. We will make and sign this treaty. Our friend can then cross the great river, but Tom Foreman and his people will put us across the dread river of death!" That must have sent a chill through the crowd, but Boudinot kept right on. "We can die, but the great Cherokee Nation will be saved. They will not be annihilated; they can live. Oh, what is a man worth who will not dare to die for his people? Who is there here that would not perish, if this great nation may be saved?"

He was their Moses, their Christ. That was his message. As all the Treaty Party leaders were. They would die, hideously if need be, so the people could live in the promised land.

The next day, Major Ridge, Boudinot, and a few others were appointed to finalize the treaty that had been rejected so decisively at Red Clay. Christmas was coming, so the work would not be finished until everyone had recovered from the Christmas revelry.

It was Tuesday evening, December 29, 1835, when a committee of the eighteen men most dedicated to the cause convened with Schermerhorn in the parlor of Boudinot's house, by the now abandoned printing shop in what remained of New Echota. A fire was blazing in the hearth to push back the chill; the room was lit by flickering candles. Schermerhorn had the treaty read out one last time. Many of the attendees smoked their long pipes as they doubtless pondered the implications of the act they were now committing themselves to. In the name of the entire Cherokee Nation, these twenty men were selling their homeland to the United States for $5 million and leading everyone to unknown lands in the west. It was audacious and unprecedented, but to them, it was the only way.

When it was time to sign, John Gunter rose first. He was from Gunter's Landing on the Tennessee; his family had long been a fixture in the nation. He'd put forward that failed amendment at Running Waters. He dipped his pen in ink and signed his name boldly, with confidence. Then came Andrew Ross, in defiance of his brother. Then John A. Bell, an emerging leader from a tight family of pro-treaty men. Then Ezekiel West. Then Boudinot. All signed with a confident flourish. Major Ridge was one of the last. He could not help thinking of the blood law he'd pushed onto the books of the Cherokee Nation almost a decade before, the one promising death to any unauthorized individuals who sold the nation's land.

After Major Ridge had bent to affix his X, he rose to deliver words that would always follow him: "I have signed my death warrant."

The signed treaty was delivered to the full council in the morning. There, it was approved unanimously, and the council asked Major Ridge himself, as the most prominent man, to gather a small delegation to bear the document to Washington, where John Ridge and Stand Watie would be waiting. Ross was there as well, trying, futilely, to win over Jackson one last time. The other two Ridge men would add their signatures, and the major was instructed to try to gain Ross's, and, ideally, those of his supporters as well. But if they proved impossible—and no one held out much hope—he should deliver it directly to the president to present to the Senate for ratification.

The councillors gathered up the blankets they'd brought to New Echota and handed one to each of the delegates. The blankets were tokens of the faith they held for each other, reminders of the place they were from, but they were warming, too, and would be needed on a long journey in midwinter.

With that, Major Ridge led his men to Washington to complete the matter.

11

OUR STRENGTH IS
OUR REDEEMER

John Ridge and Stand Watie were already in Washington to add a hint of national unity to Ross's latest delegation to Jackson, but they ended up only subtracting from it, as usual. Nothing came of it, in any case. Unaware of the events in New Echota, Jackson had agreed to see Ross at eleven o'clock on January 7 but scarcely bothered even to pretend to listen to him, and the meeting was brief.

So things were at their usual impasse when Major Ridge arrived at the beginning of the next month, aching from age and ill health after a long, freezing ride. He'd brought the New Echota Treaty, its twelve pages somewhat rumpled, from his saddlebags, and handed it to his son and Watie at Mrs. Arguelles's boardinghouse. They must have known what it meant for the country, and for them. One can imagine the grave looks, the solemnity, as they leafed through the long document, written in a smooth, confident hand, with only a few cross-outs and last-minute insertions, with eighteen signatures at the bottom, many of them just X's. It's not known if the two men hesitated before they added their names to all the others, bringing the number of signers to an even twenty.

They took the signed treaty on to Ross at his hotel in hopes that he might sign it, too. But Ross angrily dismissed the document as a "forgery palmed off upon the world as a treaty by a knot of unauthorized individuals." If he was to sign any treaty, it would be one of his own devising. Ross bade the gentlemen take their pages away.

Afterward, Boudinot was disgusted that anyone could be so stubborn while the nation was being ransacked and its citizens were being flogged.

> In this state of things, utterly unable himself to consummate a treaty which he may think preferable, Mr. Ross is using his influence to defeat the only measure that can give relief to his suffering people. . . . He says he is doing the will of the people, and he holds their authority; they are opposed, and it is enough. The will of the people! The opposition of the people! This has been the cry for the last five years, until that people have become but a mere wreck of what they once were; all their institutions and improvements utterly destroyed; their energy enervated; their moral character debased, corrupted and ruined.

But Ross's inaction stopped nothing. When Jackson received the treaty from Major Ridge, he saw it as the answer to his prayers. It did not matter a jot whether The Ridge and the others spoke for the nation, or just for themselves. This was a treaty that would remove the Cherokee from the east. It would do. He forwarded it immediately to the Senate for urgent consideration.

Appalled, and incredulous at the speed of the action against him, Ross sent word to the second chief George Lowrey to call an emergency meeting of the council at Red Clay to repudiate this absurd initiative by twenty misguided citizens. Despite horrible weather and an outbreak of smallpox, 400 people attended. The council immediately put out a resolution declaring the treaty void, and runners fanned out across the nation to gather signatures to send to Washington in furious protest.

Incredibly, they gathered more than 16,000—more signatures than adult Cherokee, and most of them the easily falsified X's of a people who were still widely illiterate. Ross added the stack of pages to a rousing cry of indignation scripted by his eloquent new ally John Howard Payne. It carried weight with the liberal pro-Cherokee forces that had earlier backed the Treaty Party— Edward Everett, Theodore Frelinghuysen, and the rest. They turned away from the Ridges and the others now, much to their distress. Opinion everywhere was running against them. The frenzy reached Concord, Massachusetts, where Ralph Waldo Emerson vented his ire at Jackson for dealing with the perfidious Ridges who'd dared act against the Cherokee, all on their own.

> Such a dereliction of all faith and virtue, such a denial of justice, and such deafness to screams for mercy were never heard of in times of peace and in the dealings of a nation with its own allies and wards, since the earth was made. Sir, does this government think that the people of the United States are become savage and mad? From their minds are the sentiments of love and a good nature wiped clean out? The soul of man, the justice, the mercy that is that heart's heart in all men, from Maine to Georgia, does abhor this business.

Amid the clamor, three senators—Calhoun, Clay, and Webster—all assured Ross the treaty was done for. But they'd underestimated Jackson, who would not be denied. When the votes were counted that May, enough of the senators who'd so loudly voiced disapproval earlier had quietly shifted their position to acceptance, and Jackson prevailed by just one vote beyond the two-thirds needed.

And so, on May 23, 1836, the New Echota Treaty became the law of the United States—and this was one law that Andrew Jackson had every intention of enforcing. It was decided: all the Cherokee would be removed from the east, voluntarily if possible, at gunpoint otherwise, by May 23, 1838, exactly two years hence.

If the Treaty Party leaders were relieved to see the matter through, they now recognized that, more than ever, they were marked men who had roused an entire country against them. The two Ridges, joined now by Boudinot and Stand Watie, were under no illusions about their popularity. Every day brought fresh rumors of another plot against their lives. The four turned cold to Schermerhorn, and fatalistic. Bullets, knives, and tomahawks were coming for them; they just didn't know from where. "The Cherokees have a good share of common sense," John Ridge noted drily. "Some may be secretly induced to assassinate, by John Ross & friends, but it will be done so secretly that only one or two may fall." One or two would be accused of the crime, he meant. All four Ridges would die; they were grimly sure of it.

It led John Ridge to despair. Why were his people so blind to the obvious? Why were the Ridges not admired, not even tolerated, for their heroic service to the nation? Why did everyone pour hatred down on them instead? Why any hatred at all?

> What will that be to the joy which the treaty will ultimately give to the Indians? The thousands who will emigrate and be happy? The thousands who will be relieved from the lowest state of wretchedness and who, now reduced almost to nakedness and starvation; buffeted and lacerated by the settlers among them; driven, with their women and little ones, from the cabins and their fields, to the woods and mountains, stripped of the little property they once possessed; wandering outcasts, and dependent on the cold charity of their new oppressors?

The Ridges would *save* the people from this fate, not cause it. Yet their own fate was to be hunted down and shot like rabid dogs. It was all so heartless, and so wrong.

Afraid for their lives, and for those of their families, the four members of the Ridge clan packed up and hurried home after the Senate vote. It was spring now, and that made for a breezy ride through the warm green world of the Blue Ridge Mountains, the old Smokies of Major Ridge's childhood, and the rolling hills of Georgia. As they neared home, the travelers were shocked to see that the spring had not brought its usual bounty. The Georgians had continued to infiltrate Cherokee homes, evicting their residents with a flash of a winning ticket. The spring rains had come, but their bounty had come not to the Cherokee, but to the invaders. As the Ridges came back to the Oostanaula, they passed clumps of Cherokee slowly walking along, or sitting listlessly in the shade, their faces downcast, their once bright clothes worn and faded. When the Ridges finally reached their own homes, they were relieved to find things as they were. With the plentiful rains, their crops were thicker and higher than ever. And their houses shone. Governor Lumpkin had been true to his word: no one dared claim any of the Ridge homes. Their families were overjoyed to see them, relieved, almost disbelieving to find them well.

Conscious of their good fortune, all the Ridges made sure to set plenty of their food aside for the hungry who trooped by their doors. In the next few weeks, however, the numbers were so great that the major's stores were nearly emptied of his once high mounds of corn, and John Ridge was running out of stores, too. He had to buy beef, since he'd slaughtered all his cattle, and was down to just three hogs. "I yet keep an open house for the Cherokees," he said.

Only Boudinot was visited by grief. Harriet had suffered complications from the grueling, stillborn delivery of her most recent child that spring while Boudinot was away in Washington, and she was in a terrible state. When Boudinot arrived, he found Samuel Worcester by Harriet's bed, along with the schoolmistress Sophia Sawyer, both sick with worry.

Harriet had never been cut out for hardship, no matter how much she'd insisted that everything was fine in her letters home. She'd sent two of the girls, Eleanor and Mary, to be schooled by Miss Sawyer, and had spoken highly of "the proficiency of the dear little creatures." But this was back in 1832, in the excitement of the Supreme Court's Worcester decision, when she was freely "bragging" about "how Indians can live—how family, & how a nation of Indians can live." She was delighted that the Ridge men had taught her son William Penn to "jump like a boy, & make bows like a gentleman." And her "Mr. B," her "kind affectionate devoted Husband" had taught her so much about the "consciousness of doing right."

But now the enthusiasm had passed, and she'd declined much as the nation had. Postpartum, she'd succumbed to what Boudinot called a "dangerous illness." Seeing her so pale, exhausted, and sweaty, Boudinot could see that her case was "hopeless."

The end came on August 16, at exactly nineteen minutes past one o'clock in the afternoon, as Boudinot, ever punctilious, noted in a strained letter to her parents. By three o'clock, he had "consigned her earthly remains to our mother earth," in a grave he would soon leave behind.

Harriet had at first been "taken with great distress and anxiety" when she realized that this might be the end, but she'd died a Christian, Boudinot reassured the Golds. She had rallied to urge her children, sobbing by her bed, to observe all God's commandments after she was gone. When the pain lifted briefly, she had turned "unusually placid—there was a benignity and smile about her countenance that I had never noticed before"—and read some biblical commentary. Several Ridges came to see her, to offer what cheer they could, including Sarah Ridge's Northrop parents, who'd come from Cornwall much as the Golds had a few years before. But as her distress rose—"bodily," Boudinot emphasized, only—she admitted that she desired to live no longer. At this, Boudinot put her through a catechism:

"You can look to the Redeemer and consider him yours?"

"Yes."

"You are happy notwithstanding all your bodily pain and affliction?"

"I am happy."

Then "her paroxysm returned, and here the conversation ended."

Boudinot drew out the letter almost mercilessly, detailing exactly how those paroxysms weakened her, how her mind started to wander, how her already soft speech dropped to a whisper, and how, at the end, she could scarcely be understood. He was sure that she meant to say, "All is well," but her body was seized by convulsions, her lungs failed, and "her immortal spirit forsook its early home to join the righteous and just men made perfect, and 'to sing the conqueror's song.'"

Excruciating in its details, much of the letter followed the conventions of Christian assurance to the earthly survivors. If the Gold family had ever had reason to question Boudinot's piety, they had none now.

Boudinot had to get the permission of a neighbor to bury his wife "on a hill near the little spring occupied, I think, by Mr. Tarvin," he told his relatives, on the path to his brother's house. Her casket was taken to this quiet spot by friends, plus a retinue of officers and privates of the detachment of federal soldiers who were stationed in New Echota for their protection.

Even in his grief, Boudinot had to know that sympathy for him was limited. The hard times had only fed the rage the Rosses were directing toward the Ridges. To John Ridge, that was ridiculous. The Georgians, not the Treaty Party, were the ones responsible for the misery everywhere about them.

Worse, he wrote to Jackson, the Georgians had claimed that the Cherokee had "intentions of war" and so aroused themselves to a "strong warlike sentiment" of their own. There had been times when Cherokee warriors rose up against white settlers with tomahawks, but those times were long past. Even if they could have summoned the will to fight, they lacked the means, since the Georgians had stripped most of them of their rifles, much as these were needed for the hunt, leaving them defenseless as the Georgians went marauding over the countryside.

And everywhere, it seemed, the Georgians were pressing their advantage. While Major Ridge's house and barn had been spared, his land had not. Right there at the Oostanaula, a Georgian named Cox had claimed a broad strip of Ridge's cropland on the other side of the river from his house and defied the major to do anything about it.

It was worse for his son. A blustery, duel-happy major general in the Alabama militia, John H. Garrett, had gone after a farm John Ridge ran in Alabama. He'd charged into the farmhouse, evicted Ridge's tenant, a luckless fellow named William Childers, and moved into it himself. And he'd taken over Ridge's ferry, too. At the time, John Ridge was off in Washington, but Sarah had turned for help to Major Currey, who passed on her complaint to the governor of Alabama, who did nothing. That summer of 1836 when Ridge returned from Washington, Garrett had started putting up his own buildings on the Ridge property.

John Ridge was beside himself. In theory, he had legal recourse, as the New Echota Treaty had required the federal government to protect the Cherokee from just this sort of outrage. To do his part, Jackson had dispatched 7,000 federal soldiers under the command of General John E. Wool to maintain order, forestalling rash acts on both sides, while government agents prepared the Cherokee for evacuation. But nothing was done to help Ridge.

In New Echota, Lumpkin—the former governor, now Jackson's new Indian commissioner—was busy with Wool's soldiers appraising the belongings that the Cherokee would have to leave behind. Cherokee drifted in by foot, wagon, and oxcart. Lumpkin's men were rarely generous in their assessments, and Wool, as an army general, was disgusted that, by Jackson's order, an odious civilian like Lumpkin outranked him. This had, he said "no parallel in the whole military annals of our country." It was sickening. "I can only say that I cannot be recalled too soon from this command."

The Ridges were caught up in the rotten business, too. As one of the few prominent Cherokee in favor of removal, John Ridge had agreed to help Lumpkin with the Cherokees' property claims, even though it meant riding about the country appraising homesteads and barns of the few Cherokee willing to emigrate—and desperate to get as much cash as they could. Inevitably, they blamed the Ridges if the money proved short. Ridge also helped select the missionaries and teachers to go west, and this made him seem even more of a traitor to his people.

It didn't make things any better when Lumpkin found several of the Ridges, including John Ridge himself, engaging in "extravagances" at federal expense. Lumpkin chalked this up to a habit of luxury from Ridge's days visiting official Washington. But it may have stemmed from Ridge's feeling that this was his due for such foul work. After having a talk with him, Lumpkin reported that Ridge and friends had "laid aside their extravagant assumptions, returned to their sober duty, and no further difficulty occurred on that head." An extra humiliation.

Still, General Wool became quite fond of John Ridge, both of them being caught up in such detestable business. When he heard of Ridge's problems with his farm in Alabama, Wool sent federal troops to remove Garrett from the property, and return Childers. Garrett was duly dispossessed, but he didn't stay away. As soon as Wool's men left for New Echota, he returned with an injunction from the local chancery court that declared him the true owner after all. Out went Childers again, this time for good, and in went Garrett.

This time, when Ridge objected, General Wool told him that he wasn't going to risk a war over this, and Ridge should simply charge the United States for such "spoliation."

The whole thing was outrageous, Ridge stormed at Jackson:

Now we come to address you on the subject of our griefs & afflictions from the acts of the white people. They have got our lands and now they are preparing to fleece us of the money accruing from the treaty. We found our plantations taken in whole or in part by the Georgians—suits instituted against us for back rents from our own farms. These suits are commenced in the inferior courts, with the evident design that, when we are ready to remove, to arrest our people, and on these vile claims to induce us to compromise for our own release, to travel with our families. Thus our funds will be filched from our people, and we shall be compelled to leave our country as beggars and in want.

But it was more than the thefts. It was the vicious hatred behind them, as Georgians were not just fleecing the Cherokee and turning them out of their homes; they were going after the Cherokee with whips to punish them for finding any of this unjust. It was too cruel, he wrote.

Even the Georgian laws, which deny our oaths, are thrown aside, and notwithstanding the cries of our people, and protestation of our innocence and peace, the lowest classes of the white people are flogging the Cherokees with cowhides, hickories, and clubs. We are not safe in our houses—our people are assailed day and night by the rabble. Even justices of the peace and constables are concerned in this business. This barbarous treatment is not confined to men, but the women are stripped also, and whipped without law or mercy.

General Wool must stop such horrors, he told Jackson. Otherwise, "we shall carry off nothing but the scars of the lash on our backs, and our oppressors will get all the money."

Like John Ridge, Wool was expected to execute orders that only undermined the worthy cause behind them, and he found it no less excruciating. Once a self-taught lawyer in the Hudson Valley, he'd turned career soldier; he had been shot through both thighs in the War of 1812 and would rise up to serve as a brigadier general in the Civil War at seventy-seven, the oldest general on either side of the conflict. No one was trained for a cattle-rousing operation like this "dirty assignment," as he called it, but Wool was particularly ill-suited. Himself an orphan raised by his grandfather, he came quickly to feel for the evicted Indians.

The whole scene since I have been in this country has been nothing but a heartrending one, and such a one as I would be glad to get rid of as soon as current circumstances will permit. Because I am firm and decided, do not believe I would be unjust. If I could . . . I would remove every Indian tomorrow beyond the reach of the white men, who, like vultures, are watching, ready to pounce upon their prey and strip them of everything they have or expect from the government of the United States. Yes, sir, nineteen-twentieths, if not ninety-nine out of every hundred, will go penniless to the West.

While he felt nothing for Lumpkin, he considered John Ross the real enemy. If it weren't for him, the Cherokee would already be gone, and far more happily. But the Cherokee did whatever Ross said, and they'd believed him when he claimed they could put off the inevitable forever. Meanwhile, they suffered for him unduly. No matter how "poor or destitute," Wool noted, they refused to accept rations or clothing from the United States, even though it meant that thousands of them resorted to "living upon the roots and sap of trees."

Wool got so mad at Ross that he threw him into jail, along with Elijah Hicks and a couple of Ross's full-bloods, to try to knock some sense into them. The move only hardened Ross's opposition, and, without just cause, a chastened Wool had to release all four the next morning.

Couldn't Ross see that the game was up? That fall of 1836, the presidency passed, not to Senator Henry Clay as John Ross had hoped, but to Martin Van Buren, the bewhiskered Dutchman who had served not only as Jackson's vice president but as his secretary of state and ambassador to Britain. Jackson had no greater enthusiast. As secretary of state, Van Buren had loyally offered to resign along with the others in Jackson's purge of his cabinet, only to be spared out of reciprocal loyalty. He was never going to break with Jackson's removal policies now.

No matter. Ross mounted a big black horse and went around the countryside, preaching the same message, the one that his people craved to hear—stay where you are, remain in your homes, have faith, all will be well. Hungry and poor as they were, the Cherokee flocked to him once again to touch his hand, his clothes, as if he were holy.

Occasionally, Ross would offer the American government a few scraps to suggest he might accede to their wishes, but Van Buren was not fooled. In control of the federal mails, he'd started intercepting Ross's private correspondence, which told a different story.

As fall deepened into winter, Major Ridge dared not stay in this dangerous country any longer, and he told Currey he'd leave with the next round of emigrants on January 1, 1837. Once he gave notice, he received generous federal compensation for his property—$24,127 for his house, ferry, and "improvements" like his hay barn, making him the third-richest man in the nation, after John Ross's brother Lewis and Joseph Vann, son of the erratic James, who would be going west with him.

But the years were wearing on the major, and it had been a close question whether the federal-run emigration committee, which decided on the travel arrangements, would find him "capable" of making the journey. But his son John sat on the committee, and it cleared him for departure. Major Ridge had planned an overland route, thinking it would be easier than navigating the turbulent river waters. He'd had his stagecoach well appointed for the trip, and he collected serviceable carriages for his Negroes to ride along with him, plus a wagon or two for as many of his furnishings as he could cram on top.

He'd have left earlier but for the marital intentions of his daughter, John's spirited younger sister Sarah, called Sally. To Miss Sawyer, the schoolmistress, Sally was "a young lady of superior talent," who favored blue calico dresses. But, as a rough-riding horsewoman, she seems to have been more tomboy than lady. Still, she was pursued by any number of beaux, all of them white. One was a small, alert Georgian lawyer, George Washington Paschal, who'd volunteered for General Wool's outfit and become his adjutant and come to share the general's fondness for the Ridges. To advance his suit, Paschal had given Sally a pony, which he proudly showed off to her at a stable. Keen to ride the animal, she immediately climbed on. The pony's bridle needed adjusting, but as Paschal tried to fix it, it slipped out of his hand. The pony exploded out of the barn. He bounded along for thirteen miles hoping to free himself of his rider. But Sally "rode him down," said a family friend, "and ever afterward the pony seemed a dispirited animal." After Sally accepted Paschal's marriage proposal, he may have ended up feeling similarly.

Politically, it was an awkward union—the major's daughter and a Georgian soldier in the federal army—but, even as he gave in to a general weariness, Major Ridge put on a grand wedding. Paschal resigned from the army and was set to emigrate with his bride when he fell victim to the sort of scheme that was bedeviling the Cherokee. Following Wool's orders, Paschal had destroyed $300 worth of the whiskey being illegally peddled to the Cherokee by a shyster named Kirkham. Kirkham brought suit, and the sheriff wouldn't let Paschal leave until he paid the plaintiff for the lost whiskey, plus court costs. After that, Paschal was only too glad to put Georgia behind him.

Major Ridge had rallied for the wedding, but his speech had softened alarmingly, he was growing thin, and his skin was losing its sunset glow. Unsure of his strength, he rarely strayed far from his house, and, as the January departure date approached, he realized he was in no condition to trek west. The illness may have been spiritual as much as anything. To lose his land, lose his people—it was almost unbearable. There was a time when a man like him would simply go off into the mountains and never come back.

Sally and Paschal left on the overland route on January 1 as planned, but without the major. For a time, it looked as if the major himself might never go, since his health was so uncertain. But he felt better as spring neared, and he decided to join the contingent leaving on March 3, so it would be warm when he arrived in the west. Since the ground was likely to be slushy with snowmelt, he'd decided to take up Wool's offer of a government boat down the Tennessee, and then ride other rivers west from there. He would go with his wife, Susanna; their feebleminded Watty, now well into his thirties; and their son John's daughter Clarinda, whose mind was not too sound, either. They joined a detachment of 466 emigrants, half of them children, who would float west under the direction of General Nathaniel Smith, who'd taken over after Currey died that winter, little missed. They'd leave from Ross's Landing, the bustling ferry port run by the Ross brothers, now lined with grogshops and shipping warehouses that thrived on the western migration John Ross professed to despise. The commerce would turn Ross's Landing into a genuine city, Chattanooga.

The government had built a small navy of eleven flatboats, each 150 feet long and topped with an enclosed, squared-off cabin that covered most of the deck. Each cabin offered four compartments where passengers could take shelter from the elements. Animals were penned at the stern, and meals were cooked over open fires on top. For a voyage that was projected to take more than a month, the boats bore 150 bushels of corn, 78 barrels of flour, and 12,000 pounds of bacon among other comestibles. A few missionaries had come to see them off, and they must have been worried to see the illustrious Major Ridge, obviously infirm, helped aboard. No one could be sure he'd make it. "It is mournful to see how reluctantly these people go away," wrote one. "Even the stoutest hearts melt into tears when they turn their faces toward the setting sun—& I am sure that this land will be bedewed with a Nation's tears."

A Dr. John S. Young was put in charge of the major's boat, and he must have been dismayed to see how slow the going was once they set off. March had come in blustery, and the wind pushed hard against the boats, tipping them this way and that as they tried to make their way down the curving river, with its nasty Muscle Shoals, without crashing into shore. They made only five miles the first day and did not much better after that. When they finally reached Gunter's Landing, Dr. Young kept all the Indians aboard to keep them out of a town that seemed to be set up to get them drunk. In the morning, they transferred to the big steamer *Knoxville*. Seeing the fragility of his most eminent passenger, General Smith had awarded Major Ridge's family the finest accommodations: a plush cabin that normally went for $300. Everyone else on board had to make do with tight, spare quarters for just $20 apiece.

The rains hadn't come and the river proved too low for safe passage, so, after a few slow miles, the Indians were shifted to railroad cars to speed west on iron rails as far as Tuscumbia, an unimaginably hair-raising experience for a people who'd never even seen a train before. There they returned to boats once more—sixty-two-ton keelboats this time, rugged and sailless, with open-air hearths for warmth and cooking, plus snug cabins, to brave the wintry cold. The winds came up as they descended the Tennessee to the Ohio, and then the Mississippi, and rain struck aslant, making cooking impossible. Three weeks in, the boats finally reached Montgomery Point on the Arkansas shore. From there, it was up the Arkansas River to Little Rock, where the Cherokee poured out onto the banks to pitch tents and take down whole trees to burn for cooking. Their bellies full of firewater, they passed the night, said some German travelers who came upon them, singing "their national songs with a mournful and heavy tongue."

It was a brutal passage, and Dr. Lillybridge, the physician for the journey, recorded ills of every description: "colds, influenza, sore throat, coughs, pleurisy, measles, diarrhea, bowel complaint, fevers, toothache, wounds from accidents and fighting, and gonorrhea." Both Susanna and Major Ridge needed medicine for hacking coughs, and passed most of the trip huddled in their cabin.

West had always been the way to death for the Cherokee, to the place where the sun dropped out of sight. It is hard to imagine that The Ridge did not see himself as reaching the end now, aboard a steamer chugging to a foreign land he could not picture. Finally, late on the night of March 27, the boats pulled up at Van Buren, the boisterous frontier town just on the Arkansas side of the Arkansas River. A place for whiskey, and the sins that whiskey led to, it was the closest thing to a hub of commerce in those parts. Passengers were free to disembark, but it was late and dark, and the Ridges decided to stay on board and ride a few miles more to Fort Smith. Built high on a bluff overlooking the Arkansas, it had long been a symbol of federal might, but its soldiers had left some years ago for Fort Gibson, thirty miles deeper into the perilous frontier in what is now Muskogee County, Oklahoma. The military left Fort Smith to a couple of old soldiers who turned it into a whiskey store, selling as much as six barrels per customer, leaving a fair number of them literally dead drunk.

It was hardly the most reassuring place for the Ridges to touch down into their new life. They off-loaded their packs and animals but stayed only long enough to acquire some wagons and fresh horses. Ailing as he was, the Ridge saddled up and led his party back toward Van Buren after all.

He'd spent some time over crude maps of the new territory and could see that Van Buren would offer the best route north to the place where he had decided he would settle—up the Line Road along the Arkansas border. They'd keep on for a good fifty miles, several days' ride, with wagons in tow, leaving the heartland behind for the vast open spaces of the rolling foothills of the Ozarks. Major Ridge had picked a spot way up on the northeast corner of the Cherokee lands. To see it on a map, it seems a place chosen solely for its remoteness. It was named for the narrow, winding, slow-moving water that must have seemed sweet as it wandered through. It was called Honey Creek.

A 1957 rendering of the Trail of Tears by the Pawnee artist Brummett Echohawk.

ECHOHAWK 1957

PART THREE

VENGEANCE
BE MINE

1837-1846

1

HONEY CREEK

I n 1832, five years before the Ridges arrived in Indian Territory to start their new lives, the writer Washington Irving had come to the area in search of adventure. Irving was a fast-talking New York sophisticate, a bit jowly as he neared fifty. He'd come off a long sojourn in the literary capitals of Europe after his early success in America with tall tales like his ghoulish "Legend of Sleepy Hollow." Like his sometime friend John Howard Payne back in Georgia, he came west for material, and he thought he might find something salable among the Indians.

Coming west mostly by coach from Saint Louis, Irving arrived in Fort Gibson, a high-picketed stockade on the Arkansas River, on the far border of the Cherokee portion of Indian Territory, forty miles down from whiskey-addled Fort Smith. With the blessing of the Indian superintendent, Henry Leavitt Ellsworth, a straitlaced easterner who would end up the U.S. patent commissioner in time for Samuel Colt's quick-firing revolver, he joined up with a couple of European dandies for a dude tour of the west. One of them was a "Mr. L.," an English aristocrat of "a thousand occupations"—meaning none—and the other was a Swiss count "full of talent and spirit, but galliard in the extreme." Tonish, a "swarthy, meagre, wiry French creole," did all the work for these worthies as "the squire, the groom, the cook, the tent-man, in a word, the factotum." But their hunting scout, Beatte, was the marvel of the piece—a half-French, half-Osage buffalo hunter who'd been educated somewhat by missionaries along the Neosho River that forked north off the Arkansas, just before it hit Fort Gibson. Hunting rifle on his shoulder, powder horn and bullet pouch at his side, knife in his belt, and a few coils of rope at his saddle bow, Beatte was ready for anything.

Entertaining as such salty characters were, it was the land that held Irving's attention as Beatte led the party west. They rode along the Arkansas past a few lonesome Creek settlements—their denizens of "gypsy colors." There began the rolling vastness of the prairie, fringed by forests of gigantic oaks that were draped with grapevines, and studded by pine that had been clawed by bear that clambered up. They meandered by charming, whimsical brooks, across long stretches of buffalo grass, over rocky hilltops with breathtaking views of wide skies to distant horizons, and finally circled back across the Arkansas River on barks of buffalo skins. The party hoped to bag one of the buffalo that ranged everywhere, but the herds proved too far out of reach, so the men had to settle for elk and deer. Irving had come for drama, but found surprisingly little beyond an assortment of colorful characters, and a savage menace that never materialized into anything too awful. His little party was never once attacked by shrieking Pawnee, assaulted by drunken Creeks, swallowed in a man-eating sinkhole, drowned in a raging river, or victimized by horse thieves. To a writer, that was disappointing.

Instead, they found honey. In "bee trees," where wild bees had built hives in the decayed trunks, and made all of Indian country abuzz. To the Indians, the sound was an alarm that white hunters had swept the buffalo west, leaving the prairie to the quiet industry of bees. "The heralds of civilisation," Irving calls them. Indians took to honey like a drug. "Nothing, I am told, can exceed the greedy relish with which they banquet for the first time upon this unbought luxury of the wilderness." It made Indian territory a paradise of honey. Bee-hunters tracked the bees back to their homes in the sweet hollows of the bee trees. The Indians would hack the bee trees down and then descend on them "with spoon and hunting knife, to scoop out the flakes of honeycomb with which the hollow trunk was stored." Few combs ever made it home intact. "Every stark bee-hunter was to be seen with a rich morsel in his hand, dripping about his fingers, and disappearing as rapidly as a cream tart before the holyday appetite of a schoolboy." Bees from other colonies swooped in to "banquet" on the "the ruins of their neighbours," while the hive builders staggered about, uncomprehending, and "buzz[ed] forth doleful lamentations over the downfall of their republic."

This was the honey for which Honey Creek was named. Succulent, free, heady—and dangerous.

If Major Ridge had had more English, and was more voluble, he might have described his journey from Van Buren in similar terms. As it was, his wife Susanna remembered it later as "an entire wilderness." After his coughing fits aboard the steamer, plenty of Cherokee had given Major Ridge up for dead, and rumors to that effect filtered back east. But he rallied and led what he'd brought of his family, plus some friends, the Fieldses, relatives of the man who took a knife for the Ridge Party at Lavender's store, up north along the Line Road that traced the border of Indian Territory with Arkansas along the 100th meridian as set by Congress. It was claimed to be a military road, one of the few that the government had pushed through, but it was little more than an uneven, hilly two-track path that required repeated fords across treacherous unbridged streams. There was a store or two along the way, but not much for sale beyond whiskey, which Major Ridge now passed up with some indignation, surely. Everyone had to be on the lookout for the highwaymen who lurked in the woods to spring upon the unwary.

Eventually, the sky opened up as the flat-ridged Ozarks on the east angled down into sloping valleys on the west. A few farming villages dotted the landscape, each one little more than a clutch of huts, fanning out to others on slender footpaths. Finally, many miles in, came Honey Creek, a lazy stream, meandering down from southwestern Missouri on its way to the wider Neosho that pushed through Indian Territory.

The sight had to have lifted their hearts a little—the wide valley was abloom with the wild rosebuds that sprinkled the fields with crimson; bees everywhere were at work. In the oak forest, a smattering of dogwoods shimmered with the white-cross blossoms that the Christians took as proof of God's deliverance.

A few rickety buildings—houses and barns—left behind by earlier settlers who couldn't make a go of it stood near the water. Major Ridge set himself up in a farmhouse with Susanna, their son Watty, and their granddaughter Clarinda. Dusty, cobwebbed, and rickety in its abandonment, the place was a sad comedown from The Ridge's proud, tight Georgia mansion, with its handsome furniture and English plate. But it kept the wind out, and the rain off. It would do.

Stand Watie took over one of the adjoining buildings, set to work putting it to rights, and fixed up some outbuildings for slaves. He'd soon add stables and a corral for racehorses, a great passion of his. Rising to the challenge of this new world, Major Ridge revived, and he joined in the effort of rebuilding, and then hitched his workhorses to plows to clear some fields for farming. It was bitter, exhausting work, even with the slaves he'd brought along. Food was scarce, and comforts were few. But it was a new beginning. "We had to undergo many privations in [the] new Country," Susanna recalled later. "But we bore [them] all under the belief that we had found a comfortable home for our children and grandchildren."

The crops were in before spring got too far along, and, with the money from his improvements at the Oostanaula, Major Ridge added some cattle, hogs, and other livestock, and put up barns to house them. The place was no plantation, just a few fields stretching out from some meager houses huddled together across a broad, windswept valley. But the houses gradually became homes, and the rich soil drew on plenty of sun and water to send up green shoots of corn and barley. It wasn't much, but it was enough, and it was all theirs.

And it was well away from the troubles they feared would follow them, as it was way up in the northeast corner of a territory that took the shape of a rotated L, its long stem pointed down, carved out of the vaster Indian lands that would be home to over a dozen dislocated tribes all around them, up against Arkansas to the east and the Kansas territory to the north, with Missouri just past the northeast corner. This would be the new Cherokee Nation. Most of the Cherokee population would be concentrated farther south along the long stem, in-country from Fort Gibson, the terminus of the Trail of Tears for so many.

John Ridge couldn't free himself to follow his father until the following September. It must have been a daily torment to stay on, for his last letter to Lumpkin, written on the eve of his departure, was a startling cri de coeur. "Tomorrow at about 9 o'clock I shall leave this place," he declared, and "bid an everlasting farewell to the land of my birth." How would he be remembered? he asked himself. "In the history of the Nation, if there is a page assigned to my name *and that of our house*, I know not what will be said. Foul misrepresentations have been made by our opponents as to our motives, and we have passed thro' the ordeal of the awakened prejudices of the ignorant portion of our people." If he was misunderstood, though, he had himself partly to blame, and he left the nation with greater sympathy for Lumpkin than he'd ever have imagined. "I cannot leave you without pronouncing the verdict of my appreciation upon your labors, and the humanity which you have manifested for my people."

Lumpkin saluted him in return. "Sir, you have made this sacrifice. You have made this effort, in the face of death, and the most determination from high sources, to save your people from certain impending ruin and destruction. We trust—we hope—we think—success will crown your efforts. May the God of our fathers prosper your way! May you long live to be useful to your people."

It was an extraordinary turnabout. John Ridge had always thought of himself as the tribune of his people, and the scourge of the whites who had abused them. Yet he now found sympathy only from those very whites, indeed, from the most prominent of them, and received detestation from everyone else. Who was John Ridge now? When he looked in the mirror, what did he see?

John Ridge's improvements on his property fetched almost $20,000, and his crop and hogs about $1,750 more, sums that he was duly paid by his own fortunate drawer, Griffin Mathis, who was far more principled about such transactions than most. The claim on his ferry from General Garrett was still outstanding and would have to wait.

John Ridge met up with Sarah and the children at Wills Valley, which descends from Tennessee into Alabama; the children had passed the summer in the valley, studying at a missionary school safely away from the rigors of New Echota. Cousin Boudinot was there with his family, too, and he had acquired a new wife, Delight Sargent, a saintly half-blood he'd married in his eagerness for a helpmeet. It was from there that both families would make their plans for their final passage west. John Ridge sent most of his slaves and horses ahead with his dislodged tenant, William Childers, while he kept back a retinue of three—a cook, a driver, and a children's maid named Mary.

The two cousins joined their families with two more families eager to leave, and the four loaded everything they could onto wagons and then boarded carriages to take the overland route to Cherokee west. It was a hard passage north through Kentucky, and then crossing the Ohio at Berry's Ferry, a few miles from Paducah in the far western part of the state; and from there crossing southern Illinois, passing along the broad alluvial plain, with its occasional marshlands, by the Mississippi; finally crossing over the river by ferry to Cape Girardeau, about a hundred miles due south from Saint Louis; and going down the Missouri until they hit the undulating hills of the vast Ozark Plateau, green valleys rising into rocky outcroppings. Gradually, as they followed "a good road through a rocky and romantic country," according to John Ridge, the plains grew wilder, and wildlife appeared—elk, deer, hares, pheasant—almost as if they were moving back to the time when Cherokee last were hunters. To his young son, John Rollin Ridge, even then showing signs of the literary man he would become, it was "a zestful voyage of discovery among new flora and fauna." And there they came at last to Honey Creek. They'd made the eight-hundred mile trip in just seven weeks.

William Childers had gone ahead with Ridge's slaves, and when Ridge arrived, he made Childers his purchasing agent to buy hogs, plus enough corn to feed them. He came back with forty-one, producing almost six thousand pounds of pork, which sold briskly to settlers who'd scarcely ever seen such a luxury.

Cousin Boudinot and his new wife, Delight, had come along, and between the two families there must have been over a dozen Ridges, plus a few more friends who'd joined in. Combined with the major and Stand Watie, they made a small village. "It is superior to any country I ever saw in the U.S.," John Ridge declared after he'd had a chance to ride about the territory. "In a few years it will be the garden spot of the United States." And they wouldn't have to fend off anyone. "Perfect friendship and contentedness prevail over his land," he declared. Then again, they were pretty much all by themselves up there well to the northeast. It would be the first true enclave of the Cherokee, and Jackson was counting on them to set an example, as he saw the Ridges as genuine Cherokee statesmen, principled men with a serious following among the mixed-blood elite, and possibly others as well. To Jackson, this was the beginning of everything he'd hoped. To Ross, back in the east, it was the beginning of everything he'd feared. He was happy to see the back of the Ridges, of course, but he had to know that their example would only encourage Jackson to push for more removal. It was like water bursting through a dam: once the first rush of it breaks through, the rest will all drain out, too. His own people might not see it that way, but Jackson would, and this would be all that mattered.

The earnest Miss Sawyer had gone east when the Ridges left Georgia, but, once John Ridge got settled, he invited her to join them there at Honey Creek, as he could see the children would need instruction if they were to make anything of themselves. He put up a two-story log schoolhouse for her a short walk from his house, just like the setup in New Echota. Happy to return to her labors, Miss Sawyer was pleased that John Ridge had come out "in favor of the Christian religion." She'd evidently been starting to wonder.

John Ridge had moved his family into one of the tumbledown houses along the creek, but it was not up to his standards. They all got through that first winter, but when spring came, he bought $150 worth of lumber for a much nicer place. This one would have five windows across the front, a solid door, and a tight floor that was unusually sound for such a remote locale. But it was hardly the mansion he'd left. "A good double log house," a visitor called it, which suggests there was a limit to its grandeur. Still impaired by his gimpy legs, he'd left the construction to others. That spring he had Childers set the slaves to fencing in an astounding 150 acres for his livestock, and the pleasure of claiming land as his. Soon to come were a smokehouse, outhouses, cribs, stables, and pastures for his horses.

Boudinot did not remain long at Honey Creek, but shifted thirty miles south to Park Hill, where he moved in for a time with his old friend, the long-suffering Reverend Samuel Worcester, and together they resumed their efforts at translating the bible into Cherokee, book by book. "The Messenger," the Cherokee called Worcester now.

John Ridge soon partnered with his father to set up a general store for all the emigrants moving in. It cost more than $1,500 to build, and required more than ten times as much lumber as his house. It would be a kind of trading post like John Ross's, but far bigger, as he had all the new territory for himself, with people coming literally by the boatload, if not the caravan. Did John Ridge mean to serve these new arrivals, or to exploit them? Was this altruism, or capitalism? It's an open question, for, by now, John Ridge's heart was not what it had been back in the days when he roamed the Atlantic coast extolling the Cherokee from every pulpit. The Cherokee had turned on him; there was no other way to see it. And his veins now stirred with a desire not so different from the age-old Cherokee quest for vengeance. In the face of the massive rebuff by his people, he did not turn the other cheek in Christian humility. Rather, he sought to strike back, not with a tomahawk, but in a new sort of revenge that was possible only under capitalism. He might not be the most popular of the Cherokee, but he vowed to be the finest. His superiority, so visible in the McKenney portrait, would now be manifest in every aspect of his character.

John Ridge's store offered everything the Cherokee emigrants would need to get established: food, hats, clothing, shoes and leatherwear, lamps, carpets, writing implements, combs, farm tools, assorted hardware, lumber, rifles. But he also offered a product that would be their undoing, and gave the lie to all the others. Spirits. Whiskey, mostly, but also rum and even wine. The very intoxicants that his father had inveighed against, and that had undermined the nation. Miss Sawyer was appalled. "He has tampered with the cause of temperance," she complained, "by selling wine, until he has been disgusted with wine drunkards, & says he will sell no more." *Says.* One can hear her scoff. Indeed, he returned to selling this vice, repeatedly.

2

THE BUSINESS OF REMOVAL

The Ridges were among the last few Cherokee who'd been eager to leave. General Nathaniel Smith was able to send barely 400 Cherokees west that fall of 1837. Many others had fallen sick with dysentery and diarrhea at the camps beside the demarcation site on the Tennessee before they had a chance to leave. The general was hoping to do better the following spring, but he did worse, as just 250 headed off on April 5 on the steamboat *Smelter*, which was dragging behind it a number of families in a single keelboat that soon swamped.

By now, 2,000 Cherokee had gone west, most of them from the Treaty Party. But 15,000 others stayed put, awaiting word from John Ross about what to do. Well into that spring, Ross was off in Washington, vainly trying to get President Van Buren to disavow the "dirty paper"—the New Echota Treaty. But he had no such inclination; and even if he had disavowed it, Georgia would never have followed suit. By then George Gilmer had rotated back into the governor's chair, where he'd received confidential reports from his spies that the Cherokee in the state were "saucy, stubborn, and rebellious." They'd been spotted clearing fields, putting up barns, and planting crops "as though there was not the least hope of early removal."

This was infuriating, and Gilmer made Van Buren know he would not stand for it. Van Buren, in turn, let Ross know that he'd never relent. To bring the point home, he withdrew the sympathetic General Wool on May 8 and put in Major General Winfield Scott—bearish, six foot four, with a sagging gut, a sour disposition, and eagerness for advancement—as commander of the 7,000 federal troops, with the charge of removing the Indians by May 23, as planned, or facing the consequences. His mission was no longer to assist the removal, but to impose it. C. A. Harris, the new Indian commissioner, told Ross to let his people know "in forcible language, the unavoidable conclusion that a ready and cheerful acquiescence on their part can alone save them from serious calamities."

At this, Ross decried the persecution of his people, but aroused only two flurries of protest: in Marietta, Ohio; and in Philadelphia. Some Quakers asked Ross to address them at Philadelphia Hall on May 23, but he didn't dare leave Washington. There, he made time to see a certain O. S. Fowler of Philadelphia, a "practical phrenologist," or student of cranial features. Sympathetic to the Cherokee cause, Fowler wished to produce a plaster cast of Ross's skull to show that a Cherokee was the full intellectual equal of a white.

With the deadline fast approaching, Ross offered to guarantee removal after all—but only in two years' time, and only if the government rejected the financial terms of the New Echota Treaty and boosted payments for the relocation to a staggering $13 million. Van Buren would not hear of any delay, but he did allow the Senate to make supplementary payments that pushed the total allotment to $6,647,067, plus another $100,000 for contingencies and $33,333 for annuities, all to be disbursed through the Ross government. But the May 23 deadline would remain in effect.

Ross's brother Lewis saw the writing on the wall. "It is evident that the Gov'mt is determined to move us at all hazards," he wrote to John, "and it only remains for us to do the best we can." He doubted they could negotiate a better treaty than this one. "Schermerhorn's screw is severely felt by us all," he concluded glumly.

Lewis Ross's children followed the developments from Lawrenceville, New Jersey, where they attended boarding school, somewhat mystified by the events back home. Lewis's daughter wrote to her uncle John hoping "our people will not be moved west," as if she were not one of them, and, irritated by President Van Buren, recommended that her uncle "cut his head off." A son added in the same vein: "Do you think anything can be done for the Cherokees?" And his brother asked their father if he knew if a new treaty was in the offing, as he was "frequently asked these questions."

None of these young Rosses ever saw their homes in the nation again.

In Washington, General Scott assured Ross he had no desire for bloodshed, but he would remove the Cherokee by force if they would not leave on their own. It was with some exasperation that, when Ross was still unmoved on May 10, with the deadline less than two weeks off, he proclaimed the hard facts of the matter directly to the residents of the nation.

> Cherokees! The President of the United States has sent me with a powerful army, to cause you, in obedience to the Treaty of 1835, to join that part of your people who are already established in prosperity on the other side of the Mississippi.

They should leave now, he declared, before he had to push them out at gunpoint. "My troops already occupy many positions," he warned, "and thousands and thousands are approaching from every quarter, to render assistance and escape alike hopeless." He put it starkly: "Will you, then by resistance compel us to resort to arms . . . or will you by flight seek to hide yourself in mountains and thus oblige us to hunt you down?" He implored the Cherokee to make straight for the embarkation centers on the Hiwassee in Calhoun, Tennessee; at Ross's Landing, soon to be Chattanooga, on the eastern swoop of the Tennessee River; or at Gunter's Landing, at its southernmost dip in Alabama. He would provide food, clothing, and shelter for all who needed it while they waited for the next boat west.

To such a stark declaration, Ross remained silent. Without his guidance, all but a few Cherokee stayed where they were. General Scott did not back down. "My orders from Washington require that the collection of the Indians

for emigration shall go on, and it shall." With that, he directed his occupying army to go ahead. Of the 15,000 Cherokee to be evicted, Scott assumed
that four-fifths were Ross's followers who'd need to be ripped away from their
houses, regrettable as that might be. The rest might still be open to persuasion. Either way, his soldiers needed to brace themselves. "Avoid harshness
and cruelty," General Scott counseled his men. "Every possible kindness . . .
must, therefore, be shown by the troops." If any soldier acted badly, the rest
should "seize and consign the guilty wretch to the severest penalty of the laws."

Placing his headquarters in New Echota, as if it were *his* capital now, Scott
divided the nation into three districts—eastern, western, and middle—but
he built stockades throughout to hold recalcitrant Cherokee as they awaited
deportation by boat down the Tennessee River.

When the May 23 deadline passed without any sign of movement, Scott's
men started in on their grim task. More than 7,000 uniformed federal soldiers, all of them well armed, fanned out through the nation to descend upon
the Cherokee in their homes. There, so long misled by their principal chief,
these Cherokee must have been dumbfounded to find insolent, rifle-toting
soldiers, swarming in to roust them from their homes as if the Indians had no
more right to stay there than field mice.

A half century later the Cherokee ethnologist James Mooney interviewed
survivors who well remembered the horror of that time. They recalled how
bands of soldiers stole silently across fields or through the woods to surround
the Cherokees' snug cabins, and then burst in, rifles cocked and bayonets
fixed, ready to shoot or stab anyone who resisted. Then, "with blows and
oaths," they forced the Cherokee outside to tramp off to spare stockades that
were miles away. Others were grabbed where they were working in the fields
or just ambling down the road. Women were yanked away from their spinning wheels and barked at to come *now*. Small children were seized as they
played and sent to join the long files of wailing Cherokee. Too often, as the
evicted turned for a last look at the homes they'd built and lived in for decades, they saw them in flames, torched by a rabble of jeering whites.

Some of the more daring Cherokee responded with contempt, but many
more could see that, when they were taken by surprise, defenseless, wildly
outnumbered, with their families about, resistance was futile. When the sol-

diers thundered in on one aging Cherokee patriarch at dinner, he bade the men wait long enough for him to gather his extended family around him for quiet prayers to the Great Spirit to protect them, then he let the soldiers lead them all away into exile.

Too often, after the Cherokee families had been ripped from their homes, white mobs swarmed in to pick the houses clean, then empty the barns, round up any livestock, and even dig up graves to steal the silver pendants and other valuables sometimes buried with the dead.

One Georgia volunteer, a veteran soldier, told Mooney that the Cherokee removal was "the cruelest work I ever knew." But, of course, the Cherokee found it even crueler.

The Baptist missionary Evan Jones watched as the Cherokee were rooted out, one by one. "The poor captive, in a state of distressing agitation, his weeping wife almost frantic with terror, surrounded by a group of crying, terrified children, without a friend to speak a consoling word," he wrote. He watched the soldiers march the families away like cattle, poking any resisters with a bayonet, or whacking them with long sticks that whistled down on shoulders or the side of the head, to keep them all stumbling along, "mortified," wrote Jones, "by vulgar and profane vociferations" by the soldiers that didn't need to be translated. Soldiers sent everyone plunging across even the swiftest streams, the water sometimes as high as their heads, not allowing them to stop to remove their shoes, which were often lost in the passage. When youngsters fled in terror into the woods, parents were not allowed to collect them, leaving them to grow up alone in the wild, if they lived at all, while their elders were sent to the Indian Territory in Oklahoma. If any Cherokee, whether men or women, complained too hard or dared to push back at these hardened soldiers, they were stripped naked, roped to a tree, and given a hundred lashes on their bare backs, their shrieks piercing the air.

It did not have to be this way. Illegal as Ross had declared it to be, the New Echota Treaty had been the law of the United States for two years, plenty of time for the Cherokee to settle up their affairs and leave in order. That would have been anguishing, no question, but far better than suddenly being driven from their lives at gunpoint, whipped and beaten, forced to leave behind everything they could not wear or carry, with the summer heat rising. "If Ross had told them the truth in time," John Ridge complained, "they would have sold off their furniture, their horses, their cattle, hogs, and sheep, and their growing corn." They could have used that money to start afresh.

By June 6, the first 800 of the rounded-up Cherokee were sent west from Ross's Landing on six double-decker keelboats lashed three on a side to a 100-ton steamboat that sent acrid smoke into the air as it tugged its cargo downriver. It was slow going with all that weight, and ungainly as the keelboats lurched about. The frigid water must have only increased the Cherokees' sense of surging peril. Down the Tennessee to those treacherous Muscle Shoals rapids, all of them dangerously low that dry spring, as the Tennessee River dipped into Alabama. Here, each boat was set free to maneuver on its own, and several slammed onto the rocky shore "with some violence," severely damaging one, and raising terror, but causing no injury. The water smoothed after that and the Cherokee passed the night in the woods by Gunter's Landing. From there to Decatur, where they waited overnight for a long train of thirty-two cars. Stuffed inside, the Cherokee must have been stupefied to speed to a new world aboard such an iron monstrosity. From there to Tuscumbia, just before the Tennessee passed out of Alabama into Mississippi, where whiskey brought a flurry of brawls and 100 emigrants melted away into the forest overnight. But the remainder continued on about fifty miles to Waterloo, where the Smelter pulled a pair of keelboats heavy with Indians up the Tennessee River into Kentucky. They turned at Paducah to follow the Ohio to the Mississippi and swing back to reach Memphis, a huge zigzag that took three hundred miles—twice the distance as the crow flew. From there to Montgomery's Point in Arkansas, where the Arkansas River peeled off to Little Rock, and finally to Fort Smith and then the blessed destination of Fort Coffee, named for Jackson's favorite general, where the boats could be beached at last. Remarkably, no one died on this harrowing journey, but of the 875 who undertook it, only 489 arrived. The rest were simply gone.

Another band of 875 captives followed a week later, and they had worse luck. One man drowned in the river, trying to retrieve his hat, and three children were lost to disease. When their steamer ran aground on the Arkansas, impassable now in the drought, they had to finish the journey largely on foot. In the rising swelter, the daily marches began well before dawn. Even so, nearly every day a dozen Cherokee would drop dead from heat, exhaustion, or thirst. By the end of June, 300, nearly a third of the total, had fallen ill. All July they staggered on, and when they reached Lee's Creek halfway along, half were sick, and the green peaches and raw corn they feasted on only made them sicker. Of the original 875, only 602 made it to the creek, where the records end.

General Scott ordered 1,000 more Cherokee to leave on June 17. Having languished so long in the makeshift pens, these were the least hardy—hungry, sick, barely clothed—and they were distressed by the news of the hardships to come. Three days into the journey, some Cherokee back home begged General Smith to call a halt to this murderous expatriation. "Spare their lives," they pleaded. "Expose them not to the killing effects of that strange climate, under the disadvantages of the present inauspicious season." But the boats continued on. The days were even hotter now; the sun was burning bare skin. The rains still did not come, and the lowering rivers forced the first boatloads of Cherokee onto wagons at Bellefonte, Alabama. The next group gave up on the rivers altogether, and left on foot for the long march west.

There was something wrong in heaven, too, for the rains never did come that spring, or that summer, either. The drought burned crops, dried up springs, deadened spirits. Even the shallowest-draft boats could not slip past the craggy boulders that emerged from the depths, and the overland route offered little better. Far longer and more arduous, it lacked the spring water to slake the Indians' burning thirst.

Scott had no choice but to stop the removal until September. By then, surely, the rains would come again.

In their optimism, the Cherokee took the suspension to mean that the federal government was giving up on its campaign altogether, just as Ross had promised it would. Joyous with relief, those who still had houses returned to their lives as if the threat had passed.

Through all of this ordeal—the evictions, the forced marches, the temporary imprisonments, the loading of Cherokee onto boats—John Ross was nowhere to be found. He had remained in Washington and didn't leave until roughly when the last boat did, in the middle of June. Even then, he didn't come straight home, but went first to Salem, North Carolina, to collect his daughter Jane, his favored child of the six, who was being schooled there at the Moravian Seminary.

It took him a full month to return with her to the nation; they arrived at the Cherokee agency on the Hiwassee on July 13. It created a sensation, a second coming, this sudden arrival of a short, dusty, burdened man in black. People flocked to him from every direction, surrounding him with a great sea of the destitute, all in fading colors, pressing in to touch his hands, his clothes, anything.

But he did not bring relief. Back with Quatie at last at Red Clay, just inside the Tennessee line from Georgia, Ross sent out runners to alert Cherokee everywhere that, whatever they might now be thinking, the bitter truth was that the long fight was over and they had lost. They must now leave. Ross made clear that everyone should evacuate west, starting on September 1, just as Scott said.

Coming from him now, after so many years of hope, the news must have been heart-stopping. How could this possibly be?

A week later, on July 21, Ross convened the general council at Red Clay to pass an official resolution that was not made public. This one put him in supreme command of the emigration as "superintendent of removal and subsistence," a title of his own composition. As his first official act, he awarded his brother Lewis the lucrative contracts to provide transportation and supplies. The delegation that had just returned from Washington would serve as his executive committee, although it would scarcely be consulted. Long the object of his fierce resistance, the removal would now be entirely his operation.

Scott was only too happy to let Ross take charge of this wretched enterprise, but Ross let him know he wasn't going to work free. Rather, he demanded $65.88 per person to cover all the transportation costs, from wagons to physicians, of an eight-hundred-mile journey he expected to take eighty days. By then, the initial Senate appropriation for the purpose had already been exhausted, and Scott balked at a new price that would run $800,000 more.

Ever the trader, Ross knew when he had a customer over a barrel. Instead of reducing his offer, he raised it to cover costs he'd previously forgotten. The Cherokee would need not just the expected rations, but also coffee and sugar.

And soap, too, which he considered "indispensable." Three pounds of it for every 100 rations, at 15 cents a pound. He insisted the cost was the lowest possible. "It is our anxious wish in the management of the business to be free at all time from the imputation of extravagance."

Scott was stuck. If he wished the Cherokee removed, he would need Ross to do it. He was not about to quibble over the price. "The estimate therefore of emigration costs submitted to me . . . with the small addition of soap is hereby approved." Ross had the Cherokee; General Scott did not. It was that simple.

But the agreement meant signing over the job to the man who not only had always opposed it, but did not answer to the military. While this may have been acceptable to General Scott, it infuriated his commander, General Nathaniel Smith, and it panicked the many white contractors who had lined up business with the government and now scrambled to strike deals with Ross's brother Lewis, who stood to make $140,000 from these private contracts. When Scott tried to put the removal contract out for bids to keep the costs down, he got a blast of Ross's righteous anger. How dare Scott ask him and his brother to skimp on their moral obligation to their downtrodden people? No, only the Rosses could be trusted to handle the business properly. To which a browbeaten Scott could only agree.

When, at the Hermitage outside Nashville, Andrew Jackson heard that his bête noire John Ross was in charge of the removal, he could scarcely contain himself. Tired and ailing at seventy-one, he fired off a furious letter to Felix Grundy, the attorney general, in Washington.

The contract with Ross must be arrested, or you may rely upon it, the expense and other evils will shake the popularity of the Administration to its center. What madness and folly to have anything to do with Ross when the agent was proceeding with the removal on the principles of economy that would have saved at least 100 per cent from what the contract with Ross will cost. . . .

I have only time to add as the mail waits that the contract with Ross must be arrested, and General Smith left to superintend the removal. The time and circumstances under which Gen'l Scott made this contract shows that he was no economist, or is, sub rosa, in league with Clay and

Co. to bring disgrace on this administration. . . . P.S. I am so feeble I can scarcely wield my pen, but friendship dictates it and the subject excites me. Why is it that the scamp Ross is not banished from the notice of the administration?

But it was too late. Ross could not be removed from the enterprise.

3

EXODUS

eeing that the Rosses had taken charge of the removal, the remaining members of the Treaty Party, nearly 700 of them, decided to leave on their own on September 1. But the rains had still not come, so the rivers were impassable. They waited as long as they could, but finally decided there was nothing to do except take the more grueling overland route. Led by the Treaty Party elite, they gathered at the agency at Hiwassee and then, with only a few wagons trailing along beside, left on October 11, the downed leaves tossed by a vicious, icy wind that portended an early winter. They walked the length of Tennessee—ten, twelve miles a day—finally reaching Memphis in November, just as the first snows hit. There, they fought a whipping wind to ford the wide Mississippi, and continued across a snowy, windswept Arkansas, passing a frozen Little Rock in mid-December and finally reaching Fort Smith a few days into the new year on January 7, 1839.

Finally, the Ross Party had the nation to itself, and Ross took full advantage.

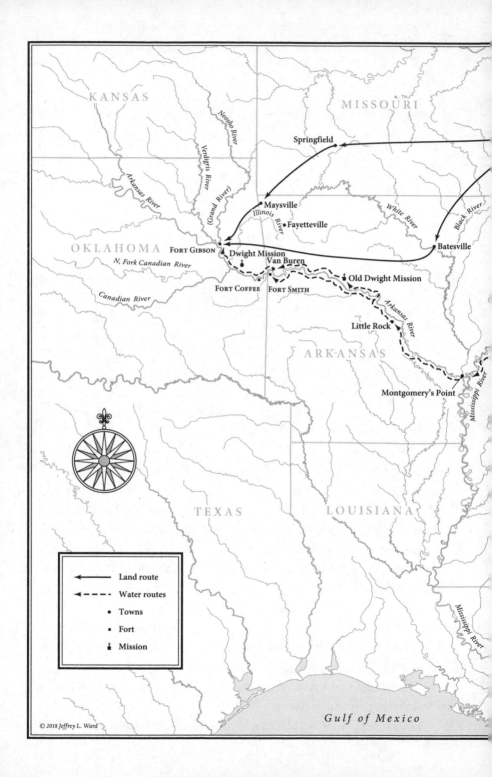

KANSAS

MISSOURI

Neosho River

Verdigris River

Arkansas River

(Grand River)

Springfield

White River

Black River

Maysville

Illinois River

Fayetteville

OKLAHOMA

FORT GIBSON

Dwight Mission

Van Buren

Batesville

N. Fork Canadian River

FORT COFFEE

FORT SMITH

Old Dwight Mission

Canadian River

Arkansas River

Little Rock

ARKANSAS

Montgomery's Point

Mississippi River

TEXAS

LOUISIANA

Land route

Water routes

Towns

Fort

Mission

Mississippi River

Gulf of Mexico

© 2018 Jeffrey L. Ward

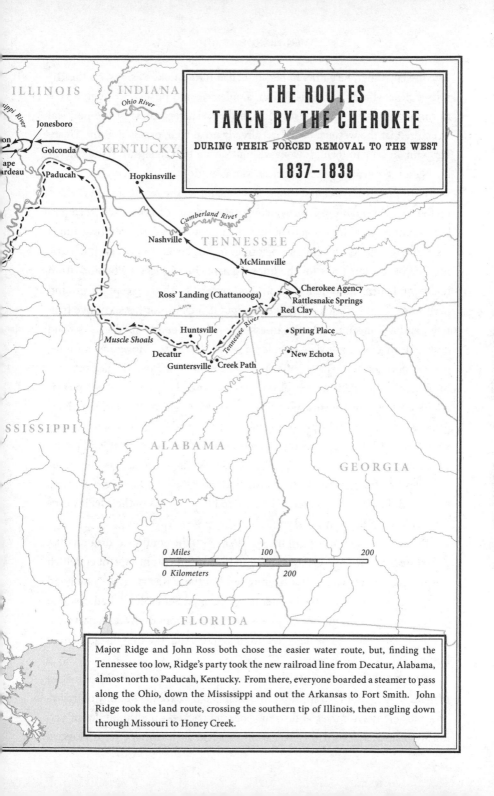

ILLINOIS   INDIANA

Ohio River

Jonesboro

on

Golconda   KENTUCKY

ape
rdeau   Paducah   Hopkinsville

Cumberland River

Nashville   TENNESSEE

McMinnville

Ross' Landing (Chattanooga)   Cherokee Agency
Rattlesnake Springs
Red Clay

Huntsville   *Tennessee River*   • Spring Place

Muscle Shoals

Decatur   • New Echota
Guntersville   Creek Path

MISSISSIPPI   ALABAMA

GEORGIA

0 Miles   100   200
0 Kilometers   200

FLORIDA

THE ROUTES TAKEN BY THE CHEROKEE

DURING THEIR FORCED REMOVAL TO THE WEST

1837–1839

Major Ridge and John Ross both chose the easier water route, but, finding the Tennessee too low, Ridge's party took the new railroad line from Decatur, Alabama, almost north to Paducah, Kentucky. From there, everyone boarded a steamer to pass along the Ohio, down the Mississippi and out the Arkansas to Fort Smith. John Ridge took the land route, crossing the southern tip of Illinois, then angling down through Missouri to Honey Creek.

Late in September, he gathered his council at Rattlesnake Springs, on the Hiwassee near what is now Charleston, Tennessee, and pushed through a vote to continue its laws and constitution in the west, regardless of the political structure that the western band had already organized, or any that the Treaty Party might seek to form. It went without saying that the head of the Cherokee Nation government would be, as ever, John Ross.

With that, Ross declared that it was time for all the rest to go. He divided up the 13,000 remaining Cherokee into detachments of 1,000 each, trying to keep families and clans together, and then apportioned the removal funds accordingly. Like General Wool before him, Ross tried to give each departing Cherokee a fair price for the improvements he was leaving behind, from houses and farm equipment to chairs and cutlery. Nothing except the ground itself was off limits. Richard Wilkenson put in a claim for his sixty-five fruit trees, and a Chickamauga woman asked for the value of "six ducks, a plaid coat, a feather bed, a turkey gobbler, a set of china, two blowguns, a fiddle, garden tools, an umbrella, a coffee pot and a plow." For Ross, the last remaining Cherokee left their houses of their own accord. They could close up their affairs on their own terms; no soldiers needed to shove them along. They gathered peaceably at the points of embarkation to board the boats when they were ready. All this was as it might have been for everyone. As it was, plenty of the dispossessed were still jailed in those embarkation centers—even luminaries like the Reverend Jesse Bushyhead and Reverend Steven Foreman, speaker of the national council, who tried to lift the spirits of their fellow captives by leading them in worship.

But Ross could not control the weather. With the continued drought, the departure date for "his" Cherokee had to be postponed until October, which was worrisome, as winter was coming on. But there was at least some good news: Joseph L. Roberts, the cashier for the United States Bank, had boarded a stagecoach for Georgia bearing a $500,000 check from the War Department of the United States, to be delivered to Ross in person, the first installment of his $6 million fee for removal.

Check in hand, Ross at last made arrangements with Captain John Page of the U.S. Army for the removal of himself and his extended family of thirty-one, plus eighteen horses and oxen. Then he packed up all the piles of yellowing historical records of the nation that had so transfixed John Howard

Payne, plus a few treasured personal effects. The most prized might have been the ornate, signature-laden Master Mason certificate from the Olive Branch Lodge in Jasper, not far from Ross's Landing, attesting to his membership in that illustrious Scottish order, the Freemasons. This was a precious document, never publicly displayed, that said a lot about this Cherokee's true identity.

The dry weather held back their departure until October 1, when they could put it off no longer. John Benge, a descendant of Chief Bench who had fought with The Ridge against the settlers, led the first contingent. Now, at last, the rain came, but only enough to chill the emigrants to the bone. It did little to lift the rivers high enough to allow them to leave by boat. "In the chill of a dazzling rain on an October morning I saw them loaded like cattle or sheep into six hundred and forty five wagons and started toward the west," wrote an army private, John Burnett. "Chief Ross led in prayer and when the bugle sounded and the wagons started rolling many of the children . . . waved their little hands good-bye to their mountain homes." Benge's company bravely went first; it was soon followed by another detachment, headed by the officious editor Elijah Hicks; and then came eleven more, staggered a few days apart, as if each had to summon the courage to follow the one before, knowing that hundreds upon hundreds of miles lay ahead, a steady, death-defying slog of young and old, all on short rations, scarcely clothed, with the winter coming down hard upon them. The wind already had a bite to it, a hint of the freeze to come. The once green fields were just pale husks flattened against the cold earth, the barren trees' dark black limbs reaching to gray skies. The soul of the land was leaving.

It made a sad progression, like the retreat of a defeated army, regiment after regiment of broken troops. Life was no longer in balance, but tipped just one way, toward misery. Even the ones who weren't sick or frail or old or weary already seemed to be, so daunted were these courageous people by the prospect of a terrible journey to nowhere.

Still, they rallied, and forced their feet to trudge forward across the gathering bleakness, doing their best to ignore the icy temperatures, the sores, the aches, the monotony. Benge's group reached Nashville in two weeks, with Hicks coming a few days later. Measles, whooping cough, pleurisy, bilious fever—many were the diseases that they brought with them, making the camps into pockets of the undead. Hicks put at least forty on his sick list, and buried five of them before he pushed on. By the time they reached Port Royal, halfway between Saint Louis and Cincinnati on the Kentucky line, Hicks's people were hard to rouse, slow to leave in the morning, and keen to stop, as if the bonds that held them to their original homes were being stretched to the limit and they could go no farther without snapping. A full-blood named Nocowee weaved about as he pushed along, seemingly determined to drink himself to death. The old chief White Path staggered for miles before collapsing in Hopkinsville, on the Kentucky side from Nashville. He was buried where he fell, his shallow grave marked by a pole topped with a white linen flag.

The last groups didn't leave until early November, when winter was fully upon them. Icy blasts of wind ripped across the flatland, and soon brought drenching rains that delivered more torment, soaking everyone to the skin, and, as temperatures dropped, freezing everyone's clothing.

A couple from Maine happened to come upon a band of 1,100 departing Cherokee, an endless, bedraggled column of gloom, with just sixty wagons for the feeble pulled mostly by oxen, sometimes horses. One of the Mainers wrote an account for the *New York Observer* that January. "We found them in the forest camped for the night by the road side," he told readers, "under a severe fall of rain accompanied by heavy wind. With their canvas for a shield from the inclemency of the weather, and the cold wet ground for a resting place, after the fatigue of the day, they spent the night." It was painful to see them, the drawn faces, the limp bodies, some standing to stay dry, others lying down to rest, perhaps even to sleep, on the freezing slop. The writer couldn't get over the suffering: "The Indians as a whole carry in their countenances every thing but the appearance of happiness. Some carry a downcast dejected look bordering upon the appearance of despair." But not all of them, he noted perceptively. Stoicism was not always the rule—there was smoldering anger, too, that such hardship had befallen them, and it seemed ready to flare at any moment. Many of the Cherokee bore, said the author, "a wild frantic appearance as if about to burst the chains of nature and pounce like a tiger upon their enemies."

The suffering was not distributed equally, either. "Some of the Cherokee are wealthy and travel in style," he noted. "One lady passed on in her hack in company with her husband, apparently with as much refinement and equipage as any of the mothers of New England." They still brought hardship with them; it was just harder to see. For the lady had a sick child in her arms "and all she could do was to make it comfortable as circumstances would permit." Her wealth did not protect her. She would stop a few miles farther "in a stranger-land and consign her much loved babe to the cold ground . . . without pomp or ceremony, and pass on with the multitude."

The Maine couple encountered the Indians a few times more as they journeyed west, sometimes pitching tents for the night, at other times stumbling along. It was too much for the couple. "I turned from the sight with feelings which [I] cannot express and 'wept like childhood then,'" wrote one of them. The procession was at least three miles long. There were the sick, borne in wagons; many others on horseback; a few in fine chaises; and "multitudes" on foot. Many of them labored under the burden of all they could take with them. Even though the ground was now frozen, or awash with icy mud, most of the Cherokee were shoeless, wearing only "what nature had given them," and their clothes did not protect them from the cold. Ten miles a day they covered, stopping occasionally to bury their dead, or, if the ground was frozen too solid for digging, to just leave the corpse behind, unburied.

The Cherokee walked every day but Sunday, when they stopped for Sabbath services in which they appealed to the Great Spirit, not the Christian God who'd deserted them. On they staggered, crossing the frozen Ohio River on foot at Berry's Ferry. They pitched their feeble tents on the near banks to tend hundreds of the sick and dying, most of them brought on wagons that were turning into funeral carts. They crossed the Mississippi at Cape Girardeau, a short distance on, and then carried on all across Missouri, whipped by the wind, pelted by sleet, more Cherokee dropping by the day. Those with the money for chaises came through fine, but not the others, according to the *Arkansas Gazette* of December 26, "most of them poor and exceedingly dissipated." Evan Jones, the Baptist missionary with a later band that took a southern route through Arkansas, despaired a few days later that they'd gone 529 miles by his calculations and still had 300 to go. "It has been exceedingly cold," he wrote, with many "thinly clad." They'd taken to lighting a bonfire every few miles so that everyone could pause briefly to warm up before continuing, to "the great alleviation to the sufferings of the people."

It was so cold that the Reverend Jesse Bushyhead, leading a group that had tried to go by boat, had to stop for an entire month, since the Mississippi was locked in ice. They pitched their tents among the trees in the mounting snow and did their best to stay alive.

Elijah Hicks's party, the second to go, was the first to arrive in Indian Territory. That was on January 4 of the new year, after a bitter journey of three months. Then came a company led by the full-blood Hair Conrad three days later; Benge brought in his group three days after that. John Ross, who had come by boat, arrived on February 1. All but one of his party of thirty-one made it. His wife, Quatie, was the one who did not. She'd given her shawl to a sick child and then had come down with pneumonia; she died at Little Rock, where the boat had come to shore. If John Ross grieved, he did so silently. Theirs had been a complicated relationship, since he had spent so much of his time in Washington while she labored on in the nation. There was the language gap between them, compounding the distance. Now that she was gone, he buried her in a shallow unmarked grave that was soon hidden under the snow, and he continued on with his people.

The Cherokee came to the new land at intervals of a week or more through to March, when the Reverend Evan Jones's people arrived after a wicked journey of nearly six months of vicious winter. Many were missing from each detachment, many more were sick, and some had simply left along the way. Of the 1,250 Cherokee who had started out with Evan Jones, 1,033 appeared in the territory on February 2. Seventy-one had died, but five babies had been born.

Of the 15,000 Cherokee who undertook the journey that became universally known as the Trail of Tears, roughly 2,000 died, and countless more simply disappeared en route. Two thousand more died after they arrived, from disease, starvation, and the misery that comes from such suffering.

An elderly full-blood summed up the tragedy:

Long time we travel on way to new land. People feel bad when they leave old nation. Womens cry and make sad wails. Children cry and many men cry, and all look sad like when friends die, but they say nothing and just put heads down and keep on go towards west. Many days pass and people die very much. We bury close by trail.

4

"THE CHEROKEE ARE
A COMPLAINING PEOPLE"

The previous spring, with his store built but not yet stocked, John Ridge had returned east, but not to Washington for politics as always before. Instead, he went to New York for commerce. Leaving the children in the care of Miss Sawyer, he took his wife, Sally, with him, as she could use a break from the frontier. It was March 1838, just as the May deadline for removal under the treaty was drawing nigh. He'd come to collect merchandise to sell to the later emigrants who would not be able to bring much of their own.

In New York, though, he was disturbed to discover that the right-thinking religious elite, once the most fervent backers of his Cherokee cause, had turned against him, and not idly. They now hated Ridge with the venom they'd previously reserved for Jackson. In their estimation, the Cherokee weren't victims of the whites anymore. They'd been done in by their own kind, by the Ridges' Treaty Party. "Instead of receiving the late Treaty as a blessing to the Cherokee," John Ridge raged, the New Yorkers considered it a source of all his people's "afflictions." He fired off indignant rebuttals to the newspapers, but they failed to turn the tide.

Disgusted, the Ridges pushed north to see Sally's aging parents, the Northrups, who'd by now left inhospitable Litchfield for tiny South Lee in the Massachusetts Berkshires. Never the hardiest, John Ridge must have been exhausted by all the turmoil, not just in the nation, but now in New York, too, for he took to his bed after the couple arrived at the Northrups' home and scarcely roused himself from it for weeks. It must have been a torment for Sally to see her man so low. But she felt the pull of her children off in the distant west. In late July, even though her husband was still unwell, Sally could stay away from them no longer and began the long trek back to Indian Territory on her own. It was mostly by stagecoach, not horseback, but it made a daring passage for an unaccompanied woman. It wasn't until September that John Ridge rose to follow her. He may not have been fully well, but he had to go, for the last rounds of emigrants were finally leaving the east and would soon be arriving in the west, and John Ridge needed to sell to them when they got there.

In his own trek west, he got only as far as Kentucky when he spotted an alarming item in the *Louisville Journal.* Apparently, John Looney, the second principal chief of the western Cherokee, had called for an emergency meeting of ten tribes in the territory, both eastern and Plains, to "polish the chain of friendship" between them. Obviously, something had happened to tarnish that chain—but what? Had the waves of fresh Cherokee emigrants upset the delicate balance among the tribes already in residence? Later newspaper reports revealed that General Edmund Gaines, the aging commander of the Southwest Military District, dubbed "Granny" by his detractors for his anxious manner, had feared the whole frontier was about to erupt from the pressures of these new arrivals, terrifying white families along the border, who turned to him for safety.

Ridge rushed to the *Journal* offices to assure the editors that Looney's big meeting would surely be "entirely pacific—entirely deliberative—and by no means of hostile character." But this was just a hope. The territory had to be at peace or all his well-laid plans for his store would break apart. The Cherokee might turn back, or refuse to come, and those who remained could make the nation a worse hell than the one they'd left.

John Ridge raced back to Indian Territory in late October, to be well in place when the emigrants finally arrived after weeks of arduous travel with little more than the rags on their backs. No food, no money, no home, and no hope that anything would improve anytime soon. Rather than consult with Looney to calm everyone down, Ridge rode north to prepare his store. Knowing that even the most prosperous emigrants came short of cash, he offered terms few other storekeepers could match—purchases on credit, up to $10,000. John Ridge knew that if the emigrants did not have the money now, they would soon. The per capita allowance provided for in the New Echota Treaty would be distributed to these Cherokee, and he would take it.

The Old Settlers, as the original émigrés became known, had a government, but it wasn't much by eastern standards. They had no proper constitution and there were few laws, largely because there was little need for many, just as there had long been little need for laws in the east. There was a national capital in Tahlonteeskee, twenty miles west of Fort Smith. But it was no New Echota, just a single rustic council house in a field where the principal chief gathered with a few councilmen, plus judges and sheriffs and whatever chiefs cared to show up to do a week or two of government business, and then return home.

Treaty Party emigrants like the Ridges were happy to leave politics to the Old Settlers. And that sat well with the Old Settlers, too. They were not happy that twenty Treaty Party men, no matter how illustrious, had sold out everyone else. Personally, though, they had nothing against any of them—except for one. There was uneasiness regarding John Ridge. When he'd gone east that spring, rumors flew that he was planning to sell off a piece of the western territory for his own profit. The notion was utterly unfounded, but it took hold all the same. Even when no sale materialized, the Old Settlers remained wary. John Ridge was a man to be watched.

Truth to tell, the Old Settlers weren't so sure about Boudinot in Park Hill, either. As wealthier emigrants came in, the town was emerging as the social capital of Cherokee west. John Ross would soon move in about a mile away, and other mixed-blood Cherokee aristocrats would follow. Boudinot was there to help Worcester with the great effort of translating the King James Bible and then publishing it on a massive printing press Worcester had floated down the

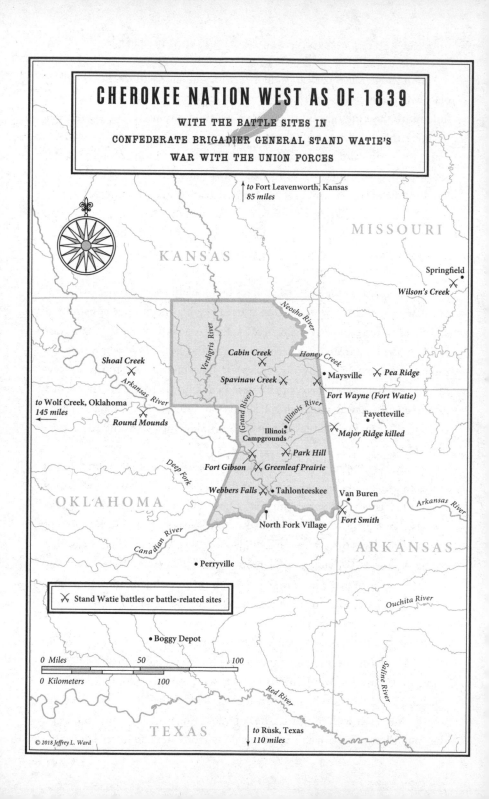

CHEROKEE NATION WEST AS OF 1839

WITH THE BATTLE SITES IN
CONFEDERATE BRIGADIER GENERAL STAND WATIE'S
WAR WITH THE UNION FORCES

to Fort Leavenworth, Kansas
85 miles

MISSOURI

KANSAS

Springfield
Wilson's Creek

Neosho River

Verdigris River

Cabin Creek

Honey Creek

Shoal Creek

Maysville

Pea Ridge

Spavinaw Creek

Fort Wayne (Fort Watie)

Arkansas River

(Grand River)

Illinois River

Fayetteville

to Wolf Creek, Oklahoma
145 miles

Round Mounds

Illinois
Campgrounds

Major Ridge killed

Deep Fork

Park Hill

Fort Gibson

Greenleaf Prairie

Webbers Falls

Tahlonteeskee

Van Buren

Arkansas River

OKLAHOMA

North Fork Village

Fort Smith

Canadian River

ARKANSAS

Perryville

✗ Stand Watie battles or battle-related sites

Ouchita River

Boggy Depot

0 Miles · 50 · 100

0 Kilometers · 100

Saline River

TEXAS

Red River

to Rusk, Texas
110 miles

© 2018 Jeffrey L. Ward

Arkansas River. But Worcester had been embittered by his long prison ordeal and started using the press to crank out harsh religious tracts with terrifying titles like "Incorrigible Sinner Forewarned by His Doom" along with circulars to recruit a "Temperance Army" to keep the Cherokee away from the whiskey peddled by Boudinot's cousin and so many others eager for a fast buck.

The Cherokee tended to leave the other Ridges alone, way off in Honey Creek. But Boudinot was unavoidable, and his presence in Park Hill rankled some of his neighbors. Worcester himself considered the New Echota Treaty "entirely unjustifiable" and believed that the Ridges, Boudinot included, should never have pushed it on the nation. Nonetheless, several prominent Cherokee members of Worcester's congregation found it such a "great sin" for Worcester to keep Boudinot on that they abandoned his church, and some Old Settlers sent a formal request to the national council to force Worcester to be done with him. But Worcester could not bring himself to abandon his old friend, not yet, anyway. He persuaded the western principal chief to hold off at least until the next council meeting in the fall. But even so, Worcester told the American Board that the council might order Boudinot's "removal," as Worcester put it, at any moment.

That was hard on Boudinot, understandably. Ever tender, he and his pious second wife, Delight, were struggling to make a go of it, and, along with his six children, he was still in mourning for his late first wife. Boudinot described the children proudly by birth order to their grandparents, the Golds. First came the scholarly Mary; then the independent Sarah; "quite large" Eleanor; keen William; then Cornelius, "still lame" like his uncle; and finally Frank, "the darling and pet of his new Ma." And evidently also of his Pa, who could not contain his admiration for the boy's "high arching noble forehead, with black quick and sparkling eyes."

But this was written the previous May, shortly after they'd arrived west, in a letter that told the Golds that he'd have to hold off from a promised visit as it would be "a long tedious and expensive journey." South Lee might have been reachable for cousin John, but he was rich. For Boudinot, Cornwall was too far away. Things had worsened since.

The Ross faction began to arrive in earnest that winter, waves of them, many of them just husks, wasted by disease, fatigue, and near-starvation. Since they had nowhere else to go, most of these new emigrants ended up

at the Illinois Campgrounds near Fort Gibson, where the meager federal rations would be dispensed. The meat was mostly spoiled, inedible; and there
wasn't nearly enough of anything else to go around. The War Department had
contracted with the firm of a pair of former army majors, Glasgow and Harrison, to deliver the rations, and apparently they'd skimped on edible food and
pocketed the savings. John Ross protested, but he and his brother had been
in on this too as the general contractors, and Glasgow and Harrison claimed
to be mystified: no other tribes under contract had had any such problems—
a statement that was demonstrably untrue. With a shrug, they dismissed the
matter: "The Cherokees are a complaining people." And the higher-ups saw
no reason to disagree.

The collision of the old and new bands of Cherokee put the commander
of Fort Gibson, Matthew Arbuckle, in a terrible bind. At fifty, he was a veteran of the Indian Wars who'd fought the fearsome "Fowltown Indians" in the
First Seminole War in 1817 before coming to the territory. As Fort Gibson's
first commander, he'd been the one to place it by the Neosho River, which
periodically rose up to overrun the fort, rotting out the foundation, its fetid
waters releasing a miasma that, by 1835, had killed almost 600 soldiers since
the founding of the fort in 1824. It seemed all too symbolic, this spreading,
invisible contagion, as if there were a secret poison in this part of the world
for which there was no antidote.

A stalwart character with ample hair that, in his one surviving photograph, seems to be blown from behind, Arbuckle was desperate to keep order.
It was his job to make the frontier at least *look* safe to the whites watching
anxiously from over the Arkansas border. The tension and uncertainties got
on his nerves. At one point, he was convinced that a Cherokee chief, Situ-
wakee, was preparing to storm the fort. Arbuckle sent a detachment of 200
dragoons to hold him off, only to find Sitawakee quietly chatting with John
Ross in front of his fire, peaceful as could be. Ross was rarely amused, but he
found that hilarious.

When the dispute between the different Cherokee factions rose up, Arbuckle made enemies on all sides. The Late Emigrants continued to mass at
the Illinois Campgrounds through the spring of 1839, twice as many as the
Old Settlers who'd been there for years. These newly arrived Cherokee had
resolved to bring the constitution of 1828 with them, along with their elected

officers, starting with John Ross. The Old Settlers, however, had their own government, and their own elected officers. They'd recently lost their long-time principal chief, in December. When his second, John Rogers, declined to serve, they were now guided by a neophyte, John Brown, until a proper chief could be elected in October. Brown had no interest in ceding to Ross, and the Old Settlers generally had no desire to be politically subsumed by the more numerous Late Emigrants. And there was a lot of money at stake, too, because the principal chief would be the one to dispense the federal annuity payments to the full tribe. Which one would it be—Brown or Ross?

The issue flared into open hostility that alarmed Miss Sawyer. "The critical situation of the Nation I cannot communicate," she wrote that May. It was even worse than back east. "The atmosphere of the old nation in its most disturbed state, compared to this, was like the peaceful lake to the boisterous ocean."

Ross did his best to assure the Old Settlers that he had no intention of imposing his government on their people. "He & his people were ready to come under the government and laws already existing there," said the missionary Cephas Washburn. The problem was that no one believed him.

For now, the Ridges stayed out of the political fray, content to attend to business in the North. They left it to the two bands, old and new settlers, to sort out. The two planned to do just this at a big meeting of both sides at Tahlonteeskee, the barren capital, on June 3, 1839. More than 6,000 Cherokee descended on the grounds. There, Ross called for a peaceful union of old and new, drawing on the Bible to observe, as Lincoln would, that "a house divided against each other cannot stand." For a time, harmony reigned, and the two sides shared campfires and blankets.

But the Old Settlers were afraid that unification would mean their eradication. Fearful, they insisted that all communication be written down—in English, still the language of diplomacy—so they'd have a record of any agreement, to avoid misunderstandings later on. They grew alarmed when Ross asked for a committee to create a set of laws for the new nation. The two sides would be equally represented, but the westerners had scarcely ever thought in terms of laws, and didn't see the need. They were put off when Ross put forward an elaborate bill to develop a system of laws in this new territory. Such formality was not the Old Settlers' way. They removed Ross from the joint council and closed off the prospect of a committee on laws. John Brown thought he'd showed unity enough just by meeting with these upstarts. Affronted, John Ross feared that the westerners planned to "annihilate" the easterners, and the westerners no doubt returned the sentiment. The easterners wished to put the question of laws to a vote, but, since the easterners had a majority, the westerners had no intention of agreeing to any such thing.

And then, as always, there was the money. After telling off Ross, Brown wrote in secret to tell Montfort Stokes, the federal agent, to dispense the annuities through him, not Ross. Ross fired off a letter of his own, telling Stokes to hold on to all the money for now, until "a reunion of the people shall be effected."

The breach might have been fatal but for Sequoyah. A resident of the west, but venerated in the east, too, he was a grand, unifying figure, and he emerged from his quiet seclusion to push through a resolution for everyone to meet again on July 1, after tempers had had time to cool.

But then the Ridges showed up. They came late to the meeting—all four of them, including Stand Watie, who was now a full partner. They took no part in the public discussions, but were seen quietly conferring with the western principal chief, Brown, just before he spiked Ross's laws committee. This did not sit well with the easterners. They thought that the Ridges had caused enough trouble. The three of them should mind their own business in Honey Creek, and Boudinot should stick to his translations in Park Hill.

Just the sight of the Ridges whispering with Brown was like a spark on dry leaves. Soon there was a blaze that leaped up to the sky and raged everywhere. That night, June 20, more than 100 of Ross's followers gathered in secret not far from his home on Park Hill. Everyone there had lost someone during the removal, or afterward; many of them had lost close family members, whose deaths all too often were slow and torturous. Now these Treaty Party men were defying them in the west, too? Would this never end?

Blood law—this was the thought raging in everyone's mind that night. No one was to sell Cherokee land without official permission. *No one.* John Ridge had written this law himself, at his father's instigation. The fury had been smoldering for some time, possibly from the moment the ink was dry on the page just after Christmas 1835, now almost three and a half long years before. Did they not know that *the land was not theirs to sell?* Land belonged to everyone. That was the Cherokee way. The lordly Ridges might have possessed the nation's finest houses, most extensive farms, most valuable ferries, and, now, its richest store, but they'd never owned the nation, and, for all their airs, they never would own it. That one act of theirs at New Echota had affected Cherokee everywhere, bringing down the wrath of the federal government and the state of Georgia on them, routing them from their homes, pushing them through the long freezing deadly march west only to find more misery when they arrived. And now the western settlers were dead set against them.

This was the talk that night. Loud, frenzied, raw, outraged, liquored-up. Someone brought out the original text of the blood law, as written by John Ridge himself, and read it out in stentorian tones. The Ridges' own words— did they really think those words did not apply to themselves? Were they above that law too? Others called out the names of the other Treaty Party men to be charged with the capital crime of selling the eastern lands of the nation. Not just Major Ridge, John Ridge, Elias Boudinot, and Stand Watie, but three others, as well: John A. Bell, James Starr, and George Adair. All seven of the accused were prominent, successful men who had found riches here in the west when everyone else was struggling just to survive. To the Ross men, their wealth was exceeded only by their arrogance. This must end, the throng declared. *They* must end.

After the names were read out, the clans of the accused were called. Deer, Wolf, Bear, and the rest. The clans had been receding as modernity came on. Few Cherokee full-bloods, even, observed the ancient prohibition against marriage within the tribe, or insisted on the original blood revenge, or followed matrilineal lines of property descent. All this was slipping away, but tonight, the clans would assert themselves once more. Three men from the clan of each defendant would serve as the judges of their own kind. The seven accused would not be able to defend themselves, and no evidence or testimony would be presented. But there would be solemn deliberations. If some of the particulars of the law were overlooked, the essential thrust was not.

Three elders from the Deer Clan pronounced the formal verdict for Major Ridge. Guilty. And elders from the clans of the others quickly followed suit. Guilty, all seven. The room must have echoed with the word. All seven must die two days hence, at dawn.

John Ross wasn't there, but his son Allen was, and he saw a pile of wooden chips dropped into a large black hat, one chip for every man present. Fourteen of them bore an X in black ink, to indicate "EXECUTIONER," a word Allen Ross capitalized in his account. Everyone was to reach into the hat and draw out a chip. Everyone but Allen. "When I came to draw the chairman stopped me," he wrote, "and told me that I could not draw as the committee had another job for me on that day." He was to find his father and keep him in his house all night, and all through the next day and night, too. But he was not to say why.

Two executioners were assigned to each victim, but as many as fifty took part in delivering what they saw as justice to the convicts. After the meeting broke up, more than two dozen men galloped through the next night to reach Honey Creek early Saturday morning, June 22. It was still dark when they roped their horses to some trees across the field from the two-story log house John Ridge had built for his family. It was the last of the predawn moonlight, and silent except for a light rustling through the hay as the men sneaked across the field to the house itself, where they peered in the windows, dark, menacing shapes under soft hats. They saw John Ridge asleep downstairs beside his wife, Sally, their three children slumbering nearby. Most of the men split off to surround the house, ready to stop Ridge if he burst out a window. The two executioners remained on the porch with a few others until everyone was in place. Then, just as dawn was breaking, one of the killers eased up the heavy iron latch and swung open the door.

Pistol drawn, the lead executioner crept toward the sleeping John Ridge, his heavy boots treading light on the hardwood floor, to bring the tip of the gun barrel to Ridge's temple. He held it there only for a moment, and then squeezed the trigger.

Nothing. The gun delivered only a click of the hammer. At that, Ridge started, and several others stormed in to pounce on him and drag him in his nightclothes to the door while Sally screamed from the bed. Frail and weak, John Ridge scrabbled desperately on the hardwood floor to defy his assailants, his bony legs kicking feebly. He grabbed for the doorposts before the men yanked him through and then dragged him down the front steps to the bare ground, where they laid him out, surrounded. There, the proud Ridge did not plead for his life, but argued for it, tried to reason with this mob, but the men hollered to drown out his words. Two men pinned his arms to the ground and others held his feet, and then the rest took out their skinning knives to slice them through Ridge's nightclothes to his slender body, one after another, everywhere. The cuts were not deep enough to kill, just enough to torture, and each one brought a piercing scream of pain. Sally was shrieking from the porch, held back by other conspirators, and Ridge tried to call out to her, but he couldn't be understood for the blood gurgling from his slashed throat. Finally, the men put away their bloody knives, and John Ridge slumped back onto the ground, struggling for breath. Seeing him there, prostrate, the first executioner smashed a muddy boot down on his head, and another did the same, and then another, and then all of them, as if they wanted to mash John Ridge into the dark soil of the despised new land. Finally, when everyone had had a crack at him, they left him there to die, slowly, in agony, as so many of their friends and relations had died. Blood-drenched, mangled, hideously contorted, he lay sprawled on the ground until Sally rushed down to him, the horror-stricken children creeping after her, all convulsed in sobs.

Incredibly, he was still alive, and Sally and the children managed to lift him up and carry him back into the house. They laid him out, groaning from his many wounds, on a table, pulled a sheet over his blood-drenched body, and stared at the horror of it all.

There before them, his literary son John Rollin wrote later, lay their father, once the glory of the nation, "pale in death," Sally beside him "hands clasped and in speechless agony." His mother, Susanna, was there, too, having rushed down from her house at the commotion, "her long, white hair flung loose over her shoulders, crying to the Great Spirit to sustain her in that dreadful hour." Neighbors crowded in, too, some of whom, John Rollin darkly declared, must have known of the assassination attempt, since the Ridges' enemies were everywhere, and had "come to smile over the scene." And then, slowly, as everyone gazed down at him in horror or wonderment, the life seeped out of John Ridge until he was no more.

Another band of killers, thirty strong had ridden to nearby Park Hill that night. They were coming for Boudinot, who'd been staying with his family— Delight and the six children—at the Worcester house while he built his own nearby. Arriving just past midnight, the killers watched the Worcester place from the distant trees, waiting for Boudinot to emerge from the front door in the morning.

Sure enough, a little after daybreak, out came Boudinot with a few last good-byes, and then he strode alone across the hayfield to join in with the carpenters at his own house, which was rising a few hundred yards away. As he neared the work site, three or four Cherokee, all good-sized men, came up to him with worried talk about a sick child. Could he possibly find some medicine? Like Worcester, Boudinot served as a local apothecary, and he kept a few potions at Worcester's mission. He did not know the men, but, in Christian charity, he bade them come along with him to see what he could find. As they made their way back across the field, one of the men dropped slightly behind—and then ripped a bowie knife into Boudinot's back, dropping him headfirst onto the grass with a cry. Then the Cherokee cracked a tomahawk into the back of Boudinot's skull, and, in a fury, brought it down on him a half dozen times more. The assailants then rushed off, leaving Boudinot facedown, unmoving, his hot blood soaking into the grass, his skull cracked open.

Hearing Boudinot's cry, the carpenters rushed to him and raised such a clamor that his wife and Worcester both came tearing from the house. Finding her husband's body, limp, hideously blood-spattered, Delight reached down to cradle him in her arms as she sobbed uncontrollably. "They have cut off my right hand," Worcester cried.

By then, a third band had set off to Honey Creek to catch Major Ridge. There were just a half dozen killers this time. They found out from a neighbor that the major had already left for some business in Van Buren, the whiskey town a good thirty miles south. The men galloped after him, determined to catch their man before he learned about the others. They followed him due east to the Arkansas border, then south down the Line Road until they found his horse tied to a hitching post. It stood by a farmhouse where the major must have been passing the night. The men waited in the trees until sunup. Then they crept to a window, where they saw the major enjoying some breakfast with his host, unaware of the gathering trouble. The killers galloped on toward Van Buren to lay a trap for him when he came along. They found a spot by a bridge over White Rock Creek, maybe a dozen miles ahead, and

In the new Cherokee capital of Tahlequah in 1843, John Ross called a convention of nineteen other tribes that had been forced west, in hopes of creating a common alliance. But his faction of the Cherokee nation was engaged in a civil war with the Ridges' Treaty Party, and nothing came of the gathering.

Stand Watie became the undisputed leader of the Ridge Party after his uncle, cousin, and brother were murdered by Ross's men. A shrewd and persistent antagonist to John Ross, Watie served as a brigadier general in the Confederate Army to battle him.

The all-suffering Sarah C. Watie was Stand's fourth wife, and the mother of his five children, three of whom died young. After she fled to Texas during the Civil War, she wrote to her husband: "I look for you soon on account of having no place."

The Cherokee principal chief John Ross in the statesman garb of his later years.

Mary Stapler married John Ross at eighteen when he was fifty-four. They met when she was in a Pennsylvania boarding school three years before. Six years into their marriage, she bloomed into a woman of considerable sophistication.

Left: Albert Pike made an unlikely military leader of the Cherokee. He had a fondness for a meerschaum pipe, sentimental poetry, unmarried women, Sanskrit, and, as reflected here, freemasonry. *Right:* Limiting himself to one term, an impatient President James K. Polk finally brought peace to the Cherokee in 1846, when he persuaded Ross and Watie to put aside their enmity.

Left: John Howard Payne is now remembered as the composer of "Home, Sweet Home," but he was also a bit player in the Cherokee drama. Eager to write a book about the Cherokee removal, he fell in with John Ross and ended up his chief publicist in Washington, DC. *Right:* The dashing Creek warrior Opothleyahola fought with Major Ridge against the Red Stick rebels, but when he joined the Union Army, a furious Watie drove him into the snows of Kansas, leaving him to freeze to death.

Left: In this Ross marriage certificate, the ship represents the Mariners' Church in Philadelphia, where the wedding was performed, since Mary Stapler's Quakers refused to sanction her marriage to an Indian. Her family filled out most of the attendees; no one from Ross's family attended. *Right:* The Watie children: the girls Jacqueline and Ninnie on the sides, the boys Watica, Saladin, and Cumiskey down the middle. Only the girls survived their father. Starting at fifteen, Saladin served under his father. He survived the war, but died of unknown causes three years later.

Top: John Ross's treasured Rose Cottage was named for the roses that lined the long drive. He lived here with his wife, Mary, until Union soldiers forcibly removed him to Philadelphia. While he was away, Stand Watie burned the house to the ground. *Bottom:* During a rare interval of peace in 1851, the nation put up this female seminary, shown with a graduating class. Its first headmistress was a Holyoke graduate, who had an early fright when some pranksters showed up at her door in the feathers and face paint of Plains Indians.

The Battle of Pea Ridge turned against the Confederacy when two of its commanders were shot dead by snipers within minutes of each other. This etching depicts the last hour of the battle.

Cherokee Braves Flag carried by Colonel Stand Watie's Cherokee Mounted Rifles.

Elias Cornelius Boudinot was the calculating son of the saintly *Phoenix* editor. He represented the Cherokee in the Confederate Congress and partnered with Stand Watie in several ill-fated business ventures.

The last Confederate general to admit defeat, Stand Watie tried to restore his vanished fortune by growing tobacco he thought should be tax-free since the Cherokee Nation was independent of the United States. When the 1870 Supreme Court disagreed, Watie was left nearly destitute.

The self-taught ethnologist James Mooney lived for almost thirty years with a band of Cherokee who'd hidden in the mountains of North Carolina to escape removal. Mooney was determined to collect every last scrap of Cherokee heritage before it vanished.

The last of the great Cherokee shamans, Swimmer was the keeper of the Cherokee traditions.

there they waited, guns at the ready, in the shadowy underbrush just off the road. It was an hour, perhaps more, before Major Ridge came cantering along. He had a servant following behind. Just as the major reached the bridge, the men burst out at him, guns blasting. Ridge's horse reared up and tossed its rider, who landed hard on the bridge. He was probably already dead from his wounds, but the killers surrounded him all the same and emptied their guns into his quivering body as the servant raced off in a panic to report the terrible news. Guns empty, the men took off, leaving behind them a crumpled, blood-slimed corpse under the oak branches that curved over the bridge.

Major Ridge had been right that night at New Echota. He had indeed signed his own death warrant. Each of them had.

Stand Watie was scheduled to die, too. He might have been an afterthought compared with the three other, more prominent men of the Ridge family, but he'd signed the New Echota Treaty in Washington without regret, and now he had to pay, just like the others. But a sympathetic Choctaw learned of the murders of the other Ridges, and galloped to tell Watie before killers came for him at the Ridge store at Honey Creek where he was helping out. When the Choctaw arrived, he found several strangers already milling about, appearing to size up the merchandise as they waited—so the Choctaw thought—to catch Watie alone. The Choctaw took Watie aside, ostensibly to discuss the price of some sugar, and whispered the dreadful news. Shaken, Watie immediately slipped out the back and jumped onto the Indian's horse, named Comet for its speed, to get away. But rather than take refuge, he raced south to warn a sister, who'd moved in near Worcester's place in Park Hill, of the frightening hazards to the family. As he neared her house he spotted several dozen men on horseback lurking about. He quickly dismounted, slapped his horse to run it off, and, hearing more men coming on horseback up the road, hurried past an orchard to a deep pit the children called the Devil's Sinkhole by the side of the road. Saplings crisscrossed the opening to keep anyone from tumbling in, and Watie slipped down into a gap between them, grasped one, and then hung off it as the enemy passed by nearly overhead. When all was quiet once more, he pulled himself up and hurried on.

More than his brother, and certainly more than the crippled John Ridge or the elderly Major Ridge, Watie was a man of action. All he lacked was seniority, and that would come quickly, as he was the last of the Ridges, the only one left standing. But he was already a man to reckon with, more than people recognized. They would soon.

Glancing about to make sure he was not being watched, Watie hurried on to his sister, who frantically told him that some men had already come through asking about him. She told him to flee right away. Watie asked if it was true about their brother, Boudinot. His sister nodded tearfully. His body had been laid out at Worcester's house. Watie would not leave until he'd seen it.

When Watie arrived at the Worcester house, a gang of armed men milled about outside, but Watie pushed right through them without stopping, and they didn't dare oppose him in front of everyone. For a crowd had gathered in the little dining room where Boudinot's body was laid out on the table under a white sheet that was smeared with his blood. Everyone went silent on seeing Watie there, and let him pass, his boots heavy on the wood floor. Reaching the table, Watie peeled back the shroud and stared down at his dead brother's face. The soulful eyes and warm lips had gone a horrible gray, and the head was hideously askew and misshapen from the ax blows. Watie stared for a long time in silence, then yanked the shroud back up over his brother again and turned away. Before he reached the door, he shouted to the crowd that he would give $10,000 for the names of his brother's killers. *"Ten thousand dollars!"* he repeated. Then he was gone, the last of the Ridge men.

Watie's name told his history. His Christian mother had baptized him Isaac, but he preferred Da-gata-ga, meaning Stand Firm, or Two Who Would Stand As One, the name given by his Cherokee father, as if Watie had an invisible twin to protect him. Stand Firm he did, and Stand he was. In the modern manner, Watie had taken his father's last name, rather than let the elders dream one up for him, but he'd contracted it from the original Oo-watie so it would sound less Indian.

All this was back in the old country, where he was raised in a Cherokee settlement consisting of a few huts, several acres of crops, and hunting land near present-day Rome, Georgia, not far from his uncle's place at the Oostanaula. The houses ran along a slender stream called Coosawattee; Watie's was one of the more modest. Unlike his brother, David Watie had not grown rich, nor celebrated; he was just settled and reasonably secure. Unlike his fascinating brother, Buck, or his brilliant, crippled cousin John Ridge, Stand Watie was barely educated. He'd had trouble getting his mouth around English, with all its crunching consonants and noisy vowels, so different from the satisfying breathy singsong of Cherokee, and even now, in his thirties, he handled the new tongue roughly. Unlike the others, he was no orator, and whenever he gave a speech, he never began it without saying so, or finished it without his listeners' agreeing with him. Among the many moods of the Cherokee language, one conveyed insistence. That was useful for Stand Watie, whose utterances could have an impatient edge. By now, though, his more distinguished brother and cousin had seen *their* words, written and spoken, collected and set down. Not a single word of Watie's had been saved. He did not know Shakespeare, but he would have known what it was like not to have been born great, but to have greatness thrust upon him. After the events of June 22, his letters would be treasured, and, invariably brief and to the point, they convey the force of his convictions.

Still, he was a man between two worlds. In becoming Elias Boudinot, Watie's brother Buck had adopted the ways of the whites, as had his elevated cousin, John Ridge. By contrast, Watie's father and uncle had remained firmly within the Cherokee tradition, and, with their gleaming copper skin, looked the part. Stand Watie, of a middle complexion, swung between the two poles. While his brother and cousin commanded the nation's attention, Watie quietly helped out with his father's ferry service, humbly doing his bit. He also kept a shop, and thanks to his politically connected uncle, was clerk to the Cherokee Nation during the troubles. He'd married three times, but all three wives had died, one in childbirth, adding a sullenness to his character. He could also be roused to sudden fury. When, in 1819, his friend, district sheriff Charles Hicks, had been shot to death by a criminal suspect evading arrest, Watie took justice into his own hands. The killer disappeared into the hills, but Watie tracked him for days and then surprised him with a bowie knife in his chest.

For a man so thickset, Watie was surprisingly agile, with fast hands. When he was younger, he'd been selected for the annual ball-play exhibition of the nation's best players. He was quite the horseman, too. He rode firmly, with command. Once asked to get word to the federal Indian agent a hundred miles away over rough, unfamiliar, Georgia terrain, some of it settled by hostile tribes, Watie returned in less than a single day, message delivered, a staggering feat for horse and rider alike. Action and patience were the two sides of his being, and the dichotomy made him somewhat unpredictable, perhaps even unknowable. Still, when people spoke of Watie, they talked about his cunning, but about his toughness most of all. It was a quality that rose fitfully, though. It took him a while to settle on who he was.

It might have been prudent for Watie to flee to Arkansas, as many other members of the Treaty Party did, and wait for the nation to calm down. But he returned to Honey Creek. The distance from Ross's Park Hill would bring safety enough, and there he could gather a few hardy loyalists to strike back. Fortunately, Bell, Starr, and Adair had survived, too. Together, the four would form the new leadership of the Treaty Party, but Stand Watie would be the man in charge. If the Ross men had assumed that they could kill off the Treaty Party with three murders, they were mistaken.

5

"THEY CAN LEAVE US"

When Ross's son Allen insisted his father stay inside on June 22 while the three Ridges were slaughtered, Ross must have wondered why he was being confined. Did he really not think anything was up? A missionary, Reverend Cephas Washburn, happened to stop at Ross's house before he'd received word of the murders that fateful morning and found the principal chief in "a bad humor." Preoccupied, it seemed. "From indications we remarked as soon as we left, that something was wrong—or that something was in preparation which we did not understand." All those who had gathered two nights before to convict the Ridges had been Ross men, and many of them members of Ross's handpicked lighthorse brigade, the old police force of Major Ridge's that Ross had revived in the territory to help keep order. It made for a very large conspiracy, and it was hard to imagine that Ross, his eyes and ears everywhere, had no inkling. Could his son really deceive him with some story? Or did Ross know better than to ask?

Whatever the facts, John Ross was always adamant in maintaining that he knew nothing of any plot. So on June 22 he acted as surprised as anyone when an Indian raced up to the Ross house and shouted out the grim news about Boudinot. Professing astonishment, Ross immediately sent his brother-in-law John G. Ross to Worcester's house to find out what had happened.

There are degrees of knowing. Ross may not have known the specific plan; his henchmen could easily have kept the details from him. But he surely knew of the general fury against the Ridges, since he himself had done so much to stoke it. There must have been loud talk about finishing off the detestable, troublesome leaders of the Treaty Party once and for all, and if Ross did not try to quiet the hotheads down—and there is no evidence that he did—they may have assumed his tacit approval. This wasn't complicity, exactly, but it didn't make for absolution either.

The question is, after John G. Ross rode back with the dreadful news of Boudinot's death by tomahawk, and then the other reports came in, how did Ross take it? A decade before, when Ross and the major were building the nation together, Ridge had been a friend, possibly even a close friend. Since then all three Ridges had emerged as bitter and possibly dangerous enemies who'd defied Ross at every turn. Tormented him. *Infuriated* him. Did Ross harbor no regrets, no sorrow?

Stolid as he often seemed, Ross could be obscure, too, his true feelings hidden behind the mask of a politician. He was a calculating man. Was he glad to see the end of the Ridges? Or genuinely regretful to learn of their deaths? Did he mourn, spill tears? A real outpouring of grief would have gone a long way to counter the suspicion that the principal chief had wanted the Ridges dead. But it is hard to picture him convulsed with grief at the news, and no account survives to say how he reacted.

General Arbuckle couldn't picture such a thing, anyway. Arbuckle was not a Ross man. To Arbuckle, Ross was nothing but a nuisance in a territory that already gave him enough trouble. He did not see Ross as the man to unify the nation—his perception was more the opposite—and he was convinced that the sooner the Cherokee realized this, the better. No, he saw in Ross a scheming opportunist who would do anything to take power and keep it. In his estimation, there was no way Ross had *not* been behind the very convenient deaths of the three leaders of the Ridge Party.

For his part, Ross sensed that Arbuckle was prejudiced against him, and did his best to proclaim his innocence. Scarcely had the Indian left the house before Ross dashed off a letter to Arbuckle telling him the news it was his "painful duty" to report: "Elias Boudinot is killed." The passive voice is artful, as it avoids any awkward reference to a killer. And he added that Delight Boudinot had advised him to flee when she heard, as Ross reported breathlessly, that Stand Watie was "coming forthwith to take my life!" Surely, Delight would never have expressed such concern for Ross if she thought he was behind her husband's death. Quite so. But had she warned Ross? From the evidence, it appears highly unlikely. But if it was a lie, it was an effective one, and a mark of what Ross was willing to do or say to get out of a jam.

"Why I am to be murdered without guilt of any crime I cannot conceive," Ross airily told Arbuckle, and asked him to make an "unbiased investigation" before there could be "an effusion of innocent blood." His own, primarily.

Arbuckle's reply was everything Ross feared. He'd already heard all about the murders, and he had reason to believe that Ross was sheltering the killers *right there in his house.* "The troops sent out will take charge of them if turned over," he curtly informed Ross, "and convey them in safety to this point." The troops *already* sent out? And *if* turned over? And if not? What then? Was Arbuckle planning to arrest him for murder?

By that afternoon, Stand Watie had assembled a posse of about fifteen men to ride down from Honey Creek to find the killers. By then, hundreds of Ross's followers had already raced to surround the home of the principal chief, well armed, sure that he would be the target of Watie's wrath. Afraid to start a war with the Treaty Party men, Ross asked Arbuckle to send out a detachment to keep the peace, but Arbuckle didn't want to get into the middle of a war, so he invited Ross to take safety in the fort instead. Afraid that Arbuckle would arrest him the moment he showed up, Ross preferred to stay home with his backers, who soon became a small, boisterous army of 500, eager to take on Watie and his Treaty Party men, and finish the job.

Such a force made Watie worry about his own safety, and he took refuge in Fort Gibson with his men. There, Watie hunkered down with General Arbuckle, who made little secret about where his loyalty lay, to decide how to proceed.

With Watie at Fort Gibson, Ross men swarmed to Honey Creek to make a "public plunder" of the Ridges' property and stripped the little settlement almost bare. "They destroyed or stole my poultry, killed my cattle and hogs," Sally Ridge wrote, as mystified as she was furious, "and not satisfied with camping by my fields and eating just what they wanted, they turned their horses into the field, evidently designing to destroy all the corn in their power." It was an utter horror, alone with her children in the house where her husband was slain, his blood staining the floor, and these angry men coming for her. Every night, all she could think was that "our sufferings would be terminated by assassination of the murderers of my husband."

A week later, she could take no more, and packed up everything she could. She was done with Cherokee territory. She fled with her children to Fayetteville, safely inside Arkansas, leaving behind all that remained of her husband's merchandise, her only possessions of much value. Still, the literary young Rollin was relieved that the family escaped "beyond the shrieks of the murdered."

Major Ridge's frail widow, Susanna, could not bring herself to leave. She was too old, too sad, to move again. In her grief, she didn't think any Ross men would come for her, but she would greet them with resignation if they did.

Miss Sawyer followed Sally Ridge to Fayetteville, but first she had to wait to close up the school in Honey Creek. After the murders, hardly any pupils showed up, and who could blame those who stayed away? She felt for the grieving Sally. "I saw her sinking under the weight of sorrow," Sawyer wrote, "fearful apprehensions & undecided anxieties." Unbowed herself, Miss Sawyer would start a female seminary in Fayetteville to turn homespun frontier girls into proper, Christian women.

After the murders, the Old Settlers figured they'd run things until everyone calmed down. But in the present crisis, with Watie sheltered at Fort Gibson, and a loyal army around him, Ross had another idea. Taking advantage of the disarray of his opponents, and utterly defiant about any role he might have played in the tragedy, he insisted that the big gathering at Illinois Campgrounds, which Sequoyah had endorsed, should take place on July 1 as planned. Under the circumstances, Ross doubted that any Treaty Party followers would show up to oppose him; they would fear they might meet the same end as the Ridges. He doubted that many Old Settlers would come either. Sure enough, they wanted to put the meeting off until July 25, when all sides could be fairly represented. If Ross promised not to have anyone killed for his views, perhaps they could talk business then.

Arbuckle passed this offer on to Ross with his endorsement, and he added that if the parties couldn't unite, he feared the nation would have to be broken up to avoid civil war. Ross gave no quarter. "Is it required, that the late emigrants relinquish all their rights, and appear before the Western Chiefs in the attitude of suppliants?" he demanded. No, Ross would have his convention.

Two thousand people came, almost all of them from his own party, just as he'd expected. All the same, he announced an "Act of Union" that proclaimed his government the one leadership body, and himself its head. His first act as a Cherokee Caesar was brazen: he offered blanket pardons to the Ridges' murderers. To him, the killings were not crimes at all, but legal "executions," making the killers not just innocent men, but heroes. The *victims* were the criminals. He summarily declared that all the signers of the "illegal" New Echota Treaty still living were "outlaws," not entitled to the protections of the Cherokee Nation. The surviving signers could now be shot on sight, with impunity—unless they publicly apologized for their traitorous ways within the next eight days and took an oath to Ross's new government. To back up this message with force, Ross created eight new lighthorse companies of police, answerable only to him, to hunt them down if they resisted.

It was astonishing. In a stroke, the murder victims became perpetrators, and those not yet killed were slated to die with government sanction. When Watie heard this, he told the *Arkansas Gazette* that he would sooner die than grovel before John Ross.

Pressing his advantage, Ross soon followed up with a new constitution just like the old one. "We the people of the Cherokee Nation," it began, just as before, although that "we" now covered a substantially different population. He had it ratified by an assembly of just 200 this time, all but fifteen of them in the Ross Party, making the act scarcely less high-handed than what the signers at New Echota had done. While he was at it, Ross pushed a vote to depose Old Settler chiefs John Brown and John Rogers, and to present a new slate of public officials, starting with himself as the principal chief, and two other Rosses in key posts: his nephew William Shorey Coody as presiding officer, and his wealthy brother Lewis as treasurer. In a sole conciliatory gesture, he gave a third of the remaining offices to Old Settlers, but they didn't have much power. He made it clear to his opponents that if they didn't like his new government, they needn't stay. "The world is large," he declared. "They can leave us."

In response, Watie's Treaty Party joined with the Old Settlers to declare that the Old Settler government, not this new regime of Ross's, was the sole "body politic" in the nation, and to charge that Ross was behind the conspiracy by which the Ridges were "cruelly and inhumanely assassinated." Watie declared that he would take up arms—but only "for our personal safety." It was Ross's "mobocracy" that was plotting war. He wrote to Ross that he wanted peace, but if Ross's men "again commence killing us, we will certainly resist them with all the power and energy we are masters of, without consulting consequences."

If anything, tempers ran higher than they ever had run in the east, when Georgia and the United States diverted some of the internal tensions. Now it was Ridge versus Ross, straight up, with the Old Settlers added to the Ridge side. In Arkansas, citizens grew so anxious about a Cherokee civil war spilling across their border that they organized a militia—vigilantes, really—of their own called the Cane Hill Independence Regulators to go after the Ridges' murderers, and they shot three Ross men rumored to have been involved. It was frontier justice—shoot first, make inquiries later. Fearing further trouble, Arbuckle asked the Arkansas governor to post the state militia at the border to wall off any Ross men bent on bursting into his state for reprisals. And, on his side, Arbuckle sealed the border of the Cherokee Nation against any whites who might come storming in to take matters into their own hands.

Startled by Arbuckle's display of power, Ross assured him that "all matters of controversy will soon be brought to an amicable close." Arbuckle replied that Ross might start by hunting for the killers himself, or Arbuckle would assume that Ross was in on the plot. When Ross did nothing, Arbuckle sent out squadrons of dragoons to round up the men he had reason to think responsible. In such a gossipy country, it didn't take long to get a good list. Their tongues loosened by whiskey, the killers themselves had taken to boasting about their accomplishment, and word spread. The identities of the suspects wouldn't have surprised anyone, for they were mostly higher-ups in the Ross Party with a long history of grudges against the Ridges. One of them was Bird Doublehead, the oversize son of the villainous tribal chief Doublehead whom The Ridge had dispatched more than twenty years earlier. It was well known that Bird had been waiting for a chance to avenge his father. It seemed he'd enlisted a pair of brothers, Jefferson and James Hair, along with some others to waylay Major Ridge as he crossed the bridge. A couple of full-bloods named Shell Turtle and Money Taker had taken the lead in killing Boudinot, although it wasn't clear who stuck in the knife and brought down the toma-hawk. And three wrathful Spear brothers—Joseph, James, and Archibald—had led the daybreak attack on John Ridge.

Dozens more took part, but the driving force behind the conspiracy against the Ridges was said to be James Foreman, the immense and surly head of Ross's lighthorse brigade. Foreman had fought the Ridge Party for years. He'd been the one to cut down Major Ridge's Treaty Party colleague John Walker Jr. years before with a barrage of bullets, much as the major had just been taken down. People said that Foreman was out looking for Watie in order to finish the job. Knowing that, Watie was now on the lookout for him.

Once he got the names of the suspects, Arbuckle enlisted Treaty Party men to guide his soldiers to their likely hiding places. The men had all made themselves scarce, and when they did move about in the open, they traveled in packs, full of scorn for the blue uniforms of Arbuckle's brigades, and the soldiers thought it best to leave them alone, at least for now. Besides, if they risked mak-ing an arrest, there was no guarantee that justice would be served in Ross's court.

Despite the rising demands from Washington for action against the Ridges' killers, no one was apprehended for the crimes. Ross did nothing to help, and mostly concentrated on keeping himself alive. Protected by a small army at his house, he surrounded himself with six well-armed bodyguards whenever he left, the cost billed to the nation.

As the summer went on, however, Ross men started turning up dead, victims of summary justice from the other side; the corpses were washed up on the sandy shore of the Arkansas River, or were found lying by the side of a road, the faces bearing a look of surprise. None of the Ridges' main killers was killed in retribution, but a man named Sanders, thought to be involved in Boudinot's murder, died in a brawl; and Edward Gunter, who'd come after Watie, fell to consumption. All the same, more Treaty Party men were picked off in reprisal.

It was the old blood law. One of yours for one of ours.

6

INDIAN JUSTICE

By now, Stand Watie was no longer the afterthought who deferred to his educated and eloquent relatives. Those relatives were all in their graves— two in a grassy field at Honey Creek, one at Park Hill—leaving him the undisputed head of the Ridge family, and of the Ridge Party, too. It was not a post he'd ever sought, but it was the one he had, since there was no one else. To mark it, the Treaty Party sometimes bore a new name, the Watie Party.

But if Watie was to gain any security in the nation for himself and his people, he would have to appeal to the only force stronger than the hundreds of Ross's henchmen, with thousands more ready to run to his aid from the countryside. That was the federal government in Washington. Watie and his close friend and fellow target of Ross's, John A. Bell, rode there to deliver a list of "grievances and wants" personally to President Martin Van Buren. Foremost among them: protection from Ross's henchmen, and the arrest of the Ridges' killers.

On the way to Washington, Watie and Bell stopped in to see former President Andrew Jackson at his plantation home, the Hermitage, outside Nashville. The relentless force behind removal, now well retired from the presidency, Jackson had nothing but loathing for Ross, who had resisted him so adamantly for so long. He dashed off a fierce letter for the two men to take to Van Buren, lambasting Ross's "outrageous and tyrannical" conduct. Justice must now be served, Jackson demanded. "When oppression comes, and murder ensues, resistance becomes a duty," he told Watie. "Let the arm of freedom lay the tyrants low & give justice & freedom to your people."

In Washington, however, the first order of business for Watie and Bell was to hit one of the city's finer haberdasheries for clothes that would make official Washington take these country bumpkins more seriously. Watie came away with an elegant green frock coat, Bell a mulberry version, plus velvet vests, fine pantaloons, and smart overcoats for both. Their wallets were lightened of a prodigious $100 each, but there were few better-dressed men in the capital when they repaired to the Globe Hotel to await their appointment with the new president.

Prepped by Jackson, the squat, muttonchopped Van Buren received the two men and their delegation sympathetically, happy to carry on his predecessor's business. He was fully aware of his obligations under the New Echota Treaty to put down any "domestic strife" in the nation, and he would not abandon the Treaty Party now. He passed the Cherokee on to his secretary of war, Joel Poinsett, in the department offices that now occupied an imposing Federal-style brick structure, one of four identical military buildings that took up a full city block. Inside, the walls gleamed with oil portraits of Poinsett's predecessors.

In Poinsett's spacious office by the main stairs, Watie pressed the Treaty Party's case against Ross, claiming that Ross had "misrepresented our motives, charged upon us treasonable designs and resorted to every unscrupulous means to array the bitter prejudices of the less informed and more savage of our tribe against us." This was only too true: Ross had promised to sacrifice these Watie Party infidels "on an altar of revenge." Watie charged that Ross was planning to abuse the annuity system by taking the money to pay off national debts—if not his personal ones—rather than pass it to individual Cherokee as intended, leaving many "on the very verge of starvation." He mocked Ross's grand notion of "Cherokee law" as simply Ross's law, carried out by his chiefs, "patroles," and police companies in his interests alone. Just that December, Ross's men had broken into a man's house while he slept and nearly hacked off his hand with a hatchet.

Watie told Poinsett that his people could never live "side by side" with Ross's people. The dream of a single Cherokee Nation was over. The time had come for the federal government to split the nation in two, the North for the Watie Party and the Old Settlers, the South for Ross's men.

A dashing, windswept South Carolinian, Poinsett had studied medicine at the University of Edinburgh; trained for the military in Woolwich, England; taken tea in Moscow with Czar Alexander; served as a secret emissary to Chile and Argentina to pry them loose from Spain; and been the first American minister to Mexico, returning with a bright Christmas plant he named after himself, the poinsettia.

Poinsett didn't need Watie—or Andrew Jackson, for that matter—to tell him that Ross posed a dire threat to the success of the Cherokee Nation. If Ross got his way, there would never be peace. He should never be allowed "to exercise any tyranny toward those persons who may be odious" to him by branding them "outlaws." Poinsett would tell Arbuckle to order Ross to back off and turn over the murderers. If he didn't, Arbuckle should arrest him, too. Otherwise, Poinsett had to agree with Watie. The nation was not big enough for both parties.

Watie might have won official Washington, but he was losing the Cherokee Nation. For while Watie was away, Ross persuaded the local Indian agent Montfort Stokes to back his "unity" government, and he assembled another convention of his backers to endorse the new constitution and affirm his own position as the primary chief. And he installed his new government in Tahlequah, not far from Park Hill, and declared it the new capital.

When Ross discovered that Watie had won over Poinsett, he traveled to Washington to set the secretary of war straight. On the way, he dropped off his thirteen-year-old son Silas at Lawrenceville, which had emerged as the Ross family boarding school, with Princeton to follow. In Washington, Poinsett could hardly have been more frosty, assailing Ross as the "instigator and abettor of the foul murders." Stunned, Ross snapped that he would never recognize the government's authority over a private act of "one Indian against another," a rather delicate term for a series of political assassinations. The Cherokee Nation was sovereign and independent, he insisted. The United States should keep its hands off—except, of course, where the annuities were concerned.

Not wishing to be left out of the discussions in Washington, a group of Old Settlers also raced east to present themselves to Poinsett. Watie and Bell were still there pressing their case. At one point, representatives from all three groups crowded into Poinsett's first-floor office, all of them talking at once. Watie reiterated that his faction would never get along with Ross's people, and the nation would simply have to be divided. And, by the way, while Ross had talked of adding secondary schools, Watie wished to build a *college* to "present to the world a spectacle different to what is now seen in our country."

The Old Settlers sniped that they were never going to go along with a tyrant like Ross who trampled on minority rights. But Ross insisted he was the only one in a position to lead the single, unified government that, he believed, was needed to run the territory. He would never permit the humiliation of seeing his land chopped in two—especially if the federal funds were halved accordingly.

Ross demanded that Poinsett release the annuity funds immediately, and, while he was at it, he should make payment on Ross's personal claims for his improvements in Georgia, too. Although the property had officially been valued at $50,000, among the priciest in the nation, Ross was asking for an additional $164,250 in damages because of the harm to his public image. That was not exactly a conciliatory move. By contrast, Watie asked only for $2,392 for his improvements in Georgia.

Seeing all the acrimony, Poinsett found the notion of two separate nations increasingly appealing. It would bring peace, and bring *him* peace. But he wasn't keen on deploying federal troops to bring it about, not after army soldiers had just gone through the strain of enforcing removal. Piqued as he was at Ross for taking the law into his own hands, he didn't endorse Arbuckle's plan to remove him from office, either.

The whole thing was a mess, and the United States had more important issues to deal with, chiefly in Mexico, which had just lost Texas to independence. Ironically enough, General Sam Houston, once a runaway with the western Cherokee in Arkansas, had led the Texas troops to victory. Arbuckle decided the best way to deal with the Cherokee was to stall. He'd appoint a commission to investigate the financial claims, and in the meantime hope the two sides would relax their grip on each other's throats.

To try to keep the peace, Arbuckle had assembled military forces not just at Fort Gibson, but at Fort Smith past the Arkansas border, and at Fort Wayne, thirty miles north, all of them stuffed with soldiers poised to jump at the least provocation. Ross knew that his men were the primary targets, but he figured that Arbuckle wouldn't dare sic federal troops on him—and then be blamed for the uproar that was sure to follow. It was true: Arbuckle didn't want to get into the middle of a war on the frontier. He hoped only to make Ross think that he might indeed press to divide the nation, which would frighten Ross into giving the other parties more of a say in his "unity" government. Ross was content to wait Arbuckle out. As 1840 wore on, events may have turned against the principal chief, but the nation was still his, at least for now.

Among Watie's skills—shopkeeper, horseman—he was also a lawyer, having learned the trade as clerk of the nation. He held power of attorney for John Ridge's estate, but he had not handled any cases in the territory until a friend in the Treaty Party, Archilla Smith, asked Watie to defend him against a murder charge. A staunch ally of the Ridges back in Georgia, Smith had signed the New Echota Treaty and come west with Major Ridge and Stand Watie in the spring of 1837. Rather than go north with the Ridges, Smith had stayed near Fort Gibson in a rough settlement of emigrants where several tribes mingled uneasily.

Like many on the frontier, Smith was not one to shy away from a fight, and he didn't back down when, several months after the Ridges' murders, a Ross man named John MacIntosh came after him. The two had words, there was a scuffle, and MacIntosh ended up with a knife in his chest. Word of the killing got back to Ross, and a few weeks later his lighthorse brigade stormed into the camp and led Smith away in chains. Furious at the news, some Treaty Party men went to Ross's house and gathered threateningly outside.

To Stand Watie, however, Smith's arrest was hardly justice, but another chance for Ross to remove an enemy, as the penalty for murder was death by hanging. Watie agreed to defend Smith, an act of some daring, since the trial would be in Ross's new capital, Tahlequah, where treaty signers could still be legally shot on sight.

At that point, Tahlequah consisted of just a few nondescript, earthen-floor log houses, with words like "The Council sit here" painted on the side. One of them was the courthouse. For the trial, a jury of twelve men, all of them known to Smith, sat along one wall and Smith sat with Watie across from them. One Ross man, Looney Price, was the presiding judge; and another, Isaac Bushyhead, was the prosecutor. According to the sworn testimony, when MacIntosh came into the camp, he immediately seized Smith's horse. Smith shouted at him to let go. When MacIntosh wouldn't, Smith got out a bowie knife and slashed at him. Finally, MacIntosh gave out a cry, smashed Smith in the face with his fist, and galloped away, only to tumble dead onto the ground a few dozen yards off. Only one witness, a Creek named John, claimed actually to have seen Smith stab MacIntosh. Smith leaped up to deny it, but the judge silenced him.

The prosecutor, Bushyhead, claimed that law alone was the remedy for such a crime. But clearly politics was in play, too. A Ross man had been stabbed to death, and a Treaty Party man was in the dock. Nevertheless, Watie at first defended Smith purely on legal grounds and picked at the discrepancies in the testimony—the number of stabs, the distance MacIntosh rode before falling out of the saddle, the time of day. Given all the confusion, how could anyone be sure Smith was responsible for MacIntosh's death? After deliberating through the night, the jury could not reach the required unanimous verdict, and Looney Price ordered a retrial with a fresh jury. By then, Price had fallen ill, and was unable to continue as the presiding judge in the new trial. Ross replaced him with Isaac Bushyhead's brother Jesse, despite the obvious conflict of interest. Jesse was the esteemed minister who had led one of the Cherokee bands west, and who now served as the chief justice of the Cherokee supreme court.

When the case resumed, Watie now asserted that it wasn't just the inconsistencies in the testimony that should free his client. He argued that the murders of the three members of the Ridge family had created a terrible atmosphere of fear for such "a conspicuous sharer" of the treaty cause as Smith. If Smith had indeed stabbed MacIntosh to death, Watie now argued, his client might well have done it in self-defense, thinking MacIntosh might kill him otherwise.

Stolid, gruff, Watie was never an easy man to read. His rage had flamed after the Ridges' murders, but it seemed to cool down after his trip to Washington. Now, when he was defending Smith, it rose again. Perhaps he saw in Smith a quality he'd tried to deny in himself—a man who defended himself impulsively, without heed for the consequences. Unfortunately for Smith, that rationale came too late. As prosecutor, Isaac Bushyhead mocked Watie for insisting earlier that Smith hadn't killed MacIntosh, and admitting now that maybe he had. Which was it? As for the larger political question stemming from the Ridges' murders, Bushyhead refused to engage it. Once his friends were killed, Smith had no right "to kill anyone in return."

As the presiding judge, Jesse Bushyhead told the jury to ignore all other considerations and focus solely on one: did Archilla Smith kill John MacIntosh? If they believed the answer was yes, they must convict. Once the question was put that way, the jury had no choice, and quickly reached a unanimous decision. Guilty of murder in the first degree. Jesse Bushyhead imposed the sentence: death by hanging.

Outraged by the verdict, more than 100 Cherokee, mostly from the Treaty Party, petitioned Ross to pardon Archilla Smith, but Ross refused, and the next morning, a wagon came for Smith. He rode to his execution on a chair that rested on a plank over his open coffin. Since the proper gallows hadn't been completed, he'd be hanged from a nearby tree. When Smith arrived, a crowd was waiting, including several members of his family, all of them weeping profusely. Still sitting on his chair in the wagon, Smith angrily declared that his death sentence came not from his Creator, but from Ross. "Hatred has brought me to this." Exactly at noon, the sheriff fitted Smith with a noose and had him stand up on the chair. Then the sheriff threw the far end of the rope over a tree limb and tied it down. He gave the wagon's horses a slap, and the wagon lurched forward. The rope proved too loose, though, and Smith's feet came down to the ground, leaving him dangling there, until a couple of Cherokee jerked the rope tight and snapped Smith's neck.

Stand Watie was not in attendance. Perhaps he could not bear to witness John Ross's power to kill with impunity—or to see Smith die for fighting back when he himself had not.

• • •

If the two Bushyheads overseeing Smith's trial refused to acknowledge that the killings of the Ridges led to the death of MacIntosh, they had to see that the death of Archilla Smith had fatal consequences. Not a week passed before Thomas Terrell, a member of the first jury and one of Smith's guards for the second trial, was killed in what one witness called a "drunken fray" by Dennis Wolf. Terrell had been a Ross man, and Wolf was a backer of the Treaty Party. This time, Wolf was let go after the court deemed the death "accidental." But he was set upon by another Terrell as soon as he left the courthouse. Wolf survived the encounter, but five Terrell brothers were soon slaughtered in their beds in reprisal.

7

$1,094,765

T he mounting fury of the Treaty Party against John Ross had many sources. His complicity in the Ridges' murders, his authorizing the hunting down of the signers of the New Echota Treaty as "outlaws," and now his role in the prosecution of Archilla Smith. All of it displayed the grating ways of a despot, not an elected leader. But of all the insults, the heaviest and most enduring involved money. As principal chief, Ross had sole control of the annuity payments—the millions that the United States had agreed to pay for all the eastern land, and for the "improvements" the Cherokee had built on it, from farmhouses to schools. The payments were meant to go to the entire nation, but they had to pass through Ross's hands first. Graft was always a temptation for a chief, and it is not clear if Ross resisted.

"His ruling passion is avarice," lawyers for the Old Settlers charged in a lawsuit they brought against him later. "He has been able to gratify it to an extent almost unprecedented." His Georgian antagonist Wilson Lumpkin believed the money made him "king of the Cherokees." As Lumpkin said: "The control of this immense amount of money, in the absence of any enlightened supervision or check on his financial aspirations, is the key that unlocks the secret cause of his lone career of absolute reign and power, as well as his great popularity, at home and abroad."

By 1840, he'd led the nation for twelve years, since 1828, without once submitting to reelection every four years as required by the constitution. All that time, he had supposedly devoted himself entirely to a job that paid somewhere on the order of $3.50 a day. And yet, by the time of the removal, he had emerged as one of the three richest men in the new nation, and his brother Lewis was the richest of all. John Ross had built an impressive house for himself in Georgia, started a ferry, bought fifty slaves, laid out lavish fields, and, with Lewis, established a thriving store. Even aside from the claims of malfeasance regarding the annuity, there were rumors that he'd taken gross advantage of the 1819 Tellico Treaty to accept federal offers of land on a promise to become an American citizen, only to sell the land at enormous profit, up to $8,000 per lot, and remain Cherokee. Critics were disgusted that Ross should assail the Ridges for their "illegal" land sale, its proceeds to go to the nation, while he sold countless tracts solely to enrich himself. As one summed it up: "This patriotic man sold his share in the country, put the money in his pocket, went back for another share, liked [sic] upon the national annuities, became the mortal enemy of 'land settlers' and decried in stentorian tones any land sale proposals."

Government bribes were a time-honored means of winning over Indian chiefs, and there was no more valuable chief to win over than John Ross. He had, after all, been the major impediment to removal—until he won exclusive control of all the federal contracts and became its most energetic backer. It was easy for him to take a fat cut. By one accounting, it cost Ross only $20 to move one Cherokee west, but he ended up charging the government $103 and pocketed the difference. Paid by the number of emigrants, and by the length of the journey, Ross exaggerated the first and extended the second, or so it was claimed. General Winfield Scott, in charge of the move, noted drily that Ross's fees did not "on the whole, fall strictly within the arrangement." Ross attributed any overages to his determination to do right for a suffering people, but the suffering itself argues otherwise.

In fairness, many others had their hands out, as Ross also employed 174 subcontractors, all of them happy to profit at federal expense. The Washington firm of Glasgow and Harrison alone received $674,527 for dubious services—including $13,500 the firm paid a Major A. J. Rains to withdraw his claim of corruption. Still, accountants for the Old Settlers determined that if Ross's itemized costs were subtracted from his billings, he cleared $1,094,765.

Such extravagant numbers flew about in the breeze of the territory, and there was talk of impeachment. Ross responded by changing the subject, as if such matters were unworthy of his attention. Besides, his backers remained loyal whatever he did. The full-bloods retained a primitive faith in him that would never be shaken, as if he were not a leader but a god.

Still, by 1841 the questions of impropriety had risen to the point where the federal government hired an investigator, Major Ethan Allen Hitchcock, to look into them. In his lengthy report, he described the scene in Tahlequah when Ross arrived on horseback to address the corruption charges that swirled about him. Despite the controversy, Ross entered town like Lumpkin's Cherokee king, an object of universal reverence. Hundreds of Cherokee were standing around when Ross tied his horse to a tree in the middle of the council ground, yet, Hitchcock wrote, "Indian-like no one approached him." Hitchcock himself had no such compunctions, and he walked right up for a brief chat, and then a few of the Cherokee dared approach Ross, and then many more crowded in to shake his hand. It took a full hour before Ross could free himself to take his place under a large shed that sheltered the national committee and national council, with many hundreds of Cherokee arrayed about it to listen in despite the death threats received by the most demanding questioners. Ross had shrewdly brought with him, as a silent endorsement of his character, Jesse Bushyhead, the chief justice who remained much admired despite his role in the Archilla Smith case. While the Cherokee officers sat hushed before him on benches of split logs, Ross gravely mounted the pulpit. Everyone expected that he would finally address the corruption issue, but he hardly touched the subject. He wished instead to dangle a rare piece of good news before his listeners. He'd just come, once again, from Washington, and this time brought with him a wonderful letter from the new president, John Tyler, the high-cheekboned Virginian who'd risen from the vice presidency after the sudden death of the incumbent, William Henry Harrison, just a month into his term.* A career politician, having served Virginia as a U.S. representative, governor, and senator, Tyler had taken an unexpected interest in Cherokee issues, going so far as to consult the original statements of Washington and Jefferson to decide what was fair. Tyler had given Ross a letter that seemed to promise much of what he'd sought in terms of sovereignty and funds. Waving the letter in triumph, then pointing to Tyler's signature, Ross declared it was the answer to all their prayers.

And the corruption charges? Ross referred to those matters, Hitchcock wrote, "very briefly," saying he would wait until a full accounting could be made. "An intelligent white man residing here gives the opinion that Ross will yet fall a victim to these measures," Hitchcock concluded, referring to Ross's handling of the federal funds. Ross never did offer an accounting, or refer to the matter again. One critic disparaged him as "an artful, cunning, shrewd, managing, ambitious man." But those qualities served Ross well, and his detractors ended up grasping only air. At one point, a rumor circulated that Ross had been caught red-handed with $500,000 in federal funds. The Hotspur Rollin Ridge was thrilled that Ross's "character will perhaps be hereafter understood." Nothing came of it.

Despite his doubts, Hitchcock concluded that Ross was not only "an honest man," but "a patriot laboring for the good of his people." But by then, he may have fallen under Ross's spell, as Ross could still charm those he needed to. Even so, Hitchcock noted that several of Ross's relatives, such as his brother Lewis, had "realized fortunes through his instrumentality." And this was 1841, when Ross still lived in a modest cabin. His fortune would soon be far greater, as would his house.

That fall of 1841, around the time of Hitchcock's visit, there were national elections for the lower offices. The higher offices like principal chief wouldn't come around for two more years, if indeed Ross allowed a vote to be held. While he had been able to dispel suspicions about his finances, the execution

---

* It was often said that he'd died of pneumonia brought on by the two-hour inaugural address, a record that still stands, he had delivered coatless and hatless despite chilly and damp weather. More recent medical investigations suspect that the foul gas rising off open sewage near the White House was the more likely cause.

of Archilla Smith must have hung over the nation, as the Ross Party lost its majority to an alliance of Old Settlers and Treaty Party candidates.

Although Watie was the titular head of the Treaty Party, he himself did not seek office. After the Smith trial, he'd returned to a quiet life in Honey Creek, where he ran a small store, replacing the grander Ridge enterprise; farmed; and raised horses. In time, he'd keep a half dozen horses, all bred for speed, in a corral at Honey Creek, and he'd race a couple of them, sometimes for purses that reached an astronomical $500,000, inflated by the high rollers who were starting to float down the Arkansas looking for adventure. Gambling had become a popular pastime in the seething nation. The drunken David Vann's son Joseph was soon smitten, raising speedy thoroughbreds of which the fastest was the celebrated Lucy Walker. Dubbed "Rich Joe," Vann was so taken by the mare that he named his luxury steamboat after her, and one October took the *Lucy Walker* down the Ohio to the annual races in Louisville with a bevy of gentlemen in beaver hats and cutaways, their ladies in elegant crinolines. A fiend for speed, Vann was determined that his steamer be the fastest on the water, and he maniacally stoked the fires to drive it full blast—until the boiler exploded, killing all but thirty of the 136 passengers on board. Vann was literally burst apart. All that was found of him was one arm, in a sleeve adorned with his monogrammed cuff link, dangling from a far tree.

Now that John Ridge's widow Sarah had removed her family to Fayetteville, taking Miss Sawyer with her, Susanna—also a widow, lonely and distraught—was the only Ridge to remain in Honey Creek. Watie himself, having buried three wives, lived alone. He seemed content to stay well away from the political action in the capital.

For a man who'd been at the violent center of the national controversy over the Ridges' deaths, and so much else, Watie seemed to have resigned himself to a life of quiet solitude. A Cincinnatus who had returned happily to his plow, he seemed done with politics. Although he'd won the sympathy of the federal government, it had taken no action on behalf of his followers. Watie had not avenged the deaths of his close relatives, not secured a share of the annuity payments, not established an independent state, and had not significantly diminished John Ross's power or standing in the nation. Instead, he had retreated alone to Honey Creek, almost as if he were daring Ross's men to come for him.

At least one other Ridge was not nearly so complacent, and his attitude revealed what Watie's lacked. That was his nephew John Rollin, often shortened to just Rollin, who was fuming, and he would continue to fume for years. "Although I have always been taught never to harbour feelings of revenge it is impossible for me to control them," he wrote to Watie later. "It will always give me pleasure to hear of the deaths of the murderers of my relations." Watie didn't see the point in adding another corpse to the count, and bringing more of Ross's men gunning for him.

But the feelings that had been ignited in Archilla Smith's trial continued to smolder. On May 9, 1842, the notorious Ross man Anderson Springston, who'd been in on the shooting of John Walker, was himself shot dead just inside the Arkansas border. A white man did it, but the Ross Party accused the Ridge men of putting him up to it. A rumor flew that Watie was finally planning to take his long-awaited vengeance. Supposedly it would occur at a horse race where leading Ross men were going to be in attendance. But there was nothing to the rumor. Watie had never intended to watch the race, let alone to kill anyone there.

He did leave Honey Creek, though. He had some business in Van Buren. As a precaution, he decided to bring along a friend, James P. Miller, for an extra pair of eyes, and another gun if need be, while he made his way along the two-track road that wove through the trees. It was late afternoon when they reached the little frontier town of Maysville, just over the Arkansas border, near the turn south onto the Line Road. David England's grocery was the only establishment in town, and the two men were ready to break up the long ride. They tied their horses to the hitching post, pushed open the grocery's swinging door, and entered the cool shadows of the store.

Although it was called a grocery, England's shop had a little of everything, from kerosene lamps and tack to barrels of molasses and wheels of cheese—with a jar of peppermint candy on the counter for children, gratis. Watie and Miller weren't there for any hard goods. They just wanted some restorative whiskey from the bar in the back.

In the dim light, Watie could see there was a customer already at the bar. He was good-sized, at least six four, solid, and broad-shouldered. He was well known to Watie, who may have felt him there before seeing him. It was James Foreman, the leader of the Ross gang that had slaughtered the three Ridges.

Everybody knew that now. "A giant in size and strength," someone called him, "given to dangerous and deadly strategems." He was the one who, years back, had clipped John Walker, Jr., having teamed up with Anderson Springston, Foreman's half brother, now dead.

Watie had heard that Foreman was planning to "put him out of the way," and that he had lately been careering about the nation with seventy men for the purpose. Only two men were with him now: his uncle Alexander Drumgoole, and his other half brother, Isaac Springston.

Miller didn't like it. He told Watie they should probably leave. But Watie shook him off. He'd come for a drink, and he'd have it. He called out for whiskey, and England set a glass down in front of him and gave it a pour. Before Watie could have his drink, Foreman swept up Watie's glass.

"Stand Watie," he said, raising the glass in a mock toast. "Here is wishing that you may live forever." Then he knocked Watie's drink back and set the empty glass down on the counter.

The gesture reeked of insolence, but Watie maintained an even tone. "Jim, I suppose I can drink with you." He weighed his next words. "But I understand a few days since that you were going to kill me."

"Say yourself!" Foreman shouted, furious to be called out.

Watie grabbed the glass from Foreman's hand, smashed it down on the floor, and glared at him. Foreman was a head taller than Watie, and thicker, too.

Foreman snatched from Drumgoole a thick bullwhip, the kind that can snap a man's neck, stepped back, and brought it whistling down on Watie's shoulders. But Watie was well padded by a leather jacket and, shielding himself with an arm, he dodged away. Foreman was gathering the whip back for another stroke when Drumgoole jumped on Watie's back and tried to put his hands around Watie's neck. Watie staggered about the store with Drumgoole heavily on top of him, grasping for his windpipe. Foreman yelled to Springston to fetch his "pieces"—his guns. As Springston dashed off, Watie managed to fling Drumgoole out a side door and into the yard, where he lay heaped on the grass. Inside the store, Foreman yanked out a board from England's stack of lumber and was about to crash it down on Watie's head when Watie produced a bowie knife and shoved it into Foreman's chest. At first, Foreman seemed merely surprised to feel the blade inside him. He stepped away from Watie and out to the yard, and continued to stroll along, as if he were in fine health despite the blood spilling down him. After about twenty yards, he wheeled about. "You haven't done it yet!" he cried.

Then Watie pulled out his Colt, took aim, and shot Foreman in the chest. Foreman seemed to shrug off the bullet, too, and continued walking as though nothing much had happened. Finally, as he reached a gap in the far fence, his steps slowed and he started to weave. Then he collapsed face-first, and he never moved again.

Springston came back with a rifle shortly afterward, but it was too late. Seeing what had happened, he didn't dare turn the gun on Watie. Drumgoole picked himself up and glanced at the dead man off at the far end of the yard. He left Watie alone too.

8

THE DEFENSE

Stand Watie had stood firm, and John Ross was disgusted. At Park Hill, he sent out his lighthorse guard to arrest Watie and haul him back to stand trial in the nation. But Watie was not going the way of Archilla Smith. He surrendered to the authorities in Arkansas, in Maysville's Benton County, beyond Ross's reach. He was offered bail and swiftly collected "more than fifty gentlemen," according to one account, willing to put up the money to guarantee Watie's appearance at trial.

Out on bail, he remained in Fayetteville, which was safer than Honey Creek, and did his best to carry on with his life. Three months later, he did something quite unexpected under the circumstances. He married Sarah Bell, sister of his close friend and ally John A. Bell. In a surviving photo, she looks like a minister's wife, her hair tightly parted, her dark dress brightened with a prim bow. She stares gamely into the camera with sad eyes, her features otherwise blank, as if she can no longer respond to what life has thrown her way.

The photo is undated, but it is likely that her suffering had begun by then. She would have five children by Watie, but lose three of them, each death harder to bear than the last. After the wedding Sarah settled in with her new husband in Fayetteville. Rollin Ridge was hunkered down there for the same reason. He warned his uncle that if he crossed the border, "neither law nor justice would save you from the death they so unjustly wish you to die." The fact that they hadn't killed him already "shows the cowardice of the whole Ross party."

The marriage of Stand and Sarah was as much a political union as a romantic one, for it deepened his alliances within the Treaty Party as almost nothing else could have. The Bells were all staunch members. James M. Bell was likewise a wanted man for signing the New Echota Treaty. Sarah's father, John Bell, Jr., had led a contingent of Ridges out of Georgia; her mother, Charlotte Lightfoot Adair, was one of the Adairs of Adairsville, Georgia, whose father was a supreme court justice; and her grandfather was the celebrated Irish trader and ethnologist James Adair. The Bells were also connected by blood or marriage to other powerful pro-treaty clans, the Thompsons, Beans, and Mayfields and the soon-to-be notorious Starrs. Finally, in joining with Sarah, Watie was also joining a colony of anti-Ross emigrants who had settled in East Texas, following the legendary warrior Chief Bowles, who'd fought under Dragging Canoe.* Sarah ultimately would move there.

Justice could be slow on the frontier, and it was a full year before Watie appeared at the prisoner's table before the Honorable Joseph M. Hogue in a crude building of hewed logs that barely kept out the wind. It had been thrown up just a few years before when Benton County split off from the larger Washington County to handle all the squabbles created by the crush of pioneers coming west for a fresh start.

As Watie sat coolly in the prisoner's chair, a proper jacket over a colorful shirt and loose tie, he must have felt more anxiety than he displayed. In the outback, the difference between innocence and guilt could be alarmingly

---

* Overwhelmed by Texas Rangers seeking to oust the Cherokee from the state, Bowles faced them down on horseback while his followers fled to safety behind him. The advancing rangers shot Bowles's horse out from under him, then blasted the chief in the leg so he couldn't run off. Bowles sat on the ground, singing a war song as a ranger captain approached, pistol drawn. The captain shot him in the head and then used Bowles's own sword—given to him by Sam Houston—to slice off a swath of skin as a souvenir.

slight. To improve his odds, Watie hired no fewer than six lawyers to defend him, while the state relied on a single prosecutor, the rather beleaguered Alfred M. Wilson. And Watie's lawyers were all prominent men—a state senator, state representative, major general, and state supreme court justice among them. The last was George Washington Paschal, the white soldier who had married Major Ridge's daughter Sarah, and he was the key to Watie's fortunes. Besides being on the state supreme court, he was the law partner of the redoubtable Alfred Arrington, whose legal acumen, theatrical bravura, and disdain for convention were legendary. This was a man who would argue not just the facts, but their history, their meaning, their *morality*. A man of large-lunged grandiloquence, he would loom up over the awestruck jurors like a backwoods Jeremiah.

The law wasn't really Arrington's calling so much as his belief, or rather his manipulation of the beliefs of others. Arrington had in fact started out as a Methodist minister. He wasn't a big man, but with his long arms, spectral gaze, and mesmerizing voice, Arrington could, it was said, "electrify an audience beyond all living men." Thousands had gathered at campgrounds to hear him rhapsodize about God in the open air. Twelve years into his ministry, he got a little carried away and, possibly in the belief that he could convince his listeners of anything, he began to push a startling new message—about the joys of infidelity. At the time, he was married to a local girl, Sarah Connors, from a respectable family—but, remarkably, he extolled the pleasures of forbidden women, and he spoke from experience. He'd planned to elope with one on a Sunday after church, but, unfortunately for Arrington, her husband got wind of the plan and preferred to keep his wife for himself. Arrington carried a gun but prudently did not use it in the ensuing three-way confrontation of errant wife, distraught husband, and eager lover. Things retreated to the status quo ante. Mrs. Arrington must have been forgiving, for she hung in with Arrington ever after, and bore him five children. But that was it for Arrington's ministry.

Life on the frontier was sufficiently far-flung that Arrington had to move only about ten miles to start over in a new pursuit that likewise depended on utter self-confidence, and the histrionics to back it up. The law. He specialized in sensational murder cases, which were plentiful in an outback where whiskey, firearms, and grudges frequently converged. Arrington's rousing defenses soon won acquittals much as his pious eloquence had secured conversions. And on those rare occasions when the jury did not go along, Arrington took his case outside the courthouse. After a timid jury let a notorious Indian-killer, Willis Wallace, go free, Arrington rounded up 100 Cherokees to seize him in Fayetteville Square—until Wallace wheeled into view a massive cannon he'd somehow commandeered from the state arsenal. Even Arrington had his limits.*

In the trial, Wilson kept it simple. Watie killed Foreman. No one disputed it. Guilty.

To Arrington, the case just started there.

It wasn't *what* Watie did, it was *why*. The short answer was obvious: he might have been killed by Foreman otherwise. After his three relatives were murdered, Watie had much to be wary of, and reason to strike first if danger loomed. "We expect to prove that [Watie] was hunted down and followed up—waylaid, and every attempt made to take his life," Arrington declared. "If ever there was a case where a man acted in self-defense, from a necessity enforced upon him by imperious circumstances, this was that case."

But Arrington took the notion of self-defense far beyond the events at English's grocery to the broader history of the nation that lay behind it. In his telling, Foreman was not the threat. That dubious honor fell to the notorious John Ross. It was Ross versus Ridge again, or so it seemed. In Arrington's telling, Watie would not be on trial for what he did on May 9, 1842. *Ross* would be on trial for what *he* did on June 22, 1839, plus the events that led up to it, and what came after. If this was a straight murder case, Watie might swing just as Archilla Smith did. But if it was a matter of politics, there was another calculus. For the politics of the Ridges' murders had pushed the nation into civil war, leaving Watie to be judged by its rules. Kill or be killed. A kind of savagery, perhaps, but a savagery that fitted the chaotic circumstances.

Arrington boldly made these assertions in his final summary, a remarkable panegyric that, printed verbatim, fills seventeen dense pages out of Paschal's forty-four. In his opening lines, he asserted that Watie's life was at risk from James Foreman not solely on the evening at England's store, but ever

---

* Arrington later recounted this and other of his back-country tales in a fictionalized account called *Desperadoes in the South-West*.

since Foreman killed Major Ridge and said he was gunning for Watie next. As Arrington put it, from that day on, Stand Watie had a right to kill James Foreman. Even if Foreman did not make the slightest move against him, Watie could shoot first to defend himself preemptively. In effect, Foreman was the outlaw, not Watie.

It didn't matter to Arrington that this hadn't occurred to Watie himself. After an early determination to get the Ridges' killers, he'd pretty much decided to leave them be. His nephew Rollin might be spoiling to kill, but Watie wasn't. And even Rollin thought only of revenge, not of personal security. When Watie saw the hulking Foreman in the bar, he did not reach for his gun, but waited until the provocation was too great to be ignored. And *even then* he responded only with harsh words. The knife came out only to keep Foreman from slamming a thick piece of lumber down on his head.

"The right of self-defense is a natural right," Arrington bellowed. But to him it went further than Watie could have imagined, to include a dispensation to defend himself by *attacking*. To Arrington, this was a right that derived from no constitution but from the laws of nature, in which survival is one's first duty. This had always been the Cherokee way, long before the first settlers arrived, and it says something about Watie and the "civilizing" impulse that this had not, actually, been his way at all.

By pushing the source of the threat back to the time of the Ridges' deaths, Arrington also adjusted the context. The conflict wasn't personal, but moral. For those deaths, in turn, could be traced back to the New Echota Treaty, whose signers the Ross men now wanted to exterminate. But unlike Ross's henchmen, who gathered in secret conspiracy, the signers of the treaty had done their work in the open. They had sought not vengeance, but a better life for their countrymen. In Arrington's telling, the signers were the true patriots, "the first, the best friends of the Cherokee people." Yet Ross had done his best to stymie their efforts for his own profit, and then embarked on a conspiracy to vilify, ostracize, and finally eliminate them.

Yes, *conspiracy*. There was no other word, Arrington declared.

If there were no such conspiracy, how happens it that so many murders all of the signers of the treaty, occurred on all the same day, at nearly the same hour, although miles and miles separated the scenes of ruthless outrage?

How happens it, that the special friends of Ross were in every instance the perpetrators? How happens it that these men were also the deadly foes of the twenty men who were slain? How happens it that the day before the slaughter, crowds were collecting around Ross? How happens it, that the morning of his awful outrages, hundreds of armed men, and among them hands even yet warm and smoking with the fresh blood of the victims, moved on the same central point, the house, which a trite trifling hyperbole might turn into the very hell of the principal demon?

It was quite a performance, but Arrington wasn't done. He spared no gruesome detail in describing how the fiendish Ross men had mercilessly slaughtered the three defenseless patriots: Boudinot "assailed and tomahawked, without warning as without pity"; John Ridge "dragged . . . from his own bed, beside his sleeping wife, from the embrace of his unconscious little ones"; and Major Ridge "in a remote glen, shot from his horse and butchered."

And Stand Watie was the outlaw? He was the one obliged to kiss John Ross's ring? Who would let stand such injustice—and who would not slay his persecutor if he had the chance?

At the end of this appeal, Arrington turned to Watie, silent in the prisoner's dock, and hailed him as the embodiment of "all that is daring and generous in the Indian character." He hoped that Watie would ever remain "patient but heroic; slow to avenge, but quick to defend life." Knowing his client's "soul and conduct," Arrington declared that anyone would be proud to call him "friend and brother." Then he fell silent at last.

Quite outdone, Wilson tried to claim that Arrington had addressed everything but the case, and to remind everyone that Watie, not Ross, was the defendant here. But the bell could not be unrung. The jurors deliberated only briefly, "about five minutes," according to Paschal, before delivering a unanimous verdict of not guilty to make Stand Watie a free man.

Stand Watie had been on trial for his life, but his life had also been on trial. As he sat there, the testimony and argument swirling around him, he had to wonder exactly why he'd killed Foreman. Was it just a spasm to save himself, or was he battling something larger and more profound? Was he fighting Foreman or Ross? Was he saving his own life, or defending a greater cause? At that point, Watie was so tightly identified with the Treaty Party that the two weren't easy to separate, but, more than for his three dead relatives, there was a difference. Just as his Cherokee nature could be parsed out of his modern trappings, and vice versa, so could Watie be teased out from his party. Unlike his relatives, he'd never sought the mantle of leadership, and he had never embraced it all that eagerly.

Even now, that August 1843, when the nation was once again called to vote, and Ross put himself up for reelection, Watie did not rise to oppose him. Instead, he threw his support to the Old Settler candidate, Joseph Vann, not to be mistaken for Joseph "Rich Joe" Vann, who'd died in the steamboat explosion. Backed solidly by the full-bloods, Ross won by a two-thirds majority. While Watie accepted the defeat, three members of a prominent Treaty Party family were defiant. George West attacked Isaac Bushyhead, the prosecutor in Archilla Smith's trial, as he finished his count of the votes at a polling station, and, in a frenzy, hacked him to death with a bowie knife. Then West's father, Jacob, grabbed Bushyhead's assistant David Vann (a cousin of Joseph) as he tried to climb onto his horse to get away, while other Treaty Party loyalists started whacking at Vann with clubs. "Kill him!" the senior West urged. Still others, including George West's brother John, jumped Elijah Hicks, the former *Phoenix* editor, but other Ross loyalists managed to pull them off Hicks before anyone else was killed.

At the news, about 200 Ross men rushed to form the usual protective circle around Ross's house. Ross himself sent the lighthorse guard to capture the elder West, who was soon brought into custody, summarily tried, and hanged for the murder. His son John was also caught and sentenced to a hundred lashes. The instigator George West was never found.

But that was just the start of it, for others took up where the Wests left off. Once again, however, Stand Watie was not one of them. The onus was taken up by the Starr gang, a pack of militant desperadoes so named because it was thick with the sons of a signer of the New Echota Treaty, James Starr, a close friend of the Ridges. It was led by Tom Starr, although he was just twenty, the youngest of the Starr children, twenty-one in all. Unspeakably vicious, Tom Starr cut a memorable figure even on a frontier known for wild men. He stood a mammoth six foot five, with eyelashes plucked out for ghoulishness, a necklace strung with the dried earlobes of his victims, and the whole effect topped off by Starr's signature fox fur cap, the orange-red tail flopping behind him as he galloped along in search of more Ross men as prey. Rollin Ridge declared that most people would "rather meet the devil himself than Tom Starr."

Still furious that John Ross's henchmen had put his father on the death list back in 1839, Tom Starr enlisted his two gun-happy brothers Bean and Ellis, plus James McDaniels; Sewell Rider; another West boy, Ezekiel; and a few others to make up a small company of the vengeful to tear about the countryside, slaughtering Rosses. In September 1843, just after the election, they shot a Ross spy named Kelly, and then went after a trader, Benjamin Vore, who was tight with Ross. The Starr gang burst into his home, shot Vore dead, then killed his wife and a guest of theirs and set the house on fire. When a five-year-old staggered out from the blaze, Tom Starr grabbed the boy and flung him back into the fire.

Outraged, the national council voted a $1,000 reward for the capture of any of the Starrs responsible. Daniel Coodey, another of the relative Rosses, took charge of some lighthorse troops to trace the gangsters, following the tracks of some shod mules they'd stolen. The trail led to the yard of a William Harris in a Cherokee settlement by the Ouachita River just down from Fort Smith, where several other mules and a large number of horses were penned up, all of them probably stolen. Coodey dismounted, and found Harris inside. When Coodey pressed his pistol against Harris's chest, he admitted that the Starrs had left the animals with him for safekeeping. He claimed to have no idea where the Starrs had gone, but his son blurted out that he'd just seen Tom's brother Bean Starr at Dempsey Fields a half mile away. Coodey's men tore off and found Bean as he was galloping toward the fields from the other side. When Bean saw Coodey and his men, he jerked his horse around to get away, but Coodey's men fired off ten shots before he could get out of range. Two bullets cracked his arm and a third went clean through him. That slowed Bean considerably, and Coodey grabbed him. Fearing a noose, Bean told Coodey all about the gang's activities: robbing people, burning down houses, and yes, stealing horses. He revealed that his brother Tom had just shot a man named Buffington, and that the gang expected Treaty Party men everywhere to rise up against Ross any day. He himself wished he'd never gotten involved. He was sure that his brother was going to come and kill him after everything he'd just said.

He was wrong about that. For Coodey did it himself, most likely point-blank. After Coodey filled Ross in, Ross got a separate report that the Starrs were now coming for Coodey. He promptly sent Johnson Foreman to go with Coodey to the Starrs' sympathizer William Dutch, to warn the Starr gang off. As they were coming up on the house, they caught a boy fleeing from it, and brought him inside while they talked to Dutch. Menacingly.

But that was just the start. On November 14, Ross men came for Stand Watie's brother Thomas. He was asleep at a friend's farmhouse when the men found him. They pointed guns at his head. "Let me put on my clothes," Thomas pleaded. He was slowly climbing out of bed when one of the men crashed a tomahawk down on his skull, and two others finished him off with bullets. His wife was in another room, and she came racing in to find her husband's hacked corpse sprawled on the bed, blood everywhere.

Even that didn't do it for Watie. When he heard about his brother's murder, Watie was gathered with about sixty men at Fort Wayne in the heart of the Treaty Party's stronghold. He seethed for revenge, but took none. This was probably prudent, as he was both outnumbered and outgunned. With the Ross men looming everywhere, Watie was better off staying inside the fort. He was in no position to mount any attack.

So once again Watie left any reprisals to the Starrs, and one of them, a man named Smith, picked off a member of Coodey's detachment to avenge Bean's death. The lighthorse then came for Smith and left him dead by the side of the road as a warning to others.

The Starrs paid no heed. Ross himself was heavily protected by soldiers, so the Starrs went after his favored daughter Jane instead. She was married to Return J. Meigs Jr., the son of the former Indian agent who'd been tight with her father, and a half dozen of the Starrs descended quietly on the Meigses' house one night. Jane and their children weren't there. But the Starrs surprised a couple of servants and demanded to know if Meigs was about. Meigs was in another room when he heard the gangsters. Terrified, he dashed out the back way and was running for the trees when the Starrs fired at him, but missed in the dark. They ransacked the house, made off with a few hundred dollars, then burned the place down.

As they were leaving, they spotted a couple of Ross loyalists coming up the road and recognized them as the men who'd captured Wash Starr for killing a Ross man named Charles Thornton. Luckily for him, Wash had gotten away, but the Starrs chased down the two Ross men and stripped them. They tied one to a tree and whipped him half to death before dispatching him with a bowie knife in the heart. Then they knifed open the other one and plucked out his bowels before slitting his throat.

Meigs flew to Coodey's soldiers, and his wife and children rushed to join him there. At daybreak, some Ross men galloped after the Starrs, but they found only the hideous remains of the two Cherokee.

"There is now no security in the country," William P. Ross told his uncle in passing along this gruesome news. And Jane had to agree in her own note to him. Everyone lived in "fear of being robbed & murdered by these barbarous fellows." She ended: "I am so nervous I can scarce write at all."

Since Coodey couldn't round up the sons, he went after the father, James Starr, not that he was doing any of the killing. He acted at the request of the national council after Ross said he was "cognizant" of acts "obviously intended to exhibit their contempt for the Ross government." One morning, thirty-two mounted Ross men in face paint swarmed the Starr farm south of Honey Creek. James Starr was on the front porch washing his face when they charged up, firing away. Starr fell dead, shot through the heart, and then in a lot of other places, too. His crippled son Buck tried to hobble off into the woods, only to be mowed down. Making no pretense of being anything more than a lynch mob, the assailants shouted that they were going to kill all the men and boys in the house, but Starr's wife wrapped three of her little grandchildren in her skirts and stared the gunmen down. They left her alone and charged on to deal with Sewell Rider, who lived nearby. They found him doing laundry in his yard and dropped him with one shot. They went on for Ezekiel West, but couldn't find him. But they did capture his brother John, stripped him, tied him to a tree, and gave him a hundred lashes with a hickory switch, splashing him with ice water after each ten to keep him from passing out and missing the sensation of the rest.

Shocked by all the mayhem, Watie appealed to Arbuckle to stop the slaughter, and he told Ross to disband his lighthorse brigades, which had nothing to do with the law. Ross ignored him. When one of Arbuckle's own captains, Nathan Boone, told Washington that the Starrs were no better than the Rosses, Arbuckle had to back off. That drove more treaty partisans to seek safety at Fort Wayne. As for the Starr gang, what was left of it skipped out to Arkansas, thinking it best to lie low for a while. Tom Starr was spotted strolling about Evansville, not a care in the world.

To keep Washington from turning against him, Watie told his men to "abstain from excesses, and to suffer wrong rather than be the aggressors." The violence convinced him that the nation was indeed better off in two. With all the killings, Watie said, his people's "peaceable residence among the Ross party is impossible." Besides, separation was the only way the Treaty Party would ever get its fair share of the annuity money. The Ross government replied that the Treaty Party should simply give up, disband, leave the fort, and devote themselves to "the promotion of order and harmony among our people."

Watie decided to argue for separation in Washington. Before he went, he put the fort in the hands of his brother John, who erected an outer perimeter of picket fencing. If the Rosses stormed Fort Wayne—now dubbed Fort Watie—John told his brother he would fight to the last man.

John Ross's politically minded nephew William P. Ross was disgusted that the Watie Party was trying to use the deaths of James Starr and some of his marauding sons to win sympathy from General Arbuckle. "A strenuous effort will be made to create the impression that these men have been killed out of political animosity," he declared. "But it will not do." Of course, the Ross forces were doing their best to do the same. With each side cloaked in righteousness, the killing went on and on. Murder became so common, said one Cherokee, that it was like hearing "of the death of a common dog." From the end of 1845 to the end of 1846, thirty-four killings were recorded, nearly all of them political.*

After Watie left for Washington, his brother-in-law John Candy in Park Hill tried to fill him in on the murderous developments.

---

* The number may seem small, but this was out of a population of about 15,000. If that ratio were applied to the present-day United States, such a civil war would claim almost 800,000 people.

You will doubtless recollect that Stand [no relation to Stand Watie] the murderer of James Starr was killed and scalped and that Faught was caught for decoying him and has since been hung. Since that time Old Cornsilk has been killed & robbed of a negro. Mrs. Pack has had some negro children kidnapped. Barrow Justin has been caught, tried and hung yesterday. Ecoowee became States witness against him. Bug John Brown & his company caught a horse thief and they have killed him. It is now rumored that he and his company (that is Brown) have cut up another man in Flint in his own home. . . . I forgot to mention that another man was killed at Ellis Hardin's. This man, it is said, was one of the company in Downing's gang on the mountains. He was scalped.

I think there is now to be no end to bloodshed. Since the Starr boys & the Ridges have commenced revenging the death of their relatives. A dozen or so are implicated and I am afraid that some of them will be more desperate than the first ones.

But none of this kept Candy from blaming John Ross for the calamity. "The quest may be asked. Who first began the troubles in the Cherokee Nation? The answer is obvious. We know it well."

Rollin Ridge was in Fayetteville, and he sent updates to his uncle, too.

"No very important transactions have happened since your departure, except the killing of five or six Indians of the Ross party, including Old Ta-ka-to-ka by Tom Starr and his confederates. Caleb Duncan was way-laid a short time ago, by several of the Wards, who snapped a pistol three times at them; when about to be surrounded, he wheeled his horse and escaped by flight."

Unlike his uncle, though, Rollin wished to take matters into his own hands. "One thing in particular I wish to know," he coolly inquired, "and that is when (if ever) John Ross designs to return, and by what rout he would probably come." Surely through Arkansas, Rollin was thinking. "A great degree of interest is manifest here concerning him and I desire to be acquainted with his movements on our particular account, which, when summed up and determined, will satisfy me."

Watie was not encouraging, and in his next letter Rollin turned to more cheerful news about a "prettily shaped girl, of about 16 or 17 years, who is very friendly." But even if she were to slip away, he told his uncle, "there are thousands of other soft breast, gentle eyes, and slender waists in the world." But Rollin continued to pester his uncle.

> I wrote you only a few days ago, and told you all that I desired to say, except of an article which I wish extremely that you would get for me, that is a Bowie knife. I would like one not very large, nor very small, but rather small than large."

He didn't have to say why. It was getting irritating. Watie knew only too well that before Ross's body was cold, there wouldn't be a Treaty Party man left alive in the nation, because Ross's followers would be so crazed for revenge. And then what?

Watie had sent his wife Sarah with the children to Arkansas, too, but, unlike Rollin, she hadn't found any comfort there. It must have been agonizing for her. Watie was staying at a decent hotel and with visiting dignitaries in fine clothes while she was trying to keep body and soul together amid the mayhem. Sarah did not have her husband's talent for hardship. And she must have known it, for she wrote not to Stand but to her brother, James M. Bell, off with him in Washington. She was filled with an anxious bitterness she couldn't bring herself to reveal to her husband, although he must have known of it.

> You must write to me soon I am so anctious to hear from you all but I do not expect you cast one thought on me since you left. You must not drink any while you are gone. I want you to write to me soon. I am allmost crazy to hear from you all, some times I sit down and cry my eyes out but it all dont do any good but it dont make business any faster. Major [her oldest, Saladin] is well and tries hard to stand alone and will walk soon. I would wright more but the baby is crying.

9

"THE GROVES OF THE BRANDYWINE"

Ruinous as this period of general slaughter was for the nation, it was a time of unparalleled happiness for John Ross.

He was in love, so heavily by the spring of 1844 that he could scarcely think of anything else. His courtship was so intense it seemed he might die if he could not possess the object of his ardor, Mary Bryan Stapler, a bewitching, lily-white "Quakeress." Every billet-doux to her was urgent with underlines and ecstatic with exclamation marks, and it conveys his joyous, lusty desire. It seems he'd adored her from the moment he'd laid eyes on her when she was fifteen—yes, fifteen—just three years before. He'd been introduced by the ubiquitous Thomas McKenney in 1841 when she was off in a Pennsylvania boarding school for girls, Linden Hall, and Ross was a lonely widower of fifty-one in Washington. From that moment on, he was upside down. The teenage Molly, as she was then known, could hardly have been more different from her stalwart, nearly full-blood predecessor Quatie, the mother of his five children. If Ross had always before presented himself as an obdurate, defiant, and somewhat opaque principal chief, now he was a dizzy, boyish, scheming Lothario. Previously, Ross had found something almost obscene in the intermarriages of John Ridge and Elias Boudinot, and had forbidden them in his own family. Now he was lurching giddily into one of his own. Formerly a figure of stately self-confidence, Ross was now worrying himself sick over whether a cute teenager really liked him. If before, he passed himself off as more Cherokee, now he was desperate to be more white.

She was not the first white girl his eye had landed on. Before her, he had been enthralled by the sophisticated Elizabeth Milligan, daughter of the proprietress of an elegant Washington boardinghouse Ross frequented. But his heart wasn't in it, as became obvious when he proposed at the end of a long and rather tedious letter detailing his labors in "the path of duty." "May I not then hope to be pardoned through your kind indulgence, for concluding with a petition craving your reply on the subject of my desire for negotiating a treaty with you for the purpose of uniting our hearts in the bonds of Matrimony."

The answer was no, or so we can assume, since that was the last letter of the correspondence.

But Molly had a hold on him from the start when she wrote to Ross, purringly calling him "uncle," complaining that she'd had to write to him first, and hoping he might somehow be able to spring her from her "imprisonment" at the boarding school where her father had placed her after her mother died. Ross bit, signing himself "Kooweskoowe"—his Indian name, which he never otherwise used—and the game was on.

Playful and flirty, Molly proved quite the coquette despite her years, and quite the writer, too, not just romantic but also clever. In that very first letter in August 1841, just as the Cherokee Nation was exploding, she punned freely on the idea of courtship as a matter not just of romance but of law, which was fitting for a politician like her suitor. What "case," she asks, might he make with her? And who else might he be "courting"? Unfortunately, the Quaker higher-ups at the school soon discovered that John Ross was no uncle of hers, and they put an end to the correspondence.

It wasn't until 1844 that the letters picked up again—with Mary at home in Wilmington, Delaware, Molly no more at eighteen and plainly bored, expressing some pique that Ross seemed to have forgotten about her. "Has time and absence quite obliterated from the memory one whom thee honored the name of Neice," she wishes to know, giddily lapsing into Quaker usages, and adopting the chaste-seeming "thee" and "thou" to conceal a desire that would be manifest soon enough. "I cannot allow myself to think that we have been forgotten." By "we" she means her and her elder sister, Sarah, almost thirty, who'd served as surrogate mother after their real mother's death. He should, she says, pay them a visit at her family's "Humble Home" by the Brandywine, where the "songsters" had just returned after the chilly winter and the flowers were springing up, too. "Some of our walks are truly romantic," she needled him.

"Ah, Mary," Ross almost immediately replied from Washington, his heart up. "I perceive you are still the same bewitching and playfull Molly, who was wont to touch the heart for the sake of mirth." What, exactly, did she intend? That line about being forgotten, for instance. "It is to the point," he says. "And in repeating that I have not and never will forget you—the assertion is as full of sincerity as striking a nail on the head!" Not the most felicitous turn of phrase, perhaps, but it was boldly frank for him. He'd be delighted to hear those "songsters" on a private ramble about the "groves of the Brandywine" with their "gay & pretty May flowers of the valley, the sweet odour of the sylvan Brooks" and so on for several more lines like a love-struck Malvolio before he fairly hollered: "O! what a delightful season for the meeting of absent friends—and for the hearts of all who love to be united in the various charms of life." But then he consulted his calendar and returned to earth. Regrettably, official business would keep him away from such a delightful get-together, at least for now.

Such effusions gave the first hint of the tender soul within the iron potentate. Clearly, the girl had claimed a big chunk of his heart. But he still had his position to think of. "I beg you not to expose these crazy lines to the inspection of any person but your ownself," he implored her, then added a postscript, wishing "Professor Morses telegraph" had a line between Washington and Wilmington just for the two of them.

Mary assured him that her sister Sarah was the only one to know of the correspondence, and she would never tell anyone else "till I hear from thee." She went on: "Do not let it be long for delay is dangerous." Then she concluded with a giggle: "I have turned to be quite a little quaker girl."

That she had. In his next letter, Ross inched a desiring hand toward her, unsure how his touch would be received, but unable to hold himself back. Did she love him? Was that really possible? He broached the momentous topic as a crafty syllogism that would lead to only one conclusion.

First—I and *you* . . . makes . . . Two
Second—*you* and *me* . . . makes . . . both
. . . So, if *you* love me—I love *you!*
And *as*—I *do love you*—Do *you love me*?

Afraid he might have overdone it, he turned playful. "I am fond of the 'friends,'" he joked, her faith now having distinctly salacious overtones. "And am well pleased to see that you have turned to be quite a quaker girl!!!"

That was in the letter of June 16. On June 17, not having received it or heard from him, Mary was afraid she'd been too forward. She was "electrified by the shock of disappointment [and] a little sprinkled with the tears of mortification." Even so, she wrote, he should please tell her how he felt—*now*. She signed it coolly—"thy adopted *Niece*."

By June 26 she'd gotten his syllogism of June 16 offering his love and seeking hers. She'd not yet responded, as she didn't know quite what to say. Was he serious? Was she? For all of his attractions, he was a Cherokee chief from a faraway territory he'd said precious little about—and not a word about the corpses mounting up everywhere, the threat of division, the factional hatred, the dangers posed by the vengeful Stand Watie.

This was a time for caution; that she knew. "As regard my heart it is still in my own possession, and so far has resisted all attempts to besiege it," she curtly informed him. "When I started in life I determined never to give my hand without my heart, until I can yield both, I remain as I am, although I am by no means invincible." As for his syllogism—it was too abstract for her, "not being a good mathematician and rather dull of comprehension." She would need to see him in person before she declared herself. "I do not think I can give the solution until I can in thy aid by asking a clearer explanation."

In Washington, Ross declared that he didn't know what to think, either. When he'd received her previous "favor," from June 17, he felt the "heat of its contents as they came hot from your pen." It was delightful, but worrisome, too. He feared being consumed "by the flame of that dreadful element" or, worse, by its "extinguishment." Love had been all her idea. "A thing you yourself had invented." And now, when in return he'd revealed his love, and needed some reassurance from her, he was being pushed into this terrible purgatory of uncertainty. It was unbearable! "In breathless anxiety I was awaiting to receive your response. I have very unexpectedly been ejected from the stand I had taken, but a tact which can only [be] tolerated by that cruel temporizing policy of the Sex—yea the *fairer Sex*—who are wont to adopt by a cunning coquettish negotiation, to cheat and rob the poor unsophisticated and confiding man of his only heart. And then leave to pine away and die upon the green fields of love—unpitied and unwept."

This was the man who had stood up to Andrew Jackson? Had regarded the Ridges' deaths with icy indifference? Had faced down murderous factions? Any pathos, however, lasted scarcely a paragraph before he returned to the "question as stated" and asked again for her hand—but hand *and* heart this time, in those "bonds of matrimony." No equivocation permitted. Yes or no. If the answer was no, please say so, and do not "flatter him with hopes, & then see him die with grief for your sake."

He let the letter sit unsent overnight, and in the morning decided he should sweeten it a little, and held out once again the prospect of that lovely walk together along the Brandywine. Then, still unsure he'd struck the right note, he let yet another day pass while he went shopping. And then he added another postscript: that he'd just been to a jewelry story and bought her a "gem that is to be a bosom Companion for me all the days of my life!"

She replied a week later. Come see me.

But he could not. That very day, he was negotiating the future of the nation with the new President Tyler, composing a lengthy report to his assistant John Lowrey back in the nation, and grappling with the issue of his self-dealing that was being raised by Colonel Hitchcock. He could not leave now, or anytime soon.

Acutely disappointed, Mary reviewed the entire correspondence between them and realized the obvious. She had not actually seen him in two years. Who was he? She craved to know.

The very next day, he canceled all his appointments, boarded the train south, and stood in front of her, in Wilmington. And they took that stroll along the Brandywine, unchaperoned.

Five days later, he could not stop thinking about that walk. "My own mind has ever since been in emotion," he wrote, his heart like a "wounded, fluttering bird."

Back in Wilmington, Mary was consumed with John Ross. "My mind often wonders over the many miles that lay between us, and places me by your side, and I endeavor to imagine what you are then doing, and at night your image visits my slumbers." She'd given him her heart—but had he given his?

In New York on July 30, Ross was frantic to hear from her, and actually went to the post office in hopes of finding a letter, but no. He could think of nothing else but her. "Why then," he demanded, "should we no longer be separated, if our hearts do not deceive us, and our affections for each other be really formed?" He turned almost desperate. He must have her *now.* "All things being satisfactorily settled—delay for the consummation of the Union would be worse than useless—as nothing but suspense, anxiety and pain can be experienced from such a course!" Consummation—the meaning could scarcely be clearer. "I will never deceive you having thus frankly disclosed to you my own feelings." And hers? "I hope you will not hesitate to communicate yours in like candour to me."

Two days later, on August 1, Mary judged his letter "truly acceptable." She was his. With her whole heart, she emphasized.

After that, there were only the details, about when to tell her family (immediately), whether he would now resign as he'd promised (no, actually), what his friends might say (whatever he wanted them to), whether she could bring her sister (yes), when they would marry (in time for him to return for the October council), how to ask her father (by requesting his assent "without delay").

When the marriage was finally arranged, Ross could hardly contain his excitement in communicating with his good friend McKenney. He'd been visiting McKenney in a cottage in Maine when she had agreed to marry him, but he had not breathed a word about the courtship. In a letter to McKenney now he bubbled over—"Are you surprised to hear of it? If not, pray then, who do you believe that lassie is? I think you may guess & guess, over & over again, and not hit upon the right one! And when the name is revealed to you, I believe that you will wonder! Well then, without further exciting your curiosity, or keeping you in suspense, I will deliberately and softly whisper into your ears, that, it is the same identical little school girl, whom you once called Molly. And at this time know as Miss Mary Stapler of Wilmington, Delaware!! Yes, my friend, strange and unexpected as this news may be to you, yet, it is nevertheless true."

He added a boastful postscript, terming his Mary a "captive quaker lassie, to preside over his wigwam." This was jocular, but it played off the fear of savage Indians making off with white women—to ravish in the wild, or so their families feared. But this captive, Ross joked, was to be installed as a matriarch. One wonders: did Mary know all this?

The wedding was on September 2 in Philadelphia, at the Washington House Hotel on Chestnut Street. Flanked by a Masonic temple and a rifle range, it was nonetheless a fashionable area where ladies might stroll about in bonnets, and men in smart hats. The Quakers refused to bless Mary's union to a man outside the faith, so the wedding was performed by Pastor Orson Douglass of the Mariners' Church. Ross had hoped to wear his usual black silk vest, but Mary preferred satin, and satin it was. Although the wedding was to be "private," Ross invited McKenney, but he couldn't come on such short notice, and the ceremony was attended almost entirely by relatives, with Mary's brother—not her father, significantly—giving her away.

If this marriage of white and red didn't provoke the same hysteria as the Boudinots' and Ridges', it also did not pass unnoticed in Philadelphia. A brief wedding announcement ran in all the major newspapers, but the *Public Ledger* ran a feature that hinted at scandal as it mentioned that the Quakers had expelled Mary over the marriage. The article also noted the age disparity between the eighteen-year-old bride and her fifty-five-year-old groom, "the celebrated Cherokee Chief" and "half-breed Indian," who was "considered to be worth a half a million dollars."

But one eminent member of polite society was gracious. The former first lady herself, Dolley Madison, perhaps nudged by McKenney, sent flowers to the bride, and Mary pressed a few petals in a book and always kept them.

The couple departed immediately for the west to arrive in time for the national committee meeting in October, Ross's first as the reelected principal chief. It had been convened to address the mounting violence in the nation.

They arrived in Van Buren, which was as uproarious as ever, and no joy for a young lady from Wilmington. Ross most likely secured his usual six-man armed guard to escort them home. Whatever her apprehensions, Mary had to have been comforted by the first glimpse of Park Hill. Despite all the political turmoil, there were signs of prosperity in the nation, and these were especially pronounced at Park Hill, which was becoming quite the place for Cherokee aristocrats. The grandest was surely George Murrell, an enterprising white merchant from Lynchburg, Virginia, who'd married a niece of Ross's, Minerva. (When Minerva died later, Murrell married another Ross niece, Amanda.) Murrell was busy building a new plantation to top his fox-hunting estate, Tally-ho, in Louisiana. This new one, to be called Hunter's Home, would have dozens of hounds bounding over the fields in pursuit of imported foxes, and gentlemen of various shades, all in fine coats, galloping after them. It was to be a pretty, clapboard-sided place with a two-story porch and an elegant fan of lights over the front door. Inside, the floors of hard pine would be covered with Oriental rugs, the interior doors painted to look like mahogany, and the parlor heavy with Victoriana from a curving sofa to the gilt mirror over the mantel. In the drawing room there would be a cage of a hundred twittering yellow canaries.

Ross's house was just as spectacular. The half-mile drive up from the road was lined with the roses that gave the cottage its name, spilling over the rail fence that ran on either side, past a vast apple orchard, bright with fruit that fall, and a thousand ornamental trees scattered artfully about. It led up to an imposing two-story house that wasn't as darling as Murrell's would be, but more impressive, more stately, with its four stout columns holding up the front porch, a pair of solid chimneys at either end of a pitched roof, an interior gleaming with *genuine* mahogany, and priceless rosewood, too, and an endless dining table that would serve twenty-four with English china and polished silverware. And all about the house, stables for fifty horses; a kiln, smokehouse, dairy, blacksmith house, and laundry; and the huts for the hundred slaves who worked the fields, staffed the house, and drove the carriages, by far the most in the nation, and the clearest measure of his riches.

Did Mary gasp at all this—and did John Ross beam? It is impossible to know, for once she joined Ross in matrimony, her letters to him ceased for twenty years, and he rarely mentioned her. But she did sit for a portrait four years later, when she was ensconced at Rose Cottage. By then, the Molly of Ross's courting days had evolved into the sophisticated, ladylike Mary, nicely bejeweled, in a fine dress, her hair up, mouth tight, a hand curled lazily under her chin as she scrutinized the viewer with a discerning gaze. Around the same time, Ross was captured in black silhouette as a proper gentleman in a long coat, one hand across his breast, the other clutching a top hat, every inch the eastern gentleman even as he resided with his bride in the thick of Indian Territory, which was still riven by civil war.

President John Tyler left office without seeking election for a presidential term of his own, seeming to take all of Washington's sympathies for the Ross Party with him. He never was able to fulfill the promises Ross had clung to in his letter of 1841. That fell now to Jackson's acolyte James K. Polk, who'd been selected by the Democratic Party as a compromise candidate on the eighth ballot, and then unexpectedly defeated the aging Whig lion Henry Clay to become, at forty-nine, the youngest president to date, and possibly the boldest, a "Young Hickory" to his mentor's old one. Knowing that he was hardly anyone's first choice, he pledged to limit himself to just one term in a bid to unify support, and set an ambitious agenda that included pushing America's southwest border from the edge of Colorado to the Rio Grande. That left little room for any protracted negotiations over the fate of the Cherokee. Previously, the Treaty Party and the Old Settlers had been the ones to call for a breakup of the nation, a position that Ross could discard as the politicking of a disgruntled minority. As for the persistent violence in the nation, he attributed that to "stealthy incursions of a number of banditti," not to factional strife. Whatever it was, Polk was tired of it and took up the idea of a division as the surest and quickest way to bring peace to the territory so he could turn to other matters. On June 2, he introduced a bill to Congress to send another commission to the territory, this one to determine the exact border between the two new nations.

Clearly, Polk was serious. This was fine with Watie, and he declared himself ready to abide by any commissioners Polk appointed. Ross, however, was horrified by the prospect of his dominion being reduced by half, and this made him suddenly amenable to allowing all three parties to remain within the existing borders. On that basis, the negotiations commenced in earnest, and after just a month of wrangling, an agreement emerged that all sides declared they could live with. It proved a remarkable document, in its way more impressive even than the Cherokee constitution, which had relied so much on the Constitution of the United States. Styled as a treaty—the Treaty of 1846— it had thirteen articles covering just about every area of dispute. It called for allowing all fugitives to return safely from Arkansas, or wherever they might be hiding; ending the lighthorse brigades so hated by the Watie faction; and dismantling quasi-military organizations like Watie's troops and Ross's guard. All party distinctions would cease; everyone was a Cherokee now. A general amnesty was declared for those accused of committing crimes during the troubled times, Starrs included, so long as they returned to the nation by the end of the year. From now on, however, all laws were to be enforced equally on everyone, guilt to be determined by jury trial. As the original constitution had declared, everyone in the nation was equally entitled to life, liberty, and property; permitted to assemble peacefully; and allowed to petition the Cherokee government, or the federal one, for redress of grievances. The Old Settlers gave up the idea that they alone owned the nation. In return, they were guaranteed a share in the per capita payments that Ross had tried to reserve for Late Emigrants alone. The Treaty Party received a special allocation of more than $100,000, of which $5,000 was to be paid to the heirs of the three dead Ridges, and the rest would pay the hefty travel expenses of the delegation and settle individual claims of Treaty Party members regarding their improvements and despoliations in the east. The Cherokee were granted clear, permanent title, not to the nation's land, as they all had sought, but only to their individual lots. That was the sole disappointment shared by all. But it was made up for by the U.S. government's promise to restore the payments that had been unfairly deducted from the initial $5 million appropriation for removal, and to pay off all the outstanding per capita money due to the tribe.

In the end, the payments were not paid as promptly as promised. The first tranche of money would not be delivered for another five years. But the intention proved enough, and all representatives from the three parties agreed to accept the terms. When they all had signed, Watie and Ross stood up to do something unimaginable. They shook hands in a gesture of good faith. A political marriage of opposites that was in its way even more startling than Ross's legal one to an eighteen-year-old Quakeress. And the two men then worked together to persuade the government to shift the location of the commission addressing the property claims from Washington to the Cherokee Nation, which would be infinitely more convenient. With that adjustment, the bill was put forward for congressional approval. It passed with just one vote to spare, and peace came at last to the Cherokee Nation.

It is hard to say how a result that had previously seemed inconceivable had now been attained, and so swiftly. Part of it was certainly due to Polk's demeanor: he expressed no scorn for the Cherokee in their plight, just impatience to resolve it. In that sense, it was not punitive, but genuinely optimistic. Ross was faced, for the first time, with the very real prospect of losing something dear to him—the prestige of being principal chief of the entire nation, and not just a portion of it. It is possible that his daring new marriage freed him from some of his old intransigence. But underneath all of it lay the recognition from all the parties that, after so many years of bloodshed and acrimony, enough was enough.

The postwar Cherokee delegation to Washington in 1866, including three Ridges: John Rollin Ridge and Saladin Watie, to the far left, and Elias Cornelius Boudinot, standing second from right.

PART FOUR

FATEFUL
LIGHTNING

1846-1871

1

SLAVES TO FORTUNE

The Reverend Evan Jones, who escorted a band of full-bloods west along the Trail of Tears, had been a dutiful missionary to the Cherokee ever since he arrived in the "howling wilderness" of Tennessee in 1821. A mild-looking man distinguished by unusually long sideburns and small-lensed spectacles, he'd signed on with the Baptist Foreign Mission Board to bring the Lord to the Cherokee shortly after he'd come to America as a thirty-three-year-old Welshman. He seemed to welcome the harshness of life as a dirt-poor schoolteacher and itinerant preacher. He also had a penchant for trouble.

At his Valley Towns mission along the Hiwassee, his young sister-in-law, Cynthia Cunningham, was found dead in her bed one night, a tiny baby boy slathered in blood at her feet. Dark rumors swirled about Jones after he quickly buried the dead woman with the baby hidden under her burial dress. No one officially accused him of murder, or of adultery, but he was indicted for "aiding, helping, abetting, comforting, assisting and maintaining" Cynthia as she did "choak and strangel" the baby. No evidence or testimony was ever produced to support such a charge, and he was cleared. But the suspicion dogged him ever after, and darkened both his reputation and his mood.

While Congregationalists like Reverend Samuel Worcester, a rival who came to the Cherokee about the same time, focused on saving the aspiring mixed-bloods who responded to their educational program, Baptists like Evan Jones concentrated on the more numerous full-bloods. This brought Evan Jones into an alliance with John Ross, who was himself inclined to the full-bloods for political reasons; it's why Ross enlisted Jones to head up one of the emigrant parties headed west. But, as a Baptist minister, Jones brought a problem with him, one that would ultimately wreck the peace brought by the Treaty of 1846. Slavery.

In his census of 1859, the Indian agent George Butler noted that there were 4,000 Negroes in the Cherokee Nation, nearly a quarter of its 21,000 population, and most of them were slaves. They were field hands and house servants, but also emblems of prosperity. The Cherokee had routinely enslaved captured enemies (if they didn't torture them to death), but they didn't think to acquire black slaves until Jefferson pushed farming on them and they noticed that their fellow Southerners found it a lot easier if they left field work to slaves. The Africans also brought valuable agricultural knowledge, and a measure of status, like the handsome carriages rich Cherokee liked to show off. Slaves weren't cheap; only one family in ten could afford even a single slave. So slavery widened the already pronounced divide between rich and poor, further separating the mixed-blood elite from all the full-bloods.

The tension might have been manageable, just another aspect of a dynamic society, if slavery weren't splitting the entire United States in two. The two halves could scarcely have been more different anyway. One was industrial, fast, and cosmopolitan, the other agricultural, languid, and insular. Once the North started getting moral about a "peculiar institution" for which it had no particular economic need, but which the South depended on as a way of life, catastrophe loomed. The Cherokee had never thought very much about whether slavery was wrong. They assured themselves that they enslaved blacks not because of race, but because of the blacks' lack of clan, which made them nonpersons. But the truth was that the Cherokee rarely enslaved whites who were likewise without clan. Whites could join a clan through marriage; blacks would be given a hundred lashes if they tried.

In the rising abolitionist clamor, the Northern Baptists who had funded Jones insisted he remove any slaveholders from his rolls of the faithful. As a Baptist missionary, he was a circuit rider who made a two-hundred-mile loop serving a few hundred irregular attendees at his open-air services. After a year of stalling, he admitted that four of his congregants owned slaves—exactly six slaves in all. The board demanded he expel these errant Baptists from the church.

Personally, Jones was against slavery, but he had never thought it a bar to the faith. Besides, it was the rich mixed-bloods, not his full-bloods, who held slaves in any number. He dutifully banished the four slaveholders, but secretly offered them a "dismission" that would allow them to join another church elsewhere. When Reverend Samuel Worcester learned this, he passed the word on to the Baptist board, creating a scandal. There had been bad blood between the two missionaries ever since Jones had lambasted Worcester for giving up his court case against Georgia and encouraging the Cherokee to go west. This was payback. As it happened, Worcester held slaves himself (although he invited them to eat with his family at table), and claimed he'd have resigned his missionary post rather than force abolitionism on anyone.

The revelations about dismission caught the attention of the new Indian agent, George Butler, a famously pro-slavery Southerner who didn't enjoy the notion of a Baptist missionary embarking on any sort of abolitionist crusade. And Southern Baptists were sorely dismayed to learn that their northern brethren were making an issue of slavery south of the famous 36–30 parallel where it was legal, as decreed by that carefully wrought Kansas-Nebraska Act of 1854.*

That 36–30 line ran across the top of the Indian territory of the Cherokee. Territories above it could now decide for themselves by popular vote if they were to enter the union as slave states or not. In Kansas, directly over the border, Northerners and Southerners flooded in to try to tip the balance in their

---

* It had been crafted by George Butler's brother, South Carolina senator Andrew Butler. When Massachusetts senator Charles Sumner berated him for his pro-slavery views, Butler's nephew Preston Brooks famously caned Sumner nearly to death on the floor of the Senate.

favor, deluging the territory with fierce partisans who were now drawn into close quarters with their most dire enemies. One of the newcomers was the messianic John Brown, who waged war on slaveholders in what the newspaperman Horace Greeley came to call "Bleeding Kansas."

The turmoil threatened to spill over into a Cherokee Nation that had finally been enjoying some peace. Tom Starr had long since ceased his marauding, and no Wests rose up to take his place. Murders had become, once again, rare enough to be a topic of interest. Two colleges had gone up on Park Hill. The inauguration of one had been celebrated by a promenade of gentlemen and ladies to the music of a military band from Fort Gibson.* The nation had a new newspaper, the *Advocate*, edited by John Ross's urbane nephew William P. Ross. Tahlequah had blossomed with state buildings, and its grid of streets sprouted decent homes and a thriving merchant district.

But slavery underlay much of this progress, and many Cherokee were proud that it did. When the Rosses rode about in their gay carriage, two shining horses with a driver up front, they made a point of positioning a little black boy in uniform on the back. At dinners where educated Cherokee daughters performed on the piano and violin, liveried slaves poured the wine. The more prosperous farmers imported the mechanized reapers, mowers, and harvesters of Cyrus McCormick for farms that could now encompass 1,000 acres— but also required scores of slaves to work them.

And now slavery was to be denounced? Only a few missionaries were calling for an end to the practice, but even a few were too many. In October 1855, the Cherokee national council had to decide if it should join with its Southern neighbors to make the nation officially slaveholding, and expel any missionaries who preached otherwise.

After the Treaty of 1846, Stand Watie had been living quietly with Sarah in Honey Creek. The two had produced children almost annually into the 1850s, five in all. He'd turned his little shop into a dry goods and general store under the name Stand Watie and Company, and with a partner, J. S. Knight, gone into the lumber business with a steam sawmill. He also joined with his

---

*The principal of one of the colleges, Miss Ellen Whitmore, a recent graduate of Mount Holyoke, had a terrible fright late one night when a couple of Plains Indians in headdresses and face paint appeared at her door, but it was two students playing a prank on her.

long-haired and heavily mustached nephew Elias Cornelius Boudinot, the ambitious son of his murdered brother, to build farms along the Arkansas and Neosho Rivers. With the swelling proceeds, Watie built a grand house for his growing family on Brush Creek, just outside Fayetteville in Arkansas, with two large rooms downstairs set off by a breezeway, and a full basement done in limestone.

All of this, of course, needed slaves. To defend the practice, Watie had returned to elective politics, and served on the national council, where he stood firmly with those who proclaimed the Cherokee "as Slave holding People in a Christian like Spirit."

And this upset John Ross. He could see that slavery was about more than just slaves—it was about the Cherokees' place in the United States. He personally kept plenty of slaves, but, as usual, his personal views weren't the issue so much as the politics of the matter. If the Cherokee Nation went with the South over slavery, it would receive the ire of the North, on which it depended for annuity payments. If it sided with the antislavery North, it would infuriate its Southern neighbors.

But slavery threatened to cleave the nation from the inside, too, as a class issue. After all, only the rich mixed-bloods like Watie (and Ross himself) owned slaves in any number, and the full-bloods didn't want to see the country ravaged just to protect them.

To Ross, the answer was to try to play it down the middle, and keep his distance from both sides. When the legislature went ahead and passed a bill declaring the Cherokee Nation pro-slave, Ross vetoed it. The upper house, heavy with mixed-blood slaverholders like Watie, voted to override, but the lower house, composed mostly of full-bloods who did not own slaves, backed Ross to sustain his veto. The nation remained unaligned—for now.

But, of course, slavery, like removal, allowed no middle ground. Either you were for it, or you were against it. Even if Ross would not allow any official recognition of the pro-slavery position, it would come forth. Quietly, hidden away in the woods, a secret society was banding together into a political network that would force Ross's hand. It was called the Keetowah Society, named for the now sacred first town in the original Cherokee Nation. But it was a largely Baptist organization started by the Reverend Evan Jones, who was infuriated that the moralizing Baptist higher-ups were plotting to cut off his funding, pull him from the territory, and undo all the good works he had done in God's name since 1821. And all of this in the name of fighting slavery, which, in his view, had nothing to do with the church or his preaching.

The Baptist hierarchy had been suspicious of Jones ever since rumors of infanticide had swirled around him, and it had lately been nagging him about his accounts, tiny as the sums were. All this got Jones's back up. If the Baptists now sought to cleanse the land of slavery, Jones would be only too happy to oblige. Usually inclined toward passive aggression, he soon became a man possessed, a furious renegade who would defy his board by promoting its cause to a horrifying extreme. It was perfect—Jones would go after the Baptist board he scorned by championing the full-bloods he loved. He'd save them from the mixed-bloods who seemed determined to bring the wrath of the North down upon them all.

As the name suggested, the Keetowah Society harked back to the old ways of the Cherokee, before they were corrupted by all the inrushing whites. Its membership was strictly limited to the "uneducated," meaning the full-bloods, and everything about the organization emphasized full-blood traditions. All meetings took place around a council fire, with tribal dances and the recitation of sacred myths along with Christian psalms. It was a Cherokee class war in the name of Baptist abolitionism. The Keetowahs would drive out the mixed-bloods, nothing less, and run the government their own way.

Alarmed, the slaveholding mixed-bloods organized their own secret organization, the Knights of the Golden Circle, in fervid opposition. Its membership was restricted to believers in slavery. Significantly, members did not need to be Cherokee but could be whites, and the latter were most likely to be the Southern whites from neighboring states who were the Knights' natural allies. If the Keetowahs' intentions were political, the Knights' were paramilitary, as they were keen on "capturing and punishing any and all abolitionists" in the nation, starting with the Keetowahs.

George Butler, the Indian agent, made clear which side he was on. Once he learned that Evan Jones, in his new abolitionist fervor, had impeded the sale of a Negro, he tried to get Jones expelled as an enemy of the nation. Jones objected on the grounds of religious freedom, but when John Brown tried to spark a slave revolt in his famous raid on the federal arsenal at Harpers

Ferry, Virginia, in October 1859, the pro-slave contingent demanded that Jones be evicted before he could try something similar in the nation. Butler ordered Evan Jones out, and also his mild, full-bearded son John B. Jones, who, as a Cherokee-speaking minister in his own right, had helped organize the Keetowahs. But when the sheriff went out to seize them at their house just east of Tahlequah, he found nearly a hundred gun-toting Keetowahs waiting for him, and he prudently reconsidered.

The Reverend Samuel Worcester would have been targeted for eviction, too, but he'd died a few months before. Exhausted and dispirited, he'd suffered from painful boils all over his back, and his hips had given out. His last letter to the American Board asked that the commissioners send someone else to replace him, but they never did. Worcester was buried beside his wife, Ann, in the Park Hill burial ground, under a simple stone saying that it was to him that the Cherokee "owe their Bible and their Hymn Book." That was all. Once he was gone, the American Board closed down his mission permanently, wanting no part of slavery.

That left the Joneses. When Butler proved unable to eject them, prominent Arkansans installed a loyal Arkansan as superintendent of Indian Affairs, and he named a more forceful agent, Robert Cowert, to do the job. Cowert was directed to enlist the U.S. Army to go at Jones's annoying Keetowahs, but even he didn't consider that warranted just yet. When a few hundred slaveholders petitioned for young John B. Jones's removal before he could succeed in "scattering his principles of Abolitionism like fire brands throughout the country," Cowert ordered Jones to leave the nation at once or "military force" would expel him. And if it did, a lynch mob was likely to be awaiting him on the far side of the border. One such mob had recently hanged a Reverend Mr. Bewley for his "antislavery sentiments." Outraged, Evan Jones confronted Cowert at the Indian agency in Tahlequah, but Cowert was untroubled by the prospect of Jones's being hanged by Southern vigilantes. Evan Jones turned to Ross for help, but he replied only with "assurance of his sympathy." So John B. sold everything he owned and quietly slipped out of the nation with his wife and children under the watchful escort of some kindly Cherokee. That left his father to fight on alone.

Having at last put at least one Jones to flight, the Knights grabbed their guns to go after the Keetowahs—now called the Pins, for their crossed-pin insignia—and the Pins responded in kind. It was the Watie Party against the Ross Party all over again. Leery of going back to the bad old days of Tom Starr, Stand Watie stayed out of it, but he kept tabs on the developments. As he wrote to his wife, off visiting relatives in Texas: "Bob Parks shot John Ramsey, broke his arm and shattered his shoulder which may kill him. I am told that Bob was justified in shooting him." He noted that a Mrs. Morris and three of her children were to be executed on bogus charges. "Shame to our country," he raged. But he was pleased that one of the Knights, George McPherson, "broke custody," and escaped with his life.

Racked from within, the nation was under assault from without, too. The new railroad companies that were springing up everywhere hungered for track routes to cut through the nation up from Texas and out to California, with the prospect of bringing in yet more hostile settlers with them. And the federal government was getting tired of dealing with so many different tribes, with their separate customs, histories, and demands, and wished to lump them together in a single Indian Territory, its residents to be citizens of the United States, with the idea of its becoming another state, albeit one overseen by the federal government. That would finally spell the end of the Cherokee Nation.

2

"AS BROTHERS LIVE, BROTHERS DIE"

n 1860, it was clear that a great war was coming to America. With the election that November of a tall, gawky, creaky-voiced Republican congressman from Illinois named Abraham Lincoln—a "Free-Soiler" firmly opposed to the expansion of slavery—Southern states were determined to detach themselves from a federal government that seemed determined to end their way of life. Ross was agonized. As war fever mounted, his neutrality was annoying both sides, but to choose one side was to infuriate the other. He needed the annuity payments from Washington to fund his government, and he relied on the U.S. Army to honor federal treaty obligations to protect the Cherokee from harm. But his Southern neighbors needed to keep the Indian Territory to wall off U.S. forces that might otherwise flank them, interrupting critical supply lines up from Texas. While Ross figured the industrialized North would prove the mightier power, the agrarian South, with its acceptance of slavery and the congenial plantation life it fostered, was far more hospitable to Cherokee customs.

But perils lay on both sides of the divide, and the South was growing especially distrustful of Ross's intentions. The *Arkansas Gazette* feared he was harboring a mass of "savages" who, spurred on by abolitionist zealots, would soon be howling for Arkansan scalps. Not so, Ross insisted. "We are not dogs to be hissed on by abolitionists." But the insinuation stuck. The new governor of Arkansas, Henry M. Rector, warned Ross that if he didn't hold the line against the North the Lincoln administration would take over the Indian Territory's "fruitful fields, ripe for the harvest of abolitionists, freesoilers, and Northern mountebanks." He urged Ross to follow the Choctaw and declare his loyalty to his "natural allies" instead.

Still Ross declined, and he held that position even after the states of the Deep South began to secede, one by one, starting with South Carolina in December 1860. Texas sided with the South in February. Its governor, the former runaway Sam Houston, was evicted from office when he refused to sign a loyalty oath to the Confederacy. He was replaced by Lieutenant Governor Edward Clark, who dispatched three emissaries to persuade Ross to join the rebellious South, too. Still nothing doing. And Ross didn't change his mind when Confederate artillery fired on the Union garrison at Fort Sumter in South Carolina's Charleston harbor on April 12, 1861, to plunge the United States into war. Ross defined intransigence, and not for the first time.

Arkansas formally joined the Confederacy by convention that May. Elias Cornelius Boudinot, who'd been partnering with his uncle Stand in business, was developing political ambitions, too, and won an appointment as convention secretary from Southerners keen to lure the Watie faction to their cause—and to put Ross on notice that he should follow suit. Nonetheless, when, after the vote, Arkansans wrote to Ross demanding to know his intentions, he coolly demurred yet again. Then the captain of Fort Smith—no longer in federal hands now that Arkansas had joined the Rebels—warned Ross that "the notorious Abolitionist, robber, murderer and rascal" Senator James H. Lane of Kansas was raising a Union regiment to come crashing down on the South. Would he resist if Lane invaded? This time, Ross declared his loyalty—to the Union side, as he considered the nation still bound by its treaty with the United States. In a letter, he implored Lane to stay away. "We do not wish our soil to become the battle ground between the states."

But he had more to fear from the South, and more immediately, as Texas troops were creeping into the nation, forcing the Union to abandon all the federal forts except Gibson, and leaving the Cherokee Nation ripe for the plucking. As far as the South was concerned, Indian Territory was already theirs. Asserting authority over it, the nascent Confederacy summarily announced that it would take over payment of the annuities due from the United States, effectively claiming all of the Indian Territory, the Cherokee Nation included. All that remained was to inform Ross of this fact. For the purpose, it enlisted a local Arkansas attorney, Albert Pike, as its Indian commissioner, to ride to Park Hill to let him know. Once Ross had come around, as Pike was sure he would, Pike would recruit two Cherokee regiments to defend the territory from any Union attempt to take back the Cherokee Nation. The deal would be done.

In an era when all of American life was divided into North and South, Pike was a hard man to peg. He was a big, burly three-hundred pounder with a profusion of Walt Whitman whiskers and a fondness for a meerschaum pipe, sentimental poetry, loose women, foreign languages (from Greek to Sanskrit), and Freemasonry. He was no soldier, and hardly a statesman. He'd started out as a Massachusetts schoolteacher but come west for the adventure and washed up at Fort Smith in 1832, the same year as Washington Irving. Settling in Arkansas, he tried journalism, dabbled in politics, turned to the law as a circuit rider long on oratory and saloon sociability, got a taste of war as a member of the Arkansas home guard in Mexico, and then took the case that would make his name: the Creeks' financial claims against the government. He won the Creeks a full $800,000, and himself almost $200,000, most of it paid in solid gold. In tight with the Creeks, and worldly, Pike was appointed the Confederacy's first commissioner of Indian Affairs. If that meant abandoning any last ties to the North, and the abolitionism of his youth, so be it. As he wrote:

> Southrons, hear your country call you!
> Up! Lest worse than death befall you!
> To arms! to arms! to arms! in Dixie!

Before going to see Ross at Park Hill, Pike spent a few days at Fort Smith with its new commander, the Texan Confederate general Ben McCulloch, who was in charge of all the incoming Texas forces. And there, the two of them received some unexpected visitors. Five "Southern Cherokees," as they called themselves, led by Stand Watie, came by to say they were set to raise a military regiment of their own, whatever Ross did. They didn't intend to fight against the Union, though, at least not yet. They just wanted to put down Evan Jones's Pins, sympathizers with the North who were operating under the protection of the Ross Party. If allowed to roam freely, the Pins were sure to drag the nation into yet another internal fight.

Watie would not have known what to make of the fat, garrulous Pike, but he was surely drawn to the firm, self-confident General McCulloch, who was family of a sort. He was a good friend of Davy Crockett from Tennessee (who was in turn friendly to the Cherokee), and had served with Major Ridge against the Creeks in 1812, before going on to make a name for himself under General Zachary Taylor by leading some rough-hewn, pistol-toting Texas Rangers to push the Mexicans back across the Rio Grande.

But opportunists are by definition good at seizing an opening, and Pike saw one in Watie. If Watie was spoiling to take the battle to the Pins, then Pike was only too happy to let him. Watie would tie them down while Pike tried to win for the Confederates the rest of the Indians in the territory. As Pike figured it, the Choctaw and Chickasaw to the west had already declared themselves Confederates. The Quapaws, Seneca, and Seneca-Shawnee to the northeast were mostly stragglers who could easily be ignored or cajoled; it didn't much matter which. The Plains Indians like the Comanche, Tonkawas, and Shawnee farther west still mostly stayed out of national entanglements. They were best bribed to lay off any raids along the Texas border, freeing up the Southern troops there for the larger battle. That left the more populous Seminoles and Creeks to the south. Pike bet that if the Cherokee came in for the Confederacy, those two tribes would fall into line rather than risk being isolated.

But this meant winning Ross. That, Pike explained to Watie, had to be the first order of business. Well, fine, Watie said, but suppose Pike failed to bring him around? Suppose Ross stuck with the Union after all, and then went after

Watie's men for attacking the abolitionist Pins? Would Pike protect Watie's men not just from the Pins, but from Ross's men, too? Pike assured him the Confederacy would indeed stand by him—anything to isolate Ross.

So Watie struck a deal. If the Confederacy backed him, he'd back the Confederacy. More precisely, if the Northern forces raised by Senator Lane crossed the border into the Cherokee Nation, Watie would join the Confederates to repel them. Anything to keep out the "Kansas rascals." And Pike would have Watie's back if Ross turned Union against him.

Now, how to win Ross over? Pike figured that, for all Ross's bluster, he had to be feeling a little beleaguered with Washington the capital only of what was left of the Union, not of the entire United States, and its troops confined to Fort Gibson. It didn't even have an Indian agent in the territory anymore, not after the last one, Elias Rector, had gone over to the Confederacy. The Confederates, not Washington, now promised to deliver the precious annuities. The land was turning Confederate beneath Ross's feet. If he held out for the Union, Watie's Confederates would come after him like the Watie men of old, the slaves might rise up in the chaos, and the Knights might attack the Pins with renewed vigor. All of this would put the Cherokee government itself in grave peril, and quite possibly endanger Ross's life into the bargain.

Theatrical by nature, Pike was determined to make a display of force when he marched into Tahlequah. He paid out of his own pocket to recruit a long column of uniformed soldiers, plus an impressive train of supply wagons, to create an imperial aura as he made his way to a parley with the principal chief. Unfortunately, heavy rains washed out much of the road, and left his wagons mud-splashed and his men bedraggled when they finally pulled into the capital. The Cherokee who lined the streets to watch the spectacle weren't sure what to make of it.

But it surely made John Ross smile. Now a ripe seventy-two, he was somewhat shrunken by age, his wrinkled skin cracked with folds, his eyes receding under a craggy forehead, and his voice gone raspy. But he'd lost none of his spine. When he drew the enormous Pike into his office with McCulloch and Watie, he turned on him the force he had once directed at Andrew Jackson. No. That was his answer. No. It did not matter that the United States had thrown him over, or that Stand Watie was breathing down his neck, or that his government was nearly insolvent. If Watie was for the Confederacy, he was against it. He unloosed a blizzard of words: "A comparison of Northern and Southern philanthropy, as illustrated in their dealings toward the Indians within their respective limits, would not affect the merits of the question now under consideration, which is simply one of duty under existing circumstances." It boiled down to this: He would stick with the Union, come what may. If the Union troops now massing in Kansas stormed into the nation, he would not oppose them, but would honor his federal treaties and welcome them. And as for any further hostile encroachment from Texas, he would regard that as a "foreign invasion" and would "assist in repelling it."

Clearly, Pike had overlooked the depth of the hatred between Ross and Watie. By bringing Watie into the fold, Pike had pushed Ross out of it. Simple as that. The Treaty of 1846 was well behind them now. In the face of this new threat, Ross did not trust Watie nearly enough to join him in repelling it. If that made him an abolitionist Yankee-lover, so be it. As Pike said ruefully later: "If Stand Watie and his party took one side, John Ross and his party were in the end sure to take the other."

In some disgust at such an absurd display of politics, McCulloch stormed off to raise a Confederate regiment in nearby Sculleyville, just south of Fort Smith. Pike left in a huff, too, to lead his grand procession north. If he couldn't win Ross over, he would try the Creeks.

Amid a cloud of biting flies in the rising summer heat, Pike went to the Creek capital at North Fork Village, on a knobby peninsula on the Canadian River about forty miles due west of Fort Smith. On the way, he dropped in on the Choctaw and Chickasaw, and they let Pike know their support for the Confederacy was unwavering. The Creeks, however, proved not nearly so receptive. Ross had sent a letter to the tribe's ancient patriarch, Opothleyahola, an illustrious Creek leader since the time of the Red Sticks rebellion, to plead with him to stay neutral. Pike feared Ross was thinking of creating a "great Indian confederation" of all the tribes, independent of North *and* South, with himself at the head. He did win the backing of some Creek chiefs at North Fork Village, but there weren't many, and it took a lot of money and promises. And Opothleyahola was not one of these backers, which was worrisome. Pike went on to round up the other tribes who were willing to come to him to negotiate. One chief greeted Pike with a bear hug that left him feeling "squeezed in a cotton press" and another fell asleep during Pike's lengthy entreaty, requiring another chief to rouse him by tickling his bare feet, much to the general amusement of the assembly. By August 1, Pike notified Ross that he was nearly surrounded, as Pike had secured agreements with the Choctaw, the Chickasaw, a good portion of the Creeks, and several Plains Indians to come in for the Confederacy. And about the $500,000 that the Confederates had promised him as the first batch of annuity money? It was now "withdrawn." He should try to get it out of the Yankees instead.

That, at last, had an effect on Ross. And Stand Watie was starting to worry him. In July, some of Watie's men had tried to raise the Confederate flag in the Tahlequah town square. They'd been stopped by Watie's archenemy Bird Doublehead with about 100 Pins, but Ross had to ask Doublehead to please avoid such confrontations in the future, since he didn't wish to antagonize Stand Watie further.

Then came the startling news that the Union forces had been routed in the war's first big battles, at Bull Run in Virginia and at Wilson's Creek in Missouri. Perhaps the Union was not invincible after all. The defeat in Missouri was especially alarming because the Southern newspapers were claiming that the battle was turned by none other than Stand Watie, whose men had seized all but one of the North's artillery pieces in the rout. This proved to be an exaggeration, and there was even some question as to whether Watie was there. But just the thought was enough. If Watie was emerging as a powerful military commander on the winning side, and Ross was tied to the losing Union, Watie might challenge Ross for the Cherokee leadership, and triumph. That was a frightening prospect.

On August 21, Ross assembled 4,000 Cherokee, most of them his loyal full-bloods, in Tahlequah, and told them he had changed his mind. It was time for an "alliance" with the Confederacy after all. It was a time for unity: the Cherokee needed to be allied with the other Indian tribes Pike had recruited, and with the neighboring Southern states. (And with Stand Watie's Southern Cherokee, although they went unmentioned by Ross.) "Union is strength, dissension is weakness, misery and ruin!" Ross shouted. "In time of war, if war must come, fight together. As Brothers live; Brothers die." If this contradicted everything Ross had said before, no matter. He was at his most emphatic, and the multitude agreed deliriously with his latest opinion.

To show he meant it, Ross directed his nephew (by marriage) John Drew to raise a regiment of 1,200 to serve the Confederacy. To Pike this was very good news, but Watie was naturally apprehensive. To him, the men might better be said to serve *Ross* in the name of the Confederacy. Combine that 1,200 with the legions of Pins, who "already have more power in their hands than we can bear," as one Watie leader put it, and add to it Ross's self-proclaimed "sole right" to do business with North *and* South, and Watie had plenty of reason to fear Ross's highly publicized switch to the Rebel side. And Pike's support was proving to be less than total. When Watie's supporters demanded that Pike break up the domineering Pins, Pike replied that, alas, this was beyond his power.

In September, at his headquarters at Fort Smith, McCulloch officially welcomed Watie, a "gallant man and true friend to our country," into the Confederate army as a colonel, his men now to be known as the Cherokee Mounted Rifles. Privately, McCulloch was cautious about letting these men in too far and told Pike to keep Watie's forces well away from Ross's soldiers under Drew "for fear of a collision if they should come into contact with each other." McCullough sent Stand Watie's regiment to defend the northern border from any marauding Kansans, while he kept Drew's men well to the south near Tahlequah.

When Ross sent the joyous word out to other tribal chiefs that the Cherokee had gone with the Confederates and hoped they all would unite with him in a "common destiny," all the notables were receptive except one: the Creek patriarch and Union loyalist Opothleyahola, who was furious at Ross's turnabout. Just two months earlier, Ross had promised Opothleyahola that he would never fight against the Union, and now he was pledging to do just that. Stunned, Opothleyahola demanded that Ross send another letter, sure that this one had to be a hoax. But it was not, of course, and when Ross convened all the newly united Confederate forces at Park Hill, Opothleyahola's Creeks stayed away. They would remain true to the Union.

For the others, though, it made for a festival day. Park Hill filled up with "strangers," as one Ross man put it. Osages, Quapaws, Shawnee, and Seneca were only too pleased with the arrangement they'd made with Pike, allowing them to enjoy the protections of the Cherokee army without having to put up any men themselves. Watie brought his regiment down from the north, colors flying—much to the consternation of the Ross men. They weren't happy to see their enemies strolling about Park Hill, fully armed. His brother-in-law James M. Bell brought a company that included the businessman-politician Cornelius Elias Boudinot, who was now a Confederate soldier. Drew's men were there in far greater numbers.

For Ross, the decision to side with the Confederacy was largely financial. Gratified that the Rebels were now willing to pick up the federal annuity payments after all, he pressed a further claim. He demanded that they assume the still unpaid federal $5 million obligation for the nation's eastern lands. On top of that, he agreed to obligate Cherokee troops only to defend the Cherokee Nation and not to chase after the enemy elsewhere.

When the South agreed to all Ross's terms, Ross stood with Watie as Watie handed Pike a Cherokee flag, and Pike gave Watie a Confederate banner in return. Later, Ross would sign his name to a forceful "Declaration of Independence" written by Pike that slammed the Union for drawing "inmates" and "the scum of the cities" from the North "to burn, to plunder and to commit the basest of outrages on the women." Such accusations would serve to justify the secession of the South. But standing with Watie, Ross did something even more dramatic. He presented his hand to his longtime rival, and the two men shook, just as they had after President Polk's Treaty of 1846.

3

CIVIL WAR

Not all the Indians rallied to Ross, however. Opothleyahola stoutly refused to join Ross's "brotherhood of the Indian nations in a common destiny." In McKenney's gallery, as a younger man in Georgia, he cut a fine figure in a coat of robin's-egg blue, jaunty scarf, and stylish cap, topped with a starburst of feathers; and he still retained that magnetism. Other pro-Union Indians started streaming in from the hills, bringing along livestock, their families, and whatever possessions they could haul by wagon with them, to gather by Opothleyahola's house on the Little River, a tributary of the Canadian that flowed due east to the Mississippi through the center of the nation. Not just Creeks, but a number of disaffected Plains Indians and some dissident Seminoles came, too. They set up tents across the valley, with nightly bonfires for dancing and storytelling. Four thousand came in all, about a quarter of them warriors.

This did not sit well with the Rebel-friendly Creek chief, Motey Canard, who considered Opothleyahola's detachment "hostile." At Park Hill, Ross was "shocked with amazement" that a Creek might turn against a fellow Creek. When some of Opothleyahola's men made off with cash from the Creeks' national treasury, Canard vowed revenge.

Pike was away in the Confederate capital at Richmond. He left the former Indian agent Colonel Douglas H. Cooper in charge of a sizable Rebel Indian force—Choctaw and Chickasaw, mostly—plus some Texas cavalry led by the rugged, big-bearded Colonel James McIntosh. Cooper charged the camps around Opothleyahola's house in the middle of November 1862, sending the Union Creeks south. A battle at Round Mounds—named for its hills—four days later ended in confusion when darkness fell. Afterward, Cooper tracked Opothleyahola's people into Cherokee country at Bird Creek, which branches off the Verdigris that drifts down toward Fort Gibson. There, Watie's rival John Drew sent a major to try to talk peace. Something about Opothleyahola inspired sympathy, and Drew's resolve to fight weakened. He let two of his captains go over to Opothleyahola's side, taking 300 men with them.

Without them, Cooper had to retreat to Fort Smith, where he demanded that John Ross force his traitorous nephew John Drew to restore the troops. When Ross claimed to be powerless, Cooper vowed to exterminate Opothleyahola and anyone who followed him, Drew's men included. It was late December now, and winter had come on, heaping up snow and sending an icy breeze across the wide valleys. After a search of several days, Cooper's men discovered the Union Indians hiding among some wind-whipped boulders in the Osage hills by Shoal Creek in Chustenahla. There, Cooper sneaked around to attack them from the rear while McIntosh's Texas cavalry charged up the Verdigris River to hit them from the front. Tucked behind boulders, fighting for their lives, the Union Creeks held off the Rebel forces at both ends for hours.

Then, in mid-afternoon, 300 Cherokee horsemen came blasting through the snow along the Arkansas River, led by a fire-breathing Stand Watie, with his pink-cheeked nephew Elias Cornelius Boudinot racing at his side. Turning to fend off Watie's men, the Union Indians exposed a flank to the Texans, who crashed down on them, slaughtering hundreds, and putting to rout hundreds more. They fled through heavy snow and bitter winds clear to Kansas, many of them dying of starvation even before the bitter cold could get to them. Terrified mothers killed their babies so the enemy could not grab them. Some refugees ate their horses and hid inside the carcasses.

The newspapers hailed Watie as the hero of the battle, although Cooper and McIntosh deserve equal credit. And there were wild claims that Watie went on to lay waste to more towns well inside the borders of Kansas. The rumors were false, but they showed that Stand Watie was beginning to achieve legendary status. Worse for Ross, President Jefferson Davis made Albert Pike a brigadier general in full military command of the entire Indian Territory. John Ross held no military rank, controlled no army, and now he'd lost supreme governmental authority as well. Still, it was Watie he went after. From his "Cherokee Executive Department" at Tahlequah, Ross claimed he'd planned to assist the Rebel attack against the Creeks but was put off by "some unwarranted conduct on the part of many base, reckless and unprincipled persons belonging to Watie's Regiment." Apparently, Watie's men had trampled on the rights "of peaceable and unoffending citizens." It was all Watie's fault that Ross hadn't showed up.

The Creek survivors who straggled into the Kansas campsites of the Union army must have made a grim sight. Half-dead from exhaustion, disease, and hunger, the survivors were met by Union surgeons with hacksaws, eager to cut off any limbs lost to frostbite. Hundreds died, Opothleyahola himself among them; all the corpses were dropped into mass graves that scarcely dipped into the frozen ground.

Into this terrible scene came the Reverend Evan Jones. The high priest of the Pin vigilantes who sympathized with the Union, he'd been hiding out in Kansas after having been evicted from the nation. Jones was so removed from things he didn't hear that Ross had joined the Confederacy until he reached the camps. Jones simply could not believe it. He told the Union's Indian commissioner, W. P. Dole, that Ross must have gone Rebel out of "imminent and perilous necessity."

Jones was sure that Ross could be peeled away from the Southern cause. To try, the War Department decided to make a personal appeal to the principal chief at Park Hill. The department would take the last of Opothleyahola's army, plus what was left of Drew's defectors, and try to sneak them down past Watie's sentries into the territory to find a route to get Union troops to Ross, then spirit him north if he proved willing, or kill him otherwise.

For now, the Union forces were busy trying to take back Missouri, which had been pro-slavery since the Compromise of 1820. By the fall of 1861, Union troops had joined with antislavery "jayhawkers" from Kansas under the command of a grizzled fifty-seven-year-old former engineer, Major General Samuel Curtis. A West Point graduate, class of 1831, Curtis had left the military for politics to become mayor of Keokuk, Iowa, and then a Republican congressman. When war broke out, he raised a Union regiment and became a brigadier general with 10,000 men to drive the Confederate forces out of Missouri.

Meanwhile, the Confederates enlisted Missouri's former governor, Sterling Price, age fifty-three, dubbed "Old Pap" for his genial ways, to seize the federal arsenal at Saint Louis, commandeer its railroads, and kick the Union out of the state. Price commanded the Missouri state guard, the military arm of the state's secessionist government. He teamed up with Ben McCulloch, now a brigadier general in charge of the region's entire Confederate army, to create a vast army of 17,000 men, easily the largest in the west. But each commander was so headstrong that neither would cede authority to the other. So President Jefferson Davis put them both under the command of Brigadier General Earl Van Dorn, a planter-aristocrat from Davis's own Port Gibson, Mississippi. He'd fought Mexicans and Comanche, and now lusted for greater glory still. His ambition, he confided to his sister, "rages like a house on fire." Van Dorn planned to gather his forces in the safety of the Boston Mountains of northwest Arkansas late in February 1862 and strike the federal forces from there.

But Curtis was not a man to sit tight. In early February, he'd smacked into Price's troops and sent them howling south in an endless, desperate train. Everything from oxcarts to painted stagecoaches scrambled along the road. The methodical Curtis pursued the Confederates over the border, even though his army was drastically undersized. Whatever he lacked in manpower, he made up for with the heavy guns of the Missouri artillery he dragged along, and with the brisk cohesion of a nimbler army.

Van Dorn set up his camp in Fayetteville, where many members of the

Ridge family were still exiled. He used Miss Sawyer's female seminary as an arsenal and took over the Overland Mail Company as stables. Frightened Southerners had flooded in from all corners, turning a tidy town of 2,000 into a snowy chaos of thousands more. When McCulloch found his way down there, he broke open the military stores to everyone before they could fall into federal hands, creating a frenzy of plunder. When a breathless Sterling Price hurried in shortly afterward, Van Dorn was staggered to learn that Curtis's federal troops were snapping right behind him. They'd made camp just fifteen miles north at Cross Hollow, enjoying the makeshift shelters Price had abandoned in his frantic retreat.

A prudent man might have stayed put, or lured the Union troops yet deeper south, further extending their already stretched supply lines, and let winter do its savage work. But Van Dorn was too cocky for caution. He would attack with all the vigor of the overeager.

Last to arrive in Fayetteville, just in time for battle, were Pike's Confederate Indians. They made a remarkable entrance, some smartly mounted, the rest on foot, with the massive Pike himself at the head, riding in a splendid carriage alongside his Negro manservant, Brutus, who carried the official papers in a carpetbag. By one account, Pike was "decked out like Sioux in feathers, leggings, and beaded moccasins," but that is hard to imagine, even for Pike. (Van Dorn would never take him seriously in such a getup.) Still, the image has symbolic truth, as Pike had gone native to an extraordinary degree, and he identified with his Indian fighters. None of them were in uniforms, which were thought to be "wasted" on Indians. A few might have been able to cadge Confederate gray caps to squash down over their long black hair, which would stream out from underneath. But otherwise they dressed for battle in whatever clothes they came in, adding war paint for ferocity. The stern Stand Watie rode in with Elias Cornelius Boudinot beside him, leading his Cherokee Second Rifles of mixed-bloods, mostly, followed by what was left of Drew's Cherokee First Rifles, to whom Watie was obliged to defer, much to his annoyance. Behind them came John Jumper's Seminoles, and then the Creeks led by General Daniel McIntosh, son of the traitorous William, long-haired and long-bearded as if he were a mystic. Pike did his best to train them in basic military maneuvers. He'd clump his men into groups, then give a shout to send them charging toward the far trees with great war whoops while they shot off their rifles at an imagined enemy. Not entirely trusting such battlefield maneuvers, they downed cups of the alcoholic "black drink" to make them bulletproof and chanted pleas to the Great Spirit to protect them from harm.

On March 4, the Indians were sent through a late-winter snowstorm up the Bentonville Road to join McCulloch at Smith's Mill, perhaps twenty miles north. Trouble had already flared between Watie and Drew by then. Watie's nephew Charles Webber had killed and scalped an irksome full-blood named Chunestootie in Drew's company. Watie took Webber's side, but regretted it when a Watie man then summarily shot a defector from Drew's force who'd returned to the Confederate fold. Nothing would stanch the bad blood between Ross and Ridge.

Back in his Indian-fighting days, Van Dorn, a cavalryman at heart, used to frighten Comanche by driving at them and scaring them into flight—right into a trap he'd laid for them and a general slaughter. He planned now to do the same to the Union. He'd have McCulloch surge at Curtis's men from the front, but only after he himself raced around to the rear to slice the men up as they fled.

McCulloch's men proceeded as planned, Pike's Indians trailing behind them under the command of General McIntosh. But Van Dorn's cavalry, slowed by the infantry slogging behind, weren't able to get into position to take any advantage. Besides, Curtis was no Comanche; he was not one to flee anything. Still, to get ahead of Curtis, Van Dorn had frantically sent his exhausted, starving troops up a narrow trail, sloppy with March snow, and rendered almost impassable by all the felled trees that Curtis's engineers had dropped on it. Union scouts spotted them laboring there and called in artillery fire that further pinned Van Dorn down.

Meanwhile, McCulloch's steady advance was halted when he ran into some hardened troops under Curtis's junior commander, Colonel Osterhaus, who blasted away at them from the trees. McCulloch had to stop and form a line to send his men charging at Osterhaus's company across an open field.

This is where the Cherokee came in. There were 1,000 of them, divided into Watie's and Drew's forces, many on horseback, a cap or strip of tattered gray the only indication that they were on the Confederate side. They stood way down to McCullough's right like an afterthought, well away from the center of the action, doubtless mystified to be a small part of such a big raging war, cannon and rifle fire going off everywhere, much of it coming from well beyond where anyone could see. Nonetheless, when McCulloch gave a signal, Pike let his Indians loose with a rebel yell, and they all came screaming out of the woods with war cries that soared above the boom of cannon and the bang of rifle fire. The Cherokee had rifles, but most preferred to use their bows as they charged, letting loose a fusillade of arrows. Racing toward the trees, Watie spotted another of the Union "shooting wagons," as the Cherokee called them, thundering forth. With a shout, he led a gang of mounted Cherokee to storm the cannon "like tigers," one of them later said, and dispatch the shocked cannoneers. The big gun silent, several of the Cherokee finished off the wounded, and then brought out their bowie knives to hack off scalps, lift them to the sky, and prance about with joy.

Watie took no part in this defilement, but he didn't stop the ones who joined it. Knocked back by the Rebel charge, Osterhaus regrouped and returned fire, sending the Confederates fleeing back across the field, the Cherokee with them, where they settled in among the trees. For well over an hour, Pike awaited further instructions, but nothing came.

In the lull, McCulloch ventured forth on horseback to do some reconnaissance. There was nothing like seeing with his own eyes how things stood. Not one for a proper uniform, McCulloch was dressed in a dove-colored jacket and blue pantaloons, his Maynard rifle slung over his shoulder. He was still a good seventy yards from the enemy when a single shot from an Iowa sharpshooter dropped him off his horse, dead. His second, General McIntosh, manfully took McCulloch's place to lead the next assault, until a Union bullet caught him, too, and he toppled from his saddle.

That was pretty much it for the Confederates. The deaths left the lumbering Pike, of all people, to command the Confederates' right wing. Too inexperienced in war to be taken seriously as any kind of field general, Pike had hardly been told the battle plan or the overall layout. Not knowing what else to do, he hid in the trees and desperately sent word to Van Dorn, now miles away on a slog of his own, for instructions. It wasn't until Van Dorn was finally set up in field headquarters at Elkhorn Tavern—a two-story bar and hotel that was almost the only building around—that word came back. Come.

Van Dorn's whole army was there, what was left of it, many of the troops lying half-dead in the ankle-deep snow. The Indians fell in among them, trying to stay warm. With Van Dorn's supply wagons stuck miles back, just about everyone was hungry and angry.

When dawn broke, Van Dorn formed a long line to go after Curtis once again. Pike put Drew's Cherokee at one end, Watie's at the other. Curtis, far more orderly, was well dug in, fully aware that the Confederates were leaderless. When the Rebels made a chaotic charge, his federals were ready. By afternoon, the Confederates were running for their lives, and there was nothing Van Dorn could do to stop them.

Only Watie's men, well up Pea Ridge—which gave the battle its name—were able to hold their ground. But when it was clear that all was lost, Watie fought his way down farther south to Camp Stephens, where the various Indian troops were to gather. By then, however, Drew's Cherokee had long since left for home—but not before they'd looted the one provision wagon that had shown up, leaving almost nothing behind for Watie's famished men.

The battle had been a disaster for the Confederates. Far from crushing Curtis, Van Dorn had been crushed. The Rebels would never again contend in Kansas or Missouri, and all of Arkansas north of the Arkansas River was gone as well. It was just the beginning of the war, but it might as well have been the end.

Van Dorn retreated south to Van Buren, and from there tried to put the best face on things, commending the bravery of his officers, lamenting their "misfortunes" in the deaths of McCulloch and McIntosh, and overlooking his own ineptitude. When he wrote to ask Curtis for permission to bury his war dead, Curtis replied bluntly that captured Confederate surgeons were already going about it. An adjutant explained his irritation: "The general regrets that we find on the battlefield, contrary to civilized warfare, many of the Federal dead were tomahawked, scalped, and their bodies shamefully mangled." He was also dismayed that Pike's Cherokee "shot arrows as well as rifles," violating the rules of proper military conduct. The newspapers featured the story of these "Indian savages," and, as Curtis put it, "the barbarity their merciless and cowardly natures are capable of." Eyewitnesses confirmed that eight Union soldiers were scalped, and the bodies of many others "were horribly mutilated, being fired with musket balls and pierced through the body and neck with long knives." The newspapers freely upped the number of those scalped to 100. The *Chicago Tribune* singled out Pike for "eternal infamy"; the *New York Tribune* inveighed against him as a "ferocious fish"; and the *Boston Evening Transcript* declared that "a more venomous reptile than Albert Pike [never] crawled on the face of the earth." The Indians themselves were not held responsible for their acts. Presumably, they just couldn't help it, in contrast to Pike, who knew better.

Van Dorn was finished with Pike, and with his Indian charges, too. He was determined to renew his campaign to rid Missouri of Union soldiers, but without the aid of any "savages." Pike would be sent back to the Indian territory with the men he still commanded, but they would be restricted to tasks more befitting Van Dorn's idea of Indians' skills—"cut off trains, annoy the enemy in his marches, and to prevent him, as far as possible, from supplying his troops from Missouri and Kansas." In a later order, Van Dorn's adjutant spelled it out. The Indians could be rewarded with any spoils, "*but you will please endeavor to restrain them from committing any barbarities upon the wounded, prisoners or dead who may fall into their hands.*" In passing these orders on to Watie, Pike expressed his pique that he would now have to leave all of western Arkansas to the Union. Pike himself would regroup in Texas, establishing a base of operations there, and rely on Watie to take up the fight in the territory along the lines that Van Dorn proposed, with raiding parties to "annoy" the Union. He'd leave the job of keeping the Union out of the rest of Arkansas to Thomas C. Hindman, a five-foot former novelist whom Pike found useless. It seemed only Watie could hold off a Union advance now.

At Park Hill, John Ross viewed the developments with mounting distress. Without Pike, he relied on Hindman to keep the Union out of the territory, but Hindman turned Ross over to Pike, which was ridiculous. That left Ross with Watie, the last person he wished to rely on. He wasn't getting anything out of the Confederates, either. No one was. It seemed that the Confederacy was all smoke. Watie's fellow Treaty Party man William P. Adair, key to his outfit, wrote to tell him that, low as he was, his brother was worse, his ammunition scarce, food scarcer, and now no paper to say more than this: send a military surgeon to his wife or she'd be dead "in 30 hours."

Meanwhile, Union colonel William Weer had taken over the "Indian Expedition" to bring Ross to the Union side or kill him. Weer had his own Tenth Kansas Regiment for the purpose, plus four other companies, including some of Opothleyahola's warriors and a few of Evan Jones's Pins. Near the end of June, it was time to strike. Deploying the Indians as scouts, Weer led his men south through Cowskin Prairie amid the usual plague of black flies under a broiling sun. Everyone was on the lookout for Watie's men, who seemed to be everywhere. On July 3, they spotted an encampment of Watie's soldiers, and some of Drew's, too, and charged at them, catching Watie off guard for once. That went badly for Watie's Confederates, and Watie himself barely managed to slip away into the darkness. Nearly 100 of Drew's men threw down their arms and volunteered to come over to the Union side, handing over an immense mule train as well.

With Watie absent, Weer pushed down deeper to Wolf Creek, ten miles from Tahlequah, but the stresses of war were getting to him. The colonel found confidence in a bottle, but also ill temper and unreliability. Still, Weer sent a communiqué to Ross via an expedition surgeon, requesting an interview. Ross replied that, as he was now "honor bound" to the Confederacy, he had to decline. Under the circumstances, that was brassy.

And, to Weer, puzzling. The Reverend Evan Jones had assured the Union command that Ross was at heart a Union man who'd joined the Confederacy only out of fear of Watie's reaction if he did otherwise. Not so? What were the man's true colors? With Ross, this was always the question. By declaring himself "honor bound" did he mean *only* honor bound? If it was completely up to him, would he behave differently?

Half-drunk, Weer decided it didn't matter. He'd seize Ross regardless. And so he sent a small detachment of soldiers, a mingling of white and Cherokee, under Major H. S. Greeno to size up the situation at Rose Cottage, where Ross was ensconced with his Mary. Watching from a safe distance, the contingent found the place in terrible decay. The roses along the fences had dried up, the lawns had yellowed, and the house had lost its sparkle. It was also surrounded by a kind of palace guard, many of them drawn from the remaining portion of Drew's company, who stared menacingly at Greeno's party as it conducted its surveillance through a spyglass from a safe distance away.

Greeno set up camp a couple of miles away from Rose Cottage and awaited orders. By now, Weer had repaired to the safety of Fort Gibson, and he was soon joined there by a Major Campbell, who'd toured the territory farther south and discovered that the last of the Confederate forces were well away from Park Hill. Aside from his private guard, it seemed Ross was defenseless. Learning that, Greeno charged at Rose Cottage in haste. Seeing so many Union men coming at them, Ross's guards threw up their hands in surrender, and Greeno's men stormed inside. There, a finely dressed Ross welcomed these hostile soldiers into his parlor as if they were his guests invited for tea, not his enemy ready to shoot him. He styled himself a Union man now.

Ross remained under house arrest for two weeks until August 3, when he and Mary were taken by armed guard to Fort Leavenworth in Kansas. There, an urgent cable came in from the War Department ordering the commander to treat the Rosses with deference. The commander duly received the Rosses as honored houseguests, not as prisoners of war. Ironically, it was the expedition commander, Weer, who was the prisoner. His second in command, Colonel Saloman, had had him arrested as an "abusive and violent" drunkard, and he awaited a court-martial. So the pursuer was in chains, the pursued left free, yet more proof of Ross's political adroitness in the face of adversity that would have left a lesser man dead. The Rosses were soon taken like dignitaries by stagecoach under military escort to Philadelphia, where they were offered residence in an impressive two-story Colonial-style house on South Washington Square, free to enjoy themselves about town while Ross awaited an audience with President Lincoln.

With Ross removed, the three Confederate Indian regiments withdrew to a military camp at Wolf Creek. While Drew's men remained under suspicion at Rose Cottage, Watie's men freely roamed the nation elsewhere. Some renegades burst into the general store of Daniel Ross at Fort Gibson, arrested him on spurious charges, smashed everything they didn't steal, and dumped a hundred barrels of sugar onto the ground. This was vengeance, but it was also victory. A triumphant Watie called for a general council at Tahlequah. With Ross in flight as a Union sympathizer, Watie put himself forward as the *true* principal chief of the Cherokee Nation, and he was elected by acclamation.

In the excitement, Watie's men went marauding about Park Hill, scatter-ing Drew's guard, and going after any Rosses they could find. They butchered some men in Murrell's orchard by Hunter's Home, where some relatives of Ross had been staying. Others ransacked another Ross house, sending any remaining Union backers running north for their lives. "Many of our friends have been scattered abroad upon the world," wailed Mrs. William P. Ross, wife of Ross's nephew who had edited the *Advocate*. "Others dead, yet others are estranged from one another."

Ross begged Lincoln to send troops into the territory to put down such lawlessness. Otherwise his people faced "distress, danger, and ruin." Lincoln was sympathetic, but, after consulting with General Curtis, decided the ter-ritory was too far from Union supplies for him to intercede. Ross did get his own national council to reject Watie's claims to being principal chief. He tried to get the council to depose any Cherokee officials disloyal to the Union, and to abolish slavery. Neither edict was likely to have much effect in a coun-try that was Watie's now.

As Watie's men stormed about the nation, the Union methodically re-took its forts. Popular strength was one thing, military power another. From its base in northwest Arkansas, Union general James Blunt's Kansas Division stormed Old Fort Wayne, briefly Fort Watie, where Colonel Cooper's Con-federate forces had been holed up. Watie scrambled to repel the attack, but the Union men forced him back to Spavinaw Creek, twenty miles north of Tahlequah. When the Union cavalry continued to go after him, Watie had to retreat all the way to the Moravian mission, leaving Fort Wayne to the enemy. Meanwhile, Union colonel William Phelps held on to Fort Gibson, always a key to control of the territory, and redoubled its fortifications.

The inner war between Watie and Ross raged on. As Mrs. William P. Ross wrote in February 1863, "Watie's men have acted very badly indeed since we left. They took all of Uncle Robert's things and gave them away and Aunt Min's too and robbed Mrs. Gunter's House while she was dying." Refugees in their own land, many of Ross's loyalists depended on the Union for food. Hannah Worcester, Unionist daughter of the late missionary, wrote to her sis-ter that May: "I am dependent on what is given me for bread, but we have not suffered yet. They are expecting a large Train loaded with flour to supply the people. Hundreds of women and children, now without bread and salt, eagerly waiting for the train. . . . I fear that many will actually starve."

The Southern Cherokee fared little better, though. With food scarce, and fighting everywhere, Watie moved Sarah and the children out of Honey Creek to Webbers Falls, well south in the nation. In late fall, he sent them farther south still.

4

THE END

The tide of the larger Civil War had started to turn decisively with the new year, 1863, as the Union army prevailed that summer on the battlefields of Gettysburg and Vicksburg. In the territory, the Confederates' fortunes just about ran out. Determined to recapture Fort Gibson, Confederate colonel Cooper planned to surge down the Texas road to the fort with an army of Indians led by his Texas cavalry; but General Blunt intercepted the attack before it could form, sent Cooper's forces scurrying, and marched on to take Fort Smith.

Dispirited, a number of Watie's men switched to the Union side, and others dreamed of murdering the Confederate leadership that had abandoned them, starting with Jefferson Davis. Watie doggedly carried on, convening a national council at a campground at Webbers Falls to address the "evil times" that had fallen on them. At a planning session, he was confident that the Confederates would soon drive out the federal forces—only to learn that Colonel

Phillips, in charge of the Union Indian brigade at Fort Gibson, had marched by night to Webbers Falls, sending everyone at the meeting scrambling for safety.

To retaliate, Watie collected 1,000 men to plunder a Union supply wagon train near Fort Gibson, only to be foiled by federals who learned of his plans. Adding to his woes, Watie's son Cumiskey died of a fever that spring. Grief-stricken, Sarah took the rest of the family out of the territory entirely to join her ailing sister, Nancy Starr, in Rusk, Texas, where some exiles from the Treaty Party had set up a meager enclave below the Red River. Only the oldest son, Saladin, remained with his father. Just fifteen, with the first trace of a mustache coming, he was slender and impetuous and had a taste for fine coats. He gleefully wrestled his father, stiff with the bone ache of war, and, unlike many of his elders, was keen to fight on. His lust for battle further distressed his already distraught mother. When she heard that Saladin had killed a prisoner, she wrote to Watie that "it almost runs me crazy to hear such things. I find myself almost dead some times thinking about it. I am afraid that Saladin never will value human life as he ought." She begged Watie not to take blood revenge on the Rosses, either, tempting as she knew it must be. "I want them to know that you do not want to kill them just to get them out of your way." But her love for her husband shone through. "I can't live and not hear from you," she concluded. "You must write and tell me when it will be safe to come home."

Determined to bring the war to the enemy, Watie sought out the federals at Maysville, where he'd shot James Foreman years before, only to find a much larger force gunning for him. With the Neosho River and its tributaries too high to ford, he was nearly overtaken by Union major John Foreman's forces before he made a brief stand at Greenleaf Prairie, just south of Fort Gibson, and then slipped away once more. Surprise attacks, then a melting away. These were the methods of Watie's Cherokee.

The federals largely remained safe in their forts, but they were only as durable as their food supply. Watie's Confederates tried to starve out the brigade at mighty Fort Gibson, and gleefully snatched a herd of Union horses foraging outside the walls. The Union commander, Phillips, called for a lengthy wagon train from Kansas to resupply the fort, escorted by a brand-new Negro regiment, the Second Colorado Infantry. Watie planned to ambush it at Cabin

Creek, now Big Cabin, off the Neosho River, since floodwaters had made the creek virtually impassable. Sure enough, the train arrived and halted nose first before the near shore of the creek, unable to go farther. Watie had arrayed 1,500 men in the bush well out of sight, back from the far bank. From there, they pelted the train and its many protectors with a hail of gunfire and arrows, but the Kansas artillery replied with furious heavy mortar shelling. Watie's men held their ground, waiting for reinforcements from Arkansas under Major Cabell. But Cabell had himself been held up by floodwaters on the Grand River to the east. While Watie stewed, the Kansas infantry pushed across the creek, guns high over their heads, and the cavalry splashed after them, to storm Watie's troops on their rise. Watie had no choice but to abandon his position. When the creek waters settled the next day, the long wagon train passed on to Fort Gibson, to the joy of the Union soldiers trapped inside.

Overmatched by Union power in what was supposed to be a Cherokee stronghold, Watie fired off an indignant letter to S. S. Scott, the latest Confederate commissioner of Indian affairs, expressing outrage at Richmond's callousness toward its Indian troops: denying them their pay; skimping on their rations; and providing few guns, no uniforms, and scarcely even any clothing. Out of 5,000 men, James M. Bell reported to his sister, 1,000 went into battle unarmed "and many have not Clothing to change, without shoes" and looking "*more like Siberian exiles* than soldiers." He himself had been in "almost nude condition."

Replying for Scott, General Kirby-Smith hoped only that Watie would encourage his men to "struggle on through the dark gloom which now envelopes our affairs." He did manage to put through some rations for the starving Cherokee, and threw up a camp in Choctaw Nation for any refugees from the still rampant Pins. Elias Cornelius Boudinot—now the sole Cherokee representative to the Confederate Congress—contributed $10,000 of his own from Richmond and promised $40,000 more. He got through the Confederate congress a bill providing $100,000 in relief, but it was paid in useless Confederate "greybacks," worth just a few pennies on the Union dollar.

Where were the Confederate soldiers that President Davis had promised for the protection of the nation? It seemed to Watie that the task had been left to him alone. He tried to enlist the Choctaw and Chickasaw in a united Indian state, a Cherokee dream since the time of Dragging Canoe, but it was no use. The Choctaw scarcely rallied to help the Confederates oust a Union regiment from their own Choctaw Nation. Whenever Watie had to attend to his administrative duties as principal chief, the military effort flagged noticeably. Confederate general William Steele, battling the Union forces at Perryville, southwest of Fort Smith in Choctaw Nation, found the Indians "desponding, hopeless, and . . . thoroughly demoralized." Steele's own white regiment had few arms and no change of clothes. Most of his officers were useless, and Steele had one of them court-martialed for "disrespect." Powder secured from Texas turned to "paste" in the morning dew. And his troops deserted at a rate of up to 200 a night. Scarcely had the first bullets flown at about eight o'clock on the first night of battle before the Confederates folded and fled, leaving Perryville in flames behind them. While Steele hurried away, Blunt pushed on like Sherman, destroying everything.

Steele tried to choke off Fort Gibson, but the federals there not only held him at bay, but made their own assault on Fort Smith, the last significant fort still in Southern hands, before Steele could rush to its defense, and it fell almost without incident. Later that day, when the Southerners tried to recover at Devil's Backbone, just south of the fort, Blunt dismissed them virtually with a clap of his hands, securing the region's two dominating fortresses for the rest of the war, and vast reaches of countryside surrounding them. What the Union forces didn't control through arms they won by relieving the hunger of the Indians starving everywhere around them. Famished themselves, the Confederates had nothing to offer except promises.

Infuriated by the relentless loss and retreat, Watie charged on Tahlequah late in October. His target was not President Davis's dissolving Confederacy, or the relentless Union troops, but everything that remained of John Ross. Watie's men charged screaming into town, burned down Ross's council house, slaughtered the full-bloods still loyal to him, and captured William P. Ross. Watie might have killed William if he hadn't promised Sarah to let the Ross men be, and not to produce any more grieving Ross widows. So Watie let William go, but then continued on to Park Hill and torched Ross's beloved Rose Cottage.

With John Ross in Philadelphia with Mary, the rest of the family had to save themselves. When his son James tried to get some food through to his wife and children, he was arrested by Confederates and sent to a series of hellhole prisons in the South, dying in captivity the next year. After the death of her first husband, Return Meigs, Jr., Ross's daughter Jane had married a full-blood, Andy Nave. He was guarding their house as a Union soldier when some of Watie's marauders converged on it. Nave dashed across a field to get away, only to be caught in the back by a shotgun blast that slapped him up against a wire fence and left his corpse pinned there while Jane clutched their daughter to her and screamed uncontrollably.

From the Rosses' new home in Philadelphia, Mary passed the dreadful news about Rose Cottage to her husband, off for meetings in Washington, in one of the few surviving notes from her. "Home, my dear Husband we have no home there now, one we cherished so long & took so much trouble to beautify is now in ashes, all is ruin around." Mary sought comfort from her "Heavenly Father" while her husband raged against "the meditated harm of a murderous band of incendiary bandits!" He could too easily envision the scene described by his daughter—"her devoted Husband was so barbarously murdered, by that Notorious band of rebel robbers, who at the same time burned our family Homestead at Rose Cottage & while the fiends were robbing & searching her House for victims, she says—'Expecting every minute to see my Child dragged out.'" But Jane's sister Sallie had saved her daughter from "the bloody hands of the assassin."

Watie told his wife that he felt "sorry" Nave had been killed, as he had been "friendly" with him before the war, but "it could not be helped." He was too pestered to write more. "I am annoyed almost to death by people calling on me on business of various kinds, this and that." Sarah Watie responded bitterly. The war had taken a toll. Two children had already died of disease, and now Saladin was sick, and Watie himself acknowledged he'd been feeling poorly for some time, a frightening admission.

But being off in Texas, so far removed, posed a strain of its own for Sarah. With little solid news, amid a bedraggled enclave of Treaty Party loyalists in small, bleak farmhouses with poor crops and scarcely any livestock, she felt cranky and put upon, she wrote. "I have not been in the right good [spirit since] you left for several [reasons] non I will name here. . . . We always [go] about under more disadvantages than any one else. we always feed more folks than any body else and get less thanks. we have our troubles here as other places. . . . Let me tell you how we were caught when they got here we had not a scrap of meat or grease only some that I had thought not fit to use but I went to getting supper and made it do. . . . I look for you home soon on account of having no place." She asked him for a loom, work tools, plows, anything. "I am sorry you are not as well as you were at the beginning [of the] war so many of our friends have died . . . we have had such bad luck with our children that it keeps me uneasy about them."

In November 1863 Watie tried to whip up the general assembly of Confederate Indians with assurances that if the Cherokee "put forth united action," they would drive the Union out of the territory. What history did they seek to make? he asked. "Will it be a history which will cause your children to be ashamed, or will it be one which will cause their eyes to lighten with joyous pride?"

But the Cherokee did not rally. Watie was left to conduct more guerrilla raids, sometimes with the notorious Confederate outlaw William Quantrill, whose gang of bushwhackers included Jesse James. They tried a sneak attack on Fort Smith. When it failed, Watie stormed back to Park Hill to burn down the last of Ross's slave cabins and plunder the exquisite home of George M. Murrell. With just a few hundred ill-trained, ill-equipped soldiers, he couldn't manage much more. The year ended ominously when Watie's men attacked the Indian home guard of Union captain Alexander Spilman, only to be sent scrambling by the Union's screaming howitzers.

That winter, thousands of Cherokee roamed about the frozen countryside scrounging food—companies of soldiers little more than gangs, families broken up by all the deaths. "It seems all the time like one great funeral," Hannah Worcester said.

Things were no better in Richmond. Boudinot reported to his brother William Penn that the Union seemed to be closing in. One night, "the city fairly shook with the thunder of artillery. I was awakened by it—the firing was terrific and very rapid. I counted looking at my watch 30 guns a minute." Alarms sounded all over the city, and the government itself "packed up" and everyone hurried to the train station, only to discover that the railroad lines had been cut. Boudinot resolved to get away on foot if necessary, but General Lee rallied once more to repel the enemy, and by July the threat to the city had passed. By then, Boudinot had roused the Confederate government to make his uncle Stand a brigadier general, the highest-ranking Confederate Indian in the war. Boudinot actually carried a copy of the commission west to present to Watie in person, fearing word might not reach him otherwise.

Nothing would lift Sarah's spirits in Rusk. "I will stay here in this part of the country till July and then I expect to hear from you if you think there will be peace I will go back as far as I was." Only as far as Choctaw country, since she was still afraid of the Cherokee Nation. "It is ten times as hard to get along here as there. I am not well enough to do any thing in the way of making a living. I will do well to save my self alive for my children. Nancy is still very feeble just can walk about the house, all the rest are well."

Worried about his failing aunt, Cornelius Boudinot went to Rusk that fall to check on her and to bring "cards" to spin the raw cotton fiber that still grew there into thread for marketable cloth. As it was, federal gunboats patrolling the Mississippi cut off commerce with the west, further squeezing the economy of the Confederate southwest. While he was there, Boudinot offered to take the younger two children with him back to Richmond, where they could go to school, but Sarah wouldn't hear of it.

Watie continued to pester the Union forces. His men captured a federal steamboat, the *J.R. Williams*, pushing up the Arkansas with supplies. A blast from some concealed artillery knocked holes in its hull, and Watie's men stormed aboard to plunder its 16,000 pounds of bacon, and 150 barrels of hominy, salt pork, and flour.

That September, 1864, Watie's men seized a long federal wagon train— 250 heavy wagons pulled by 740 mules to bear much-needed food and clothing for 2,000 men garrisoned at Fort Gibson and Fort Smith. The train was escorted by 1,000 Union soldiers, but they'd slacked off with whiskey when they stopped for the night by Cabin Creek in Cherokee territory, and Watie's men sneaked up after midnight to drop artillery shells on them and seize their entire haul. Between the wagons and the train, the whole cargo was worth $1.5 million, almost a third of the outlay the United States had promised (but not yet fully paid) for all of the Cherokee Nation. "The brilliancy and completeness of this expedition has not been excelled in the history of the war," exclaimed Douglas Cooper, now a Confederate general, thrilled to have something to celebrate for once. The exploit won Watie an official resolution of thanks from the Confederate Congress, signed by President Davis. But the better praise came from his wife, who wrote in a rare bit of laconic humor: "I would send you some clothes, but I hear you have done better than to wait on me."

Watie continued to pester the Union troops through the winter and into the spring, but the Confederate cause was hopeless, and a beaten Lee finally surrendered to Grant at Appomattox on April 9, 1865. There, Grant was represented by an Indian general of his own, the Seneca chief Ely Parker, who drew up the terms of the agreement. Other Southern commanders in the east quickly followed Lee. On May 26, Confederate general Kirby-Smith surrendered his Trans-Mississippi Department. The federal government sent out agents to end hostilities with various Indian leaders in the territory. Watie, fighting to the end, was the last Indian commander they were able to reach, as he was encamped twelve miles outside the Choctaw village of Doaksville, just north of the Texas border. It was there that Watie officially surrendered, the very last Confederate officer to give up the fight.

5

"I SHALL SEE THEM
NO MORE ON EARTH"

John Ross's wife Mary was failing. Back in Park Hill, her faith had eased the pain of her being a "lonely white stranger" in her husband's country, but in the east, she was succumbing to what her husband called "that unhappy disease—the blues." Mary assured him that his letters "cast sunshine around my heart." But her emotional distress contributed to a general weakness. A congestion in her lungs was making her breathing increasingly difficult. On July 20, 1865, as the war was finally drawing to a close, her heart gave out from the strain. She was just thirty-nine, to her husband's seventy-four. The Staplers buried her in their family plot in Wilmington, as if to reclaim her from the Indians.

Grieving and exhausted, Ross returned home alone to the nation. From the steamer *Iron City* five miles below Van Buren he wrote to his sister-in-law Sarah Stapler that he knew he'd find Rose Cottage gone, and any cheer with it. "Where is that delightful House & the matron of the once happy family who so kindly & hospitably entertained our guests. Alas, I shall see them no more on earth." It was almost too much. "I am here journeying as it were, alone to find myself, a stranger & Homeless, in my own country." When he finally reached Park Hill, he saw the full horror. The burned homes, ruined farms, and charred fences; the fallow cropland; the livestock scattered, seized, or slaughtered, only the bones left. And, of course, just "ruins and desolation" where Rose Cottage had once stood. "I cannot express the sadness of my feelings in my ramblings over the place." He stayed instead at the Murrell house, or what was left of it.

He was supposed to attend a conference staged by the U.S. government at Fort Smith on September 8 to decide the nation's future, but he couldn't rouse himself to go. He sent his second chief, Lewis Downing, instead, accompanied by a dozen loyal full-bloods—Pegg, Flute, Conrad, Fish, Chee-Chee, and others.

In the Cherokee Nation, the ravages of the American Civil War had been compounded by the internal equivalent. Six thousand Cherokee, a quarter of the population, had died in the battles that occurred in every corner of the nation, or from the terrible starvation and rampant disease that followed them. It turned 7,000 more out of their homes to roam the landscape in search of sustenance and shelter. It widowed a third of all Cherokee wives, orphaned a quarter of the children, killed or scattered 300,000 head of cattle, and drove virtually everyone to depend on the federal government dispensing scant aid from the major forts, chiefly Fort Gibson.

Under the terms of his surrender at Doaksville, Watie held the Americans to the infamous New Echota Treaty of 1835 that required the federal government to provide protection to its Cherokee charges from invasion, and from each other. Now came the jockeying for supremacy between the two rival principal chiefs. Each had his liabilities. Since Ross had openly sided with the Cherokee before he turned pro-Union, he was open to charges that he had betrayed both sides. Watie had fought furiously for the South, inflicting incalculable harm on the North. In July 1865, Ross's Northern Cherokee national council tried to assume control by offering amnesty to its Southern Cherokee counterparts for any crimes they might have committed during the war—but only if they swore to uphold Ross's Cherokee constitution. Having spurned a similar demand after the murders of his relatives in 1839, Watie was no more likely to take any loyalty oath now. Besides, Ross—not Watie—was the one to throw over the nation. The nation had always held Watie's loyalty, paid for many times over in blood.

To try to work things out, the federal government sent a delegation of commissioners that included the Seneca Ely Parker to Fort Smith that September. If Ross assumed he had an advantage because he ended up a Union man, he misread the situation. His strength depended on his ability to speak for all the Cherokee, not just one faction. Watie spent his time trying to draw dignitaries from other Indian tribes into a broader Indian coalition that would dwarf the Ross faction. Watie left it to his indefatigable nephew Elias Cornelius Boudinot to represent the interests of the Southern Cherokee to the federal agents who sought national unity.

At Fort Smith, the government realized that Watie was right in thinking it should try to reconcile not just the feuding Cherokee but all the Indians in the territory, by creating a multi-tribe district overseen by Washington that might someday become a full-fledged state of its own. More immediately, the federal negotiators declared that slavery was abolished everywhere, including in the territory, and ex-slaves should be welcomed as full members of Indian society. The negotiators left it to the individual tribes to make sure the law was observed.

As for the Cherokee, the commissioners blamed the years of political in-fighting within the Cherokee Nation squarely on John Ross. They wired to Secretary of the Interior James Harlan that they intended to refuse to recognize Ross as the Cherokees' principal chief, and Harlan agreed that his removal would be of "great benefit" to the Cherokee people. The lead commissioner, Cooley, an Indian agent, drew up what amounted to an indictment of Ross's leadership, calling him a charlatan who was still "at heart" an enemy of the state he professed to lead.

Ross was an old man now, hunched, weary, and his voice quavered. But when he rose to respond, he was still fully capable of indignation.

"Sir," he began, "I deny the charges asserted against me. I deny having used any influence either with the Cherokees, Creeks, or any other persons to resist the interests of the Indians, or of the Government of the United States." No, he was as loyal to the United States as any man living. He'd been elected and reelected principal chief for forty years, and he'd done his best to serve his nation in Washington during the war by staying in constant contact with the Department of the Interior and even with the president himself. He returned now "after burying my wife and burying my son." He'd given three sons and three grandsons to the U.S. Army. And he was disloyal? "If I'd been disloyal I would not have shrunk from going in the direction where the enemies of the United States were."

When Ross was done speaking, Boudinot jumped to his feet. If Ross wanted to know who would charge him with "deep duplicity and falsity," he snapped, he himself would.

I here announce my willingness and intention to make such charges, to state such fact & to prove them too, as will prove his duplicity. The fact is the Cherokee Nation has been long rent in twain by dissensions & I here charge these upon this same John Ross. I charge him with it here today & I will do it tomorrow. I will show that the treaty made with the Confederate States was made at his instigation. I will show the deep duplicity & falsity that have followed him from his childhood to the present day, when the winters of 65 or 70 years have silvered his head with sin; and what can you expect of him now.

The Indian agent Cooley then declared that he had no desire to dredge up such ancient history. He sought only "peace and amity." To that end, Cooley thought it might be useful for the Indians to have a representative in Washington—and Boudinot might be just the man. Initially distrustful of any complicity with the federal government, Boudinot soon came around and hailed Cooley's idea as "one of the grandest and noblest schemes ever devised for the red man." For Boudinot, self-righteousness did not preclude self-interest.

William P. Ross's wife railed at the way John Ross was being treated by the commissioners and their toadies, and by President Andrew Johnson, too, calling it "shameful and a disgrace." His loyalty questioned, with opponents rising up against him, Ross took to his bed at the Murrell house and remained there. He was in no shape to weather such blows. A Dr. Brown was summoned from

Park Hill to offer herbal remedies, many of them drawn from Cherokee medi-cine, and sat with him night and day, fearful that the end was coming.

But Ross rallied, as he had done so often before, and made his way to Washington to press his argument with Secretary of the Interior Harlan and Commissioner Cooley. Assailed again for ever throwing in with the Confed-erates, Ross insisted he had done it only as a drowning man might reach for a log that came floating by. It was a dignified performance by an old man, and left Commissioner Cooley denying he'd ever wanted Ross deposed. "I feel myself as standing upon firm ground," Ross wrote to his sister-in-law in Philadelphia with new confidence. "Time will soon indicate whose official authority is resting upon a sandy foundation."

The stronger Ross's position was, the clearer it became that his faction and Watie's would need separate territories, just as Watie had long argued. While Ross spoke for his faction, Watie left the negotiations to Boudinot, as-sisted by Saladin and another Ridge cousin, the now celebrated John Rol-lin Ridge, who came all the way from California to advance the Treaty Party cause. Somewhat improbably, he had emerged as a well-known American In-dian novelist—having published to some acclaim a fictionalized account of the infamous California bandit Joaquín Murieta—and was currently serving as the editor of the *Sacramento Bee*.* The entourage would soon be rounded out by the dead John Ridge's son John Ridge Jr. It was Ridge against Ross, just as always.

The Ridges went at John Ross on the now familiar charges of embezzle-ment, but this time the specific claim was that he'd made off with $250,000 that was supposed to have been disbursed to the nation under the terms of the 1835 New Echota Treaty. Where was it, they demanded? The Southern Cherokee hadn't received a penny. Ross insisted that the money had gone to pay down the national debt, and his brother-in-law John W. Stapler, the national treasurer, testified that the money had indeed been placed in his safe in Tahlequah, and not a cent had been spent by Ross on himself. Of course, Stapler was family, and this made his claims a shade less than persuasive.

---

* Murieta is remembered today as the inspiration for the heroic Mexican outlaw of TV and film, Zorro.

The real questions were those that had plagued Ross since the issue of removal had first riven the nation: Who was John Ross? What interests did he represent? His own, his faction's, or the full nation's? Scottish in appearance, Cherokee by declaration, he had always escaped definition. Deceptiveness, duplicity—these were Ross's liabilities as well as his talents, as always. He was simply not to be trusted. And Commissioner Cooley came to share this opinion as he pushed the southern delegation's line.

But after so many decades spent grappling with official Washington, Ross knew where to apply whatever force he still retained for the greatest leverage. "He is as artful as ever," wrote J. Washbourne, secretary of the southern delegation, with grudging admiration of the longtime principal chief, "and tho' he is personally powerless, he can work through agents, as you and I know to our cost."

By "personally powerless," Washbourne was referring to the fact that a lingering illness had confined Ross to bed in a Washington hotel for more than a month. "Ross will be beaten," said one gleeful ally of the Ridges. "His day is done. Ours is rising fast and bright. We will get all we asked for." And the Ridge faction had every reason to think so.

But as long as Ross could still guide a pen across a page, he could move minds. He dashed off impassioned letters to the *New York Tribune*, and to Johnson's closest advisers, many of them known to Ross for decades, all to persuade the president that the claims against him were preposterous. If he had profited so handsomely from federal largess, why was he now a virtual bankrupt, his Philadelphia home mortgaged to the hilt, and all his furniture, too? He'd given everything he had to his people, right up until the last, when he doled out his final coins to the indigent who still made their appeals to him in Washington. How could Johnson possibly side with a hostile faction that had killed for the Confederacy and fought against him, John Ross, who had spent most of the war in Washington looking after the interests of his entire nation, often sitting beside Lincoln himself? And, surely, *he* was the sole principal chief, the only one elected by the entire nation, not just by one faction. More to the point, how could Johnson think of following a war to preserve the American nation with an act that would tear the Cherokee Nation in two?

For months, Washington officials huddled at Ross's bedside, as he was too ill to leave his meager hotel bedchamber. Exhausted and morose, he could not even rouse himself to sit in a proper chair. Commissioner Cooley, never an admirer, came by several times, and at one point marveled that Ross had now served his nation so long. Ross rose up on his pillows. "Yes, Sir. I am an old man and have served my people and the government of the United States a long time, over fifty years. My people have kept me in the harness, not of my own seeking, but of their own choice. I have never deceived them, and now I look back, not one act of my public life rises up to upbraid me. I have done the best I could, and today upon this bed of sickness, my heart approves all I have done. And still I am John Ross, the same John Ross of former years. Unchanged! No cause to change!"

On June 13, Commissioner Cooley sent a proposed treaty to President Johnson that might have been written by the Southern Cherokee themselves. It slammed Ross as a covert traitor to the Union, always a Confederate at heart, unlike the Ridges, who had always been open about where they stood. It called for a ban on slavery, the return of stolen property, and a general amnesty. But it did not call for a general Indian council as Boudinot had hoped. And one thing more: the nation had to be divided.

Days passed, however, and Johnson did not act on it. He called for another round of negotiations with Ross instead, and ultimately bowed to Ross's argument that he couldn't save one union, only to dissolve another. He believed that the borders of the Cherokee Nation should stay as they were, and that John Ross should remain the sole principal chief.

John Ross won and, as if to seal his victory, died shortly afterward, on the evening of August 1 at about seven o'clock. No eyewitness account of his death survives, suggesting that he died alone, his body to be discovered by the hotel staff. There was a funeral service at Jay's Hotel in Washington, and another in Wilmington, where his remains lay in state at the home of his brother-in-law John Stapler, the former treasurer for the nation, with a service at the Methodist Episcopal Church, although Ross never had become a member of any Christian denomination. He was buried beside Mary in the Stapler family plot.

But at the annual meeting of the national council the following October, it was decreed that his body was to be returned for burial in the Cherokee Nation at Park Hill. The council dispatched William P. Ross and two other Cherokee leaders to reclaim the principal chief when the ground thawed the following spring. His body was finally laid to rest in what became known as the Ross Cemetery by the ruins of Rose Cottage. "It is proper that here should his dust mingle with kindred dust," William P. Ross intoned. Actually, at that point it was only Lewis Ross's descendants who were interred there, not John's. Mary's remains would stay in Wilmington. William hoped his uncle's memory would "serve to unite us more closely in peace, in concord and in devotion to the common welfare. It will soften our asperities and excite the thoughtful youth of our land to patience, to perseverance, to success and to renown."

That was not likely to happen right away, for one of Ross's last acts had left the Ridge faction more riled than ever, probably just as he intended. Before he died, Ross had crafted an agreement with the federal government that ended up cutting the Ridge men out of their expense money. It acknowledged the obligation to pay the sums owed the Ridges, but created no system of disbursement; as Ross knew well, this meant the payments would never actually be made. Four of the Ridges had been paid out of a previous $10,000 allotment, but Boudinot and Stand Watie were now left with nothing. Stand Watie was home in the territory for this dispute, and wisely stayed out of it. But Boudinot objected, rousing his cousin John Ridge Jr. to charge that Boudinot had actually already gotten an ample financial piece of his own, that he had "sold himself" by taking money that was not his. Outraged by the allegation, which was never proved, Boudinot fired back that he had been "grossly swindled" by the Ross agreement that left out any payment plan, and he demanded his portion of the money that had been given to the others. Boudinot was supposed to receive a share of another chunk of money, $28,825, from the sale of some Cherokee land in Kansas, but it hadn't materialized, and in his frustration he insisted that none of the Ridges get paid until he did. That split the four irrevocably, with two taking Boudinot's side; one taking Ridge's; and the fourth, Watie, keeping his distance. The vituperation that the Ridges had previously directed at Ross they now aimed at each other. As Boudinot, the most intemperate of the four, wrote to his cousin: "I have written to your wife, brother and sisters, that all friendly relations between you and me have ceased forever, and that you have proved yourself a faithless and ungrateful friend, a slanderer and a liar, a thief and a coward." More than the cousin was lost to the acrimony. Boudinot had hoped to use the money to start a newspaper with John Ridge in Arkansas, and with it to commence political careers that might bring them fortunes as well. That was now all gone.

At sixty, Stand Watie was older than his years, with a coldness in his eyes. He often complained of a chill, which was unlike him. Sarah had finally rejoined him, and they settled in Boggy Depot well down in the Choctaw Nation, where he had spent much of the war. He was trying without much luck to start a decent farm there.

To try to revive his fortunes, Stand joined with his nephew Boudinot to grow tobacco, a crop that did nicely in the territory and benefited from being tax-free as the product of a foreign nation. It cost 43 cents a pound to produce a pound of plug tobacco, but the U.S. excise tax added another 32 cents a pound. By avoiding the tax, the Boudinot and Watie Tobacco Company had a significant financial advantage over its competitors in adjoining states. It was Boudinot's idea to exploit this tax loophole, and he put up a tobacco factory not far from Maysville, with Stand Watie a silent partner. It did well, and it continued to do well even after the U.S. Congress passed a law imposing the tax on any such product within the "exterior boundaries" of the United States, for tax collectors were leery of venturing into Indian Territory. The tobacco company might have gone a long way toward lifting Watie's spirits if tragedy had not struck, and then struck again, harder.

On February 13, 1868, his treasured son, Saladin, his junior officer in the war, died suddenly. No details survive. Afterward, Watie devoted himself to his younger son, Watica, sending him to Cane Hill College, the first institution of higher learning in Arkansas, in hopes that something would come of the Watie name. With the tobacco money, Watie planned to build a house for everyone at Honey Creek, just like old times. Watica would come back after college and they'd all live together—he and Sarah, plus his younger two daughters and their families. But in early April 1869, while he was still in college, Watica fell ill with pneumonia. Sarah and Watie rushed to his bedside only to watch him die on April 9.

After that, there wasn't much of Stand Watie left. He took over a barge on the Arkansas River and got in on a deal Boudinot was putting together to buy up land along the proposed lines of three railroads that were going to haul passengers west to California. But the tobacco company remained the real moneymaker. To the two partners' great relief, the U.S. government's commissioner of internal revenue assured them that his office had no intention of collecting any tax on their tobacco. But then, just two months later, the U.S. marshal for the Western District of Arkansas seized 7,500 pounds of processed tobacco at the Boudinot and Watie plant at Wet Prairie, confiscated all the hydraulic presses and pumps, and left 100,000 pounds of "lump" tobacco outdoors to rot. Agents then fanned out to seize thousands more pounds of finished Boudinot and Watie tobacco in stores as far as four hundred miles away. When Boudinot raged at federal officials, he was jailed on criminal charges. Boudinot threatened to sue the arresting agent for trespass, damage, and injury.

To defend himself, Boudinot hired Albert Pike, now an attorney in Arkansas once more, but the U.S. District Court ruled against him, sending him into bankruptcy. Declaring himself "crushed to the earth," Boudinot cried to Watie, "For God's sake help me out!" But there was nothing Watie could do, since he was nearly broke himself. Boudinot decided to do what the Cherokee had done in the face of Andrew Jackson's threat: take his case before the U.S. Supreme Court. There, in 1871, Pike argued what William Wirt had claimed in the Worcester case, and John Marshall had finally agreed: The Cherokee Nation was a sovereign nation, independent of the United States. Previously, that had legally exempted the Cherokee from the Indian Removal Act. Now, Wirt said, it should free them from the 1868 Revenue Act imposing a sales tax on tobacco.

Having just seen a Civil War fought over a similar states' rights issue, the Supreme Court was not eager to take on the subject of Cherokee sovereignty. The court declared it a political matter, not a judicial one. Wrote Justice Noah H. Swayne for the majority: "If a wrong has been done, the power of redress is with the Congress not with the judiciary." This, of course, presumed that the Indian Territory was subject to the will of Congress, which was exactly the question at hand. As a practical matter, it was doubtful that Congress would take an interest in freeing Indians from federal taxes.

"The Supreme Court has decided the tobacco case against me," Boudinot wrote to Watie. "It is the death knell of the nations." The sovereign treaties on which the Indians had based all their hopes were merely illusions. The American government had never intended to see the Cherokee Nation, or any other

Indian nation, as anything except subservient. "In our ignorance we have supposed that Treaties were contracts entered into under the most solemn forms, and the most sacred pledges of human faith, and that they could be abrogated only by mutual consent." No, the Cherokee were simply American taxpayers like everyone else.

The ruling dashed hopes just as Jackson had when he ignored Marshall's verdict, but this was personal, as it addressed the case of Boudinot and Watie's tobacco company, alone. And it would spell the end of Boudinot's dream of getting rich, the only way to prove himself to white society and to restore the Ridges to the prosperity they'd last enjoyed when they signed the New Echota Treaty.

The defeat in the Supreme Court was the ruin of Stand Watie, too. With what little remained of his fortune, he struggled to send his two daughters, Jacqueline and Ninnie, to school at Berryhill, northeast of Fayetteville; at one point he was mortified because he couldn't pay for both tuition and shoes. Meanwhile he labored to restore his old home at Honey Creek. Boudinot urged him to run for the national council, but he confined himself to service as a delegate to the general council for the Indian Territory, lending his imprimatur to the idea of an Indian fraternity if not a state. He was tired of bickering. When the writer Charles C. Jones Jr. sought information from him for a book on Confederate generals, he sent Jones away. The war had taken its toll. That spring of 1871, he bought some more cattle and tried to bring back his plantation all by himself. "You cant imagine how lonely I am up here at our old place without any of my children being with [me]," he wrote to his daughter Jacqueline that May. He was alone when he collapsed on September 9, 1871, and died where he fell.

Because the Grand River was flooding, his body could not be taken to Webbers Falls, where the rest of the family were living as they awaited the repair of Honey Creek. So Watie was buried near Major Ridge in the Ridge cemetery, not far from John Ridge's old house and the school he had raised for Miss Sawyer. It is not known if there was a proper service. His obituary in the Cherokee Advocate claimed there was "no Indian in the country better known or more highly esteemed." But it's doubtful that Watie, off by himself, died thinking of himself as either. Sarah and the girls settled, not in Honey Creek, but farther north, where Horse Creek joins the Grand River. His two daughters both died there, of unknown causes, in 1875, and were buried nearby. Afterward, Sarah lived on alone until 1883. When she died, she was buried near her daughters. Since then, her remains have been joined with those of her husband and two of their children under an obelisk that rises up beside a more humble stone of Major Ridge. John Ridge is nearby, under a modern gravestone, suggesting he'd never had one before. Elias Boudinot is off in Park Hill, buried in a cemetery dedicated to the Reverend Samuel Worcester, under a long, flat slab of rock, unmarked.

6

WHAT REMAINED

So ended the long war between John Ross and The Ridge, their descendants, and their followers. Starting with the battle over removal, and continuing through the Civil War and beyond, the conflict became so all-consuming, the hatred so personal, that it nearly destroyed everything, including much of what it had been intended to save. Not the Cherokee people, as they would endure, but the Cherokee identity, which was more fundamental, but more elusive, too. Were the Cherokee an adaptable people who could maintain the essential truth about themselves in a new land? Or were they a rooted people, who would never be the same anywhere else? These were the questions posed by Ridge and Ross, and they were important. But there was a far bigger one that went unasked, and unanswered, which had to do with what the Cherokee had been before the troubles hit, not what they should be afterward.

The Cherokee had always seemed oblivious to their own history, perhaps intentionally so, leaving the impression that things had always been exactly the same since time began. In the 1770s, when the naturalist William Bartram asked about some strange mounds he discovered in Cherokee territory—some as big as the Egyptian pyramids, but grassed over and flat-topped, the Cherokee said they had no idea. (It now appears they date from as early as 1000 B.C., vestiges of a previous Indian culture that had spread across the continent before the Cherokee arrived.) So the question remained, and it loomed larger as the times vaulted ahead—what lay back there in earlier eras? Who had the Cherokee been? What had they believed, done, felt? In a nation of emigrants who'd come for a new life, they were not the only ones to ponder their earlier identities as they struggled to retain them in a new land. But the Cherokee, of course, were not emigrants. Their life had been here for aeons, and they'd been expelled from it. What, exactly, had they lost?

Stay or go—the fight became so furious and so irresolvable that it obscured the agony within, of losing touch with the people they'd been before. Once the land was gone, and the people had been removed and the new territory ripped up, the historic meaning of *Cherokee* was becoming a memory and, as the decades passed after emigration, an increasingly dim and distant memory at that. The lived truth of it was back at the far end of the Trail of Tears, abandoned along with the huts and council houses that had always stood beside the rivers that ran through the valleys of the blue-green hills.

As the years after removal mounted, all the traditional lore, legends, incantations, and practices that had defined the tribe remained only in the minds of a dwindling number of old-timers who still believed them, and still clung to them, in a new territory that fostered modern ideas about commerce, medicine, and Christianity. The traditions, once so noble and enriching, became fewer and more peculiar as they were passed down by these emigrants to their children, and their children's children, until there was nothing left except antics and oddities. As the calamitous nineteenth century at last drew to a close, the old ways of the Cherokee might have faded out entirely, gone forever with nothing saved—the last and worst loss of the long war between Ross and Ridge—if it hadn't been for a stroke of luck.

James Mooney, a solitary ethnologist of Irish descent at the federal Bureau of American Ethnology in Washington, decided to make it his lifework to collect everything he could find of the old Cherokee ways—every scrap of memory, behavior, and written lore—before it vanished. Mooney was oddly like the Irish trader-ethnologist James Adair 150 years before, except that for Mooney, the Cherokee were not rising into general consciousness, but falling out of it entirely. A tough little man with a thick mustache and, according to a friend, an "intense emotional attitude," he had a touch of the missionary in him as well as he began this work in 1885, not long after Stand Watie's death, and continued it until his own death in 1921.

There might have been nothing for Mooney to find if all the Cherokee had obeyed the federal command, enforced first by General Scott and then by John Ross, to go west. But a band of a few dozen slipped away into the hills to the east and hid there, eventually developing a small presence near Asheville in the Smoky Mountains of North Carolina. These Eastern Cherokee, as they were called, remained tucked away like a lost tribe up the Amazon, deliberately secluded from the larger society that was everywhere around them. In hiding from modernity, they lived as Cherokee always had, preserved in a kind of amber until Mooney came around.

As the child of Irish emigrants in tiny Richmond, Indiana, James Mooney fancied himself a dispossessed Irishman. Fascinated by the ways of the old country that his parents had left behind, he learned Gaelic, started a chapter of the Irish Land League (a tenants' rights organization) at eighteen, and founded the Gaelic Society of Washington to preserve the ancient traditions of his people, going back to the druids. With this in his blood, he was drawn to the historic plight of the Indians, whose past had been even more cruelly snatched from them. In 1878, after unsatisfying stints as a journalist and a schoolteacher, he applied at twenty-two to the head of the Bureau of American Ethnology at the Smithsonian. That was Major John Wesley Powell, an extraordinary character who'd lost an arm in the Civil War and been the first adventurer to explore the Grand Canyon, and who was rather brusque. When Mooney offered to map all the thousands of tribes of North and South American Indians, and record all their tribal characteristics, Powell simply noted that Mooney didn't speak any Indian languages, and turned him down. He then rejected him twice more in sterner terms after Mooney refused to take no for an answer.

In 1885, Mooney nonetheless came to Washington to declare he was ready to start his mapping expedition by focusing on a tribe of Brazilian aborigines. He wangled a private interview with the imperious Powell, and this time something about the young man's grinding persistence persuaded Powell to hire him that April, although not to pursue his Brazilians. Mooney turned his attention instead to the Eastern Cherokee after he met the principal chief, Nimrod Jarrett Smith, when Smith came to the capital on a lobbying trip shortly thereafter. A massive six four, with shoulder-length black hair, Smith was, to Mooney, "a splendid specimen of physical manhood" with a "kindly spirit and natural dignity that never failed to impress the stranger." Mooney was captivated, and when Smith invited him back to see his people in North Carolina, the budding ethnologist was delighted to accept.

Once Mooney came to Cherokee country he basically never left. At that point, the Eastern Cherokee numbered a little over 1,500, a third of them fullbloods who still spoke no English and lived as Cherokee had, separated into seven clans, for countless generations, although many of the tribesmen now endured tattered poverty. Mooney plunged into his lifework as a collector of everything Cherokee, starting with their language, which he mastered well enough to conduct interviews, and extending through their myths, customs, arts, herbal medicines, dances, and habits.

He arrived just in time. The railroads were slicing deep into the Cherokee hills, whites were marrying in, epidemics were rampant, and well-meaning Quaker missionaries were drawing Cherokee children into schools that would extinguish their culture. Mooney went at his task like a one-man army. Through Smith, he developed other political contacts, cultivated local informants, enlisted subordinates, consulted specialists, snapped up artifacts such as long-stemmed pipes and blowguns, recorded tribal dances, scrutinized ceremonies and rituals, seized on everything written, and hunted down the last living sources for the remaining mysteries of the Cherokee, which were most of them. He found John Ax, who remembered everything that had happened to the tribe all the way back to the Creek War of 1812; and Suyeta, or "the Chosen One," who knew all the countless rabbit stories, and many more. Mooney dug them all out of the hills to empty their minds into his notebooks.

One rose far above all the others. If the Cherokee had a Rosetta stone that recorded and translated its ancient culture for modern minds, it was the Cherokee shaman known as Swimmer or He Who Swims. Born in the Cherokee Nation in the pivotal year 1835, when the Ridges signed the New

Echota Treaty, Swimmer was spirited away to the eastern hills by his parents as a toddler. There, in hiding, he trained in the arts of the shaman—a combination of doctor, priest, and keeper of tradition—before emerging to serve in the Sixty-Ninth North Carolina Confederate Infantry in the Civil War. By the time Mooney arrived two decades later, Swimmer had risen to become the last of the true Cherokee, the grand man whose presence was essential at every tribal function. By then, Swimmer must have known that the end of the Cherokee was coming, for he had painstakingly recorded the names and uses of all the medicinal plants; he'd memorized all the songs and learned to mimic the cry of every animal in the forest; and he knew by heart, in extraordinary detail, just about every Cherokee myth, from the epic tale of Kelu and Seti to the details of the Haunted Whirlpool, the story of the Two Lazy Hunters, the secret of the Rattlesnake's Vengeance, the explanation of why the buzzard's head was bare (it had to do with his pride), and hundreds more, all of them tiny pixels in a vast photograph of a vanishing world.

Truth be told, Swimmer didn't immediately warm to the nosy ways of Mooney. He tried to sell him some of the tribal songs for $5 each. But Mooney appealed to his tribal pride, saying his songs would be lost forever otherwise, and Swimmer came around. Mooney nowhere records much of Swimmer's own story; he disappears into the tribal history he recounted in such prodigious detail. But a single photograph evokes him, as it shows a small mountain of a man topped by an eternal head swathed in a turban; a fierce, fixed gaze; a formidable goatee; a drooping bow tie over a white shirt covered by a loose dark coat; and in his massive hand the ceremonial rattle he always carried, the symbol of his imperial status as the last great Cherokee shaman.

Mooney drew everything he could from Swimmer and, with his help and that of many others, was finally able to capture everything meaningful about the Cherokee in two extraordinary volumes, *The Sacred Formulas of the Cherokees* in 1891 and *Myths of the Cherokee* in 1900. Of all the myths Mooney collected, Swimmer alone produced three-quarters.

The year before the second volume was published, Swimmer died, in 1899, on the cusp of the new century, his great work done. He was buried, Mooney writes, "like a true Cherokee on the slope of a forest-clad mountain." His body was translated not so much into spirit as into text. In his *Myths,*

Mooney offered a tribute. "Peace to his ashes and sorrow for his going, for with him perished half the tradition of a people." What the great war in the Cherokee Nation had nearly destroyed, Mooney had saved.

Mooney didn't quite realize it, but he was himself a representative of a vanishing era, when ethnographers could still contribute to an understanding of so-called primitive people. Soon the field was being taken over by a cadre of professionals who grandly termed themselves "anthropologists," a far higher calling in their estimation, and who looked down on "mere" ethnologists as rank amateurs. It was the German-American Franz Boas, known for his work with the Inuit of the Pacific Northwest, who first promoted the term by establishing the American Anthropological Association in 1902. As a professor of anthropology at Columbia, he trained acolytes such as Margaret Mead throughout American universities to start or enhance Boasian anthropology departments of their own. Although these modern anthropologists did their fieldwork at remote locations, such as the South Seas, their contributions were measured in concepts that tried to explain all of human nature—rather than in the raw details about a particular group of distinctive individuals of the sort that Mooney had so painstakingly collected over decades and then related without scientific adornment. While much of Mooney's work went into his few publications—there were only two or three others beyond the principal two—at his death much more remained in his notebooks, written in a hasty scrawl that his successors found largely indecipherable. If Mooney did not make more of what he had, it was probably because he got too caught up in a subject he cared too much about. Dubbed the "Indian man," he slipped from being purely an investigator and become more of a participant in the life he was recording. For years, he largely lived among his subjects, doing what they did. This, in fact, led to his undoing when he turned his attention to the Kiowa in Oklahoma and ate the mind-expanding peyote of their religious rituals—and then publicly endorsed the practice. This brought down on him the wrath of a House subcommittee, and got him temporarily banned from fieldwork. He saw the Cherokee less as subjects and more as friends, and this led to a personal involvement that deepened his connection to his material but slowed his output.

Mooney never developed any universal theory of the Cherokee, and for this he has been graded down by his more highly credentialed successors in elite universities, but he didn't believe that the Cherokee required interpretation. What he did believe led to what he did do, and he did that magnificently. He conveyed the value of a scorned people through his own enthusiasm for them.

When Mooney started out, reigning luminaries in the field like John Wesley Powell saw history as the story of human progress to ever-higher states of enlightenment and understanding. To them, the value of the Cherokee lay in their extraordinary ability to assimilate, just as Major Ridge might have claimed, and thus to disappear into the greater society of ever-improving people. Mooney concluded just the opposite. When he evoked their ancient splendor in their Ghost Dance, in their profound devotion to the Great Spirit, in their trust in natural medicine, he was holding up truths that sophisticates had no place for. To Powell and his ilk, these were the primitive beliefs the Cherokee needed to cast off to join advanced society. To Mooney, these were the marks of Cherokee glory that should be extolled. And now, if people find something beautiful in the Cherokee, in their sublime connection to the earth, in their enduring faith in what they could not see, in their boundless appreciation of the weblike interconnection of all life, it was Mooney who showed it to them.

EPILOGUE

ON POLITICS

Removal is often seen today as the Cherokee Holocaust, an unspeakable tragedy that will define the tribe forever as one consigned to the Trail of Tears. Sadly, that is only too true, but it overlooks the fact that removal was probably inevitable. Twenty-one thousand people were never going to be able to hold on to their territory in the face of mass expansion by a dynamic, burgeoning nation that dramatically outnumbered them, possessed military power that had twice defeated the greatest empire on earth, was backed by an economy that had become the envy of the world, was convinced it should rule from the Atlantic to the Pacific as its manifest destiny, and completely surrounded them. Whether the Cherokee lands stretched over their original 125,000 square miles or the 7 million acres they were ceded in Oklahoma, the Cherokee Nation was never going to survive as an independent, sovereign nation within America's borders.

The tribe, at its height surely the most dynamic in America, was a glory that deserved far better. Jackson's implacable demand for removal was heartless, and Georgia's straight-out land theft by means of a lottery was criminal, but the Cherokee Nation was in no position to resist either one. And with the Civil War looming, the American government was never going to help, whatever the Supreme Court ruled.

It was lamentable, but the Cherokee Nation had no future in the east, and probably none anywhere. The only question was what would become of its people. Jackson demanded removal, but presidents before had held out the offer of assimilation, making the Cherokee Americans like anyone else. As an indigenous people the Cherokee were foreign nationals who were determined to remain independent despite the forces of integration that rose up everywhere around them. That was understandable, but hopeless. Rather than face facts, the Cherokee took refuge in varying degrees of denial, always a temptation when the future appears dire.

In this, they were not well served by either of the two preeminent Cherokee leaders of the day, John Ross and Major Ridge. Their views were diametrically opposed, but similarly detached from reality. The three leading Ridges held to their belief so tightly that they willingly died for it, and Ross clung to his so fiercely that he seems to have been complicit in the killings. Their competing attitudes drew on the divisive issues of class, race, power, and money, but at bottom, they may simply have been personal, as befitted a diminutive Scot and an imposing Cherokee who literally did not speak each other's language. The remarkable evolution of Cherokee society might have united the two men in pride over the nation's progress and heritage, but it did the opposite, as Major Ridge identified with the prosperous mixed-bloods and Ross with the full-bloods who'd been left behind. The rub between them created the national friction that would ultimately explode in flames.

But it didn't have to, and that was the tragedy. Ross and Ridge had created the modern Cherokee government together and they served it together as its top two officials. They had thought as one, but they split over Jackson's demand for removal, and the gulf between them only widened over time. It is the work of politics to resolve such conflicts peacefully, but Cherokee politics were not up to the job. For a society that had always operated by consensus, there was little tradition of compromise. The marvelous balance of opposites in the Cherokee cosmology left few means for humans to make adjustments when things went off. Prizing stability, society was too threatened by instability to address it meaningfully. The warrior culture offered few gradations between war and peace, all or nothing. When the medicine men proved powerless against smallpox, the Cherokee did not revise their system of medicine, but abandoned it in despair. When the settlers demanded land, the Cherokee blithely ceded it or fought to the death, leaving themselves worse off either way. When the modern ways of the settlers were considered superior to the traditional ones, the traditional ways were either clung to defiantly or discarded like old clothes.

The issue of removal was so stark as to be existential, and seemed to offer only two, mutually exclusive positions. Stay or go. But there were plenty of gentler variations available. If Ross had been willing to listen, he would have realized that staying was untenable, made plans to leave sooner, and sold his people on those plans, greatly reducing the hardship when removal was thrust on them later. For their part, the Ridges might have seen that the west was hardly a panacea, acknowledged that resistance was legitimate, and worked to make removal more attractive. Few Cherokee could start over as easily as the Ridges. It didn't help that Ross was principal chief for life, insulated from legitimate opposition, or that he responded to the dissent of Major Ridge and his son John by removing them from the government. Rather than try to understand the Ridges, and work with them, Ross declared them traitors who should be shot on sight, ending any discussion. The Ridges too easily turned to outraged indignation when Ross failed to share their point of view. Once the government split into two parties on the issue, only Sequoyah was left to speak for the nation, and his voice was too weak to carry any message of unity. And so politics shifted to that "other means" of General Clausewitz—to war. While Jackson's removal killed too many Cherokee, their own ensuing civil war, and their attacks on each other in the greater American Civil War, killed far more.

Everyone is self-interested, and politics is the art by which everyone's self-interest can be fairly served. It is the market system for distributing whatever benefits government can dispense. The Cherokee have been slow to embrace it. Since Stand Watie's death, finally drawing the war of Ross and

Ridge to a close, the nation has grown to become the second-largest tribe in America, with almost 300,000 people on its rolls, although most of them have increasingly tenuous connections to their ancestral past. But its politics have not come along commensurately. (In this, of course, it cannot have been encouraged with the example set by Washington.) Its government remains in Tahlequah as ever, with a supreme court, legislature, and a principal chief, but it has been crippled by internal conflicts that have proved nearly impossible to resolve. They led to a constitutional crisis in 1997 when the principal chief, Joe Byrd, facing possible charges about misuse of funds, fired fifteen of the marshals who came to search his office; and when the nation's supreme court issued an arrest warrant for him, Byrd had three of the justices impeached, then enlisted a private paramilitary force to storm the national courthouse, evict the marshals there guarding the financial documents, and padlock the building behind them. When the head of the marshal service tried to reopen the courthouse, the Byrd forces refused to oblige. A riot erupted when hundreds of marshal supporters forced the issue. Police from five counties, Oklahoma Highway Patrolmen, and officers from the Bureau of Indian Affairs were summoned to stop the violence that left six people injured. In an unprecedented step, U.S. Interior Secretary Bruce Babbitt and U.S. Attorney General Janet Reno summoned Byrd to Washington, where they raised the possibility that President Bill Clinton might invoke his statutory authority to remove Byrd from office or shut off all federal funding for his tribe. With that, Byrd agreed to reopen the courthouse. A subsequent investigative commission blamed all three branches of the government—executive, legislative, and judicial—for the impasse.

Byrd was never convicted of any wrongdoing and served out his term. But in 1999, he lost to Chadwick "Corntassel" Smith, who had been arrested and led away in handcuffs for protesting the courthouse closure, although no charges were filed. The election was so tense that the balloting was monitored by the Carter Center, which previously had supervised voting only outside the United States.

Smith's tenure went little better, as he created a firestorm when he sought to exclude from citizenship any descendants of the former slaves, the Cherokee Freedmen. Since virtually all of these Freedmen are of African-American descent, this maneuver struck many people as racist, and it was found to be unlawful by the federal government. Although the Cherokee Nation had argued the opposite side, it agreed to abide by this decision. Twice reelected nonetheless, Smith lost to Bill John Baker in 2011 in a bitter election involving two separate votes, several recounts, and a pivotal federal court order declaring that the Freedmen were indeed eligible to cast ballots. Once again, the Carter Center was called in to supervise.

Happily, Baker's tenure has so far been untarnished, and if the Cherokee Nation is not completely at peace, it seems to be mending. The Cherokee have always been an inspired, resilient people, close to the earth, and, with it, to the eternal. There is hope for the future. But the Trail of Tears has proved to be a long one.

ACKNOWLEDGMENTS

The history of the Cherokee is largely recorded in accounts written by others about them, starting with the observations of the Irish trapper James Adair from 1775 and running through the Smithsonian ethnologist James Mooney's research at the turn of the twentieth century, with any number of congressional reports, memorials, travelogues, newspaper accounts, letters, and much else in between. Despite Mooney's work, much of this material lay fallow for another half-century, until a group of scholars took a fresh interest in the people then starting to be called Native Americans. In gathering the Cherokee story, they performed a remarkable service to the Cherokee people and to America's understanding of itself through them. Many of them devoted their professional lives to this work, and all delivered the best kind of scholarship—informed, coherent, and compassionate. Too many of these writers have faded into obscurity by now, and I wish to start these acknowledgments by paying tribute to some of the greatest among them: John P. Brown, Grace Steele Woodward, William McGloughlin, Grant Foreman, Gary E. Moulton, Thurman Wilkins, and Theda Purdue. I give credit to their specific contributions in the endnotes. As a generalist, I could never have written such a detailed history of the internal politics of the Cherokee Nation without their efforts.

I've also turned to two of the most authoritative contemporary scholars of Native Americans to make sure I have kept up with the latest understanding of the Cherokee. I owe great debts to Colin Calloway, a professor of Native American Studies at Dartmouth College, and to Jace Weaver, the director of the Institute of Native American

Studies at the University of Georgia, for scrupulously going over the manuscript to correct errors of fact and interpretation. They have made this book much better for their efforts. Needless to say, I take full responsibility for any mistakes that remain.

In a far deeper sense, one can see the history of the Cherokee also written on the land itself, from the wavelike ridges of the timeless Smoky Mountains and the valleys beneath them, to the lush rolling foothills of the Ozarks of what is now eastern Oklahoma, and of course through the harsh miles of the Trail of Tears. It is in these places, and in the many Cherokee sites that remain on them, that I drew my inspiration for *Blood Moon*. And I am profoundly grateful to the many guides, authorities, historians, and curators who showed them to me and patiently explained their significance, doing their best to bridge the gap between the Cherokees' experience of America and my own. I am thinking in particular of Ethan Clapsaddle of the Museum of the Cherokee Indian in Cherokee, North Carolina, one of the places where the eastern band of the Cherokee took refuge to avoid the forced removal west in 1838. It is a terrific resource for students of Cherokee heritage and culture, not just for its exhibits of every phase of Cherokee history, but also for the kind of historical research that generated the *Journal of Cherokee Studies* in cooperation with the Cherokee Historical Association. I am likewise indebted to Keith Bailey, a curator and interpretive guide to the mysterious hundred-foot-high Etowa Indian Mounds in nearby Cartersville, Georgia. Besides filling me in on thousands of years of Cherokee history, he did me the invaluable service of insisting I climb Clingmans Dome, at more than six thousand feet, the highest peak in the Smoky Mountains. On the clearest days, one can still see a hundred miles in every direction, and because so much of it is in a still-pristine national park, I could get a sense of the mind-swelling expanse of the original Cherokee lands as The Ridge himself might have seen on one of his hunts. It was likewise a marvel to visit Ridge's mansion, now called The Chieftain, on the banks of the Oostanaula River in Rome, Georgia (hard by his son John Ridge's home, Running Waters, which sadly no longer exists); to visit David Vann's well-preserved Federalist mansion at Diamond Hill, smartly overseen by Julia Autry; to see John McDonald's original log house, where his grandson John Ross brought Quatie, in Rossville, adoringly maintained by the Chief John Ross House Association for more than half a century. It was nearly miraculous to tour the re-created capital of New Echota; to get a noseful of the fragrant replica of the printshop for the *Cherokee Phoenix* of Elias Boudinot, whose house, where the fateful New Echota treaty was signed, once stood nearby; and to see the rather lonesome Supreme Courthouse, and so many other evocative buildings that, together, make up the Washington, D. C., of the Cherokee Nation. I spent a great deal of time in and around Chattanooga, Tennessee, first called Ross's Landing, where boatloads of miserable emigrants boarded for the rough passage west. I roamed about Brainerd, once the finest school in the Cherokee Nation, and now, regrettably,

Just a cemetery off a shopping mall. I climbed up Lookout Mountain, scene of the last significant battle of the Cherokee and of a major one for the Confederates later, and disappeared into the deep cave that lies within. I drove a hundred miles up the Hiwassee River, now much swelled in places by the dams of the Tennessee Valley Authority, to see where The Ridge might have been born, not that the exact site of Savannah Ford has ever been ascertained. All that made for a glorious few weeks of summer.

They were followed by a few more spent hunting about Oklahoma to see the remnants of the Cherokee Nation West. For that, I was headquartered in Tahlequah, where the tribe maintains impressive national offices, just as it has since the days of John Ross. The nation's history and preservation officer Catherine Foreman-Grey took it upon herself to drive me all over the territory, from Honey Creek down to Park Hill to show me where the Ridges lived and died. We made a special stop over the Arkansas line in Maysville to see the site of the grocery where Stand Watie fought James Foreman to the death, and, farther south, toward Van Buren, the spot by White Rock Creek where Major Ridge was ambushed. It was solemn to see the gravesites of these fallen heroes to a cause they alone, it sometimes seemed, appreciated. In the nation's offices, the linguist Ryan Mackey spoke to me in Cherokee and explained the rudiments of its extraordinary syntax. At the Cherokee Library, I heard the long-time archivist Jerry Clark talk over the Ross-Ridge dispute with Bruce Ross, a direct Ross descendant, with a vehemence that made clear the disagreement may never be resolved. Amanda Pritchett gave me an enlightening tour of the still-elegant George Murrell House, once known as Hunter's Home. I walked through the nearby Ross family graveyard, which holds the remains of the longtime principal chief, his gravestone the most significant Ross family remnant after Stand Watie burned down his treasured Rose Cottage. But, of course, the nation that he served as principal chief for so long is still very much with us.

All such prowling is a quest to defeat time and visit lives lived long ago. Of all my searches, the most meaningful was the one farthest off the trail, when I drove four hours south of Tahlequah to Rusk, Texas, to see what was left of Mount Tabor. That was where a tiny enclave of Treaty Party supporters huddled in the tumultuous years of the Civil War. The beleaguered Sarah Watie spent long months there tending her dying sister, Nancy Starr, at the home of their brother John A. Bell. A few modern descendants, led by J. C. Thomson and Paul Ridenour, have devoted themselves to reclaiming Mount Tabor's history, and they inspired a local historian, Patty Haskins, to hunt up the ruins of John Bell's house.

Mount Tabor is now just a smattering of very modest homes of African American families, many of them descended from the slaves freed after the Civil War. Mount Tabor was once all farms, and it gave a sense of the passage of time to see that it was almost impenetrably thick woods now as Patty drove slowly along in her SUV, searching for the remains of the Bell house. Darkness had fallen by the time we arrived, and we strained to peer into the shadowy woods, lit only by peripheral light from Patty's high beams. "We're looking for a chimney," Patty told me. "It tipped down toward the road when the house fell." We made several slow passes trying to spot any fallen bricks. Finally, Patty noticed a narrow gap in the trees. "That's it," she declared. We pulled over, and I scrambled out. I tried to put out of my mind her warnings about rattlesnakes as I plunged into the trees. And there it was—the fallen wall of what was once a decent-size house, now a faint gray in the dying light. Shattered by time, the house's beams and boards lay in rotting pieces, the chimney a tumble of bricks. History is a kind of nothingness, all the actors long dead, but it occurred in places like this, where something always remains. I took pictures with my iPhone in the gathering dark. When I looked at them later, the building's remains glowed from the flash.

Now to thank the many other people who have helped me see this story of the Cherokee into print. First comes the incomparable Dan Conaway, my agent at Writers House, who was marvelously quick to see the wonder of the idea I sketched out to him about a tribe of Indians who'd fought on both sides of the Civil War. And my hat is off to his brisk assistant Taylor Templeton, too. At Simon & Schuster, my editor Jofie Ferrari-Adler caught the Cherokee fire, and has been a dream editor—a perfect blend of brilliance, responsiveness, and easy charm. His assistant, Julianna Haubner, has done wonders to extend his reach and touch. In fact, the whole S&S team has been divine, and it is a joy to call the roll: president and publisher Jonathan Karp, associate publisher Richard Rhorer, publicist Elizabeth Gay, marketing specialists Jessica Breen and Stephen Bedford, managing editor Kristen Lemire, production director Lisa Erwin, art director Alison Forner, cover designer David Gee, interior designer Ruth Lee-Mui, mapmaker Jeffrey L. Ward, production editor Kathryn Higuchi, and copyeditor Susan Gamer. Thank you, all!

I owe copious thanks, also, to Hannah Assadi, a talented novelist who painstakingly fact-checked the manuscript and prepared the endnotes and bibliography. The inventive photo researcher Carol Poticny found all the images that grace this book's pages. Philip Hylen, an interpretive ranger in the Tennessee State Parks, generously shared with me his knowledge of the Cherokee. My friend John Howell, a closet historian, read the book twice in manuscript to provide keen insights and welcome enthusiasm. My daughters, Josie and Sara—mother of the two dedicatees, Logan and Kyla—I should add, are the lights of my life, who guide me in everything I do. Lastly, I'd like to hug my extraordinary wife, Rana Foroohar, for inspiring me to reach for something as grand and important as the Cherokee story, and heap praise on her children, Alex and Darya, for cheerfully putting up with me as I did so. Such acts are the stuff of love.

NOTES

INTRODUCTION

1   *It was also fought by Indians*: Hauptman, *Between Two Fires*, x.

2   *The* New York Tribune *fulminated*: Confer, *Cherokee Nation in the Civil War*, 95.

2   *When one dwindling band*: W. David Baird et al., "We Are All Americans: Native Americans in the Civil War," January 5, 2009, NativeAmericans.com.

2   *Nearly a dozen battles were fought*: Hauptman, *Between Two Fires*, 42.

PART ONE, CHAPTER 1—A BIRTH ON THE HIWASSEE

9   *Its walls made of branches*: Wilkins, *Cherokee Tragedy*, 7.

9   *Although her father*: William C. Sturtevant, "Louis-Philippe on Cherokee Architecture and Clothing in 1797," *Journal of Cherokee Studies*, 3.4 (1978): 289–300.

9   *A few attendants fluttered over*: Ehle, *Trail of Tears*, 1.

10 *He was a man of stout*: Ibid., 3.

10 *In the Cherokee compass*: Ibid., 5.

11 *The mother gladly fed her son*: Ibid., 5–6.

11 *The Cherokee name for the settlement*: Mooney, *History, Myths, and Sacred Formulas of the Cherokees*, 15.

11 *It was one of about sixty*: Ibid., 22–23.

11 *Beside it was a ceremonial square*: Boulware, *Deconstructing the Cherokee Nation*, 16.

12 *In summer the fields*: Braund and Porter, *Fields of Vision*, 29.

12 *When the doughty naturalist William Bartram*: Ibid., 108.

12 *At a mountain peak, Bartram imagined*: Bartram, *The Travels of William Bartram*, 44.

12 *The most prominent was James Adair*: Adair, *The History of the American Indians*, xi.

13 *Bartram considered Cherokee faces*: Woodward, *The Cherokees*, 36.

13 *A young Cherokee bears not*: McKenney and Hall, *Indian Tribes*, I, 368.

14 *The only account of The Ridge's childhood*: Ibid., 399.

15 *As he grew, Pathkiller learned*: Ibid., 368.

15 *Even as a boy, he ranged*: Wilkins, *Cherokee Tragedy*, 7.

15 *As he grew, The Ridge could see*: Strickland, *Fire and the Spirits*, 100.

15 *The women held everything of value*: The transient nature of the grandfather's presence is my conjecture; it seems the most likely scenario.

16 *Adair was there one night*: Adair, *The History of the American Indians*, 116.

PART ONE, CHAPTER 2—CONTACT

17 *Pathkiller's eyes must have widened*: Mooney, *History, Myths, and Sacred Formulas of the Cherokees*, 239.

18 *Fire was the expression*: Ibid., 426.

19 *That this continent had*: Mann, *1491*, 176–79.

20 *The tribe remained utterly unknown*: Duncan, *Hernando de Soto*, 357.

20 *De Soto knew*: Ibid., 329.

20 *De Soto's men fastened*: Ibid., 333.

21 *The most illustrious captive*: Ibid., 335–36.

21 *Tuesday, May 18*: Ibid., 345.

22 *As the Gentleman from Elvas*: Ibid., 348.

22 *The diary continued*: Ibid., 349.

23 *Nonetheless, as the American Revolution*: "Remarkable Fulfillment of Indian Prophecy," *Cherokee Phoenix*, June 23, 1832, 2, col. 4.

23 *True contact did not come*: Woodward, *The Cherokees*, 27.

23 *As agents of Abraham Wood*: Ibid., 29.

24 *When the two men's interpreter*: Ibid., 28–29.

24 *To be done with these irksome*: Ibid., 29.

25 *Unknown before the Europeans*: Ishii, *Bad Fruits of the Civilized Tree*, 34.

25 *The Cherokee rarely infected*: Fenn, *Pox Americana*, 6.

26 *Horrible as this was*: Ibid., 24.

26 *Horribly disfigured, in excruciating pain*: Adair, *The History of the American Indians*, 253.

27   *These plagues cost the Cherokee*: Thornton, *The Cherokees*, 21.
27   *Into the bargain*: Ibid., 31.
27   *But the greatest exchange*: Ibid., 12.
27   *As late as the 1770s*: I am thinking of the undated map of the Tennessee government from this period.
28   *But once those first two traders*: Woodward, *The Cherokees*, 61.
28   *The Cherokee, of course, were hardly*: Boulware, *Deconstructing the Cherokee Nation*, 11–17.
28   *Finding no one in authority*: Woodward, *The Cherokees*, 61.
28   *To make the post enticing*: Ibid., 63.
29   *When Moytoy realized that*: Ibid., 64.
29   *One of them was Moytoy's serious*: Bartram, *The Travels of William Bartram*, 307.
29   *The doughy, paper-white King George*: Woodward, *The Cherokees*, 64–65.
30   *To show how little about*: Ibid., 65.
30   *For Attakullakulla's part*: Wright, *Stolen Continents*, 96.
30   *Since Attakullakulla had a little*: Woodward, *The Cherokees*, 66.

PART ONE, CHAPTER 3—THE BLOODY LAND

31   *If Attakullakulla went to London*: Woodward, *The Cherokees*, 67.
32   *When some renegade Cherokee*: King, *The Memoirs of Lt. Henry Timberlake*, 15.
32   *Attakullakulla was the one*: Ibid., 59.
32   *The most lasting thing*: Ibid., 137.
33   *Strictly speaking, the transfers*: Woodward, *The Cherokees*, 60.
33   *In 1755, however, his successor*: Ibid., 88.
33   *The fateful deal was struck*: Ibid., 88–89.
33   *Already sixty himself, Dragging Canoe*: Brown, *Old Frontiers*, 12.
34   *It was Dragging Canoe who brought*: Woodward, *The Cherokees*, 92–93.
35   *They bore an assortment*: Brown, *Old Frontiers*, 148.
35   *Attakullakulla's half-blood niece*: Ibid., 148–49.
36   *When a couple of lissome white girls*: Woodward, *The Cherokees*, 96.
36   *When the remnants*: Ibid., 96.
36   *Putting aside their war*: Wilkins, *Cherokee Tragedy*, 10.
36   *The inveterate Indian fighter*: Woodward, *The Cherokees*, 97.
37   *Tar-chee fled before the slaughter*: Wilkins, *Cherokee Tragedy*, 11.
37   *Dragging Canoe had sent out*: Le Fevre, *Deep Ruts the Wagon Made*, 13.
38   *When the British finally blundered*: Brown, *Old Frontiers*, 222.
38   *Everyone assembled by the water*: McKenney and Hall, *Indian Tribes, I*, 370–71.
39   *When the ordeal was finally over*: Ibid., 372.

PART ONE, CHAPTER 4—THE FIRST KILL

40   *To explain the change of sovereignty*: Woodward, *The Cherokees*, 105.

40   *When he learned the details*: Ibid., 103.

40   *And then he started in*: Faulkner, *Massacre at Cavett's Station*, 22.

42   *As it happened, the genial*: Woodward, *The Cherokees*, 108–9.

42   *All along the shores*: Wilkins, *Cherokee Tragedy*, 17.

42   *One of the youngest warriors*: McKenney and Hall, *Indian Tribes, I*, 371.

43   *A small force led*: Wilkins, *Cherokee Tragedy*, 18.

43   *It wasn't long before*: McKenney and Hall, *Indian Tribes, I*, 371–72.

44   *He found Tar-chee had fallen*: Ibid., 372.

44   *It was a nearly impregnable fortress*: Wilkins, *Cherokee Tragedy*, 20.

44   *But the various chiefs soon*: McKenney and Hall, *Indian Tribes, I*, 402.

45   *Back at Pine Log*: Brown, *Old Frontiers*, 293.

46   *John Watts blamed Sevier*: Ibid., 293.

47   *But Sevier had hidden*: Ibid., 297–98.

47   *As the oldest son*: McKenney and Hall, *Indian Tribes, I*, 373, 374.

PART ONE, CHAPTER 5—FOREIGN RELATIONS

47   *After Washington's inauguration*: Brown, *Old Frontiers*, 307.

47   *Washington had appointed*: Woodward, *The Cherokees*, 112.

48   *The Cherokee sent a delegation*: Brown, *Old Frontiers*, 309.

48   *Just as his predecessors*: "Treaty of Holston," Cherokee.org.

48   *To seal the deal, the United States*: According to a complaint brought by the Cherokee Nation against the United States Department of the Interior and related parties in the United States District Court of the Western District of Oklahoma, November 28, 2016.

49   *The United States would also*: Brown, *Old Frontiers*, 309–10.

49   *As did an article*: Woodward, *The Cherokees*, 112.

49   *When the Cherokee heard about*: Brown, *Old Frontiers*, 137.

50   *Spoiling for war, Dragging Canoe*: Wilkins, *Cherokee Tragedy*, 23.

50   *Dragging Canoe's men*: Brown, *Old Frontiers*, 324.

50   *All across the nation*: Wilkins, *Cherokee Tragedy*, 23.

51   *To improve his chances*: Woodward, *The Cherokees*, 113.

51   *Nonetheless, The Ridge got caught up*: Wilkins, *Cherokee Tragedy*, 24–25.

51   *But the old chaos plagued them*: Brown, *Old Frontiers*, 359–60.

51   *John Watts himself was struck*: Ibid., 360–61.

51   *Watts's uncle, the notorious Doublehead*: Ibid., 362.

52   *Doublehead's war party was lumbering*: Ibid., 374–75.

52 *It was the tradition of their Iroquios*: Ibid., 375.

52 *Then Doublehead slammed his tomahawk*: Ibid.

52 *Not just at Watts's camp in Willstown*: Walker, *Doublehead Last Chicamauga Cherokee Chief*, Kindle Location 2531.

53 *The Ridge's band was making*: Wilkins, *Cherokee Tragedy*, 23.

54 *When Governor Blount heard*: Ibid., 24.

54 *"Governor Blount always told"*: Faulkner, *Massacre at Cavett's Station*, 48.

55 *But at Pine Log his Party*: Wilkins, *Cherokee Tragedy*, 24.

55 *He cited his prophecy*: Brown, *Old Frontiers*, 390.

55 *They were about ten miles*: Faulkner, *Massacre at Cavett's Station*, 76–78.

56 *Despite Watts's insistence*: Ibid., 78–79.

56 *Other warriors joined*: Ramsey, *The Annals of Tennessee to the End of the Eighteenth Century*, 581.

56 *Finally, only the youngest*: Brown, *Old Frontiers*, 391.

56 *Years later, The Ridge related*: Wilkins, *Cherokee Tragedy*, 25.

56 *The Indians commanded a height*: Brown, *Old Frontiers*, 393–94.

57 *"We mean now to bury deep"*: Ibid., 399.

57 *There, he wrote to remind*: Ibid., 400.

PART ONE, CHAPTER 6—A BIRTH ON THE COOSA

58 *Located on a broad plain*: Moulton, *John Ross*, 5.

59 *A bluff and ruddy Scotsman*: Ibid., 6.

59 *No shaman was present*: Hicks, *Toward the Setting Sun*, 28–29.

60 *"Villains and horse thieves"*: Woodward, *The Cherokees*, 85.

60 *In 1769, he married a half-blood*: Moulton, *John Ross*, 3–4.

61 *When the Revolution came*: Ibid., 4.

61 *Covetous of his intimacy*: Brown, *Old Frontiers*, 350.

61 *Asked about his loyalties*: Moulton, *John Ross*, 4–5.

61 *Born on Scotland's raw northern*: Ibid., 5.

62 *Once Little John hit his teens*: Ibid., 6.

62 *Blackburn's Chickamauga school*: McLoughlin, *Cherokees and Missionaries*, 59.

62 *In 1809, he was found*: Ibid., 79.

62 *By then Daniel Ross switched*: Moulton, *John Ross*, 6–8.

PART ONE, CHAPTER 7—A DEATH FOR A DEATH

64 *Despite the inglorious incident*: Wilkins, *Cherokee Tragedy*, 29.

64 *In 1796, when The Ridge*: McKenney and Hall, *Indian Tribes*, I, 377.

64 *"They invited him to a seat"*: Ibid.

64 *As surprising as it was*: Wilkins, *Cherokee Tragedy*, 29.

65 *Blood law was simple*: Miles, *The House on Diamond Hill*, Kindle Location 735.

66 *Too many good men*: Wilkins, *Cherokee Tragedy*, 30.

67 *She was known to the Cherokee*: McKenney and Hall, *Indian Tribes, I*, 380.

67 *When, after a courtship*: Claiborne, *Life and Times of Gen. Sam Dale*, 212.

67 *Before any marriage, however*: Wilkins, *Cherokee Tragedy*, 31.

68 *As wives were displaced*: McKenney and Hall, *Indian Tribes, I*, 380.

68 *"Industrious" was McKenney's primary*: Wilkins, *Cherokee Tragedy*, 33.

69 *Oothcaloga was fast becoming*: Ibid., 33.

69 *"They believed in a great first"*: C. Sturtevant, ed., "John Ridge on Cherokee Civilization in 1826," *Journal of Cherokee Studies*, 1981, VI, 84.

69 *By 1796, Doublehead had bullied*: Charles C. Royce, *The Cherokee Nation of Indians*, Bureau of American Ethnology Fifth Annual Report, 174–93.

71 *"The chiefs and the people"*: McKenney and Hall, *Indian Tribes, I*, 385.

71 *Doublehead was like Dragging Canoe*: Walker, *Doublehead*, Kindle Locations 3572 and 509.

71 *"As he sought office"*: McKenney and Hall, *Indian Tribes, I*, 385.

72 *Prone to fury even*: Wilkins, *Cherokee Tragedy*, 39.

72 *On the afternoon of August 9*: Brown, *Old Frontiers*, 452.

73 *Vann was supposed to be outside*: Ehle, *Trail of Tears*, Kindle Location 1342.

73 *The Ridge let Doublehead*: Brown, *Old Frontiers*, 452.

74 *They made their way to the tavern*: Wilkins, *Cherokee Tragedy*, 40.

75 *The Ridge gestured*: Brown, *Old Frontiers*, 453.

PART ONE, CHAPTER 8—PROSPERITY

78 *The council at Brooms Town*: Strickland, *Fire and the Spirits*, 58.

78 *To enforce it, the nation established*: Abram, *Forging a Cherokee-American Alliance in the Creek War*, 29.

79 *It turned out that Blair*: Wilkins, *Cherokee Tragedy*, 42.

79 *He conducted a census*: McLoughlin, *Cherokee Renascence in the New Republic*, 295.

80 *"Females have made much"*: Cobbs, Blum, and Gjerde, *Major Problems in American History, I*, 227.

80 *those annuities were*: McLoughlin, *Cherokee Renascence in the New Republic*, 96; also, the complaint brought by the Cherokee Nation against the United States Department of the Interior.

80 *Distributed to all the Cherokee*: Wilkins, *Cherokee Tragedy*, 44.

81 *He answered Saunders*: Ibid., 44–45.

81 *"Our game has disappeared"*: McKenney and Hall, *Indian Tribes, I*, 383.

81 *By the new laws*: Ibid., 384.

82 *His opinion was his alone*: Ibid.
82 *Black Fox remained silent*: Cherokee Phoenix, December 3, 1831, 2, col. 3.
83 *It was an arduous journey*: https://www.aoc.gov/history-us-capitol-building.
83 *Upon arrival, the delegates*: Wilkins, Cherokee Tragedy, 47.
84 *Jefferson followed the meeting*: Ibid., 48–49.
84 *But The Ridge came back*: McKenney and Hall, Indian Tribes, I, 384–85.
84 *Wealthy, powerful, and dignified*: Ehle, Trail of Tears, Kindle Location 1375.
85 *The transformation was not simply*: Miles, The House on Diamond Hill, 31.
86 *He turned to his neighbor*: Wilkins, Cherokee Tragedy, 50.
86 *Ever ambitious for their children*: Ibid., 98–99.
86 *There was no proper girls' dorm*: Ibid., 99.
86 *A squared-off property*: McClinton, Moravian Spring Place Mission to the Cherokees, 6.
86 *He did not mean just religiously*: Ibid., 9.
87 *Black-haired but slight*: Wilkins, Cherokee Tragedy, 99.
88 *"If the child were"*: Ibid.
88 *The Gambolds took to John*: Ibid., 100.
89 *"My heart received the rays"*: Ibid., 101.
89 *The Ridge admitted*: Ibid., 102–3.
89 *While Christianity was taking*: McLoughlin, Cherokee Renascence in the New Republic, 180.
90 *It drew on loss and longing*: Ibid., 187–88.
90 *"About six feet high"*: Elmore Barce, "Tecumseh's Confederacy," Indian Magazine of History, March 1917.
90 *The Ridge met him*: Wilkins, Cherokee Tragedy, 53–55.
91 *"Kill the old chiefs"*: Ibid., 55.
91 *When an immense Creek*: Ibid.
92 *Unnerved, The Ridge galloped*: Ibid., 56.
92 *Thoughts of Indians battling*: McKenney and Hall, Indian Tribes, I, 386.
93 *He claimed to have been*: Wilkins, Cherokee Tragedy, 58–59.
93 *He rose, waited for the crowd*: Ibid., 59.
93 *Furious, several Cherokee jumped*: Ibid., 60.
94 *Defiant, Charley prophesied*: Mooney, The Ghost Dance Religion, 676–77.

PART ONE, CHAPTER 9—INTO THE WILD
95 *By 1812, almost 2,000*: Moulton, John Ross, 8–9.
96 *Ross had thought of taking*: Ibid., 9.
96 *In Chickamauga, the men boarded*: Moulton, The Papers of Chief John Ross, I, 17.
97 *Not really "bandits"*: Ibid.

97   *They had actually followed*: Moulton, *John Ross*, 10.
97   *It must not have made*: Moulton, *The Papers of Chief John Ross, I*, 17–18.
98   *She and Ross were married*: Moulton, *John Ross*, 12–13.
98   *In his enormous two-volume*: Hicks, *Toward the Setting Sun*, 50.
99   *In the tense months of anticipation*: Wilkins, *Cherokee Tragedy*, 60.
99   *These Creeks were the Red Sticks*: Ibid., 62–63.
100 *When a federal investigator*: Brands, *Andrew Jackson*, 195.
100 *Elected major general*: Ibid., 26–28.
101 *That was the 1,000-acre*: Ibid., 190.
101 *One bullet struck Jackson*: Ibid., 190–91.
101 *No loyalist of Tecumseh*: Wilkins, *Cherokee Tragedy*, 63.
102 *He must have poured*: McKenney and Hall, *Indian Tribes, I*, 390.
102 *He declared that if the Cherokee*: Ibid.
102 *One of the enlisted soldiers*: Wilkins, *Cherokee Tragedy*, 67.
103 *The Cherokee would march*: Ibid., 68.
104 *That created such a furnace*: Hicks, *Toward the Setting Sun*, 64.
105 *Temporarily released from service*: Wilkins, *Cherokee Tragedy*, 70–71.
105 *She refused to have anything*: Ibid., 104.
105 *"This is a phew words"*: Ehle, *Trail of Tears*, 112.
106 *Without the Indians*: Wilkins, *Cherokee Tragedy*, 72.
106 *John Ross had returned*: Moulton, *John Ross*, 11.
107 *It was his idea to exterminate*: Wilkins, *Cherokee Tragedy*, 62.
107 *"Nature furnishes few situations"*: Congressional Series of United States Public Documents, Volume 5409, 40.
107 *This fortress did not keep*: Wilkins, *Cherokee Tragedy*, 78–79.
107 *Shortly after dawn on March 17*: Ibid., 76–78.
108 *Then a few daring Cherokee*: Ibid., 76.
109 *Attacked from the front*: Jackson, *Correspondence, I*, 492.
109 *John Ross prepared the Cherokee casualty*: Moulton, *The Papers of Chief John Ross, I*, 20.
109 *After the sweeping defeat*: Brands, *Andrew Jackson*, 221.
110 *Under other circumstances*: Ibid., 222.
111 *But soon he got interested*: Wilkins, *Cherokee Tragedy*, 105.

PART TWO, CHAPTER 1—THE PERILS OF PEACE

115 *When Ross returned*: Abram, *Forging a Cherokee-American Alliance in the Creek War*, 85.
116 *But he was nearly breathless*: Ehle, *Trail of Tears*, 121.
116 *When the Cherokee demanded*: Jackson, *Correspondence*, 255–56.

116 *In protest, the Cherokee dispatched:* Wilkins, *Cherokee Tragedy,* 87.

117 *The correspondent for the:* Niles' *Weekly Register,* March 2, 1816.

117 *At one soiree:* Wilkins, *Cherokee Tragedy,* 88.

118 *The next ghostwritten by Ross memorandum:* Ibid., 89.

119 *Ross begged the president:* Ibid.

119 *Another Cherokee memorandum:* Ibid., 90.

120 *As the sole fluent English-speaker:* Ibid.

120 *While the delegation was still in Washington:* Ibid., 92.

121 *He was about the only one:* Ibid., 93.

121 *Back at the Hermitage:* Jackson, *Correspondence, II,* 243, 254.

122 *When that bluff failed:* Ibid., 243, 254.

123 *In a final insult:* Ibid., 98, 307.

123 *If the Cherokee insisted on staying:* McLoughlin, *Cherokee Renascence in the New Republic,* 230.

124 *To lure them, Governor McMinn:* Ibid., 241.

125 *Jackson's deal:* Moulton, *John Ross,* 20.

125 *In his case, he received:* Ibid., 21.

126 *Hearing about McMinn's:* Ibid., 22.

126 *Relieved by their victory:* Eaton, *John Ross and the Cherokee Indians,* 32.

PART TWO, CHAPTER 2—DELIVERANCE

129 *Educated at Brown:* Andrew, *From Revivals to Removal,* 89.

129 *He could be judgmental:* Hicks, *Toward the Setting Sun,* 90.

129 *Both Ross and Ridge would have agreed:* Ural, *Civil War Citizens,* 194.

130 *The Gambolds had feared:* Wilkins, *Cherokee Tragedy,* 105.

130 *Ever since the death:* Ibid., 106.

130 *The Gambolds took that:* Ibid.

130 *"He seemed very low":* Ibid., 107.

131 *When the Moravians:* Moulton, *John Ross,* 7.

131 *Major Ridge's children Nancy and John:* Starkey, *The Cherokee Nation,* 53–54.

132 *The teachers caught glimpses:* Ehle, *Trail of Tears,* Kindle Locations 2462–2465.

132 *The mixed-bloods like Major Ridge:* Cornelius, *Memoir of the Rev. Elias Cornelius,* 62.

132 *To everyone, Cornelius rhapsodized:* Ehle, *Trail of Tears,* 143.

133 *Reverend Elias Cornelius escorted:* Parins, *Elias Cornelius Boudinot,* 4.

135 *By the time Buck's little party:* George White, *Historical Collections of Georgia,* https://archive.org/details/historicalcolle00duttgoog.

135 *Surveying the latest lot:* Wilkins, *Cherokee Tragedy,* 123.

135 *When the missionary:* Ibid., 116–17.

136   *When John finally arrived*: Hicks, *Toward the Setting Sun*, 90.

136   *One of them was a remarkable ode*: Wilkins, *Cherokee Tragedy*, 123–24.

136   *The day started at six*: Demos, *The Heathen School*, Kindle Locations 2850–2851.

137   *John Ridge took easily*: Wilkins, *Cherokee Tragedy*, 129.

137   *That won him a lengthy stay*: Ibid., 130.

138   *Cherokee students had been*: Gaul, *To Marry an Indian*, 7.

139   *Mrs. Northrup herself*: Demos, *The Heathen School*, Kindle Locations 2898–2902.

139   *"I told her that a white woman"*: *Religious Intelligencer*, October 1825.

140   *Still, he himself had suffered*: Wilkins, *Cherokee Tragedy*, 134.

141   *John gave a stirring account*: *Missionary Herald*, XIX, January 1823.

141   *When the cousins finally returned*: Demos, *The Heathen School*, Kindle Locations 2894–2898.

141   *John brooded over the unfairness*: Ibid.

PART TWO, CHAPTER 3—A NATION OF VERBS

142   *"She has chosen the good"*: Wilkins, *Cherokee Tragedy*, 137.

142   *As speaker of the council*: Ibid., 142.

143   *This government was writing laws*: Moulton, *John Ross*, 23.

144   *Rather, it came from*: George Battey, *History of Rome and Floyd County*, https://archive.org/details/historyofromeflo01batt.

144   *Like everyone, he'd thought*: Jones, *History of the Ojebway Indians*, https://archive.org/details/historyofojebway00jone.

145   *For Cherokee consists almost entirely*: Perdue, *Cherokee Women*, 40.

145   *Sequoyah knew not a word*: Jones, *History of the Ojebway Indians*, https://archive.org/details/historyofojebway00jone.

146   *But gawking at written*: Perdue, *Cherokee Women*, 40.

147   *By 1826 the number*: Malcomson, *One Drop of Blood*, 530.

147   *The census of 1826*: McLoughlin, *Cherokee Renascence in the New Republic*, 295.

147   *What was more hazardous, the population*: Ibid.

147   *"Well armed," Meigs admitted*: Ibid., 154.

147   *The colony was ruled*: Inskeep, *Jacksonland*, 117.

148   *As part of the deal*: *Cherokee Phoenix* (February 28, 1828), I, No. 2, 2, col. 1b.

148   *He knew perfectly well*: "George William Goss, "The Debate over Indian Removal in the 1830s," http://scholarworks.umb.edu/cgi/viewcontent.cgi?article=1045&context=masters_theses, 32.

149   *As council speaker, Major Ridge*: Wilkins, *Cherokee Tragedy*, 123.

149   *"The Cherokees do not"*: *Cherokee Phoenix*, June 18, 1828, col. 4b–5b, col. 1a–2b.

149   Ross uttered a cry: Ibid.
150   He was the Creek version: Wilkins, Cherokee Tragedy, 144.
150   Then, said McIntosh: Ibid.
150   "If the chiefs feel disposed": Moulton, John Ross, 25.
151   He reminded the hall: Hicks, Toward the Setting Sun, 128.
152   The oration went on: Ibid.
152   "A plain maxim of our Nation": Wilkins, Cherokee Tragedy, 145.
153   Instead, he banished him: Hicks, Toward the Setting Sun, 130.
153   At daybreak one morning: Ibid.

PART TWO, CHAPTER 4—"BARKS ON BARKS OBLIQUELY LAID"

155   He immediately impressed Adams: Message from the President of the United
      States, 18th Congress, 1st Session, 87.
155   When the headstrong Calhoun: Moulton, John Ross, 26.
155   At that, the Georgia representatives: National Intelligencer, April 10, 1824, 2,
      col. 3.
155   For his part, Adams was struck: Adams, Memoirs, VI, https://archive.org/details
      /memjohnquincy12adamrich.
155   Far from being the uncouth primitives: Wilkins, Cherokee Tragedy, 157.
156   But one of them: Ibid., 158.
156   When word of their permission: Smith, An American Betrayal, 50.
156   Even so, they were hounded: Niles' Weekly Register, XXXVIII, July 9, 1825.
156   The news spread like the wind: Ehle, Trail of Tears, 191.
157   The puritanical Bunce chased: Gaul, To Marry an Indian, 9.
157   It claimed only that: Demos, The Heathen School, Kindle Location 3025.
157   Some of the first citizens of Cornwall: Parins, Elias Cornelius Boudinot, 5.
158   Harriet received a letter: Gaul, To Marry an Indian, 110.
159   Once she was safely: Ibid., 1.
159   Instead, Stephen wrote outraged letters: Demos, The Heathen School, 180.
159   But when word of his impending: Ibid., 190.
159   Stunned by the reaction: Ibid., 186.
159   Boudinot had been out: Smith, An American Betrayal, 57–58.
160   As the crowd roared: Gaul, To Marry an Indian, 83.
160   Once again, the newspapers weighed: Demos, The Heathen School, 186.
161   One of them, a cousin: Gaul, To Marry an Indian, 43.
161   Sometime in late February: Parins, Elias Cornelius Boudinot, 7.
162   Despite his profound misgivings: Niles' Weekly Register, XXVIII, July 9, 1825.
163   As Adams's chosen commander: Wilkins, Cherokee Tragedy, 167.
163   Their daughter looked: Gaul, To Marry an Indian, 137.

164 *After an investigation*: Wilkins, *Cherokee Tragedy*, 173–74.

164 *While McKenney was at it*: McKenney and Hall, *Indian Tribes*, I, 326.

165 *He'd already redone*: Wilkins, *Cherokee Tragedy*, 186.

165 *It was two stories of white clapboard*: McKenney and Hall, *Indian Tribes*, I, 395.

165 *"If I were a poet"*: N. D. Scales, *Cherokee Phoenix*, January 15, 1831, 3, col. 3b.

166 *He gleefully recited*: Wilkins, *Cherokee Tragedy*, 194.

167 *As Boudinot declared*: Perdue, *Cherokee Editor*, 69.

167 *To show off these triumphs*: Ibid., 15.

168 *John Ridge was backing plans*: Carter, *Cherokee Sunset*, 62.

168 *The council house offered religious*: Ibid.

168 *"We, the representatives of the people"*: *Cherokee Phoenix*, February 21, 1828, 1, col. 2a–2, col. 3a.

169 *While all citizens were free*: Ibid.

170 *In filling out the leadership*: McLoughlin, *Cherokee Renascence*, 406.

171 *That left John Ross*: Wilkins, *Cherokee Tragedy*, 208.

PART TWO, CHAPTER 5—GOLD FEVER

172 *The lease held*: Williams, *The Great Georgia Gold Rush*, 22.

172 *Word of the gold strike*: Ibid., 25–31.

172 *When he realized*: Ibid.

173 *This new blood law*: Wilkins, *Cherokee Tragedy*, 208–9.

174 *In his memoir*: Gilmer, *Sketches of Some of the First Settlers of Upper Georgia*, 234.

174 *On December 19, 1829*: *Cherokee Phoenix*, June 26, 1830, 2, col. 4a–3, col. 2a.

175 *Georgia's own law, meanwhile*: Bass, *Cherokee Messenger*, 110.

176 *As for Ridge, the* Savannah": Gilmer, *Sketches of Some of the First Settlers of Upper Georgia*, 263–64.

176 *Although Boudinot had been*: *Cherokee Phoenix*, February 10, 1830, 2, col. 4c–5b.

176 *In the* Phoenix, *Boudinot preached*: Ibid.

176 *The antislavery evangelist*: Meacham, *American Lion*, 54.

177 *He had pressed his Indian Removal Act*: Ibid., 122.

177 *As a hardy Tennessean*: *American Indian Magazine*, 1944, 6. nos. 3–4, 168.

177 *He was wary of ambitious men*: Inskeep, *Jacksonland*, 240.

179 *One of the newspapermen*: *Cherokee Phoenix*, March 26, 1831, 2, col. 3, quoting *New York Observer*.

179 *To address the central issue*: Wilkins, *Cherokee Tragedy*, 221–22.

179 *Cherokee Nation was*: *Cherokee Phoenix*, April 16, 1831, 2, col. 4, quoting *New York Observer*.

180　*When Ridge saw that a Georgia paper*: John Ridge to Elias Boudinot, *Cherokee Phoenix*, May 17, 1831, 2, col. 5.

181　*For all the high-handedness*: Ibid.

181　*The eldest, Richard Taylor*: Ibid.

PART TWO, CHAPTER 6—THE IMPRISONMENT OF REVERAND SAMUEL WORCESTER

182　*Convinced that the Cherokee*: Wilkins, *Cherokee Tragedy*, 226.

183　*In the pages of the* Phoenix, *Elias Boudinot*: Smith, *An American Betrayal*, 126.

183　*With his wife Ann*: Bass, *Cherokee Messenger*, 27.

184　*To him, Worcester was*: Smith, *An American Betrayal*, 113.

184　*There, to Gilmer's frustration*: Wilkins, *Cherokee Tragedy*, 227.

185　*By then, he'd returned home*: Ibid., 123.

185　*The two men were*: Ibid.

185　*The trial came in September*: Ibid., 123–124.

186　*Now, the punishment was mindless*: Walker, *Torchlights to the Cherokees*, 287.

186　*He bore the document*: Ibid.

186　*Gilmer dispatched the Georgia*: Moulton, *John Ross*, 46–47.

187　*Nothing came of the meeting*: Ibid., 47.

188　*By then, Harris had*: *Cherokee Phoenix*, January 21, 1832, 1, col. 1a-2, col. 3b.

188　*Harris wheeled on him*: Ibid.

189　*In the* Phoenix, *Ross didn't come*: Ibid.

190　*Cass could hardly have*: Watson, Indian Removal Records, Senate Document 512, 23rd Congress, 1 Session, Volume II, 42.

191　*"He is apparently as strong"*: Woodward, *The Cherokees*, 170.

191　*For days they waited anxiously*: Dale, "Letters of the Two Boudinots," *Chronicles of Oklahoma*, September 1928, 6, no. 3.

192　*On further reflection*: Starkey, *The Cherokee Nation*, 178.

192　*When Boudinot told him*: Langguth, *Driven West*, 189.

192　*There would be no nullification*: Ibid.

193　*Finally, troubling reports started*: Meacham, *American Lion*, 204.

193　*Incredible as it seemed to Ridge*: Ibid., 205.

194　*He must have sagged*: Wilkins, *Cherokee Tragedy*, 236–37.

PART TWO, CHAPTER 7—THE TERRIBLE TRUTH

197　*Currey patched together*: Langguth, *Driven West*, 183.

198　*From there, the emigrants*: Ibid., 195.

198　*Yet it was here*: Foreman, *Indian Removal*, 241–42.

198　*Once the full Cherokee delegation*: Congressional Serial Set, Issue 246, 381.

198　*Ross refused even to think*: Langguth, *Driven West*, 196.

199   *It guaranteed the Cherokee ample land*: Wilkins, *Cherokee Tragedy*, 242.

199   *An English traveler, George William Featherstonhaugh*: Ibid., 242–43.

200   *Even the sleepy-eyed Governor*: Lumpkin, *The Removal of the Cherokee Indians from Georgia, II*, 187.

201   *For whatever reason*: Moulton, *John Ross*, 48.

201   *No, Ross declared them nothing*: Ibid., 49.

201   *To rout his opponents*: Wilkins, *Cherokee Tragedy*, 244.

201   *Just as there would be*: Moulton, *John Ross*, 51.

201   *Boudinot replied with his resignation*: *Cherokee Phoenix*, August 11, 1832.

202   *They mournfully added*: Wilkins, *Cherokee Tragedy*, 45.

202   *In the* Phoenix, *Elijah Hicks*: Langguth, *Driven West*, 198.

202   *In an essay the* Phoenix *refused to publish*: Wilkins, *Cherokee Tragedy*, 246–47.

204   *The French traveler Alexis de Tocqueville*: Pierson, *Tocqueville in America*, 598.

204   *Since 1805, Georgia*: Williams, *The Great Georgia Gold Rush*, 52.

204   *He recruited 550 surveyors*: Wilkins, *Cherokee Tragedy*, 249–51.

205   *"Our papers from Georgia"*: *Cherokee Phoenix*, November 11, 1832.

205   *It was Christmas Eve*: Carter, *Cherokee Sunset*, 144.

206   *It was driven by the fortunate*: Ibid., 144–45.

206   *They flooded in*: *Niles' Weekly Register*, XLIII, January 26, 1833.

207   *After months of letters*: Starkey, *Cherokee Nation*, 206.

207   *Worcester recorded that a Cherokee*: Ibid., 206–7.

208   *"I told them that"*: *Missionary Herald*, Volume 29, April 1, 1833, 242.

208   *"The usual scenes"*: Wilkins, *Cherokee Tragedy*, 252.

PART TWO, CHAPTER 8—"A CONSUMMATE ACT OF TREACHERY"

209   *He offered Ross $2.5 million*: Wilkins, *Cherokee Tragedy*, 253.

209   *Ross trumpeted a letter*: "Emigration of Indians Between 30th November 1831 and 27th December 1833," Washington, DC: Printed by Duff and Green, 1835, 170.

210   *That proved no victory*: *Cherokee Phoenix*, July 20, 1833, 2, col. 2–3; August 17, 1833, 3, col. 3.

210   *Hearing about such fights*: Wilkins, *Cherokee Tragedy*, 256–57.

211   *Ross refused*: *Cherokee Phoenix*, November 23, 1833, 1, col. 3.

211   *And then the heavens*: *Cherokee Phoenix*, December 7, 1833, 3, col. 3.

211   *Eventually, six steamers*: Foreman, *Indian Removal*, 256.

212   *"The grief of the whites"*: Ibid., 258.

212   *They finally reached*: Ibid., 262.

212   *An émigré, William Bolling, wrote*: Starkey, *Cherokee Nation*, 236.

213   *"It is our desire"*: Ibid., 237.

213   *Hicks hoped the three*: Eaton, *John Ross and the Cherokee Indians*, 92.

214   *"Kitchen chiefs"*: Wilkins, *Cherokee Tragedy*, 259–60.
215   *But for that, they insisted*: Ibid., 261.
215   *The Ridges quickly disavowed*: Ibid.
215   *Ross's wife, Quatie, had fallen*: Woodward, *The Cherokees*, 176.
216   *In the morning, he packed*: Ibid.
216   *"These men," Foreman declared*: Wilkins, *Cherokee Tragedy*, 262.
217   *He began by saying*: Ibid., 262–63, for the entire encounter between Foreman and Ridge.
217   *Then the Phoenix's Elijah Hicks*: Ibid., 63.
218   *His father, John Walker Sr.*: Moulton, *John Ross*, 58.
218   *Slashing at a sheet*: Wilkins, *Cherokee Tragedy*, 264.
218   *He told Currey to let*: Woodward, *The Cherokees*, 177.
219   *Then a "silver key"*: Garrison, *The Legal Ideology of Removal*, 230.
219   *The first meeting of the new*: Wilkins, *Cherokee Tragedy*, 265.
220   *But first, Ridge would make*: Smith, *An American Betrayal*, 159.
220   *For that, Jackson came*: Wilkins, *Cherokee Tragedy*, 267.
221   *He decried it as*: Ibid.
221   *"It is very liberal in its terms"*: Dale and Litton, *Cherokee Cavaliers*, 12–13.
222   *Might Ross be allowed*: Moulton, *John Ross*, 62–63.

PART TWO, CHAPTER 9—SPECTERS IN THE SHADOWS
223   *John Ridge termed her*: http://digital.library.okstate.edu/Chronicles/v032/v032p395.pdf
224   *As it was, dozens*: Starkey, *Cherokee Nation*, 253.
224   *Major Currey later reported*: Wilkins, *Cherokee Tragedy*, 270.
224   *John Ridge wanted to present*: Dale and Litton, *Cherokee Cavaliers*, 13.
226   *Despite these two appeals*: Wilkins, *Cherokee Tragedy*, 270.
226   *"I would deem myself"*: Eaton, *John Ross and the Cherokee Indians*, 86.
227   *Ridge asked Governor Lumpkin*: Woodward, *The Cherokees*, 183.
227   *Only "procrastination"*: Ibid.
227   *Ridge added that Ross*: Breyer, *Making Our Democracy Work*, 29.
227   *"The last hold & retreat"*: Langer, *American Indian Quotations*, 41.
228   *And he asked Lumpkin*: Ibid.
228   *"Break up this incubus"*: Hicks, *Toward the Setting Sun*.
228   *He promised that he would*: Wilkins, *Cherokee Tragedy*, 272.
229   *Afterward, the men circled*: Eaton, *John Ross and the Cherokee Indians*, Kindle Locations 1672–1685.
229   *"Some starving, some half clad"*: Wilkins, *Cherokee Tragedy*, 273.
230   *He frankly told them*: Ibid.

232 *By then, Schermerhorn had come*: Ibid., 274; Moulton, *John Ross*, 67.

232 *He himself found it meaningful*: Eaton, *John Ross and the Cherokee Indians*, 89.

233 *When the motion was entertained*: Wilkins, *Cherokee Tragedy*, 275.

233 *When the Ridges were done*: Moulton, *John Ross*, 64.

234 *Still, Ross offered to have*: Wilkins, *Cherokee Tragedy*, 276.

234 *When he failed*: Eaton, *John Ross and the Cherokee Indians*, Kindle Locations 1658–1661.

235 *A former Cherokee judge*: "A Letter to Wilson Lumpkin, Governor of Georgia," http://www.intimeandplace.org/cherokee/reading/removal/ridgeletter.html.

235 *The coach had the very*: Battey, *History of Rome and Floyd County*, I, 261–62.

235 *"Our cause prospers"*: "A Letter to Wilson Lumpkin, Governor of Georgia," http://www.intimeandplace.org/cherokee/reading/removal/ridgeletter.html.

236 *By then, the* Phoenix: Moulton, *John Ross*, 65.

236 *Schermerhorn claimed*: Langguth, *Driven West*, 422.

PART TWO, CHAPTER 10—A FINAL RECKONING

238 *At Red Clay*: Woodward, *The Cherokees*, 185–86.

239 *Solemn, exotic, and remote*: "The Green Corn Dance," June 1932, http://digital.library.okstate.edu/Chronicles/v010/v010p170.html.

239 *He started with the Ridges*: Wilkins, *Cherokee Tragedy*, 283.

239 *"Mild, intelligent, and entirely"*: Smith, *An American Betrayal*, 267.

240 *True to form, Schermerhorn grandly*: Wilkins, *Cherokee Tragedy*, 283.

240 *Late on the night of November 7*: Moulton, *John Ross*, 69.

240 *Eventually, Bishop conceded*: Eaton, *John Ross and the Cherokee Indians*, Kindle Locations 1687–1692.

241 *It commanded the Cherokee*: Wilkins, *Cherokee Tragedy*, 285.

241 *As an angry Boudinot wrote*: "Documents in Relation to the Validity of the Cherokee Treaty of 1835," Reprint of Senate Document 121, 25th Congress, 2nd Session, 33.

242 *They all crowded into*: *Cartersville Courant*, March 26, 1885, 1, col. 3.

242 *Inclined toward the brusque*: Wilkins, *Cherokee Tragedy*, 286.

243 *"I am one of the native sons"*: Ehle, *Trail of Tears*, 294.

244 *"They will come again"*: Smith, *An American Betrayal*, 175.

244 *When it was time to sign*: Ibid., 176.

PART TWO, CHAPTER 11—OUR STRENGTH IS OUR REDEEMER

247 *But Ross angrily dismissed*: O'Brien, *In Bitterness and in Tears*, 233.

247 *"In this state of things"*: Ehle, *Trail of Tears*, 296.

247 *Appalled, and incredulous*: Eaton, *John Ross and the Cherokee Indians*, Kindle Locations 1775–1780.

248 *"Such a dereliction"*: Ehle, *Trail of Tears*, 303.

248 *And so, on May 23, 1836*: Woodward, *The Cherokees*, 192–93.

249 *"The Cherokees have a good"*: 13th Congress–49th Congress, Volume 7, Document 286, 161.

249 *"What will that be to"*: Ibid.

250 *In the next few weeks*: Wilkins, *Cherokee Tragedy*, 294.

250 *She'd sent two of the girls*: Gaul, *To Marry an Indian*, 180–81.

250 *The end came on August 1*: Ibid., 185.

251 *At this, Boudinot put*: Ibid., 187–88.

251 *Boudinot drew out the letter*: Ibid., 189.

251 *The Georgians, not the Treaty Party*: Ehle, *Trail of Tears*, 297.

252 *To do his part*: Wilkins, *Cherokee Tragedy*, 295.

252 *This had, he said*: Ehle, *Trail of Tears*, 309.

253 *It didn't make things*: Lumpkin, *The Removal of the Cherokee Indians*, 86.

253 *This time, when Ridge objected*: Ehle, *Trail of Tears*, 297.

254 *General Wool must stop*: Ibid., 298.

255 *"The whole scene"*: Conley, *Cherokee Nation*, 147.

255 *But the Cherokee did*: Ibid., 148.

256 *Once he gave notice*: Wilkins, *Cherokee Tragedy*, 300.

256 *To Miss Sawyer, the schoolmistress*: Ibid.

256 *To advance his suit*: *Atlanta Constitution*, October 27, 1889, 5, col. 3.

258 *For a voyage that was*: Ehle, *Trail of Tears*, 363.

258 *A Dr. John S. Young was put*: Wilkins, *Cherokee Tragedy*, 304.

258 *From there, it was up*: Gerstacker, *Wild Sports in the Far West*, 92.

258 *It was a brutal passage*: Foreman, *Indian Removal*, 276.

PART THREE, CHAPTER 1—HONEY CREEK

263 *In 1832, five years before*: Irving, *A Tour on the Prairies*, Kindle Locations 110–121.

264 *One of them was*: Ibid.

264 *They rode along the Arkansas*: Ibid.

266 *"We had to undergo"*: Ehle, *Trail of Tears*, 366.

267 *It must have been a daily torment*: Carter, *Cherokee Sunset*, 217.

267 *"Sir, you have made"*: Ibid., 218.

268 *Gradually as they followed*: Wilkins, *Cherokee Tragedy*, 310.

268 *Cousin Boudinot and his new wife Delight*: Ibid.

269   *Happy to return*: Ibid., 311.

269   *They all got through*: Ibid.

270   *John Ridge's store offered*: Ehle, *Trail of Tears*, 370.

PART THREE, CHAPTER 2—THE BUSINESS OF REMOVAL

271   *Well into that spring*: Ehle, *Trail of Tears*, 322.

272   *C. A. Harris, the new Indian commissioner*: Woodward, *The Cherokees*, 200.

272   *There, he made time*: Moulton, *John Ross*, 93.

272   *With the deadline fast approaching*: Ibid., 94.

272   *Ross's brother Lewis saw*: Woodward, *The Cherokees*, 201.

273   *Lewis's daughter wrote*: Ibid., 202.

273   *It was with some exasperation*: Ibid., 203.

273   *They should leave now, he declared*: Langguth, *Driven West*, 278.

273   *To such a stark declaration*: Woodward, *The Cherokees*, 204.

274   *A half century later the Cherokee ethnologist*: Wilkins, *Cherokee Tragedy*, 320.

274   *One Georgia volunteer*: "A History of the Cherokee Indians," December 1930, http://digital.library.okstate.edu/Chronicles/v008/v008p407.html.

275   *The Baptist missionary Evan Jones*: Baptist Missionary Magazine, 1837–38 Volume 18, 236.

275   *Illegal as Ross had declared*: Niles' Weekly Register, 1837–38, Volume 57, 43.

276   *By June 6, the first 800*: Foreman, *Indian Removal*, 291.

276   *Remarkably, no one died*: Carter, *Cherokee Sunset*, 241–42.

276   *Another band of 875 captives*: Ibid., 242.

277   *General Scott ordered 1,000*: Ehle, *Trail of Tears*, 340.

278   *It took him a full month*: Moulton, *John Ross*, 97.

278   *Ross made clear*: Ibid.

279   *And soap, too, which he*: Moulton, *Papers of Chief John Ross*, I, 634.

279   *"The estimate therefore"*: Woodward, *The Cherokees*, 210.

279   *"The contract with Ross"*: Ibid., 211.

PART THREE, CHAPTER 3—EXODUS

281   *Seeing that the Rosses*: Carter, *Cherokee Sunset*, 248.

284   *He divided up the 13,000*: Moulton, *John Ross*, 99.

284   *Richard Wilkenson put*: Woodward, *The Cherokees*, 212.

285   *"In the chill of a dazzling rain"*: Ibid., 215.

285   *Benge's group reached Nashville*: Carter, *Cherokee Sunset*, 254.

286   *One of the Mainers wrote*: Marshall and Manuel, *From Sea to Shining Sea*, 374.

286   *"Some of the Cherokee"*: Nichols, *The American Indian*, 159.

287   *The Maine couple encountered*: Foreman, *Indian Removal*, 306–7.

287   *Those with the money for chaises*: McLoughlin, *Cherokees and Christianity*, 107.
288   *She'd given her shawl*: Woodward, *The Cherokees*, 217–18.
288   *One of the 15,000 Cherokee*: *Sunday Oklahoma*, April 7, 1929, 6.

PART THREE, CHAPTER 4—"THE CHEROKEE ARE A COMPLAINING PEOPLE"

289   *"Instead of receiving"*: Wilkins, *Cherokee Tragedy*, 313.
289   *In his own trek west*: Ibid., 314.
289   *Ridge rushed to the* Journal *offices*: Ibid.
293   *But Worcester had been embittered*: Bass, *Cherokee Messenger*, 223.
293   *But Boudinot was unavoidable*: Ibid., 218–19.
293   *First came the scholarly Mary*: Gaul, *To Marry an Indian*, 200.
294   *With a shrug, they dismissed*: Moulton, *John Ross*, 108.
294   *At fifty, he was a veteran*: Foreman, *Indian Removal*, 147.
294   *Arbuckle sent a detachment*: Moulton, *John Ross*, 109.
295   *"The critical situation"*: Starkey, *Cherokee Nation*, 305.
295   *"He & his people"*: Wilkins, *Cherokee Tragedy*, 330.
295   *There, Ross called for*: Moulton, *John Ross*, 110.
296   *Ross fired off a letter*: Wilkins, *Cherokee Tragedy*, 333.
297   *Someone brought out the original*: Ibid., 334.
298   *Fourteen of them bore*: Ibid., 334–35.
299   *There before them*: John Ridge, *Poems*, Preface, https://ualrexhibits.org/tribal writers/artifacts/Poems-of-John-Rollin-Ridge.html#Preface.
300   *Finding her husband's body*: Bass, *Cherokee Messenger*, 255.
301   *But rather than take refuge*: Cunningham, *General Stand Watie's Confederate Indians*, 17.
302   *Before he reached*: Wilkins, *Cherokee Tragedy*, 338.
303   *After the events of June 22*: Knight, *Red Fox*, 30–31.
303   *While his brother and cousin*: Ibid., 31.
303   *When, in 1819, his friend*: Cunningham, *General Stand Watie's Confederate Indians*, 17.

PART THREE, CHAPTER 5—"THEY CAN LEAVE US"

305   *A missionary, Reverend Cephas Washburn*: "The Trial of Stand Watie," September 1934, http://digital.library.okstate.edu/Chronicles/v012/v012p305.html.
307   *Scarcely had the Indian left*: Carter, *Cherokee Sunset*, 271.
307   *He'd already heard*: Starr, *History of the Cherokee Indians*, 114.
307   *With Watie at Fort Gibson*: Parins, *John Rollin Ridge*, 32.
308   *Still, the literary young Rollin*: Ibid., 34.
308   *Miss Sawyer followed Sally Ridge*: Ibid., 33.

309   *Arbuckle passed this offer*: Starr, *History of the Cherokee Indians*, 26.

309   *All the same, he announced*: Moulton, *John Ross*, 115–16.

309   *Pressing his advantage*: United States Congressional Serial Set, Volume 474, 112.

310   *In response, Watie's Treaty Party*: Reed, *The Ross-Watie Conflict*, 108.

310   *In Arkansas, citizens grew so anxious*: Moulton, *John Ross*, 115.

310   *Startled by Arbuckle's display*: Franks, *Stand Watie*, 62.

310   *When Ross did nothing*: Ibid., 65–66.

PART THREE, CHAPTER 6—INDIAN JUSTICE

312   *Watie and his close friend*: Franks, *Stand Watie*, 63.

313   *He dashed off a fierce letter*: Ibid., 67.

313   *Watie came away with an elegant*: Cunningham, *General Stand Watie's Confederate Indians*, 19.

313   *In Poinsett's spacious office*: Franks, *Stand Watie*, 91.

314   *He should never be allowed*: Congressional Edition, Volume 354, 416.

314   *For while Watie was away*: Moulton, *John Ross*, 118.

314   *In Washington, Poinsett could hardly*: Ibid., 122.

315   *At one point, representatives*: Franks, *Stand Watie*, 69–70.

315   *Ross demanded that Poinsett release*: Ibid., 39.

316   *Among Watie's skills*: Ibid., 74.

316   *The two had words*: Payne, *Indian Justice*, 1.

316   *Watie agreed to defend Smith*: Ibid., xxxiii.

317   *At that point, Tahlequah consisted*: Ibid., 16.

317   *Only one witness*: Ibid., 20.

317   *The prosecutor, Bushyhead*: Ibid., 35–36.

317   *Nevertheless, Watie at first defended*: Franks, *Stand Watie*, 76–77.

317   *Given all the confusion*: Ibid., 77.

317   *When the case resumed*: Ibid., 58.

318   *As prosecutor, Isaac Bushyhead*: Payne, *Indian Justice*, 102.

319   *Not a week passed before*: Ibid., 104.

PART THREE, CHAPTER 7—$1,094,765

320   *The mounting fury*: Moulton, *John Ross*, 150.

321   *As one summed it up*: Reed, *The Ross-Watie Conflict*, 67.

322   *In fairness, many others*: Ibid., 124.

322   *In his lengthy report*: Hitchcock, *A Traveler in Indian Country*, 38.

322   *While the Cherokee officers sat*: Ibid.

323   *Ross referred to those matters*: Parins, *John Rollin Ridge*, 38.

323   *Despite his doubts*: Moulton, *John Ross*, 131.

324 *After the Smith trial*: Miles, *The House on Diamond Hill*, Kindle Location 3776.
325 *"Although I have always"*: Dale and Litton, *Cherokee Cavaliers*, 64.
325 *As a precaution*: Franks, *Stand Watie*, 80–81.
325 *Although it was called a grocery*: Ibid., 81.
326 *"A giant in size"*: Cunningham, *General Stand Watie's Confederate Indians*, 22.
326 *Watie had heard that Foreman*: Franks, *Stand Watie*, 81.
326 *Foreman snatched from Drumgoole*: Ibid.

PART THREE, CHAPTER 8—THE DEFENSE
328 *He surrendered to the authorities*: Franks, *Stand Watie*, 83.
329 *After the wedding Sarah settled*: Ibid.
330 *To improve his odds*: Ted Worley, "The Story of Alfred W. Arrington," *Arkansas Historical Quarterly*, Winter 1955, *14*, no. 4, 315–39.
330 *He wasn't a big man*: Stevenson, *Something of Men I Have Known*, 254.
331 *After his three relatives were murdered*: Franks, *Stand Watie*, 85.
332 *In Arrington's telling*: "The Trial of Stand Watie," http://digital.library.okstate .edu/Chronicles/v012/v012p305.html.
332 *"If there were no such conspiracy"*: Worley, "The Story of Alfred W. Arrington."
333 *He spared no gruesome*: George Paschal, "A Report of the Trial of Stand Watie, Charged with the Murder of James Foreman," http://brbl-dl.library.yale.edu /vufind/Record/3447210?image_id=1399056.
333 *At the end of this appeal*: Ibid.
334 *Even now, that August 1843*: Moulton, *John Ross*, 136.
334 *It was led by Tom Starr*: McLoughlin, *After the Trail of Tears*, 50.
335 *Outraged, the national council*: Shirley, *Belle Starr and Her Times*, 80.
335 *When Coodey pressed his pistol*: McLoughlin, *After the Trail of Tears*, 52–53.
336 *On November 14, Ross men*: Franks, *Stand Watie*, 96.
336 *Ross himself was heavily*: McLoughlin, *After the Trail of Tears*, 49.
337 *As they were leaving*: Moulton, *Papers of Chief John Ross, II*, 273.
337 *Since Coodey couldn't round up*: McLoughlin, *After the Trail of Tears*, 50.
338 *To keep Washington from turning*: Franks, *Stand Watie*, 97.
338 *With all the killings*: Ibid., 97–98.
338 *John Ross's politically minded nephew*: Dale and Litton, *Cherokee Cavaliers*, 32.
339 *"You will doubtless recollect"*: Ibid., 33.
339 *Rollin Ridge was in Fayetteville*: Ibid., 35.
339 *"One thing in particular"*: Ibid., 36.
339 *Watie was not encouraging*: Ibid., 38.
340 *And she must have known*: Ibid., 37.
340 *"You must write to me"*: Ibid.

PART THREE, CHAPTER 9—"THE GROVES OF THE BRANDYWINE"

341   *His courtship was so intense*: Moulton, *The Papers of Chief John Ross, II*, 240.

342   *But his heart wasn't in it*: Ibid., 102.

342   *But Molly had a hold on him*: Ibid., 197.

342   *In that very first letter*: Ibid., 94–95.

342   *It wasn't until 1844*: Ibid., 197.

343   *"Ah, Mary"*: Ibid., 199.

343   *"I beg you not to expose"*: Ibid., 200.

343   *Mary assured him that her sister*: Ibid., 203.

344   *"First—I and you"*: Ibid., 208–9.

344   *She was "electrified"*: Ibid., 209–10.

344   *"As regard my heart"*: Ibid., 211–12.

344   *When he'd received her*: Ibid., 213.

345   *And then he added another*: Ibid., 215.

346   *Five days later, he could not*: Ibid., 229.

346   *In New York on July 30*: Ibid., 230–31.

346   *In a letter to McKenney*: Ibid., 240–41.

347   *The wedding was on September 2*: Moulton, *John Ross*, 143.

347   *A brief wedding announcement*: Ibid., 143.

348   *They arrived in Van Buren*: Ibid., 144.

349   *President John Tyler left office*: United States Congressional Serial Set, Volume 476, 41.

350   *Styled as a treaty*: Franks, *Stand Watie*, 103–4.

PART FOUR, CHAPTER 1—SLAVES TO FORTUNE

355   *The Reverend Evan Jones*: McLoughlin, *Champions of the Cherokees*, 17–18.

355   *No one officially accused*: Ibid., 105.

356   *In his census of 1859*: Perdue, *Slavery and the Evolution of Cherokee Society*, 11.

357   *After a year of stalling*: McLoughlin, *Champions of the Cherokees*, 298.

357   *He dutifully banished*: Ibid., 297.

358   *One of the newcomers*: McLoughlin, *After the Trail of Tears*, 81–84.

358   *The more prosperous farmers*: Ibid., 77.

358   *In October 1855*: Ibid., 144.

359   *To defend the practice*: Hoig, *The Cherokees and Their Chiefs*, 214.

359   *When the legislature went ahead*: Franks, *Stand Watie*, 115–17.

359   *Quietly, hidden away in the woods*: Ibid., 114.

360   *Its membership was strictly limited*: McLoughlin, *Champions of the Cherokees*, 345.

360   *Alarmed, the slaveholding mixed-bloods*: McLoughlin, *After the Trail of Tears*, 158–59.

360   *Jones objected on the grounds*: McLoughlin, *Champions of the Cherokees*, 365–68.

361   *His last letter to the American Board*: Ibid., 372.

361   *One such mob*: Ibid., 373.

362   *As he wrote to his wife*: Dale and Litton, *Cherokee Cavaliers*, 96.

PART FOUR, CHAPTER 2—"AS BROTHERS LIVE, BROTHERS DIE"

364   *The Arkansas Gazette feared*: Woodward, *The Cherokees*, 255–56.

364   *Nonetheless, when, after the vote*: Dale and Litton, *Cherokee Cavaliers*, 106.

364   *This time, Ross declared*: McLoughlin, *After the Trail of Tears*, 172.

365   *He'd started out as a Massachusetts schoolteacher*: Cunningham, *General Stand Watie's Confederate Indians*, 33.

366   *Before going to see Ross*: Franks, *Stand Watie*, 117.

366   *As Pike figured it*: Cunningham, *General Stand Watie's Confederate Indians*, 34.

367   *So Watie struck a deal*: Dale and Litton, *Cherokee Cavaliers*, 106.

367   *It didn't even have an Indian*: Moulton, *John Ross*, 167.

367   *He paid out of his own pocket*: Brown, *A Life of Albert Pike*, 357.

367   *When he drew the enormous Pike*: "War of the Rebellion," http://ehistory.osu .edu/books/official-records/019/0499.

368   *And as for any further hostile*: Woodward, *The Cherokees*, 264.

368   *As Pike said ruefully*: Cunningham, *General Stand Watie's Confederate Indians*, 45.

368   *Ross had sent a letter*: Brown, *A Life of Albert Pike*, 358.

368   *He did win the backing*: Duncan, *Reluctant General*, 178.

369   *By August 1, Pike notified Ross*: Franks, *Stand Watie*, 118.

369   *The defeat in Missouri was especially alarming*: Woodward, *The Cherokees*, 265.

369   *On August 21, Ross assembled*: Ibid., 266.

370   *Combine that 1,200 with the legions*: Confer, Marak, and Tuennerman, *Transnational Indians in the North American West*, 214.

370   *In September, at his headquarters*: Cunningham, *General Stand Watie's Confederate Indians*, 45.

370   *When Ross sent the joyous word*: Moulton, *John Ross*, 173.

370   *For the others, though*: Woodward, *The Cherokees*, 267.

371   *When the South agreed*: "Cherokee Declaration of Clauses, October 28 1861," http://www.cherokee.org/About-The-Nation/History/Events/Cherokee-Declaration-of-Causes-October-28-1861.

PART FOUR, CHAPTER 3—CIVIL WAR

372 *Opothleyahola stoutly refused*: Woodward, *The Cherokees*, 271.

373 *This did not sit well*: Ibid., 270.

373 *He left the former Indian agent*: Ibid., 271–72.

373 *Then, in mid-afternoon, 300 Cherokee horsemen*: Cunningham, *General Stand Watie's Confederate Indians*, 52.

374 *The newspapers hailed Watie*: Moulton, *Papers of Chief John Ross*, 2, 509.

374 *He told the Union's Indian commissioner*: Woodward, *The Cherokees*, 274.

374 *To try, the War Department*: McLoughlin, *Champions of the Cherokees*, 402.

375 *Meanwhile, the Confederates enlisted*: Hess and Shea, *Pea Ridge*, 20.

376 *Last to arrive in Fayetteville*: Cunningham, *General Stand Watie's Confederate Indians*, 50.

376 *None of them were in uniforms*: Woodward, *The Cherokees*, 275.

377 *On March 4, the Indians were sent*: Franks, *Stand Watie*, 123.

377 *This is where the Cherokee*: Cunningham, *General Stand Watie's Confederate Indians*, 59.

378 *Not one for a proper uniform*: Ibid., 60.

379 *Van Dorn retreated south*: *New York Times*, March 17, 1862.

379 *The newspapers featured the story*: Brown, *Life of Albert Pike*, 396.

380 *He was determined to renew*: "The War of the Rebellion," Volume 3, United States War Department, June 16, 1880.

380 *At Park Hill, John Ross viewed*: McLoughlin, *Champions of the Cherokees*, 402–3.

381 *Meanwhile, Union colonel William Weer*: Woodward, *The Cherokees*, 278.

381 *Still, Weer sent a communiqué*: McLoughlin, *Champions of the Cherokees*, 403.

382 *Ross remained under house arrest*: Woodward, *The Cherokees*, 280.

383 *In the excitement, Watie's men*: Ibid., 284.

383 *Ross begged Lincoln*: Ibid., 282.

383 *As Mrs. William P. Ross wrote*: Ibid., 285.

PART FOUR, CHAPTER 4—THE END

385 *The tide of the larger Civil War*: Franks, *Stand Watie*, 136.

386 *To retaliate, Watie collected*: Ibid., 137.

386 *When she heard that Saladin*: Dale and Litton, *Cherokee Cavaliers*, 128.

386 *She begged Watie not*: Franks, *Stand Watie*, 139.

386 *The Union commander, Phillips, called*: Cunningham, *General Stand Watie's Confederate Indians*, 100.

387 *Overmatched by Union power*: Dale and Litton, *Cherokee Cavaliers*, 137.

387 *Replying for Scott, General Kirby-Smith*: Franks, *Stand Watie*, 144.

387 *He tried to enlist*: Edwin Bearss, "General William Steele Fights to Hold on to Northwest Arkansas," *Arkansas Historical Quarterly, 25*, no. 1 (Spring 1966): 36–93.

388 *Infuriated by the relentless loss*: Franks, *Stand Watie*, 148.

389 *From the Rosses' new home*: Moulton, *Papers of Chief John Ross, II,* 547.

389 *Watie told his wife*: Dale and Litton, *Cherokee Cavaliers*, 144–45.

389 *With little solid news*: Ibid., 146.

390 *In November 1863 Watie tried*: Franks, *Stand Watie*, 150.

390 *That winter, thousands of Cherokee*: Woodward, *The Cherokees*, 288.

390 *Boudinot reported to his brother*: Parins, *Elias Cornelius Boudinot*, 59.

391 *"I will stay here"*: Dale and Litton, *Cherokee Cavaliers*, 163–64.

391 *Worried about his failing aunt*: Franks, *Stand Watie*, 162.

391 *That September 1864, Watie's men seized*: Woodward, *The Cherokees*, 289.

391 *But the better praise came*: Dale and Litton, *Cherokee Cavaliers*, 200.

392 *On May 26, Confederate general Kirby-Smith*: Franks, *Stand Watie*, 180.

PART FOUR, CHAPTER 5—"I SHALL SEE THEM NO MORE ON EARTH"

393 *Back in Park Hill, her faith*: Moulton, *John Ross*, 181.

393 *From the steamer* Iron City: Ibid., 184.

394 *The burned homes, ruined farms*: Ibid., 185.

394 *Six thousand Cherokee*: Hauptman, *Between Two Fires*, 423.

394 *In July 1865, Ross's Northern Cherokee national council*: Franks, *Stand Watie*, 183.

395 *Watie spent his time*: Woodward, *The Cherokees*, 296.

395 *At Fort Smith, the government realized*: Ibid.

395 *Ross was an old man now*: Ibid., 297.

396 *When Ross was done speaking*: Ibid.

396 *"I here announce my willingness"*: Parins, *Elias Cornelius Boudinot*, 71.

396 *The Indian agent Cooley*: Ibid., 74.

396 *William P. Ross's wife railed*: Woodward, *The Cherokees*, 298.

397 *Assailed again for ever throwing*: Ibid., 301.

397 *While Ross spoke for his*: Parins, *Elias Cornelius Boudinot*, 75–77.

397 *Ross insisted that the money*: Moulton, *John Ross*, 190.

398 *And Commissioner Cooley came*: Woodward, *The Cherokees*, 302.

398 *By "personally powerless"*: Moulton, *John Ross*, 193.

398 *He dashed off impassioned letters*: Woodward, *The Cherokees*, 302.

399 *On June 13, Commissioner Cooley sent*: Ibid., 195.

400 *His body was finally laid*: Ibid., 195–96.

400 *Before he died, Ross had crafted an agreement*: Parins, *Elias Cornelius Boudinot*, 81–82.

401 *He often complained of a chill*: Franks, *Stand Watie*, 196.

401 To try to revive his fortunes: Parins, *Elias Cornelius Boudinot*, 87–89.
401 On February 13, 1868, his treasured son: Franks, *Stand Watie*, 196–200.
401 He took over a barge: Parins, *Elias Cornelius Boudinot*, 97.
402 Declaring himself: Franks, *Stand Watie*, 202.
402 The court declared it: Parins, *Elias Cornelius Boudinot*, 102.
402 "The Supreme Court has decided": Ibid., 103.
402 The sovereign treaties: Ibid., 102.
403 With what little remained of his fortune: Dale and Litton, *Cherokee Cavaliers*, 295.
403 Because the Grand River: Franks, *Stand Watie*, 208.

PART FOUR, CHAPTER 6—WHAT REMAINED
406 James Mooney, a solitary ethnologist: Mooney, *Historical Sketch of the Cherokee*, vii.
407 But a band of a few dozen: Ibid., xi.
407 As the child of Irish emigrants: Mooney, *History, Myths and Sacred Formulas for the Cherokees*, 3–4.
407 In 1878, after unsatisfying stints: Ibid., 6.
407 In 1885, Mooney nonetheless: Ibid., 7.
408 A massive six-four: Ibid., 9.
408 He found John Ax: Ibid., 15.
408 Born in the Cherokee Nation: Ibid.
409 He was buried, Mooney writes: Ibid.

EPILOGUE: ON POLITICS
414 Since Stand Watie's death: Donna Hales, "Cherokee Constitution in Doubt," *Muskogee Phoenix*. September 7, 2006.
415 They led to a constitutional crisis: Sam Howe Verhovek, "Cherokee Nation Facing a Crisis Involving Its Tribal Constitution," *New York Times*, July 6, 1997.
415 Police from five counties: Dennette A. Mouser, "A Nation in Crisis: The Government of the Cherokee Nation Struggles to Survive." *American Indian Law Review*, Vol. 23, No. 2 (1998/1999), 364.
415 In an unprecedented step: Ibid.
415 A subsequent investigative: Ibid., 366–74.
415 Smith, who had been: Lois Romano, "A Nation Divided," *Washington Post*, July 17, 1997.
416 Freedmen were indeed eligible: Press release, "Carter Center Commends Successful Cherokee Nation Voting Day and Highlights the Need for Patience and Transparency as Process Unfolds," Carter Center, September 25, 2011.
416 Once again, the Carter: Ibid. See also, Donna Hales, "Cherokee Constitution in Doubt," *Muskogee Phoenix*, September 7, 2006.

SELECTED BIBLIOGRAPHY

Abram, Susan. *Forging a Cherokee-American Alliance in the Creek War: From Creation to Betrayal.* Tuscaloosa: University of Alabama Press, 2015.

Acklen, Jeannette Tillotson. *Tennessee Records, Bible Records and Marriage Bonds.* Nashville: Clearfield, 2009.

Adair, James. *The History of the American Indians.* Tuscaloosa: University of Alabama Press, 2005.

Agnew, Jeremy. *Life of a Solider on the Western Frontier.* Missoula, MT: Mountain Press Publishing Center, 2008.

Allsopp, Fred W. *Alpert Pike: A Biography.* Kila, MT: Kessinger, 1992.

Alvord, Clarence Walworth. *The First Explorations of the Trans-Allegheny Region by the Virginians, 1650–1674.* London: Forgotten Books, 2015.

Ammon, Harry. *James Monroe: The Quest for National Identity.* New York: McGraw-Hill, 1971.

Anderson, Mabel Washbourne. *The Life of Stand Watie.* Pryor, OK: *Mayes County Republican* newspaper, 1915.

Anderson, William. *Cherokee Removal: Before and After.* Athens: University of Georgia Press, 1991.

Andrew, John, III. *From Revivals to Removal: Jeremiah Evarts, the Cherokee Nation, and the Search for the Soul of America.* Athens: University of Georgia Press, 1992.

Armstrong, William H. *Warrior in Two Camps: Ely S. Parker, Union General and Seneca Chief.* Syracuse, NY: Syracuse University Press, 1978.

Bartram, William. *The Travels of William Bartram.* Lawrence, KS: Neeland Media, Kindle Edition, 2009.

Bass, Althea. *Cherokee Messenger.* Norman: University of Oklahoma Press, 1936.

Battey, George. *A History of Rome and Floyd County, Volume I.* Atlanta, GA, Webb and Vary, 1922.

Baxter, William. *Pea Ridge and Prairie Grove.* Fayetteville: University of Arkansas Press, 2000.

Belt, Gordon. *John Sevier: Tennessee's First Hero.* Charleston, SC: History Press, 2014.

Bolton, S. Charles. *Arkansas, 1800–1860: Remote and Restless.* Fayetteville: University of Arkansas Press, 1998.

Boulware, Tyler. *Deconstructing the Cherokee Nation.* Gainesville: University Press of Florida, 2011.

Brainard, Charles. *John Howard Payne: A Biographical Sketch of the Author of "Home, Sweet Home."* Washington, DC: Leopold Classic Library, 1884.

Brands, H. W. *Andrew Jackson: His Life and Times.* New York: Anchor Books, 2005.

Braund, Kathryn, and Charlotte Porter, eds. *Fields of Vision: Essays on the Travels of William Bartram.* Tuscaloosa: University of Alabama Press, 2010.

Braund, Kathryn, and Gregory Waselkov. *William Bartram on the Southeastern Indians.* Lincoln: University of Nebraska Press, 1995.

Breyer, Stephen G. *Making Our Democracy Work: A Judge's View.* New York: Vintage, 2010.

Broom, Leonard, and Frank Speck. *Cherokee Dance and Drama.* Norman: University of Oklahoma Press, 1951.

Brown, Jerry Elijah, and Henry DeLeon Southerland Jr. *The Federal Road: Through Georgia, the Creek Nation, and Alabama 1806–1836.* Tuscaloosa: University of Alabama Press, 1989.

Brown, John P. *Old Frontiers: The Story of the Cherokee Indians from Earliest Times to the Date of Their Removal to the West, 1838.* Kingsport: Southern Publishers, 1938.

Brown, Walter Lee. *A Life of Albert Pike.* Fayetteville: University of Arkansas Press, 1997.

Carter, Samuel, III. *Cherokee Sunset: A Nation Betrayed.* New York: Doubleday, 1976.

Claiborne, John Francis Hamtramck. *Life and Times of Gen. Sam Dale, the Mississippi Partisan.* New York: Harper & Bros., 1860.

Clark, Electa. *Cherokee Chief: The Life of John Ross.* London: Crowell-Collier Press, 1970.

Clarke, Mary Whatley. *Chief Bowles and the Texas Cherokees.* Norman: University of Oklahoma Press, 1971.

Cobbs, Elizabeth, Edward Blum, and Jon Gjerde, eds. *Major Problems in American History, Volume 1: To 1877.* Boston: Wadsworth Cengage Learning, 2010.

Confer, Clarissa. *The Cherokee Nation in the Civil War*. Norman: University of Oklahoma Press, 2012.

Confer, Clarissa, Andrae Marak, and Laura Tuennerman. *Transnational Indians in the North American West*. College Station: Texas A&M Press, 2015.

Conley, Robert. *The Cherokee Nation: A History*. Albuquerque: University of New Mexico Press, 2005.

Corlew, Robert. *Tennessee: A Short History*, 2nd edition. Knoxville: University of Tennessee Press, 1981.

Cornelius, Elias. *Memoir of the Rev. Elias Cornelius, Secretary to the American Education Society*. Edinburgh: Waugh and Innes, 1934.

Cunningham, Frank. *General Stand Watie's Confederate Indians*. Norman: University of Oklahoma Press, 1998.

Cushman, Ellen. *The Cherokee Syllabary: Writing the People's Perseverance*. Norman: University of Oklahoma Press, 2011.

Dale, Edward Everett. "Letters of the Two Boudinots," in *Chronicles of Oklahoma*, Volume 6, no. 3, 1928.

Dale, Edward Everett, and Gaston Litton, eds. *Cherokee Cavaliers: Forty Years of Cherokee History as Told in the Correspondence of the Ridge-Watie-Boudinot Family*. Norman: University of Oklahoma Press, 1995.

Davis, Donald. *Where There Are Mountains*. Athens: University of Georgia Press, 2005.

Demos, John. *The Heathen School: A Story of Hope and Betrayal in the Age of the Early Republic*. New York: Knopf Doubleday, 2014.

Denson, Andrew. *Demanding the Cherokee Nation: Indian Autonomy and American Culture, 1830–1900*. Lincoln: University of Nebraska Press, 2004.

Donnell, James H. *Southern Indians in the American Revolution*. Knoxville: University of Tennessee Press, 1973.

Dowd, Gregory Evans. *A Spirited Resistance: The North American Indian Struggle for Unity, 1745–1815*. Baltimore: Johns Hopkins University Press, 1992.

Driver, Carl S. *John Sevier: Pioneer of the Old Southwest*. Nashville: Charles and Randy Elder Booksellers, 1973.

Duncan, Barbara, and Brett Riggs. *Cherokee Heritage Trails Guidebook*. Chapel Hill: University of North Carolina Press, 2003.

Duncan, David Ewing. *Hernando de Soto: A Savage Quest in the Americas*. Norman: University of Oklahoma Press, 1996.

Duncan, Robert Lipscomb. *Reluctant General: The Life and Times of Albert Pike*. New York: Dutton, 1961.

Eaton, Rachel. *John Ross and the Cherokee Indians*. Menasha, WI: George Banta, 1914.

Ehle, John. *Trail of Tears: The Rise and Fall of the Cherokee Nation*. New York: Anchor, 1988.

Everett, Dianna. *The Texas Cherokees: A People Between Two Fires, 1819–1840*. Norman: University of Oklahoma Press, 1990.

Faulkner, Charles H. *Massacre at Cavett's Station: Frontier Tennessee During the Cherokee Wars*. Knoxville: University of Tennessee Press, 2013.

Fenn, Elizabeth A. *Pox Americana: The Great Smallpox Epidemic of 1775–82*. New York: Farrar, Straus and Giroux, 2001.

Filler, Louis, and Allen Guttmann, eds. *The Removal of the Cherokee Nation*. New York: Robert E. Krieger, 1977.

Finger, John R. *The Eastern Band of Cherokees, 1819–1900*. Knoxville: University of Tennessee Press, 1984.

———. *Tennessee Frontiers: Three Regions in Transition*. Bloomington: Indiana University Press, 2001.

Foreman, Grant. *The Five Civilized Tribes*. Norman: University of Oklahoma Press, 1934.

———. *Indian Removal: The Emigration of the Five Civilized Tribes*. Norman: University of Oklahoma Press, 1972.

———. *Sequoyah*. Norman: University of Oklahoma Press, 1938.

Franks, Kenny A. *Stand Watie and the Agony of the Cherokee Nation*. Memphis: Memphis State University Press, 1979.

Gabriel, Ralph Henry. *Elias Boudinot, Cherokee & His America*. Norman: University of Oklahoma Press, 1941.

Garrison, Tim Alan. *The Legal Ideology of Removal: The Southern Judiciary and the Sovereignty of Native American Nations*. Athens: University of Georgia Press, 2002.

Gaul, Theresa Strouth, ed. *To Marry an Indian: The Marriage of Harriett Gold and Elias Boudinot In Letters, 1823–1839*. Chapel Hill: University of North Carolina Press, 2005.

Gerstacker, Friedrich. *Wild Sports in the Far West*. Boston: Crosby & Nichols, 1864.

Gilmer, George Rockingham. *Sketches of Some of the First Settlers of Upper Georgia, of the Cherokees, and of the Author*. Athens: Digital Library of Georgia, 1855.

Gregory, Jack, and Rennard Strickland. *Sam Houston with the Cherokees, 1829–1833*. Norman: University of Oklahoma Press, 1967.

Gutzman, Kevin. *James Madison and the Making of America*. New York: St. Martin's/ Griffin, 2012.

Harrell, Sara Gordon. *John Ross: The Story of an American Indian*. Minneapolis: Dillon Press, 1979.

Hatch, Thom. *The Blue, the Gray, and the Red: Indian Campaigns of the Civil War*. Mechanicsburg, PA: Stackpole Books, 2003.

Hatley, Tom. *The Dividing Paths: Cherokees and South Carolinians Through the Era of Revolution*. New York: Oxford University Press, 2003.

Hauptman, Laurence. *Between Two Fires: American Indians in the Civil War*. New York: Free Press, 1995.

Hess, Earl, and William Shea, eds. *Pea Ridge: Civil War Campaign in the West*. Chapel Hill: University of North Carolina Press, 1992.

Hicks, Brian. *Toward the Setting Sun: John Ross, the Cherokees and the Trail of Tears*. New York: Atlantic Monthly Press, 2012.

Hitchcock, Ethan Allen. *A Traveler in Indian Country: The Journal of Ethan Allen Hitchcock*, ed. Grant Foreman. Norman: University of Oklahoma Press, 1996.

Hoig, Stan. *The Cherokees and Their Chiefs: In the Wake of Empire*. Fayetteville: University of Arkansas Press, 1998.

Horan, James. *North American Indian Portraits*. New York: Crown Publishers, 1975.

Hudson, Charles. *The Southeastern Indians*. Knoxville: University of Tennessee Press, 1976.

Inskeep, Steve. *Jacksonland: President Andrew Jackson, Cherokee Chief John Ross, and a Great American Land Grab*. New York: Penguin Books, 2015.

Irving, Washington. *A Tour on the Prairies*. Baudry's European Library, Kindle Edition (originally published in 1832).

Ishii, Izumi. *Bad Fruits of the Civilized Tree: Alcohol and the Sovereignty of the Cherokee Nation*. Lincoln: University of Nebraska Press, 1970.

Jackson, Andrew. *Correspondence of Andrew Jackson*, ed. John Spencer Bassett. 6 vols. Washington, DC: Carnegie Institute of Washington, 1926–1933.

James, Marquis. *The Raven: A Biography of Sam Houston*. Austin: University of Texas Press, 1929.

Jefferts, Joseph. *Captain Matthew Arbuckle: A Documentary Biography*. Charleston, SC: Education Foundation, 1981.

Johnston, Carolyn Ross. *Cherokee Women in Crisis: Trail of Tears, Civil War, and Allotment, 1838–1907*. Tuscaloosa: University of Alabama Press, 2003.

Josephy, Alvin. *500 Nations: An Illustrated History of the North American Indians*. New York: Alfred A. Knopf, 1994.

Kilpatrick, Anna, and Jack Kilpatrick. *Friends of Thunder: Folktales of the Oklahoma Cherokees*. Norman: University of Oklahoma Press, 1964.

King, Duane, ed. *The Cherokee Indian Nation: A Troubled History*. Knoxville: University of Tennessee Press, 1979.

———, ed. *The Memoirs of Lt. Henry Timberlake: The Story of Soldier, Adventurer, and Emissary to the Cherokees, 1756–1765*. Chapel Hill, NC: Museum of the Cherokee Indian Press, 2007.

Knight, Wilfred. *Red Fox: Stand Watie and the Confederate Indians During the Civil War in Indian Territory*. Glendale, CA: Arthur H. Clark, 1988.

Langer, Howard, ed. *American Indian Quotations*. Westport, CT: Greenwood Press, 1996.

Langguth, A. J. *Driven West: Andrew Jackson and the Trail of Tears to the Civil War*. New York: Simon & Schuster, 2010.

La Vere, David. *Contrary Neighbors*. Norman: University of Oklahoma Press, 2000.

Le Fevre, Barbara. *Deep Ruts the Wagon Made*. Bloomington, IN: 1st Book Library, 2003.

Lumpkin, Wilson. *The Removal of the Cherokee Indians from Georgia, Volume II*. New York: Dodd, Mead & Company, 1907.

Malcomson, Scott. *One Drop of Blood: The American Misadventure in Race*. New York: Farrar, Straus and Giroux, 2000.

Mann, Charles C. *1491: Revelations of the Americas Before Columbus*. New York: Vintage Books, 2011.

Marshall, Peter, and David Manuel. *From Sea to Shining Sea: 1787–1837*. Grand Rapids, MI: Revell, 1986.

McClinton, Rowena. *Moravian Spring Place Mission to the Cherokees*. Lincoln: University of Nebraska Press, 2010.

McGrath, Ann. *Illicit Love: Interracial Sex and Marriage in the United States and Australia*. Lincoln: University of Nebraska Press, 2015.

McKenney, Thomas, and James Hall. *Indian Tribes of North America, Volume I*. Carlisle, MA: Applewood, 1872.

McKenney, Thomas, and James Hall. *Indian Tribes of North America, Volume II*. Edinburgh: Ep Publishing, 1872.

McLoughlin, William G. *After the Trail of Tears: The Cherokees' Struggle for Sovereignty, 1839–1880*. Chapel Hill: University of North Carolina Press, 1993.

———. *Champions of the Cherokees: Evan and John B. Jones*. Princeton, NJ: Princeton University Press, 2014.

———. *Cherokee Renascence in the New Republic*. Princeton, NJ: Princeton University Press, 1986.

———. *Cherokees and Christianity: 1794–1870*. Athens: University of Georgia Press, 1994.

———. *Cherokees and Missionaries, 1789–1839*. Norman: University of Oklahoma Press, 1995.

Meacham, Jon. *American Lion: Andrew Jackson in the White House*. New York: Random House, 2009.

Meredith, Howard, and Virginia Sobral, eds. *Cherokee Vision of Elohi*. Oklahoma City: Noksi Press, 1997.

Message from the President of the United States, 18th Congress, 1st Session, "Compact Between U. States and State of Georgia." Washington, DC: Gales & Seaton, 1824.

Miles, Tiya. *The House on Diamond Hill: A Cherokee Plantation Story.* Chapel Hill: University of North Carolina Press, 2010.

Mooney, James. *The Ghost Dance Religion and the Sioux Outbreak of 1890.* Washington, DC: U.S. Government Printing Office, 1896.

———. *Historical Sketch of the Cherokee.* New Brunswick, NJ: Aldine Transaction, 2005.

———. *History, Myths and Sacred Formulas for the Cherokees.* Asheville, NC: Bright Mountain Books, 1992.

———. *The Swimmer Manuscript.* Washington, DC: U.S. Government Printing Office, 1932.

Moore, Stephen L. *Last Stand of the Texas Cherokees.* Garland, TX: Ram Books, 2009.

Moses, L. G. *The Indian Man: A Biography of James Mooney.* Lincoln: University of Nebraska Press, 1984.

Moulton, Gary E. *John Ross: Cherokee Chief.* Athens: University of Georgia Press, 1978.

———, ed. *The Papers of Chief John Ross, Volume I: 1807–1839.* Norman: University of Oklahoma Press, 1985.

———, ed. *The Papers of Chief John Ross, Volume II: 1840–1866.* Norman: University of Oklahoma Press, 1985.

Nichols, Roger. *The American Indian: Past and Present.* New York: McGraw-Hill, 1992.

Oates, Stephen B. *Confederate Cavalry West of the River.* Austin: University of Texas Press, 1961.

O'Brien, Sean. *In Bitterness and in Tears: Andrew Jackson's Destruction of the Creeks and Seminoles.* Westport, CT: Praeger, 2003.

Oliphant, John. *Peace and War on the Anglo-Cherokee Frontier, 1756–63.* Baton Rouge: Louisiana State University Press, 2001.

Parins, James W. *Elias Cornelius Boudinot: A Life on the Cherokee Border.* Lincoln: University of Nebraska Press, 2008.

———. *John Rollin Ridge: His Life and Works.* Lincoln: University of Nebraska Press, 2004.

Payne, John Howard. *Home Sweet Home.* Philadelphia: J.B. Lippincott, 1885.

———. *Indian Justice: A Cherokee Murder Trial at Tahlequah in 1840.* Norman: University of Oklahoma Press, 2002.

Perdue, Theda. *Cherokee Editor: The Writings of Elias Cornelius Boudinot.* Athens: University of Georgia Press, 1983.

———. *Cherokee Women: Gender and Culture Change, 1700–1835.* Lincoln: University of Nebraska Press, 1998.

———. *Slavery and the Evolution of Cherokee Society*. Knoxville: University of Tennessee Press, 1979.

Perdue, Theda, and Michael Green. *The Cherokee Removal: A Brief History with Documents*. Chapel Hill: University of North Carolina Press, 2005.

Pierson, George Wilson. *Tocqueville in America*. Baltimore: Johns Hopkins University Press, 1996.

Pike, Albert. *Narrative of a Journey in the Prairie*. Kila, MT: Kessinger Publishing, 2003.

Prucha, Francis Paul. *The Great Father: The United States Government and the American Indians*. Lincoln: University of Nebraska Press, 1984.

Ramsey, J. G. M. *The Annals of Tennessee to the End of the Eighteenth Century*. Charleston, SC: Walker and James, 1853.

Reed, Gerard Alexander. *The Ross-Watie Conflict: Factionalism in the Cherokee Nation, 1839–1865*, PhD diss. Norman: University of Oklahoma, 1967.

Reid, John Phillip. *A Law of Blood: The Primitive Law of the Cherokee Nation*. New York: New York University Press, 1970.

Shadburn, Don. *Cherokee Plantiers in Georgia 1832–1838*. Volume II. Pioneer-Cherokee Heritage Series, 1989.

Shirley, Glenn. *Belle Starr and Her Times: The Literature, the Facts, and the Legends*. Norman: University of Oklahoma Press, 1982.

Slover, James Anderson. *Minister to the Cherokees: A Civil War Autobiography*. Lincoln: University of Nebraska Press, 2001.

Smith, Daniel Blake. *An American Betrayal: Cherokee Patriots and the Trail of Tears*. New York: Henry Holt & Co., 2011.

Spring, Joel. *The Cultural Transformation of a Native American Family and Its Tribe: 1763–1995*. Mahwah, NJ: Lawrence Erlbaum Associates, 1996.

Starkey, Marion. *The Cherokee Nation*. North Dighton, MA: JG Press, 1973.

Starr, Emmet. *History of the Cherokee Indians and Their Legends and Folk Lore*. Oklahoma City: Warden, 1921.

Steele, Phillip. *The Last Cherokee Warriors*. Gretna: Pelican, 1993.

Stevenson, Adlai Ewing. *Something of Men I Have Known*. Chicago: A.C. Mclurg, 1909.

Stockel, Henrietta H. *The Lightning Stick: Arrows, Wounds, and Indian Legends*. Reno: University of Nevada Press, 1995.

Strickland, Rennard. *Fire and the Spirits: Cherokee Law from Clan to Court*. Norman: University of Oklahoma Press, 1975.

Swanton, John R. *Final Report of the United States De Soto Expedition Commission*. Washington, DC: Smithsonian Institution Press, 1985.

Taylor, Colin. *Native American Weapons*. Norman: University of Oklahoma Press, 2001.

Thomas, Milton Halsey. *Elias Boudinot's Journey to Boston in 1809*. Princeton: Princeton University Library, 1955.

Thornton, Russel. *The Cherokees: A Population History*. Lincoln: University of Nebraska Press, 1992.

Tresner, Jim. *Albert Pike: The Man Beyond the Monument*. New York: M. Evans and Company, 1995.

Ural, Susannah. *Civil War Citizens: Race, Ethnicity, and Identity in America's Bloodiest Conflict*. New York: New York University Press, 2010.

Viola, Herman. *Thomas McKenney: Architect of America's Early Indian Policy: 1816–1830*. Chicago: Swallow, 1974.

Walker, Ricky Butch. *Doublehead: Last Chickamauga Cherokee Chief*. Killen, AL: Bluewater Publishing, 2012.

Walker, Robert Sparks. *Torchlights to the Cherokees*. Johnson City, TN: Overmountain Press, 1931.

Wallace, Anthony. *Jefferson and the Indians: The Tragic Fate of the First Americans*. Cambridge, MA: Harvard University Press, 1999.

Wardell, Morris. *A Political History of the Cherokee Nation, 1838–1907*. Norman: University of Oklahoma Press, 1977.

Watson, Larry, ed. Indian Removal Records, Senate Document 512, 23rd Congress, 1st Session, Volume II. Yuma, AZ: Histree Publishing, 1988.

Wilkins, Thurman. *Cherokee Tragedy: The Ridge Family and the Decimation of a People*. Norman: University of Oklahoma Press, 1986.

Wilkinson, David Marion. *Oblivion's Altar*. New York: New American Library, 2002.

Williams, David. *The Great Georgia Gold Rush: Twenty-Niners, Cherokees, and Gold Fever*. Columbia: University of South Carolina Press, 1994.

Wilson, James. *The Earth Shall Weep: A History of Native America*. New York: Grove Press, 1998.

Woodward, Grace Steele. *The Cherokees*. Norman: University of Oklahoma Press, 1963.

Wright, Ronald. *Stolen Continents: Five Hundred Years of Conquest and Resistance in the Americas*. New York: First Mariner Books, 1992.

Zogry, Michael. *Anetso, the Cherokee Ball Game*. Chapel Hill: University of North Carolina Press, 2010.

CREDITS

Part Opener 4
Cherokee Delegation to Washington, DC, 1866. (Boudinot and Associates) L. to R.:
John Rollin Ridge, Saladin Watie, Richard Field, E. C. Boudinot, W. P. Adair.
*1046.B. Photo by A. Gardner, Washington, DC./Vinnie Ream Hoxie Collection/
Courtesy of the Oklahoma Historical Society*

PHOTO INSERTS

INSERT 1

Page 1, first
Hernando de Soto, Spanish explorer and conquistador, and his men torturing
natives of Florida in his determination to find gold, 1539–1542.
*John Judkyn Memorial Collection, Freshford Manor, Bath. Photo by Ann Ronan
Pictures/Print Collector/Getty Images*

Page 1, second
Three Cherokee chiefs on a state visit to London to meet with King George III, 1762.
Everett Collection

Page 1, third
Oenothera grandiflora—large-flower evening primrose.
William Bartram, Travels through North and South Carolina, Georgia, East and West
Florida, the Cherokee Country, the Extensive Territories of the Muscogulges or Creek
Confederacy, and the Country of the Chactaws. Containing an Account of the Soil and
Natural Productions of Those Regions; Together with Observations on the Manners of
the Indians, *1791. Courtesy of the Sterling Morton Library, The Morton Arboretum*

Page 1, fourth
John Sevier miniature.
James Peale, ART Collection/Alamy Stock Photo

Page 2, top
Major Ridge.
Circa 1830, MPI/Archive Photos/Getty Images

Page 2, bottom
Major Ridge Home as it may have looked from the banks of the Oostanaula River.
Artist unknown, Chieftains Museum/Major Ridge Home, Rome, Georgia

INSERT 1 *(cont'd)*

Page 3, top
John Ross.
John Neagle, 1848, oil on canvas, 45 × 38 ins., Museum purchase, Philbrook Museum of Art, Tulsa, Oklahoma, 1942.12.1

Page 3, bottom
John Ross House, Rossville, Georgia.
Museum of the Cherokee Indian Photo Collection, Cherokee, North Carolina

Page 4, top left
William McIntosh.
After a painting, circa 1825, by Charles Bird King/Granger, NYC

Page 4, top center
The Cherokee Scholar, Sequoyah.
Nineteenth century/Private Collection/Peter Newark American Pictures/Bridgeman Images

Page 4, top right
George Lowrey.
0126.2180. Artist Unknown, nineteenth century, Gilcrease Museum, Tulsa, Oklahoma

Page 4, bottom
Cherokee Phoenix Masthead for May 14, 1828, at New Echota.
Museum of the Cherokee Kinsland Collection, Cherokee, North Carolina

Page 5, top
The Dying Tecumseh.
Ferdinand Pettrich, Smithsonian American Art Museum. Photo by Paul Fearn/Alamy Stock Photo

Page 5, bottom left
John Marshall.
Jacob Eichholtz, 1841, Copy from an original by Henry Inman, 1831–32/Philadelphia History Museum at the Atwater Kent/Courtesy of Historical Society of Pennsylvania Collection/Bridgeman Images

INSERT 1 (cont'd)

Page 5, bottom right
Reverend Samuel Worcester, Union Mission.
2012.201.B1418.0582. Oklahoma Publishing Company Photography Collection/ Courtesy of the Oklahoma Historical Society

Page 6, top
Brainerd, a missionary station among the Cherokee.
Penelope Johnson Allen Brainerd Mission correspondence and photographs. Courtesy of the University of Tennessee at Chattanooga Special Collections

Page 6, bottom left
John Ridge.
After a painting, 1825, by Charles Bird King/Universal History Archive/UIG/ Bridgeman Images

Page 6, bottom center
Elias Boudinot.
19615.43. Oklahoma Historical Society Glass Plate Collection/Painting in the OHS State Museum of History Collection/Courtesy of the Oklahoma Historical Society

Page 6, bottom right
Harriet Riggles Gold Boudinot.
19615.31. Oklahoma Historical Society Glass Plate Collection/Courtesy of the Oklahoma Historical Society

Page 7, top left
Cherokee wooden buffalo mask, worn during Forest Buffalo Dance.
Granger, NYC

Page 7, top right
Andrew Jackson.
Thomas Sully, 1858/Private Collection/Photo © Christie's Images/Bridgeman Images

Page 7, bottom left
General Winfield Scott.
George Catlin, circa 1835/Collection of the New-York Historical Society, USA/ Bridgeman Images

INSERT 1 (cont'd)

Page 7, bottom right
Re-creation of the Cherokee Supreme Court Building at New Echota State Historic
Site in Calhoun, Georgia.
Georgia Department of Natural Resources

Page 8, top
Andrew Jackson as the Great Father.
William L. Clements Library, University of Michigan

Page 8, bottom
Treaty of New Echota, December 29, 1835.
Ratified Indian Treaty 199; General Records of the U.S. Government, Record Group 11;
National Archives and Records Administration, Washington, DC

INSERT 2

Page 1
International Indian Council held at Tahlequah, Indian Territory, in 1843.
John Mix Stanley, Smithsonian American Art Museum, Washington, DC/Art Resource, NY

Page 2, top
General Stand Watie.
12398. Oklahoma Historical Society Photograph Collection/Courtesy of the Oklahoma Historical Society

Page 2, bottom
Sarah Watie.
12699, Oklahoma Historical Society Photograph Collection/Courtesy of the Oklahoma Historical Society

Page 3, top
Chief John Ross.
4326-3264a. Photographer F. Gutekunst, 1863, Gilcrease Museum, Tulsa, Oklahoma.

Page 3, bottom
Mary Stapler Ross.
Samuel Bell Waugh, 1848, oil on canvas, 45 × 38 ins., Museum purchase, Philbrook Museum of Art, Tulsa, Oklahoma, 1942.12.2

Page 4, top left
Albert Pike in Masonic regalia.
14290. Oklahoma Historical Society Photograph Collection/Courtesy of the Oklahoma Historical Society

Page 4, top right
President James K. Polk.
George P. A. Healy, circa 1846, Niday Picture Library/Alamy Stock Photo

Page 4, bottom left
John Howard Payne.
Photo by Michael Nicholson/Corbis via Getty Images

INSERT 2 (cont'd)

Page 4, bottom right
Ho-Po-Eth-Le-Yo-Ho-Lo.
917 Collection/Alamy Stock Photo

Page 5, top left
Marriage certificate of Chief John Ross and Mary B. Stapler, 1844.
5126-52. Gilcrease Museum, Tulsa, Oklahoma

Page 5, top right
Watie children.
6474. Oklahoma Historical Society Photograph Collection/Courtesy of the Oklahoma Historical Society

Page 5, bottom one
Rose Cottage, Chief John Ross, Park Hill, Indian Territory (Oklahoma).
2012.201.b1109.0137. Oklahoma Historical Society Photograph Collection/Courtesy of the Oklahoma Historical Society

Page 5, bottom two
Cherokee Female Seminary—graduating class at Park Hill, Indian Territory (Oklahoma).
2410. Photo copy by L. C. Handy Studio, Washington, DC. 1875/Grant Foreman Collection/Courtesy of the Oklahoma Historical Society

Page 6, top
Confederates driven from Elkhorn Tavern, Battle of Pea Ridge, Arkansas, March 8, 1862.
©North Wind Picture Archives

Page 6, bottom
Cherokee Braves Flag carried by Colonel Stand Watie's Cherokee Mounted Rifles.
Courtesy of Wilson's Creek National Battlefield

Page 7, top
Elias C. Boudinot.
1049. Vinnie Ream Hoxie Collection/Courtesy of the Oklahoma Historical Society

INSERT 2 (cont'd)

Page 7, bottom
Stand Watie.
Photo by Paul Fearn/Alamy Stock Photo

Page 8, top
James Mooney.
NAA INV 02862900, Photo Lot 33, Photographer De Lancey W. Gill, National Anthropological Archives, Smithsonian Institution

Page 8, bottom
Ayunini (Swimmer).
From The Sacred Formulas of the Cherokees *by James Mooney,*
Wellcome Library, London

INDEX

An *n* following a page number refers to text in that page's footnote(s).